# America's
# Second
# Crusade

# America's
# Second
# Crusade

William Henry Chamberlin

amagi®

an imprint of Liberty Fund, Inc.

Liberty Fund

Amagi books are published by Liberty Fund, Inc.,
a foundation established to encourage study of the
ideal of a society of free and responsible individuals.

The cuneiform inscription that appears in the logo and serves
as a design element in all Liberty Fund books is the earliest-known
written appearance of the word "freedom" (*amagi*), or "liberty."
It is taken from a clay document written about 2300 B.C.
in the Sumerian city-state of Lagash.

First published in 1950 by Henry Regnery Company.

Printed in the United States of America
2nd printing (2022), printed on demand by Lightning Source, Inc.

Library of Congress Cataloging-in-Publication Data
Chamberlin, William Henry, 1897–1969.
    America's second crusade / William Henry Chamberlin.
        p.   cm.
    Originally published: Chicago: Regnery, 1950.
    Includes bibliographical references and index.
    ISBN 978-0-86597-707-5 (pb: alk. paper)
    1. World War, 1939–1945—Diplomatic history.
    2. World War, 1939–1945—United States.   I. Title.
    D753.C55  2008
940.53'2—dc22                                    2008002559

LIBERTY FUND, INC.
11301 North Meridian Street
Carmel, Indiana 46032
libertyfund.org

# Contents

# Introduction

There is an obvious and painful gap between the world of 1950 and the postwar conditions envisaged by American and British wartime leaders. The negative objective of the war, the destruction of the Axis powers, was achieved. But not one of the positive goals set forth in the Atlantic Charter and the Four Freedoms has been realized.

There is no peace today, either formal or real. Over a great part of the world there is neither freedom of religion nor freedom of speech and expression. Freedom from fear and want is not an outstanding characteristic of the present age. The right of national self-determination, so vigorously affirmed in the Atlantic Charter, has been violated on a scale and with a brutality seldom equalled in European history.

The full irony of the war's aftermath finds expression in the growing dependence of American foreign policy on the co-operation of former enemies, Germany and Japan. Three countries on whose behalf Americans were told the war was being waged, Poland, Czechoslovakia, and China, are now in the camp of this country's enemies, so far as their present governments can achieve this purpose.

Much light has been thrown on World War II by the memoirs and papers of such distinguished leaders and statesmen as Winston Churchill, Cordell Hull, Harry Hopkins, Henry L. Stimson, and James F. Byrnes. A note of self-justification, however, almost inevitably intrudes in the recollections of active participants in such a momentous historic era. It requires a mind of rare insight and detachment to recognize in retrospect that premises which were held as articles of faith during the war may have been partly or entirely wrong.

My book is an attempt to examine without prejudice or favor the question why the peace was lost while the war was being won. It puts the challenging questions which are often left unanswered, perhaps even unthought of, by individuals who are deeply identified emotionally with a crusading war.

I should like to express gratitude to the following individuals for their kindness in discussing events and issues of the war with me: Mr. Charles E. Bohlen and Mr. George F. Kennan, of the State Department, Mr. A. A. Berle, former Assistant Secretary of State, General William Donovan, former head of the OSS, Mr. Allen W. Dulles, OSS representative in Switzerland, former Ambassadors Joseph C. Grew, William C. Bullitt, and Arthur Bliss Lane. I hasten to add that no one of these gentlemen is in the slightest degree responsible for the views expressed in this book. In fact, I know some of them would disagree sharply with some of the conclusions expressed here. However, they have all contributed to clarifying in my own mind the picture of America's Second Crusade which is herewith presented.

William Henry Chamberlin

Cambridge, Massachusetts
May 3, 1950

# America's
# Second
# Crusade

# 1

## The First Crusade

Americans, more than any other people, have been inclined to interpret their involvement in the two great wars of the twentieth century in terms of crusades for righteousness. General Eisenhower calls his memoirs *Crusade in Europe*. And the mural paintings in the Widener Memorial Library at Harvard University show the American soldiers of World War I as chivalrous knights, fighting for the freedom of wronged peoples. They bear the inscription:

Happy those who with a glowing faith
In one embrace clasped death and victory.
They crossed the sea crusaders keen to help
The nations battling in a righteous cause.

This was how the war appeared from the beginning to a minority of Americans who felt close emotional ties with Great Britain and France. There were politically and socially less influential German-American and Irish-American minorities with opposed sympathies.

The majority of the American people were inclined to follow President Wilson's appeal to "be neutral in fact as well as in name," "to be impartial in thought as well as in action." The tradition of dissociation from Europe's wars was strong. It was only gradually that the United States was sucked into the vortex.

Despite the President's intellectual sympathy with the British and French political systems, as contrasted with the German, there is evidence that Woodrow Wilson, until he felt his hand forced on the unrestricted submarine warfare issue, sincerely desired to keep America out of the world conflict. His imagination was fired by the hope of playing a leading disinterested role at the peace conference. He saw the advantage of keeping one great power outside the ranks of the belligerents, capable of playing the part of mediator.

The President was not an absolute pacifist, but his scholarly training had given him a strong sense of the inevitable brutality and frequent futility of resorting to force in disputes between nations. He became increasingly attracted by the vision of an international organization capable of maintaining peace.

Shortly after the sinking of the *Lusitania* Wilson risked criticism at home and abroad by saying:

> There is such a thing as a man being too proud to fight. There is such a thing as a nation being so right that it does not need to convince others by force that it is right.

On two subsequent occasions he voiced sentiments that were truly prophetic, in the light of the crusade's disillusioning aftermath. Addressing the Senate on January 22, 1917, he pleaded for a "peace without victory":

> Victory would mean peace forced upon the loser, a victor's terms imposed upon the vanquished. It would be accepted in humiliation, under duress, at an intolerable sacrifice, and would leave a sting, a resentment, a bitter memory upon which terms of peace would rest, not permanently, but only as upon quicksand. Only a peace between equals can last, only a peace the very principle of which is equality and a common participation in a common benefit.

And on the very eve of his appeal to Congress for a declaration of war Wilson privately poured out his doubts and fears to Frank Cobb, editor of the *New York World*. Looking pale and haggard, the President told the editor he had been lying awake for nights, thinking over the whole situation, trying in vain to find an alternative to war. When Cobb observed that Germany had forced his hand, Wilson refused to be consoled. He said:

> America's entrance would mean that we would lose our heads along with the rest and stop weighing right or wrong. It would mean that the majority of the people in this hemisphere would go war-mad,

quit thinking and devote their energies to destruction. . . . It means an attempt to reconstruct a peacetime civilization with war standards, and at the end of the war there will be no bystanders with sufficient power to influence the terms. . . . Once lead this people into war and they'll forget there ever was such a thing as tolerance.

For a man to be led by what he considers irresistible necessity to follow a course of action from which he anticipates no constructive results is one of the highest forms of tragedy. It was such a tragedy that brought Wilson sleepless nights before his call to arms on April 2, 1917.

America in 1914 had no political commitments to either group of belligerents. But its foreign-trade interests were immediately and sharply affected. Each side went far beyond previous precedents in trying to cut off enemy supplies with slight regard for neutral rights. The Allies dominated the surface of the seas. They could not establish a close blockade of German ports, the only kind which was legitimate under international law. But they could and did sweep German shipping from the seas. And they stretched the rights of search and seizure and the definition of contraband far beyond previous rules and standards.

The American State Department filed sharp protests against seizures of American cargoes, but received little satisfaction. One reason why the remonstrances received little attention was the extreme Anglophile attitude of the American Ambassador in London, Walter Hines Page. Sir Edward Grey, British Foreign Minister, reports that Page, after reading a dispatch contesting the British right to stop contraband going to neutral ports, offered the following postscript:

"I have now read the dispatch, but do not agree with it. Let us consider how it should be answered!"

Sir Edward's reaction is understandable:

"The comfort, support and encouragement that Page's presence was to the Secretary for Foreign Affairs may be imagined."

The purpose of the blockade, according to Winston Churchill, who unconsciously anticipated a slogan of World War II, was to enforce unconditional surrender:

"Germany is like a man throttled by a heavy gag. You know the effect of such a gag. . . . The effort wears out the heart and Germany knows it. This pressure shall not be relaxed until she gives in unconditionally."

The German reply to the Allied blockade was a new naval weapon, the submarine. These undersea craft soon developed unforeseen power as destroyers of merchant shipping. As a wag remarked: Britannia rules the waves, but Germany waives the rules.

The German Government on February 4, 1915, after vainly protesting against the rigors of the blockade, declared the waters surrounding the British Isles a war zone, in which every enemy merchant ship was liable to destruction. Neutral ships were also warned of danger in entering this zone.

The submarine was a more visible and provocative weapon than the blockade, although Secretary of State Bryan, a staunch pacifist, professed to see little difference between the prize court and the torpedo. Submarine attacks cost lives and created headlines. Cargoes seized by British warships merely became the subject of lawsuits.

A crisis in American-German relations followed the sinking of the British liner *Lusitania* off the coast of Ireland on May 7, 1915. The ship was carrying munitions and was not convoyed. Over eleven hundred passengers, including 128 American citizens, lost their lives. There was an almost unanimous cry of horror and indignation in the American press. But there were few voices in favor of going to war. There was a strongly phrased note of protest. But tension gradually eased off as there was no repetition of tragedy on the scale of the *Lusitania* sinking.

The submarine issue came sharply to a head after the British cross-Channel steamer *Sussex* was torpedoed, with the loss of some American lives, in the spring of 1916. Wilson informed the German Government that, unless it abandoned present methods of submarine warfare against passenger- and freight-carrying ships, "the Government of the United States can have no choice but to sever diplomatic relations with the German Empire altogether."

Faced with this clear-cut alternative, the German Government yielded. It consented not to sink merchant ships without warning and without taking precautions to save lives. It tried to link this concession with a suggestion that the United States should hold Great Britain re-

sponsible for observing international law in the matter of the blockade.

The American Government refused to admit any connection between these two issues. As Germany offered no further comment, the
dispute was settled, for the moment, with a diplomatic victory for Wilson. But the danger remained that submarine warfare would be re-
sumed whenever the German Government might feel that its advan-
tages would outweigh the benefits of American neutrality. And the
President had now committed the United States to a breach of relations in the event of a renewal of submarine attacks against nonmilitary
shipping.

This consideration lent an element of urgency to Wilson's efforts to
find a basis for mediation. In the light of later events there can be little
doubt that a negotiated peace on reasonable terms in 1915 or 1916
would have been incomparably the happiest possible ending of the
war. Such a peace would probably have saved the fabric of European
civilization from the fearful shocks of communism and nazism.

But foresight does not seem to have been the gift of any of the men
who occupied the seats of power in the warring countries. Winston
Churchill, writing in a sober mood between the two great wars, in both
of which he played a leading part, summed up the mood of the belligerent leaders, which he fully shared, in the following eloquent and
somber passage:

> Governments and individuals conformed to the rhythm of the
> tragedy, and swayed and staggered forward in helpless violence,
> slaughtering and squandering on ever-increasing scales, till injuries
> were wrought to the structure of human society which a century will
> not efface, and which may conceivably prove fatal to the present
> civilisation. . . . Victory was to be bought so dear as to be almost
> indistinguishable from defeat. It was not to give even security to
> the victors. . . . The most complete victory ever gained in arms has
> failed to solve the European problem or remove the dangers which
> produced the war.[1]

1. Churchill, *The World Crisis,* 2:1–2. This passage could serve even better as an
epitaph for the Second World War than for the First.

During the years when American mediation was possible, the Germans were clearly ahead on the war map. They had overrun Belgium and northeastern France before the western front sagged down in bloody stalemate. They had crushed Serbia and pushed the Russians far back from the prewar frontier. Rumania's entrance into the war in 1916 was followed by swift defeat.

On the other hand the blockade was contracting their supplies of food and raw materials. And Germany and its allies faced a coalition of powers with a larger aggregate population and much more extensive natural resources. It would, therefore, have been advantageous for Germany to conclude peace on terms that gave some recognition to its military successes.

The Allies, on the other hand, based their hopes on wearing Germany and Austria down. Peace talks would have been embarrassing to them for two reasons. Morale would have been adversely affected. And annexationist ambitions which would have scarcely stood the test of impartial neutral moral judgment, such as the Sykes-Picot Agreement of May 16, 1916, for the partition of Asia Minor between Russia, France, and Britain, would have come to light.

So all the mediation feelers of Wilson and his confidential adviser, Col. E. M. House, came to nothing. Wilson and House favored the western powers against Germany, although they were not such extravagant British partisans as Page. They distrusted militarist influences in Germany; they felt a sense of affinity between British and American conceptions of law, government, and morality. Their mediation would have been distinctly friendly to the Allies. This is evident from the so-called House-Grey memorandum of February 1916, the most concrete result of House's journeys abroad and correspondence with Sir Edward Grey and other British leaders. This document, drawn up by Grey and confirmed by House, with Wilson's approval, reads as follows:

> Colonel House told me that President Wilson was ready, on hearing from France and England that the moment was opportune, to propose that a Conference should be summoned to put an end to the war. Should the Allies accept this proposal, and should Germany refuse it, the United States would probably enter the war against Germany.

Colonel House expressed the opinion that, if such a Conference met, it would secure peace on terms not unfavorable to the Allies; and, if it failed to secure peace, the United States would [probably] leave the Conference as a belligerent on the side of the Allies, if Germany was unreasonable. House expressed an opinion decidedly favorable to the restoration of Belgium, the transfer of Alsace and Lorraine to France, and the acquisition by Russia of an outlet to the sea, though he thought that the loss of territory incurred by Germany in one place would have to be compensated by concessions to her in other places outside Europe. If the Allies delayed accepting the offer of President Wilson, and if, later on, the course of the war was so unfavourable to them that the intervention of the United States would not be effective, the United States would probably disinterest themselves in Europe and look to their own protection in their own way.

Here was indeed a venture in high politics. Wilson was willing to commit America to participation in a European war unless Germany consented not only to give up its conquests but to surrender Alsace-Lorraine, which had been an integral part of the German Empire for more than forty years.

The American offer, although politely registered, was never accepted. The Allies wanted a knockout victory and did not wish to tie their hands by accepting outside mediation, however friendly. They probably reckoned that America would be forced into the war ultimately because of the submarine issue. And, like the Germans, they were inclined to underestimate America's military potential.

Long before America entered the war, its economy was being bolstered and sustained by huge Allied war orders. As the British and French ran short of means of payment, they floated loans of more than a billion and a half dollars on the American market, largely through the agency of the House of Morgan. Lend-lease was not thought of, but the economic aspects of the periods which preceded American involvement in the two great wars were remarkably similar.

Depression gave way to boom. There was unlimited demand for the products of the steel and other heavy industries. Prices of farm products were kept at high levels. This swollen and one-sided war trade built up a tremendous economic stake in Allied victory.

An emotional stake was also being built up, partly by deliberate propaganda, partly by the instinctive sympathy of influential groups in America with Britain and France. The task of British propaganda was greatly eased by the general disposition to accept it at face value, with little critical examination.

The best Allied propagandists were perhaps not the professionals, but the amateurs, men like Ambassador Page, who unconsciously and completely absorbed and mirrored the British viewpoint. There were thousands of Americans of this type in less distinguished positions— professors, writers, publicists, clergymen—who acted in all good faith and were all the more effective in influencing public opinion for this reason.

Moreover, Britons, in this war as on other occasions, were the most effective spokesmen for their country's cause because of their national gift of restraint and understatement. This made it easy for them to identify more or less convincingly British interests with the requirements of reason, logic, and morality.

By contrast German publicity efforts, heavily handicapped by the severance of direct cable communication between Germany and the outside world, seemed clumsy, bumbling, and heavy-footed, and generally fell on skeptical ears.

Later, during the intellectual hangover that followed the wartime emotional debauch, there was perhaps too much emphasis on paid propagandists and on deliberate falsifications. To be sure, some German "atrocities" that never occurred obtained wide popular circulation. And some ruthless measures which every army of occupation would probably have employed to suppress irregular sniping were represented as peculiarly bestial acts which only "Huns" could commit. The superheated temper of a part of public opinion could be gauged from the following comment of Henry Watterson, veteran editor of the Louisville *Courier-Journal,* on the letter of a correspondent who pointed out, in connection with the case of Edith Cavell, that the United States had once hanged a woman (Mrs. Suratt) on still more dubious evidence:

"This insensate brute is equally disloyal to his country and his kind— assuming him to be a man and not an animal—and at the same time he is as ignorant as he is treasonable."

There was a good deal of scare propaganda in the magazines and in the movies. Popular magazines published serial stories describing German hordes trampling over American soil.

There were some attempts by German and Austrian agents to stir up and exploit labor discontent in factories and to interfere with munitions production for the Allies. Supplied with information from the alert British Intelligence Service, the State Department requested the recall of the Austrian Ambassador, Dr. Constantin Dumba, and of the German military and naval attachés, Captains von Papen and Boy-Ed.

The extent of German subversive activity was considerably magnified in the public imagination. There were repeated fearful predictions of a hidden army of German reservists who would rise and fight for the Fatherland. No such "army" ever materialized, even after America entered the war.

Despite the strong economic and propaganda pulls toward a pro-Ally orientation, there was little popular demand for American entrance into the war. At the very time when House was working out his mediation formula, with its strong suggestion of American intervention, there was considerable support in Congress for the Gore-McLemore resolution, warning Americans not to travel on ships belonging to belligerent nations. This anticipated the spirit of the neutrality legislation of the thirties. Strong White House pressure was employed to get this resolution tabled.

Foreign policy was not a clear-cut issue in the election of 1916. The German-Americans were inclined to regard Wilson as pro-British. It was the difficult task of the Republican candidate, Charles E. Hughes, to capitalize this discontent and at the same time to keep the support of a bellicose wing of the Republicans, of whom Theodore Roosevelt was the principal spokesman.

Undoubtedly the slogan "He kept us out of war" helped Wilson win one of the most closely contested elections in American history. But the President, in contrast to his successor in 1940, gave no sweeping "again and again and again" pledge to the voters. He stood on the warning which he had given to the German Government on submarine warfare.

The sands of time for effective American mediation were running out as the pressure of the German military and naval leaders for resumption of undersea war became more intense. Wilson was considering a peace appeal when the German Chancellor Bethmann-Hollweg anticipated him with a note expressing willingness to enter a peace conference. This note, dispatched on December 12, 1916, was noncommittal as to terms. A week later Wilson made his last effort for the "peace without victory" which he later described to the Senate as the only peace that could be enduring. He addressed a note to all the belligerent powers, asking them to state their peace terms.

The Germans maintained their reserve. The Allies, indignant at being called on to lay their cards on the table, sent a joint reply which slammed, bolted, and barred the door to any prospect of negotiated peace. Besides the evacuation of all invaded territory, with indemnities, they called for "the restitution of provinces or territories wrested in the past from the Allies by force or against the will of their populations, the liberation of Slavs, Rumanians, and Czechs from foreign domination, the enfranchisement of populations subject to the bloody tyranny of the Turks, the expulsion from Europe of the Ottoman Empire."

Such terms could only be imposed on defeated enemies. There was also a strong annexationist flavor in the German conditions, which were published late in January. These included "a frontier which would protect Germany and Poland strategically against Russia"; restitution of France "under reservation of strategic and economic changes of the frontier and financial compensation," restitution of Belgium "under special guaranty for the safety of Germany," restitution of colonies, "in the form of an agreement which would give Germany colonies adequate to her population and economic interest."

All prospect of a peace in which the United States might have played a mediating role disappeared on January 31, 1917, when Germany announced the resumption of unlimited submarine warfare. The naval and military leaders had convinced the Kaiser that they possessed sufficient submarine strength to cut the lifeline of British communications.

This German decision was not irrational. The figures of sinkings soon rose to formidable heights. But in retrospect the calculated breach with the United States was a fatal blunder. It is very doubtful whether the United States would have entered the war actively without the submarine provocation. Wilson said to House as late as January 4, 1917:

"There will be no war. This country does not intend to become involved in this war. We are the only one of the great white nations that is free from war today, and it would be a crime against civilization for us to go in."

The Russian Revolution occurred on March 12, a few weeks after the fateful German decision. One of its consequences was to eliminate Russia from participation in the war. The Russian front crumbled during 1917, and early in 1918 Germany was able to impose the Peace of Brest-Litovsk on the Soviet Government, which had come into power on November 7, 1917.

Now it is highly doubtful whether Britain, France, Italy, and the smaller Allies, deprived of Russia's vast manpower and receiving only economic aid from the United States, could have won a decisive military victory. The war would probably in this case have ended either in a German victory or in a stalemate, with Germany perhaps making some concessions in the West, but expanding on a large scale in the East.

The German leaders, however, did not anticipate the good fortune that was awaiting them in the East. They decided to stake everything on the submarine card. Wilson promptly broke off diplomatic relations. Then there was a pause, a period of waiting for some "overt act." Sir Cecil Spring Rice, the British Ambassador in Washington, was praying for "the destruction of an American ship with American passengers."[2]

Lloyd George, the new British Prime Minister, was trying to insure America's entrance into the conflict by subtler methods. No one, as he told Page, could have so commanding a voice at the peace conference as the President. The President's presence at this conference, Lloyd George suggested, was necessary for the proper organization of the peace. These were just the considerations that were most likely to appeal to Wilson's self-esteem and to his sincere belief that he might deserve well of his country and of the world by laying the foundations of a new international order, with safeguards against war.

The President, however, showed no disposition to rush the country

2. Millis, *Road to War*, 401.

into war. He was influenced by the doubts which he had confessed to Cobb. The pace of events was hastened by the revelation on February 24 that German Foreign Secretary Zimmermann had proposed, in the event of war with the United States, a treaty of alliance with Mexico, on the following basis:

"Make war together, make peace together, generous financial support and an understanding on our part that Mexico is to reconquer the lost territory in Texas, New Mexico, and Arizona."

Japan was also to be invited to adhere to this pact. From a moral standpoint Zimmermann's proposal is indistinguishable from the territorial bribes with which the Allies induced Italy and Rumania to enter the war. But in view of Mexico's military weakness the proposal was extremely stupid and helped to speed up the development of American war psychology.

Despite the stubborn filibuster of a minority of antiwar senators (a little group of willful men, as Wilson called them), the government hastened to arm American merchant ships. By April 2 there had been enough "overt acts" to induce Wilson to ask Congress for a declaration of war. America's war aims were described in the following glowing and abstract terms in the peroration:

> We shall fight for the things which we have always carried nearest to our hearts—for democracy, for the right of those who submit to authority to have a voice in their own governments, for the rights and liberties of small nations, for a universal dominion of right by such a concert of free peoples as shall bring peace and safety to all nations and make the world itself at last free.

The crusading note was further emphasized by such phrases as:

> We have no quarrel with the German people. We have no feeling towards them but one of sympathy and friendship. . . . The world must be made safe for democracy.

Opposition voices were heard in the debate on the war resolution. Senator Robert M. La Follette delivered a four-hour speech attacking the idea that this was or could be a war for democracy, suggesting that true neutrality would have kept the United States out of the war. Sena-

tor George Norris spoke of "the enormous profits of munitions manu-
facturers, steel brokers and bond dealers" and cried out: "We are about
to put the dollar sign upon the American flag."

Six senators and fifty representatives voted against the declaration
of war. Most of them were from the Middle West, where pro-Ally feeling was less pronounced than it was in the East and the South. By becoming involved in a European war, a fateful departure was made in
American policy. Giving up our historic limited goal of protecting this
hemisphere against foreign aggression, we were committing ourselves
to an ambitious crusade with such alluring but vague objectives as
"making the world safe for democracy" and "making the world itself at
last free."

One reason for growing skepticism about the success of this crusade
was Wilson's inability to inspire the majority of his countrymen with
enthusiasm for, or even understanding of, his great design for future
world peace. One wonders how many Americans carefully studied the
Fourteen Points, laid down by the President as America's peace aims,
or the supplementary statements of principle which amplified these
points.[3]

The main principles of Wilsonism were government by consent of
the governed, national self-determination, an end of secret treaties,
a nonvindictive peace, and an association of nations strong enough
to check aggression and keep the peace in the future. The mood that
developed in wartime America did not make for intelligent popular
support of Wilson's aims. The nation had not been involved in a major
foreign war within the memory of a living man. It went on a prodigious
emotional debauch.

American soil had not been invaded and the immediate cause of the
conflict, the right to carry on one-sided trade with one set of belligerents, was not an ideal trumpet call for martial action. As Wilson's ideals,
to the average man, were too abstract and rarefied to serve as fighting
slogans, the builders of national morale concentrated on building up
belief in the supreme wickedness of the "Hun," for whom "unspeak-
able" was one of the mildest adjectives in general use.

---

3. The Fourteen Points and other essential items in Wilson's peace program
are printed at the end of this chapter.

"Four-minute men" rushed about the land, selling war bonds and hate with equal vigor. Their favorite peroration was: "I'd compare those Huns with snakes, only that would be insulting the snakes." Some pastors found relief from previously repressed lives by shouting dramatically: "I say *God damn* the Kaiser—and I'm not swearing, either."

Pittsburgh "banned" Beethoven, to the greater glory of democracy. Sauerkraut became "liberty cabbage." Producers of films and stories with stock Teutonic villains reaped a rich harvest. Some professors went just as war mad and said just as foolish things as the extreme German nationalists whose chauvinistic boastings were held up to deserved ridicule.

All this did not create a hopeful background for a just and reasonable peace. It was significant that when the President, toward the end of the war, made one of his more serious and statesmanlike addresses, the audience perversely applauded all the more trivial clichés and remained indifferent to his more original and fruitful ideas.

By the autumn of 1918 the breaking point in the world struggle had come. America had proved more than an adequate substitute for Russia. The number of American troops on the western front increased from three hundred thousand in March 1918 to two million in November. Half-starved and exhausted by the blockade, repulsed in the last desperate attempts to break through on the western front in France, Germany faced the prospect of ever increasing American reinforcements and of continually increasing American supplies.

Ludendorff, who shared with Hindenburg the command of the German armies, urged the civilian government to appeal for an armistice on October 1. The German Chancellor, Prince Max of Baden, in agreement with the Austrian Government, appealed to Wilson on October 5 for an armistice on the basis of the Fourteen Points.

There was a widespread clamor in America for unconditional surrender. But Wilson kept the negotiations in progress. When the armistice was finally signed, it was on the basis of the Fourteen Points and subsequent public declarations of Wilson, with one reservation and one elucidation. Lloyd George reserved for future discussion Point 2, providing for freedom of the seas. And it was agreed between Colonel House, Wilson's representative in Paris, and the Allied leaders that "restoration" of invaded territory should mean that "compensation will be made by Germany for all damage done to the civilian population of the Allies and their property by the forces of Germany by land, by sea and from the air."

That there was a recognized obligation on the part of the Allies to make the peace treaty conform to the Fourteen Points and to Wilson's other statements is evident from the wording of a reply to a German protest against the peace terms in May 1919:

"The Allied and Associated Powers are in complete accord with the German delegation in their insistence that the basis for the negotiation of the treaty of peace is to be found in the correspondence which immediately preceded the signing of the armistice on November 11, 1918."

Wilson did not obtain Allied endorsement of his peace conditions without a severe diplomatic struggle behind the scenes. Colonel House went so far as to intimate that if the Fourteen Points were not accepted the negotiations with Germany would be wiped off the slate and America might then conclude a separate peace with Germany and Austria.[4] This firm tone led to satisfactory results in this instance, but it was seldom employed when the practical details of the settlement were being worked out.

The hope of far-sighted liberals in America and in Europe that Wilson's principles would be the foundation of a just and lasting peace could never have been achieved for several reasons.

Wilson's prestige was weakened first of all when he issued an ill-advised appeal for the return of a Democratic Congress in 1918. The Republicans were successful in the election, and Wilson's influence was lessened in the eyes of European statesmen accustomed to the system of government by a cabinet responsible to parliament. Another tactical error was Wilson's failure to appoint a single active representative Republican as a member of the commission to negotiate the peace. (The five members were Wilson, House, Secretary of State Robert Lansing, General Tasker Bliss, and Henry White, a Republican who had lived much of his life abroad and carried no special weight in the councils of his party.)

It was probably a mistake on Wilson's part to have attended the con-

4. House, *Intimate Papers*, vol. 4.

ference personally. He would have wielded greater power and influence from Washington. And Paris was an unfortunate choice for the seat of the conference if reconciliation rather than vengeance was to be the keynote of the peace. France had suffered much in the war, and in the Paris atmosphere everyone was afraid of being reproached with pro-Germanism. As Harold Nicolson, a young British diplomat who viewed the proceedings with a keen and critical eye, remarked:

"Given the atmosphere of the time, given the passions aroused in all democracies by the four years of war, it would have been impossible even for supermen to devise a peace of moderation and righteousness."[5]

Old-fashioned secret diplomacy is open to criticism. But one reason why the Congress of Vienna, meeting after the convulsions of the Napoleonic Wars, succeeded far better than the conference of Versailles was the freedom of the statesmen there from the influence of popular passion. The chief representatives of the European Allies, Lloyd George, Clemenceau, Orlando, knew they faced the danger of being swept away by a storm of popular reproach if they did not hold out for the maximum in territory and indemnities.

So the cards were heavily stacked against a peace treaty that would reflect the Fourteen Points and Wilson's other principles. If the President, amid the terrific strain of Paris, had time to take a cool historical view of what was going on, he must have felt the rightness of his earlier preference for a peace without victory. It is to his moral credit that he sometimes fought hard for his principles.

But Wilson's support of his ideals was erratic, inconsistent, and, on balance, ineffective. The President was uncompromising in rejecting Italian claims for Fiume and Dalmatia. But he acquiesced without a struggle in a still more flagrant violation of the right of self-determination: the assignment to Italy of the solidly German-Austrian South Tyrol.

In general, this principle was stretched to the limit whenever it would work to the disadvantage of the defeated powers and disregarded when it would operate in their favor. So there was no self-determination for six and a half million Austrians, the majority of whom wished to join

5. Nicolson, *Peacemaking, 1919,* 72.

Germany, or for three million Sudeten Germans who did not wish to become citizens of a Czecho-Slovak state, or for other ethnic minorities belonging to the defeated powers.

The Treaty of Versailles was especially disastrous on the economic side. It embodied two inconsistent principles, revenge and rapacity; the desire to make Germany helpless and the desire to make Germany pay. The completely unrealistic reparations settlement was to contribute much to the depth and severity of the world economic crisis ten years later. This crisis, in turn, was a very important factor in bringing Adolf Hitler into power.

Many of Germany's economic assets—her colonies, her merchant marine, her foreign holdings, her gold reserves—were confiscated. Under the terms of the treaty Germany lost about 10 per cent of its territory and population, one third of its coal, and three quarters of its iron ore. At the same time it was saddled with an enormous and at first undefined reparations bill, far in excess of any sum ever collected after any previous war.

This bill was finally fixed by the Reparations Commission at 32 billion dollars. (French Finance Minister Klotz, who was later appropriately committed to a lunatic asylum, had at first proposed a figure of 200 billion dollars, two hundred times the indemnity exacted from France after the Franco-Prussian War.) Germany could only hope to pay this tribute, which under the later Dawes and Young plans was set at annual payments of about half a billion dollars, by developing a permanent large uncompensated surplus of exports over imports.

There were two insoluble dilemmas in this attempted financial settlement. First, a weak Germany could not produce such a surplus, while a strong Germany would be inclined to balk at payment. Second, the only feasible method of transferring wealth on this scale, the use of German labor and material on reconstruction projects, was ruled out. And, in times of unemployment and failing demand, foreign countries were unable or unwilling to purchase German goods on a scale that would make possible the desired surplus of exports over imports.[6]

---

6. For this same economic reason, inability or unwillingness of the United States to accept large quantities of European exports, the war debts of the European Allies to the United States were unpayable.

One of the many dragons' teeth sown by the Treaty of Versailles was Article 231, which read:

The Allied and Associated Governments affirm and Germany accepts the responsibility of Germany and her Allies for causing all the loss and damage to which the Allied and Associated Governments and their nationals have been subjected as a consequence of the war imposed upon them by the aggression of Germany and her allies.

This linked up Germany's obligation to pay reparations with a blanket self-condemnation to which almost no German could have honestly subscribed. In the objective retrospect of postwar years few students of the subject in Allied and neutral countries upheld the proposition that Germany was solely responsible for the outbreak of World War I. There were differences of opinion about the degree of responsibility borne by Germany, Austria, Russia, and other belligerent powers. Fairly representative of the judgment of impartial scholarship is the opinion of Professor Sidney B. Fay, of Harvard University, the conclusion of an exhaustive inquiry into the causes of the conflict:

Germany did not plot a European war, did not want one and made genuine, though too belated efforts to avert one. . . . It was primarily Russia's general mobilization, made when Germany was trying to bring Austria to a settlement, which precipitated the final catastrophe, causing Germany to mobilize and declare war. . . . The verdict of the Versailles Treaty that Germany and her allies were responsible for the war, in view of the evidence now available, is historically unsound.[7]

By the time the Treaty of Versailles was cast in final form and imposed upon the Germans, scarcely a trace of the Wilsonian spirit remained. A bitter gibe became current in Europe. It was said that Wilson deserved the Nobel Prize not for peace, but for mathematics, since he had made fourteen equal zero. It is interesting to note the judgment of a well-known British participant in the peace discussions who sympathized with Wilson's ideals. The economist John Maynard Keynes, in his *Economic Consequences of the Peace* (London: Macmillan), wrote:

7. Fay, *Origins of the World War*, 552, 554–55.

The Treaty includes no provisions for the economic rehabilitation of Europe—nothing to make the defeated Central Empires into good neighbors, nothing to stabilize the new State of Europe, nothing to reclaim Russia; nor does it promote in any way a compact of economic solidarity amongst the Allies themselves.

Wilson was partly reconciled to the sacrifice of his ideals of political and economic justice by the hope that the newly formed League of Nations, with the United States as a member, would be a force for reform and reconciliation. This hope was not fulfilled. The President experienced his final tragedy when, after his nervous and physical breakdown, the Versailles Treaty, in which the League Covenant had been incorporated, failed to win ratification in the Senate. There was an unbreakable deadlock between the President's insistence that the Covenant be accepted with, at most, minor changes and Senator Lodge's insistence on strong reservations. A majority was not to be had for either proposition and the United States remained outside the League of Nations.[8]

The submarine remained a permanent weapon of warfare against merchant shipping. For every injustice the Treaty of Versailles redressed, it created another, equally flagrant and disturbing to future peace. The failure of the new and enlarged states in eastern and southeastern Europe to band together in close voluntary federation created an unhealthy fragmentation of the European economy and made it easier for Nazi and Communist careers of conquest to get under way.

The greatest failure of all was in "making the world safe for democracy." Communism and fascism, not democracy, were the authentic political offspring of World War I.

There remains the argument that America, by taking part in the war, had frustrated a German design for world conquest. But this design looked less and less convincing as high-powered war propaganda receded into the shadows. The contention that the British and French fight was "our fight" did not convince Wilson's confidential adviser,

8. A certain school of thought is inclined to attribute most of the world's interwar troubles to the fact that the United States and the Soviet Union (until 1934) were outside the League. But these two powers have been charter members of the United Nations, without producing world harmony.

House, even in the first weeks after the end of hostilities. Discussing this question in his diary on January 4, 1919, House observes:

> I for one have never admitted this. I have always felt that the United States was amply able to take care of herself, that we were never afraid of the Germans and would not have been afraid of them even if France and England had gone under.[9]

The ghostly tramp of imagined German legions, marching through the streets of American cities, may have frightened a few nervous Americans in 1915 and 1916. But by 1933 most Americans would probably have agreed with the sentiments expressed by William Allen White in a thoughtful Armistice Day editorial:

> Fifteen years ago came the Armistice and we all thought it was to be a new world. It is! But a lot worse than it was before.
>
> Ten million men were killed and many more maimed, fifty billion dollars worth of property destroyed, the world saddled with debts.
>
> And for what? Would it have been any worse if Germany had won? Ask yourself honestly. No one knows.
>
> Is this old world as safe for democracy as it was before all those lives were lost?[10]

By no standard of judgment could America's First Crusade be considered a success. It was not even an effective warning. For all the illusions, misjudgments, and errors of the First Crusade were to be repeated, in exaggerated form, in a Second Crusade that was to be a still more resounding and unmistakable political and moral failure, despite the repetition of military success.

WILSON'S BLUEPRINT FOR PEACE
*The Fourteen Points, set forth in an address to Congress,*
*January 8, 1918*
1. Open covenants of peace, openly arrived at, after which there shall be no private international understandings of any kind but diplomacy shall proceed always frankly and in the public view.

9. House, *Intimate Papers*, 4:268.
10. White, *Autobiography*, 640.

2. Absolute freedom of navigation upon the seas, outside territorial waters, alike in peace and in war, except as the seas may be closed in whole or in part by international action for the enforcement of international covenants.

3. The removal, so far as possible, of all economic barriers and the establishment of an equality of trade conditions among all the nations consenting to the peace and associating themselves for its maintenance.

4. Adequate guarantees given and taken that national armaments will be reduced to the lowest point consistent with domestic safety.

5. A free, open-minded and absolutely impartial adjustment of all colonial claims, based upon a strict observance of the principle that in determining all such questions of sovereignty the interests of the populations concerned must have equal weight with the equitable claims of the government whose title is to be determined.

6. The evacuation of all Russian territory and such a settlement of all questions affecting Russia as will secure the best and freest cooperation of the other nations of the world in obtaining for her an unhampered and unembarrassed opportunity for the independent determination of her own political development and national policy and assure her of a sincere welcome into the society of free nations under institutions of her own choosing; and, more than a welcome, assistance also of every kind that she may need and may herself desire. The treatment accorded Russia by her sister nations in the months to come will be the acid test of their good will, of their comprehension of her needs as distinguished from their own interests, and of their intelligent and unselfish sympathy.

7. Belgium, the whole world will agree, must be evacuated and restored, without any attempt to limit the sovereignty which she enjoys in common with all other free nations. No other single act will serve as this will serve to restore confidence among the nations in the laws which they have themselves set and determined for the government of their relations with one another. Without this healing act the whole structure and validity of international law is forever impaired.

8. All French territory should be freed and the invaded portions restored, and the wrong done to France by Prussia in 1871 in the matter of Alsace-Lorraine, which has unsettled the peace of the world for

nearly fifty years, should be righted, in order that peace may once more be made secure in the interest of all.

9. A readjustment of the frontiers of Italy should be effected along clearly recognizable lines of nationality.

10. The peoples of Austria-Hungary, whose place among the nations we wish to see safeguarded and assured, should be accorded the freest opportunity of autonomous development.

11. Rumania, Serbia, and Montenegro should be evacuated; occupied territories restored; Serbia accorded free and secure access to the sea; and the relations of the several Balkan states to one another determined by friendly counsel along historically established lines of allegiance and nationality; and international guarantees of the political and economic independence and territorial integrity of the several Balkan states should be entered into.

12. The Turkish portions of the present Ottoman Empire should be assured a secure sovereignty, but the other nationalities which are now under Turkish rule should be assured an undoubted security of life and an absolutely unmolested opportunity of autonomous development, and the Dardanelles should be permanently opened as a free passage to the ships and commerce of all nations under international guarantees.

13. An independent Polish state should be erected which should include the territories inhabited by indisputably Polish populations, which should be assured a free and secure access to the sea and whose political and economic independence and territorial integrity should be guaranteed by international covenant.

14. A general association of nations must be formed under specific covenants for the purpose of affording mutual guarantees of political independence and territorial integrity to great and small states alike.

*Further points in President Wilson's address to Congress,*
*February 11, 1918*

That each part of the final settlement must be based upon the essential justice of that particular case and upon such adjustments as are most likely to bring a peace that will be permanent.

That peoples and provinces are not to be bartered about from sovereignty to sovereignty as if they were mere chattels and pawns in a game, even the great game, now forever discredited, of the balance of power; but that

Every territorial settlement involved in this war must be made in the interest and for the benefit of the populations concerned, and not as a part of any mere adjustment or compromise of claims among rival states; and

That all well-defined national aspirations shall be accorded the utmost satisfaction that can be accorded them without introducing new or perpetuating old elements of discord and antagonism that would be likely in time to break the peace of Europe and consequently of the world.

*Statements in Wilson's New York City address,*
*September 27, 1918*

The impartial justice meted out must involve no discrimination between those to whom we wish to be just and those to whom we do not wish to be just. It must be a justice that plays no favorites and knows no standard but the equal rights of the several peoples concerned;

No special or separate interest of any single nation or any group of nations can be made the basis of any part of the settlement which is not consistent with the common interest of all;

There can be no leagues or alliances or special covenants and understandings within the general and common family of the League of Nations;

And, more specifically, there can be no special, selfish economic combinations within the League and no employment of any form of economic boycott or exclusion except as the power of economic penalty by exclusion from the markets of the world may be vested in the League of Nations itself as a means of discipline and control.

# 2

## Communism and Fascism: Offspring of the War

When World War I was at its height, it must have seemed probable that the victor would be either the Kaiser or the leaders of the western powers. But the true political winners from that terrific holocaust were three men who were little known, even in their own countries, when hostilities began.

There was a Russian revolutionary, living in obscure poverty in Zürich. There was an Italian radical socialist who turned ultranationalist during the war. There was a completely unknown German soldier, an Austrian by birth, who wept tears of bitter rage when he heard the news of defeat as he lay gassed in a hospital. The names of these men were Vladimir Ilyich Lenin, Benito Mussolini, and Adolf Hitler.

Wilson proclaimed democracy as the objective of the war. And his conception of democracy was derived from Anglo-Saxon liberalism. Its bases were freedom of speech and press, freedom of election and organization, and "the right of those who submit to authority to have a voice in their own governments."

The demons to be slain, in the view of the Wilsonian crusaders, were autocracy and militarism. These abstractions were personified in uniformed and bemedaled monarchs, in titled aristocrats (so long as they were not British), in the pomp and pageantry of old-fashioned empires.

Tsarist Russia was not an appropriate partner in a crusade for democracy. But Tsarism fell just before America entered the war. There was a Japanese Emperor, whose subjects revered him as a god, in the Allied camp. But no one said much about him.

The war dealt a mortal blow to the three great empires which had dominated Europe east of the Rhine. The Tsar and his family were slaughtered in a cellar in the Ural town of Ekaterinburg. The Austrian Empire disintegrated as its many peoples flew apart. The Kaiser took refuge in the Netherlands. All the new states on the European map (Poland, Czechoslovakia, Finland, Latvia, Lithuania, Estonia) were republics.

But, although hereditary monarchy certainly lost as a result of the war, liberal democracy just as certainly did not win. On the contrary, the war begat a new type of plebeian dictatorship, which may most conveniently be called totalitarianism.

There were certain differences between the two main forms of the totalitarian state, communism and fascism. Both owed their existence to the despair, brutalization, and discarding of old economic forms and moral restraints which were associated with the war. Along with this common origin these twin offspring of the First World War possessed a more important bond. Starting from differing philosophic bases, they developed truly remarkable similarities in practice. There is infinitely more in common between communism and fascism than there is between either system and liberal democracy.

The connection between war and revolution was most direct and obvious in Russia. The downfall of the Tsar was at first greeted in the Allied capitals. It was hopefully regarded as a revolt against the pro-German influences at the Court, as an assurance that the war would be prosecuted with more vigor. But events soon disproved these hopes.

The weak Provisional Government, a combination of liberals and moderate socialists, which at first replaced the old regime, could neither direct nor restrain the vast disruptive forces which had been let loose. Respect for order and authority disappeared. Russian conditions became more and more anarchical.

The peasants swarmed over the estates of the large landowners, pillaging manor houses and dividing up the land among themselves. There was a gigantic mutiny in the huge Russian Army. The soldiers began by debating orders and refusing to attack. Then, refusing to fight at all, they deserted in hordes. Finns, Ukrainians, Caucasians, and other non-Russian peoples clamored for independence. The factory workers started with demands for less work and more pay. They advanced to the point of seizing factories and driving away owners and unpopular foremen.

A master of practical revolutionary tactics, V. I. Lenin, guided and took advantage of all these forces of upheaval. Years before, he had written: "Give us an organization of revolutionaries and we will turn Russia upside down." And less than eight months after the overthrow of the Tsar's rule, Lenin's "organization," the Bolshevik, later renamed the Communist party, was strong enough to lead a successful coup d'état against the crumbling Provisional Government. A republic of soviets was proclaimed, based on the principle of the dictatorship of the proletariat, or manual-working class, and dedicated to the ideal of world communist revolution.

The soviets were elected bodies of workers, soldiers, and, to a smaller extent, peasants, which sprang up in spontaneous, haphazard fashion all over the country after the Revolution. Delegates were elected in factories and military units and at first could be freely recalled.

After the Communists became entrenched in power, elections to the soviets became an empty formality. Supreme authority in every field was in the hands of the ruling Communist party. Lenin is said to have remarked, half jokingly, that there could be any number of parties in Russia—on one condition: the Communist party must be in power, and all the other parties must be in jail. This was an excellent description of Soviet political practice.

The world had witnessed the birth of a new kind of state, based on the unlimited power of a single political party. This party regarded itself as an elite, required a period of probation for applicants for membership, and deliberately kept this membership restricted.

Events followed a different course in Italy. Yet the political result was similar in many respects. There had been a good deal of ferment and unrest in Italy after the war, with strikes, riots, stoppages of essential services. The Italian Communists and some of the Socialists dreamed of setting up a revolutionary dictatorship on the Soviet model.

But they were anticipated and defeated by an ex-Socialist, Benito Mussolini, who had become the evangel of another armed doctrine. This was fascism.

Communism was based on the economic teachings of Karl Marx, as interpreted by Lenin and by Lenin's successor, Josef Stalin. Fascism was a much more personal and eclectic type of theory, worked out by Mussolini after he had broken with socialism. Contrary to a general impression, Mussolini was not a conservative or an upholder of the *status quo*.

The type of state which gradually evolved in Italy after the Fascist March on Rome of October 29, 1922, was a break with Italy's political past. The Fascist order emphasized the supremacy of the state over the individual. It tried to solve the clash of interest between capital and labor by making the government supreme arbiter in economic disputes. Fascism organized, indoctrinated, and drilled the youth, praised the martial virtues, gave the workers an organized system of free entertainment, tried to dramatize every economic problem in terms of a struggle in which every citizen must be a soldier.

Had there been no war, it is very unlikely that fascism, a creed which was alien to the easy-going and skeptical Italian temperament, would have conquered Italy. Many of Mussolini's closest associates were veterans who disliked socialism and communism, wanted some kind of social change, and were attracted by Mussolini's energetic personality and nationalist ideas. The Italian Leftists played into Mussolini's hands by plunging the country into a state of chronic disorder, not enough to make a revolution, but enough to reconcile many middle-class Italians to Mussolini's strong-arm methods of restoring order.

The gap between war and revolution was longest in Germany. Hunger and inflation made for civil strife in the years immediately after the end of the war. There were left-wing uprisings in Berlin and Munich and the Ruhr. There were also right-wing extremist movements against the republic.

By 1924, however, physical conditions had improved, and it seemed that a period of political stability had set in. Germany was admitted to the League of Nations. The Pact of Locarno, under which Great Britain and Italy guaranteed the existing Franco-German frontier, seemed to offer a prospect of eliminating the historic Franco-German feud.

But the hurricane of the world economic crisis, following the lost war and the inflation, which had ruined the German middle class, paved the way for the third great European political upheaval. This was the rise to power of Adolf Hitler and his National Socialist, or Nazi, party.

Of the three revolutionary "success stories" Hitler's was the most remarkable. Both Lenin and Mussolini were men of political training and experience. But Hitler had absolutely none. There seemed to be nothing to mark him out among the millions of soldiers who had worn the field-gray uniform and fought through the war.

It would have seemed improbable fantasy if anyone had predicted that this completely unknown soldier would become the absolute ruler of Germany, set out on a Napoleonic career of conquest, and immolate himself in Wagnerian fashion after leading his country to the heights of military power and to the depths of collapse and complete defeat. But in Hitler's case the factual record eclipsed the wildest fictional imagination.

Germany in years of severe crisis and heavy unemployment was responsive to a man who gave himself out as a wonder-worker, a savior. Hitler was a passionate, rapt, almost hypnotic orator in a country where there was little impressive public speaking. The very obscurity of his origin lent a romantic appeal. Perhaps the secret of his attraction lay in his apparent sympathy and affection. Sentimental as it was, and combined also with less obvious mistrust and scorn, his deceptive sympathy for the plight of the unemployed and the suffering made an impression quite unlike that made by the normal type of sober, stolid German politician, especially in such a period of despair and bitterness. Consequently Hitler exerted a powerful attraction on the German masses, who ordinarily took little interest in politics.

Hitler knew how to appeal to German instincts and prejudices. The ideal of the powerful state had always been popular. Hitler promised a "Third Reich," more glorious than the two which had existed earlier. Interpretations of history in terms of race have long possessed a wide appeal in Germany. Hitler vulgarized and popularized the teachings of Teutonic race theorists like the Germanized Englishman, Houston Stewart Chamberlain.

Anti-Semitism had been strengthened in Germany after the war by two developments. Many leaders of Communist and extreme leftist movements—Rosa Luxemburg, Leo Jogisches, Kurt Eisner, to name a few—were of Jewish origin. Many Jews of eastern Europe, fleeing from pogroms and unsettled conditions, had migrated into Germany. Some of these East-European Jews took an active part in the speculation which was rampant in Germany because of the unstable currency and the shortage of commodities.

Of course these two groups, the political extremists and the specula-
tors, had nothing whatever to do with each other. But Hitler exploited
both in building up for his audiences a picture of the Jew as simultaneously a conscienceless exploiter and profiteer and a force for the
subversion of national institutions.

Like the other modern revolutionaries, Lenin and Mussolini, Hitler
profited from the weakness and division of his opponents. The German
republic was born in a time of misery, defeat, and humiliation. It never
captured the imagination or the enthusiastic loyalty of the German
people.

The German labor movement might have been a bulwark against
the Nazi onslaught, but it was split between the Social Democrats and
the Communists. The latter, on orders from Moscow, concentrated
their fire on the Social Democrats, not on the Nazis. They were acting
on the highly mistaken calculation that Hitler's victory would be followed by a reaction in favor of communism.

Whether Hitler reflected the will of the German people or whether
they were victims of his dictatorship is often debated. No sweeping,
unqualified answer can be accurate.

That the Nazi movement appealed to a strong minority of the Germans is indisputable. Hitler got 37 per cent of the votes cast in the election of 1932, when the rule of law prevailed and all parties were free to
state their case. The Nazis got a somewhat higher proportion, about 44
per cent, of the votes cast in the election of March 4, 1933. This made
it possible for Hitler to come into power with a small parliamentary
majority, since the German Nationalists, who were then in alliance with
the Nazis, polled enough votes to insure this result.

This election, however, could not be considered free. Terror was
already at work. The Communists had been made scapegoats for the
burning of the Reichstag building. Nazi Brown Shirts were beating and
intimidating political opponents. Once Hitler had clamped down his
dictatorship, there is no means of determining how many Germans
professed to support him out of enthusiasm, how many because it was
distinctly safer not to be marked down as disaffected.

The idea that all, or a great majority of, Germans were lusting for
war is not borne out by objective study of the facts. Up to the outbreak
of World War II Hitler persisted in publicly professing his devotion to

peace. His favorite pose was that of the veteran soldier who knew the horrors of war and never wished to experience another. This attitude was designed to deceive his own people, as well as the outside world.

Many Germans hoped to the end that there would be no war. Foreigners who were in Germany at critical periods before the outbreak of war and even at the time of Germany's greatest military success, in 1940, were often impressed by the apathy, the absence of any signs of popular enthusiasm.

It is sometimes represented as a proof of deep, incorrigible depravity in the German character that the average German seems to feel little sense of war guilt. But it is doubtful whether the average Italian spends much time beating his breast in repentance for the misdeeds of Mussolini. Should the Soviet regime be overthrown, the average Soviet citizen would feel little sense of personal responsibility for the horrors of the Soviet slave-labor camps.

One of the most demoralizing effects of totalitarianism in any form is its tendency to paralyze the individual's feeling of personal moral accountability. The state is so powerful, the individual so weak, that the typical, almost inescapable, reaction is one of helplessness.

Nazism, like communism and fascism, was an ironical product of the war that was fought in the name of democracy. The hard core of Hitler's following was recruited among men who, in their hearts, had never been demobilized, who could never adjust themselves to civilian life. A great part of Hitler's appeal was to feelings associated with the lost war, the inflation, the economic hardships of the postwar period.

Communists and Fascists may be inclined to dispute the essential kinship of these two systems. But it would be difficult to deny that the following ten characteristics are very important, politically, economically, and morally. They may be listed as follows.

(1) The all-powerful and supposedly infallible leader. These three plebeian dictators—Hitler, the unknown soldier; Stalin, the son of a drunken cobbler, a hunted political rebel in Tsarist times; Mussolini, whose father was a radical village blacksmith—have reveled in clouds of sycophantic incense which would have been too strong for the nostrils of Tsar or Kaiser. "Sun of the entire world" is one of the many epithets of oriental adulation which have been lavished upon Stalin. The personal power of these modern dictators has been far greater than

that of any crowned ruler of modern times. They have been subject to no check or limit in law or public opinion.

(2) The single ruling party. Under communism, fascism, and nazism only the single ruling party has been permitted to exist legally. Parliaments in the Soviet Union, Germany, and Italy became mere rubber stamps for the registration of the party decisions. Voting under totalitarian regimes is virtually unanimous and altogether meaningless. No voice of independent criticism is ever heard.

(3) Government by a combination of propaganda, terrorism, and flattery of the masses. All three dictatorships developed very powerful methods for molding the minds of the peoples under their rule. The Soviet, Nazi, and Fascist citizen ("subject" would be a more accurate word) has been enveloped in a cloud of state-directed propaganda. From the cradle to the grave the idea is drummed into his head, through the newspapers, the schools, the radio, that he is living in the best of all possible worlds, that his highest glory and happiness are to be found in serving the existing regime, that the "toiler," the "worker," the "peasant," by this very service becomes a peculiarly noble and exalted creature.

Open counterpropaganda and free discussion are impossible. And for those individuals who were not converted, there was always the grim threat of the secret political police. This body changed its name, but never its character, several times in Russia, where it has been known at various times as the Cheka, the OGPU, the NKVD, the MVD. The Gestapo in Germany and the Ovra in Italy fulfilled the same functions.

The citizen under totalitarianism enjoys not the slightest defense against the arbitrary violence of the state. He can be seized, held in prison indefinitely, sent to a concentration camp, tortured, killed—all without the publicity which would inspire in some resisters the spirit of martyrdom. More than that, his family is exposed to reprisals if he falls into disfavor.

A Soviet law, published in the spring of 1934, authorizes the banishment "to remote parts of Siberia" of the relatives of a Soviet citizen who leaves the country without permission. Totalitarian secret police organizations habitually employ threats against relatives as a means of extorting confessions.

(4) Exaltation of militarism. "Every Soviet family, school, or politi-

cal organization is in duty bound to instill in the Soviet youth from the earliest age those qualities necessary to the Red soldier: military spirit, *a love of war*, endurance, self-reliance and boundless loyalty" (italics supplied). This statement appeared in *Komsomolskaya Pravda*, official organ of the Soviet Union of Communist Youth, on May 21, 1941. One of the reasons for abolishing coeducation in Soviet elementary schools was to give boys an earlier start on military training.

The names of Hitler and Mussolini will always be associated with glorification of war. Hitler wrote in *Mein Kampf:* "What the German people owes to the army may be summed up in one word, namely, everything." Drills, marches, and parades became second nature to the German and Italian youth.

(5) Full government control of labor power and of the national economy. In this field the original methods of the totalitarian regimes varied. But the end result was strikingly similar. Communism started out as a violent social revolution, expropriating all kinds of private property from which profit was derived and confiscating almost all private wealth.

After three decades it has evolved into a system under which a Communist managerial class, much better paid than the average Soviet citizen and with many perquisites of office, runs the state-owned factories, mines, railways, banks, and other enterprises, including the collective farms.

Under fascism and nazism, owners of property were usually not directly expropriated, except, in Germany, for racial reasons. But they were subjected to so many curbs and regulations, designed to combat unemployment, to increase military output, to make German and Italian industries self-sufficient, that the employer became little more than a managing director for the state or the ruling party. The scope of state ownership under nazism and fascism was extended, and state interference and regulation became almost unlimited.

Labor was organized, regimented, and propagandized in very similar fashion under all three regimes. All went in heavily for much publicized social benefits to workers, insurance schemes, vacations with pay, free sports and entertainments. All took away from the workers the right to form independent unions and to strike.

The labor movement in Russia was run by Communists, in Germany by Nazis, in Italy by Fascists. What this meant was that the interest of the individual worker always came second to the supposed interest of the state and the policy of the ruling party.

(6) Widespread use of slave labor. This is a natural and logical consequence of the Communist-Fascist belief that the individual has no rights which the state is bound to respect. Nazi-imposed forced labor came to an end with the military collapse of Germany in 1945. Some six or seven million workers, the majority recruited under some degree of compulsion and segregated in special barracks for wartime labor, were in German territory at that time. The majority of these uprooted human beings were sent back to their native countries. But over a million preferred the bleak and precarious life of the DP camp to the prospect of living in the Soviet Union or in the postwar Communist states of Eastern Europe.

Slave labor in Russia began on a large scale when about a million families of kulaks, or richer peasants, were dispossessed in the drive for collective farming in 1929 and 1930. A large number of these kulaks, men, women, and children indiscriminately, were thrown into freight cars and shipped off to timber camps and new construction enterprises.

Other groups swelled the numbers of this huge forced-labor system. Among these were dissatisfied nationalists in the Ukraine and other non-Russian regions, Communists who had been purged, persons suspected of foreign contacts and of too-active religious sympathies. Later, slave laborers were recruited from other sources.

There were mass roundups and deportations from Eastern Poland and the Baltic states and other regions occupied by the Red Army. There were considerable numbers of German and Japanese war prisoners. Some minor Soviet republics (the Volga German, Crimean Tartar, Kalmyk, and some administrative districts in the Caucasus) were dissolved during the war because the people were not considered loyal to the Soviet regime. Many of their inhabitants were sent to forced-labor concentration camps.

So a vast network of slave-labor reservations, which no independent foreign investigator has ever been allowed to visit, mostly located in northern Russia and Siberia, developed under the direction of the political police. Serious students of the subject estimate that there may be eight or ten million human beings in the Soviet labor camps.[1]

The conditions of the food, housing, and sanitation, and the excessive overwork are appallingly inhuman, according to the testimony of a number of individuals, Russians and foreigners, who have escaped or who have been released. Mortality is very high. The methods of punishment make Negro slavery in the United States before the Civil War seem almost humane.

(7) Hostility to religion. Dictatorships which set themselves above all restraints, which arrogate to themselves the privilege of trampling on all human rights, are inevitably hostile to any form of belief in a transcendent moral law with divine sanctions. The modern dictator's first demand on his subjects is unconditional obedience. The totalitarian state recognizes no distinction between what is due to God and what is due to Caesar. It claims all as Caesar's portion.

Communism is based on the dogmatic atheistic materialism of Karl Marx. The Soviet Government has persecuted all forms of religion, and considerable numbers of priests, mullahs, and rabbis have all been sent to concentration camps. A few were sentenced after show trials. Many more were disposed of by the simpler method of arrest and administrative banishment. And the price which the greatly weakened Orthodox Church pays for the greater tolerance which it has enjoyed since the war is complete subservience to the political demands of the state.

Many churchmen, both Catholics and Protestants, were thrown into Nazi concentration camps. Had Hitler won the war, the churches would probably have faced a still more difficult future, as is evident from the *Diaries* of Goebbels. A somewhat easier *modus vivendi* was worked out between church and state in Italy. But in Italy also there were repeated conflicts between the Fascist state and the Catholic Church over the question of education, and active members of Catholic social groups were often singled out for persecution.

(8) A primitive tribal form of chauvinist nationalism. Hitler and

1. The fullest and most informative treatment of this subject in English is *Forced Labor in Soviet Russia,* by David J. Dallin and Boris I. Nicolaevsky.

Mussolini made a national superiority complex the very basis of their creeds. The Nazi "master race" theory has repeatedly been denounced and parodied.

Soviet communism preached and still preaches a doctrine of international revolution, to be accompanied by an abolition of racial and national distinctions. But communist theory and Russian practice have become more and more divergent. Stalin, perhaps impressed by the successes of his rival dictators with their nationalist propaganda, has been cultivating a form of Russian "master race" delusion. This takes the form of announcing that some unknown or little-known Russian has anticipated almost every important discovery in natural science, exploration, and military development. Foreign literature, music, art, and science are systematically belittled merely because they are foreign and non-Communist in inspiration.

(9) The cultivation of fear, hatred, and suspicion of the outside world. These were the three stock themes of the Nazi propaganda master, Josef Goebbels, and of his counterparts in the Soviet Union and in Italy. Privations which are the natural and inevitable result of "guns instead of butter" economic policies and of bureaucratic blundering are attributed to the wicked designs and conspiracies of foreign powers. The propaganda machines are adept in conjuring up demons to serve as scapegoats—Jews in Germany, for instance; Trotskyites, saboteurs, "grovelers before the West" in Russia.

Normal free contacts with foreign countries are discouraged and forbidden. This policy has been carried to its greatest extreme in Russia. Few foreigners are admitted to that country, and they find themselves under constant police surveillance. Foreign non-Communist newspapers are not sold, and Russians may not receive them. A unique recent decree, which goes beyond anything in the Nazi and Fascist record in this field, flatly prohibits intermarriage between Russians and foreigners. Soviet wives of foreigners in most cases have not been allowed to leave Russia. It has become increasingly dangerous for Russians to associate with foreigners.

Because Germany and Italy are in a less isolated geographical position, Hitler and Mussolini never imposed such a complete blackout on foreign contacts. But there was a constant attempt by Nazi and Fascist propagandists to cultivate a spirit of bellicose suspicion of foreigners as spies. Under all three dictatorships it was stock procedure to represent independent foreign journalists as malicious slanderers.

(10) Perhaps the most ominous common trait of the totalitarian creeds is an almost paranoid conviction of world-conquering mission. Belief that the Russian Revolution is only the first step toward a Communist revolution that will encompass the entire globe is the very essence of Lenin's and Stalin's teachings. In his book, *Problems of Leninism,* which has in Russia all the authority which Hitler's *Mein Kampf* possessed in Nazi Germany, Stalin quotes with approval the following statement by Lenin:

> It is inconceivable that the Soviet Republic should continue to exist for a long period side by side with imperialist states. Ultimately one or the other must conquer. Meanwhile a number of terrible clashes between the Soviet Republic and the bourgeois states are inevitable.

Hitler's idea of Teutonic racial destiny is an equivalent of Stalin's and Lenin's faith in the messianic role of the proletariat and the international revolutionary Communist movement. Both communism and nazism created fifth columns (the Communist far more numerous and better organized) and thereby contributed one of the great divisive and subversive forces of modern times.

And Mussolini boasted that, "if every century has its peculiar doctrine, there are a thousand indications that fascism is that of the twentieth century."

An additional common trait of the Soviet and Nazi brands of totalitarianism is the capacity and willingness to commit atrocities (in the full sense of that much abused word) on a scale that makes the most ruthless and oppressive governments of the nineteenth century seem positively humanitarian. The Nazi slaughter of millions of Jews during the war would stand on a lonely pinnacle of state-inspired criminality if it were not for the much less publicized horrors which must be laid to the account of the Soviet regime.

First of these was the "liquidation of the kulaks as a class," officially decreed in March 1930. Under this procedure hundreds of thousands of peasant families whose only crime was that they were a little more prosperous than their neighbors were stripped of all their possessions and impressed into slave labor. There were no gas-chamber executions of kulaks, but many perished as a result of overwork, underfeeding, and maltreatment.

Second was the man-made famine in the Ukraine and the North Caucasus in 1932–33. This was not an unavoidable natural disaster. It was a deliberate reprisal inflicted by the government on the peasants because of their failure to work enthusiastically in the collective farms. Several million people perished in this famine. This is reflected in subsequent Soviet census reports for the Ukraine. I can testify from personal observation that a death rate of 10 per cent was normal in the very wide area affected by the famine. Death by starvation is slower and perhaps more painful than death by asphyxiation.

Third was the establishment of a vast system of slave labor as a normal feature of the Soviet economy. This system is far more cruel than was serfdom in Russia before its abolition in 1861 or slavery in the United States before Abraham Lincoln issued the Emancipation Proclamation, just because it is completely dehumanized.

An individual master might be kind or capriciously indulgent, but a secret-police organization dealing with people who are assumed to be enemies of the state is certain to employ the methods of Simon Legree without stint or variation. This is confirmed by the unanimous testimony of the Poles who were sent to slave-labor camps, assembled in *The Dark Side of the Moon* (New York: Scribner, 1947) and by such records of personal experience as Jerzy Gliksman's *Tell the West* (New York: Gresham Press, 1948), Vladimir Tchernavin's *I Speak for the Silent* (Boston: Hale and Flint, 1935), and many others.

A good deal of nonsense has been written about the Soviet regime as a riddle, a mystery, an enigma, and what not. But there is no secret about the underlying philosophy of communism. The Communist International was surely the most open conspiracy to promote violent revolution ever organized.

It is true that Soviet propaganda and Soviet censorship created some confusion about the character and methods of Soviet rule — but only in the minds of people who really in their hearts wished to be fooled. The volume of evidence that Soviet communism shared with nazism the ten common traits which have been listed was overwhelming and was certainly available to any statesman who cared to give serious study to the problem.

Soviet behavior after the war is sometimes referred to in Western countries in accents of hurt disillusionment. But this behavior was completely in line with basic Communist philosophy. It could have been, doubtless was, predicted down to the smallest detail by anyone with a reasonable background of Soviet experience and study.

Before America's Second Crusade was launched, two things were, or should have been, crystal clear. First, there was no moral or humanitarian reason to prefer Soviet conquest to Nazi or Japanese conquest. Second, from the cold-blooded standpoint of American political interest, one center of aggressive expansion in Moscow would not be more desirable than two centers in Berlin and Tokyo.

The organizers and eulogists of America's Second Crusade completely overlooked both these points. They chose to wring their hands in easily predictable frustration after the inevitable consequences of helping the Soviet Union achieve vast territorial and political expansion unfolded in relentless sequence.

# 3

## The Collapse of Versailles

It was the announced purpose of the Treaty of Versailles to replace the state of war by a "firm, just and durable peace." But the peace settlements with Germany and its allies were neither firm nor just nor durable. A century elapsed between the end of the Napoleonic Wars and the next general European conflict. But there were only two decades of uneasy armistice between the First and Second World Wars.

The Treaty of Versailles might be called too mild for its sternness and too stern for its mildness. The negotiators at Versailles fell between the two stools of a peace of reconciliation and an utterly ruthless, Carthaginian destruction of Germany as a major power.

German public opinion could not be expected to accept willingly the mutilation of the country's eastern frontier, the placing of millions of Sudeten Germans under undesired Czech rule, the inconvenient corridor which separated East Prussia from the rest of Germany, the obligation to pay tribute to the victorious powers almost until the end of the century, and what was generally believed to be in Germany "the war guilt lie."

At the same time Germany was left strong enough to cherish some hope of redressing its position. It remained the most populous country in Europe, after Russia. The people were homogeneous; there were no dissatisfied minorities of any consequence within the shrunken frontiers; Germany possessed important assets: scientific knowledge, industrial development, a national capacity for hard and disciplined work.

And the great coalition which had brought about the German downfall in the war had disintegrated. America was becoming more and more disillusioned with the fruits of its first crusade. Russia's ties of alliance with France and Great Britain had been severed by the Bolshevik Revolution. Italy had gone its own way under fascism.

There were, to be sure, French alliances with the new and enlarged states of Eastern Europe, with Poland and Rumania, Yugoslavia and Czechoslovakia. Still more important, Germany during the twenties and early thirties was effectively disarmed. It was on these bases, French armaments and alliances and German disarmament, that the new Continental balance of power reposed.

For more than a decade after the end of the war Europe's fate was in the balance. An act of generous, imaginative leadership, on the part of Britain and France, looking to some form of European union, might have strengthened moderate forces in Germany and saved the situation; but no such act was forthcoming. Narrow nationalism dominated the scene.

Between Germany and Russia, stretching from the Arctic to the Mediterranean, was a belt of thirteen small and medium-sized sovereign states (Finland, Latvia, Estonia, Lithuania, Poland, Czechoslovakia, Austria, Hungary, Yugoslavia, Rumania, Bulgaria, Greece, and Albania). The very existence of many of these states was only possible because such powerful nations as Germany and Russia were knocked out at the same time, Germany by military defeat, Russia by revolution.

The continued independence of the states in this area and their economic advantage called for some form of regional federalism. But old national antipathies and petty local interests were so strong that almost nothing was achieved in this direction.

The hopes of liberals, especially in Great Britain and in the smaller countries which the witty Spaniard, Salvador de Madariaga, described as "consumers of security," were focused on the League of Nations. But this body failed to develop the independent authority which would have been required in order to maintain peace. Its membership was never universal. The United States and Russia, among the great powers, were absent from the beginning.

By the time the Soviet Union was admitted to the League in 1934, Germany and Japan had given notice of withdrawal. And the Soviet Union's participation in the League came to an end when it was expelled in 1939 after launching an unprovoked attack on Finland.

The League never possessed the physical means to check aggression. It possessed no army, no police force. It was not a league, in any true sense of the word, just as the United Nations have never been really united. Its members were divided by clashing interests. It could not be, and was not, any stronger than the national policies of its leading members. So it is not surprising that it failed to meet one big test after another.

When Japan upset a complicated and precarious *status quo* in Manchuria in 1931, the League proved unable to cope with the subsequent crisis. It protested and remonstrated. Japan left the League and kept Manchuria.

Events took a similar turn when in 1935 Italy started an old-fashioned colonial war against Ethiopia, one of the few remaining independent areas in Africa. The League, under the reluctant prodding of the British Government, itself prodded by British public opinion, imposed half-hearted sanctions, aimed at Italian exports. Two steps that would have led to a clear showdown, the closing of the Suez Canal and the stopping of Italy's vital oil imports, were not taken. Italy conquered and kept Ethiopia — and left the League.

When World War II broke out, the League took no action at all. The European members which hoped to remain neutral did not wish to provoke the wrath of Germany by pronouncing judgment. The last flicker of the League's moral influence was the expulsion of the Soviet Union.

The experience of the League disproved several optimistic assumptions of its advocates. Contradictions of interest and policy, such as always arise among sovereign states, could not be banished by grouping a number of nations in a so-called league. Nor were governments inclined to go on a hue-and-cry against an offender, to assume a risk of war on account of acts of aggression in remote parts of the world, not very different from many which had been committed in the past.

If the League was too weak to maintain existing frontiers against violence, its usefulness was further impaired because it was never used as a forum for discussion of means of peaceful change. Article 19 of the League Covenant suggested this possibility:

"The Assembly may from time to time advise the reconsideration by members of the League of treaties which have become inapplicable and the consideration of international considerations whose continuance might endanger the peace of the world."

But Article 19 was never invoked. The League never became an instrument for promoting those policies of freer trade and migration which would have eased the tensions making for dictatorship and war.

With the League impotent, the maintenance of European peace became a matter of old-fashioned national diplomacy. Between 1933 and 1939 there was an amazing shift in the European balance of power. When Adolf Hitler became Chancellor in March 1933, German military power was inferior to British and French.

The German army was restricted to 100,000 men and was denied aircraft and tanks. (There had been some small evasions of the Versailles limitations on arms, but these were not important until the Nazi regime got into full swing with its rearmament.) The Rhineland was demilitarized; a foreign army could have marched deep into German territory without encountering troops or fortifications. The French alliances with eastern European countries created a partial ring around Germany. Moreover, Germany was suffering from severe industrial paralysis and mass unemployment. These were the consequences of the world economic crisis for a country that was thickly populated and highly industrialized.

What a change occurred in six years! The initiative had passed into the hands of Nazi Germany. Britain and France were on the defensive. Massive rearmament had helped to create full employment in Germany, although at the price of some shortages and a curtailment in living standards for the more well-to-do. The French alliances had crumbled; Germany, as events would soon prove, was far and away the strongest land military power on the Continent.

How had this upset in the European balance of power come about? It was a remarkable example of how ruthless and unscrupulous audacity on one side could prevail against half-hearted, irresolute fumbling on the other.

From the standpoint of power politics, Hitler made only one conspicuous blunder during this period, and this was quickly retrieved. A group of Austrian Nazis attempted a coup d'état in Vienna on July 25, 1934. They seized government offices and assassinated the Prime Minister, Engelbert Dollfuss. But the conspirators were not strong enough to get full control of the government. Mussolini mobilized forces on the Brenner Pass. The Italian dictator was not yet ready to accept a common frontier with Germany.

Realizing that he was not yet strong enough to risk war, Hitler hastily dissociated himself from the Austrian adventure. He removed the German Minister in Vienna, who had compromised himself with the conspirators, repudiated any complicity in the uprising, and removed the Austrian Legion (a force of Austrian Nazi émigrés) from its suspicious proximity to the Austrian frontier. The Austrian question was then shelved for several years.

After Hitler came into power the Polish ruler, Marshal Josef Pilsudski, is credibly reported to have sounded out France on the possibility of a preventive war, designed to overthrow the Nazi regime. The French were unresponsive, and Pilsudski lost much of his faith in the value of the French alliance.

One of Hitler's first diplomatic objectives was to weaken the links between France and the states of eastern Europe. So, in his first talks with Polish diplomats, he was careful to emphasize German respect for Polish nationalism, German willingness to accept the *status quo* on such thorny questions as Danzig and the Polish Corridor. Pilsudski's disillusionment with France played into Hitler's hands.

One of the first successes of Nazi diplomacy was the signing of a ten-year pact with Poland. Each government renounced the use of force against the other and affirmed the intention "to settle directly all questions of whatever nature which concern their mutual relations."[1]

Until the spring of 1939 Hitler, Göring, Ribbentrop, and other Nazi leaders tried to keep Polish confidence alive by stressing publicly and privately their pacific intentions toward Poland and their antibolshevism. Typical of this tendency was the conversation of Göring with the Polish Commander in Chief, Marshal Smigly-Rydz, in Warsaw on February 16, 1937.[2]

Göring was profuse in his assurances that Hitler was committed to a policy of rapprochement with Poland and of irreconcilable anticom-

1. For the text of this pact, see *Polish White Book*, 20–21.
2. Ibid., 36–38.

munism. This sounded all the more reassuring in Polish ears because the pre-Hitler German governments had never been willing to conclude with Poland an "Eastern Locarno," accepting the new borders in the East, as in the West.

Moreover, there had been close secret relations between the Reichswehr and the Red Army. German technical advisers had assisted the development of the Soviet aviation industry. In return German officers were permitted to experiment in Russia with weapons forbidden under the Versailles Treaty. All this was well known to the Poles, who were always afraid of a new partition of their country between its powerful neighbors.

Later, after the German military position had become much stronger, there were at least three strong German hints that Poland should join in a combination with Germany against the Soviet Union.[3] Ribbentrop proposed to the Polish Ambassador in Berlin, Lipski, that Danzig should be reunited with Germany and that an extraterritorial railway and motor road should be built across the corridor. In return for these concessions Germany would be willing to guarantee the existing frontier and to extend the German-Polish nonaggression pact for twenty-five years. Ribbentrop also suggested "a joint policy toward Russia on the basis of the anti-Comintern Pact."

When the Polish Prime Minister, Col. Josef Beck, visited Hitler in Berchtesgaden on January 5, 1939, the Führer emphasized "the complete community of interest" between Poland and Germany as regards Russia and added that "every Polish division engaged against Russia was a corresponding saving of a German division."

Finally, Ribbentrop, in talking with Lipski on March 21, 1939, argued that Germany, by defeating Russia in the last war, had contributed to the emergence of the Polish state. Ribbentrop also, according to Lipski, "emphasized that obviously an understanding between us would have to include explicit anti-Soviet tendencies."

So there is some reason to believe that Hitler's decision to destroy Poland, in agreement with the Soviet Union, was a reaction to the British guarantee, extended to Poland on March 31, 1939. Up to that time it had been Nazi policy to offer Poland the role of a satellite ally

3. For fuller details, see *Polish White Book*, 47, 53, 61.

in an ultimate move against the Soviet Union, the kind of role that was later assigned to Hungary and Rumania. The history and the present map of Europe might have been greatly altered if Poland had accepted this suggestion. But Beck adhered to a middle line. He refused to take sides with Germany against the Soviet Union as he refused to take sides with the Soviet Union against Germany. He feared equally the embraces of both his neighbors.

With Poland immobilized and with the Soviet Union weakened by the vast purges which eliminated many leading political and military figures between 1935 and 1938, Hitler could feel that his rear in the East was safe. Then he commenced to slip off, one by one, the restraints on Germany's freedom to arm at will. His method was simple but effective. He confronted Britain and France with a succession of accomplished facts. Invariably he followed each new step toward rearmament or, later, toward territorial expansion with assurances of his devotion to peace. The standard French and British reaction was simple but ineffective. It was limited to verbal protests and appeals to the increasingly impotent League of Nations.

Hitler won a legal minor victory in the Saar plebiscite of January 13, 1935. This small but highly industrialized region, rich in coal, had been detached from Germany and placed under League of Nations administration by the terms of the Versailles Treaty. There was to be a plebiscite after fifteen years, with three choices: return to Germany, annexation by France, or continuation of League rule. About 90 per cent of the Saarlanders who participated voted for return to Germany. The Third Reich gained territory and prestige.

Hitler launched a frontal attack on the Versailles system when he announced the creation of a German air force on March 9, 1935, and the restoration of compulsory military service a week later. Here was an issue on which the western powers could have made a stand without much risk. German rearmament had not advanced far enough to support a war. But nothing of consequence happened. Representatives of Britain, France, and Italy met at Stresa, in northern Italy, and came to an agreement to oppose "unilateral repudiation of treaties which may endanger the peace of Europe."

The British and French were so concerned about obtaining Mussolini's signature to this paper formula that they failed to admonish the

Italian dictator about his obvious intention to invade Ethiopia. And in June Great Britain came to a naval agreement with Germany providing that the German Navy should not exceed one-third of the British.

Even after he had obtained a free hand in rearming on land, on sea, and in the air, Hitler still faced an obstacle inherited from the Treaty of Versailles. Germany was forbidden to build fortifications or maintain troops in a wide demilitarized belt along its western frontier. So long as this arrangement remained in force, the vital Ruhr and Rhineland industries were vulnerable to a swift invading thrust from France. The demilitarization of the Rhineland was endorsed by the Treaty of Locarno, of which Britain and Italy were coguarantors.

Hitler decided to challenge this last limitation. He sent troops into the forbidden area on March 7, 1936. The official excuse for this action was the Franco-Russian military alliance, which had been negotiated by Pierre Laval, of all unlikely individuals, and which was on the eve of ratification in the French parliament. In an effort to soften the shock of this action, German Foreign Minister von Neurath proposed to the signatories of the Locarno Treaty a twenty-five-year nonaggression pact, with demilitarization on both sides of the Franco-German frontier, limitation of air forces, and nonaggression pacts between Germany and its eastern and western neighbors. Nothing ever came of this suggestion.

Hitler later declared that the sending of troops into the Rhineland was one of the greatest risks he had ever taken. It is highly probable that immediate French military action would have led to the withdrawal of the German troops, perhaps to the collapse of the Nazi regime. But France was unwilling to move without British support. Britain was unwilling to authorize anything that savored of war. There was a general feeling in Britain that Germany was, after all, only asserting a right of sovereignty within its own borders.

Hitler had brought off his great gamble, and the consequences were momentous. The French lost confidence in Britain. The smaller European countries, seeing that Hitler could tear up with impunity a treaty concluded with the two strongest western nations, lost confidence in both. There was a general scuttle for the illusory security of no alliances and no binding commitments. It was now possible for Germany to bar and bolt its western gate by constructing the Siegfried Line and to bring overwhelming pressure to bear in the East, as soon as its military preparations were sufficiently advanced.

Hitler's success in the Rhineland was possible because Mussolini had changed sides. Britain, with France as a very reluctant associate and the smaller European powers following along, had committed the blunder of hitting soft in response to the invasion of Ethiopia.

Faced with this challenge, the British Government could have chosen one of two logical courses. It could have reflected that Mussolini was a desirable friend in a Europe overshadowed by Hitler, that colonial conquest was not a novelty in British history, and let events in Ethiopia take their course. Or it could have upheld the authority of the League by imposing sanctions that would have hurt, such as closing the Suez Canal and cutting off Italy's oil imports.

Unfortunately the British people were in a schizophrenic mood. They wanted to vindicate international law and morality. But they were averse to the risk of war. As Winston Churchill put it later, with caustic clarity:

"The Prime Minister had declared that sanctions meant war; secondly, he was resolved there must be no war; and, thirdly, he decided upon sanctions."[4]

The feeble sanctions imposed by the League irritated Mussolini without saving Ethiopia. The foundations of the Berlin-Rome Axis were laid.

There was a similar absence of clearheaded logic in solving the far more important problem of how to deal with Hitler. Up to March 1936, German remilitarization could have been stopped without serious bloodshed. There was still sufficient military preponderance on the side of the western powers. What was lacking was the will to use that power.

The French had been bled white in the preceding war. When I was driving with French friends in Paris, one of them objected to taking a route that would lead past the Gare de l'Est. "So many of my friends went there as soldiers and never returned from that frightful war," she said. It was a wrench to lose the protection of the demilitarized Rhineland. But once that was lost, there was a strong and not unnatural

4. Churchill, *Gathering Storm*, 175.

French impulse to sit tight behind the supposedly impregnable Maginot Line, to concentrate upon the French overseas empire, and to forget about eastern Europe.

The psychological climate in Britain was also favorable to steps of expansion on Hitler's part which were short of war. Disillusionment with the results of World War I contributed to the spread of pacifist sentiment. A resolution against "fighting for King and country" in any cause won a majority of votes in the Oxford Union, a debating club of the intellectual elite. And the British belatedly suffered from an uneasy conscience about the Treaty of Versailles.

Many of the German demands would have been reasonable if they had not been made by a paranoid dictator and would-be conquerer like Hitler. The principle of self-determination did make a case for the absorption into Germany of a solidly German-speaking Austria and also of the Sudeten Germans who lived in a fairly compact area in western Czechoslovakia. The reparations settlement foreshadowed in the Versailles Treaty was hopelessly unworkable for reasons which have already been set forth. Equality in limitation of armaments was a fair general principle.

It was a psychological tragedy that Hitler took by force and unilateral action many things which reasonable German statesmen like Stresemann and Brüning had been unable to obtain by peaceful negotiation. French and British policy was hard and inflexible when it should have been generous and conciliatory, when there was still an opportunity to draw Germany as an equal partner into the community of European nations. This policy became weak, fumbling, and irresolute when in the first years of Hitler's regime, firmness would have been the right note.

After 1936 there was little prospect of stopping Hitler without a war which was likely to be disastrous to victors as well as vanquished. There was still, however, an excellent chance to keep the free and civilized part of Europe out of this war. One can never speak with certainty of historical "might have beens," but, on the basis of the available evidence, the failure of Britain and France to canalize Hitler's expansion in an eastward direction may reasonably be considered one of the greatest diplomatic failures in history.

Hitler had written in *Mein Kampf:*

We terminate the endless German drive to the south and west of Europe, and direct our gaze towards the lands in the east. We finally terminate the colonial and trade policy of the pre-war period, and proceed to the territorial policy of the future.

But if we talk about new soil and territory in Europe today, we can think primarily only of *Russia* and its vassal border states.[5]

That Hitler was treacherous, mercurial, and unpredictable is true. But there are many other indications that his program of conquest was eastward, not westward in orientation. His overtures to Poland for joint action against the Soviet Union have been noted. Without superior naval power, the prospects of conquering Great Britain or holding overseas colonies in the event of war were slight.

Much less was there any likelihood of a successful invasion of the American continent. Even after the Nazi archives were ransacked, no concrete evidence of any plan to invade the Western Hemisphere was discovered, although loose assertions of such plans were repeated so often before and during the war that some Americans were probably led to believe in the reality of this nonexistent design.

Hitler showed little interest in building a powerful surface navy. A former American officer who had opportunities to observe German military preparations in the years before the war informed me that the character of training clearly indicated an intention to fight in the open plains of the East, not against fortifications in the West. Emphasis was on the development of light tanks and artillery; there was little practice in storming fortified areas.

Two among many unofficial overtures which Germany addressed to Great Britain in the prewar years indicate that Hitler's political ambitions were in the East, not in the West. Hermann Göring, after entertaining the British Ambassador to Germany, Sir Nevile Henderson, at a stag hunt in his hunting lodge at Rominten, suggested that there should be an agreement between Germany and England limited to

5. Hitler, *Mein Kampf,* 950.

two clauses. Germany would recognize the supreme position of Great Britain in overseas affairs and would place all her resources at the disposal of the British Empire in case of need. Great Britain would recognize the predominant continental position of Germany in Europe and undertake nothing to hinder Germany's legitimate expansion.[6]

About the same time Joachim von Ribbentrop, German Ambassador in London, offered a virtually identical suggestion in a conversation with Winston Churchill. Germany was willing to underwrite the British Empire. It wanted a free hand in Eastern Europe. Churchill expressed his conviction that the British Government would never accept these terms. Ribbentrop said abruptly: "In that case war is inevitable."

Churchill replied with a warning:

"Do not underrate England. She is very clever. If you plunge us all into another Great War, she will bring the whole world against you like [*sic*] last time."[7]

So there was an alternative to the policy which the British and French governments followed after March 1939. This alternative would have been to write off eastern Europe as geographically indefensible, to let Hitler move eastward, with the strong probability that he would come into conflict with Stalin. Especially in the light of the Soviet aggressive expansion that has followed the war, this surely seems the sanest and most promising course western diplomacy could have followed.

Critics of this realistic policy of letting the totalitarian rulers fight it out to their hearts' content object that Hitler might have won a quick victory in the East and then turned against the West. But both these assumptions are very hypothetical. The Nazi war machine might just as probably have bogged down indefinitely in Russia, and there is no convincing evidence that the conquest of western Europe, much less of overseas territory, was an essential part of Hitler's design.

It is certainly hard to see how, either on a short-range or a long-range view, a decision to give Hitler a free hand in the East would have worked out more disastrously for the western powers than the policy which was actually followed. From every standpoint, military, political,

6. Henderson, *Failure of a Mission*, 88. This conversation apparently took place in 1937.

7. Churchill, *Gathering Storm*, 223.

and psychological, it would have been far more advantageous if Hitler's first blows had fallen on Stalin's totalitarian empire, not on Britain, France, and the small democracies of the West.

A new element of strife and tension was introduced into the European scene by the outbreak of civil war in Spain in 1936. The victory at the polls of a left-wing Popular Front coalition was followed by a period of disorder, with many political assassinations and burnings of churches. Spanish conservatives rebelled under the leadership of General Francisco Franco.

This civil war soon acquired an international character. Germany and Italy sent aid in men and supplies to Franco. Soviet airplanes and tanks, with Soviet soldiers, appeared on the side of the government. Volunteer "antifascist" units, largely under Communist leadership, were recruited in various European countries and sent to Spain. Britain and France tried to steer a neutral course of nonintervention. The prestige of Hitler and Mussolini rose further when the civil war ended with the victory of Franco in 1939, after much destruction and many acts of ruthless cruelty committed by both sides.

Meanwhile the European structure established at Versailles had been shaken to its foundations. By 1938 Hitler felt strong enough to move outside his own frontiers. His first and easiest objective was his native country, Austria. Since the murder of Dollfuss in the summer of 1934, Austria had been governed by a conservative dictatorship, headed by Dr. Kurt Schuschnigg.

There were two considerable dissatisfied groups in Austria, the local Nazis and the Social Democrats, who had been politically suppressed since 1934. Austria was a solidly German-speaking country, and there was much suffering from economic stagnation. This was especially true in Vienna, once the capital of an empire of fifty million people, now the chief city of a mountain republic with some seven million inhabitants. There was an economic as well as a sentimental case for the union of Austria with Germany.

Hitler summoned Schuschnigg to Berchtesgaden, stormed at him, and induced him to admit Nazis to his cabinet. A last flicker of independence on Schuschnigg's part, a decision to hold a plebiscite on the question of maintaining Austria's independence, brought a threat of German military action. Schuschnigg resigned on March 11, and his successor, the Nazi Seyss-Inquart, invited German troops to enter Austria. The familiar machine of propaganda and terror began to roll. A Nazi-organized plebiscite resulted in a vote of more than 99 per cent for *Anschluss*.

A witty Italian political exile once described Mussolini's attitude toward Hitler as that of a cat who had given birth to a tiger. The Italian dictator no longer felt able to oppose the German frontier on the Brenner. The western powers only offered feeble and unconvincing protests against the absorption of Austria.

This absorption meant the encirclement of long, narrow Czechoslovakia by German territory on three sides. A serious international crisis soon developed over the fate of some three million people of German origin who lived in the so-called Sudetenland area of northern and western Czechoslovakia.

These Sudeten Germans had not wished to be Czech citizens in the first place, but their protests were ignored by the peacemakers of Versailles. Although the Czech record in treatment of national minorities was better than the East European average, there was discrimination against the Sudeten Germans in state employment, and this cause of discontent was aggravated by the impact of the world economic crisis. There was much unemployment in the glass and pottery industries, in which many Sudeten Germans were employed.

Moreover, the Third Reich exerted a magnetic influence upon German national minorities. A considerable number, although by no means all of the Sudeten Germans, followed the leadership of Konrad Henlein, organizer of a Sudeten Nazi party.

A storm blew up in May 1938. Unfounded rumors of a German mobilization along the Czech frontier, accompanied by some disorders in the Sudeten area, led to a partial mobilization in Czechoslovakia. France intimated readiness to fulfill its treaty of alliance with Czechoslovakia if German troops should cross the border. Lord Halifax, the British Foreign Secretary, warned the German Ambassador that Great Britain might not stand aloof in the Franco-German war which would follow an invasion of Czechoslovakia.

Hitler for the moment accepted the rebuff, but only to spring more effectively later. He decided to make October 1, 1938, the deadline for

Operation Green, which called for military action against Czechoslovakia.[8]

Meanwhile, opinion in Britain and France was confused and divided. The military key to eastern Europe had been thrown away when Hitler was permitted to fortify the Rhineland. Poland and Hungary had territorial ambitions of their own at the expense of Czechoslovakia. The attitude of Russia was uncertain. France and Britain had no means of directly aiding Czechoslovakia, and the prospect of another war was terrifying, with chaos and communism as the most probable victors.

So there was a strong impulse in London and Paris to seek peaceful means of adjusting the controversy. Lord Runciman, a British elder statesman, went to Prague as head of an unofficial mission of inquiry. From far-reaching autonomy, which Czechoslovak President Beneš slowly and reluctantly agreed to concede, the demands of the Sudeten Germans gradually expanded to secession and union with Germany.

The climax of the crisis was reached in September. The London *Times* opened the door to territorial readjustment when it suggested in a much-quoted editorial of September 7:

> It might be worth while for the Czechoslovak Government to consider whether they should exclude altogether the project, which has found favour in some quarters, of making Czechoslovakia a more homogeneous state by the secession of that fringe of alien populations who are contiguous to the nation with which they are united by race.

Hitler delivered a speech at the Nürnberg Nazi rally on September 12 which was raucous and militant, but fell short of being an ultimatum. Sporadic fighting broke out in the Sudetenland, and Henlein, moving to Germany, for the first time demanded reunion with the Reich.

The French Cabinet was divided, and Prime Minister Daladier was eager for some British lead in mediation. It was in this situation that Prime Minister Neville Chamberlain decided to fly to Hitler's mountain retreat at Berchtesgaden and discuss the question directly. The upshot of the three-hour conversation was that Hitler consented to

8. Wheeler-Bennett, *Munich*, 61.

refrain from military action (which had been set for the end of the month) while Chamberlain would discuss with his cabinet ways and means of applying the principle of self-determination to the case of the Sudeten Germans. The question of whether to fight or yield was threshed out at top-level conferences of French and British government representatives on September 18 and 19. These conferences, in Chamberlain's words, were "guided by a desire to find a solution which would not bring about a European war and, therefore, a solution which would not automatically compel France to take action in accordance with her obligations."

The result was a decision to transfer to the Reich areas in which the Sudeten Germans were more than 50 per cent of the population. This solution was rather brusquely imposed upon President Beneš in Prague. The French Foreign Minister, Georges Bonnet, was especially emphatic in pressing for Czechoslovak acceptance.

A snag was encountered when Chamberlain went to the Rhineland resort of Godesberg for a second meeting with Hitler and found the latter insistent upon an immediate German military occupation of regions where the Sudeten Germans were more than half of the population. Hitler also refused to participate in the proposed international guarantee of the new Czechoslovak frontier until the claims of the Polish and Hungarian minorities had been satisfied.

The Czechoslovak Government at first refused to accept Hitler's Godesberg demands, which went beyond the Anglo-French plan that had been reluctantly accepted in Prague. Several days of extreme tension followed. The British Navy was mobilized. The German Army was poised to strike against Czechoslovakia at two o'clock on the afternoon of September 28. Almost at the last moment the French Government made an offer which went far to meet Hitler's demands, and Mussolini requested a postponement of the German mobilization. Chamberlain had intimated his willingness to come to Berlin for further discussion.

Chamberlain announced on the afternoon of September 28 to the House of Commons, grave in face of the threat of imminent war, that Hitler had invited him, together with Daladier and Mussolini, to a conference in Munich on the following afternoon. There was an outburst of tremendous, almost hysterical, enthusiasm. There had been little desire to die for a questionable boundary decision in eastern Europe.

Agreement was quickly reached at Munich. Hitler got substantially what he wanted. There were a few face-saving concessions, such as the establishment of an international commission to supervise the evacuation of the Sudetenland. But in the main, Germany wrote its own terms. Chamberlain returned from Munich satisfied that he had done right in averting war. He had induced Hitler to sign with him a joint declaration that the Munich Agreement and the Anglo-German naval accord symbolized "the desire of our two peoples never to go to war with each other again."

Upon his arrival in London, Chamberlain told the cheering crowd which welcomed him: "I believe it is peace in our time." And so it might have been, if the British Government had been willing to disinterest itself in eastern Europe, leaving that area as a battleground to Hitler and Stalin.

But what for Chamberlain was an end was for Hitler a beginning. The Munich settlement was capable of being interpreted in two ways. It could have been understood as a final renunciation by Britain and France of interest and concern in eastern Europe. This was how Hitler chose to understand it. Or it could have been taken as a final settlement of German territorial claims in Europe.

There was an atmosphere of precarious peace in Europe for a few months after Munich. German Foreign Minister von Ribbentrop came to Paris and signed with French Foreign Minister Georges Bonnet a declaration of friendship and mutually pacific intentions on December 6. In the text of this declaration there was nothing very striking, but there is reason to believe that Bonnet, in private talks, gave Ribbentrop to understand that France was disinterested in eastern Europe. Ribbentrop asserts that Bonnet accepted his argument that the French military alliances with Poland and Czechoslovakia were remains of the Versailles Treaty which Germany could no longer endure. He also alleges that the French Foreign Minister did not contradict the statement that Czechoslovakia must now be regarded as being within the German sphere of influence.[9]

Of course this is an *ex parte* statement of Ribbentrop and was later contradicted by Bonnet. But a disinterested observer, the Polish Ambas-

9. Wheeler-Bennett, *Munich*, 308.

sador to France, Jules Lukasiewicz, offers some confirmatory evidence. Lukasiewicz, in a report to the Polish Ministry of Foreign Affairs, dated December 17, 1938, reports a conversation with Bonnet, who admitted telling a German intermediary that he regretted the French alliances with Poland and the Soviet Union. Characterizing Bonnet as a person of weak character who adapted himself to whomever he talked with last, Lukasiewicz continues:

> France therefore remains paralyzed and resignedly confined to adopting a defeatist attitude towards everything that is happening in central and eastern Europe. . . . France does not consider anything of positive value except an alliance with England, while an alliance with ourselves and the USSR is considered more of a burden. . . .[10]

It is understandable that Hitler, in view of the atmosphere in France and Chamberlain's acceptance of his demands at Munich, hoped that he would encounter little resistance in the West to further expansion in the East. But his next move produced the challenge from London which, after further diplomatic sparring and a final German resort to arms, led to the Second World War.

Taking advantage of a separatist movement in Slovakia, Hitler in March 1939 proceeded to swallow up the shrunken remains of Czechoslovakia. The new Czechoslovak President, Dr. Emil Hacha (Beneš had resigned and left the country), was summoned to Berlin, plied with drugs to sustain his failing heart, and put under strong pressure to accept a German protectorate over Bohemia and Moravia. Slovakia was permitted to set up an independent administration and became a German satellite state.

Chamberlain's first reaction to this development was moderate. He spoke in Parliament of "disintegration" of Czechoslovakia from within and declared that no British guarantee of the country's frontiers could apply in such a situation. He took a much more militant line, however, in a speech at Birmingham on March 17. Accusing Hitler of having taken the law into his own hands, Chamberlain declared that "any

---

10. *German White Paper*, 27. This work contains documents allegedly discovered in the Polish Ministry of Foreign Affairs after the German Army occupied Warsaw.

attempt to dominate the world by force was one the democracies must resist" and that "Britain would take part to the uttermost of its power in resisting such a challenge if it were made."

Chamberlain's shift of attitude was apparently attributable to a combination of causes. His Foreign Secretary, Lord Halifax, was prodding him to take a stronger line. There was a rising tide of protest against "appeasement" in Parliament and in the country.

The Birmingham speech heralded a striking shift in British foreign policy. Hitherto the British Government had been extremely cautious about making firm commitments to defend any part of Europe east of the Rhine. Now it began to toss guarantees about with reckless abandon, and with little regard for its ability to implement these guarantees if they were put to the test.

Very fateful was the decision to guarantee Poland against attack on March 31, 1939. This was the climax of ten days of feverish and complex negotiations. The last chance for Poland to align itself with Germany against the Soviet Union, perhaps receiving compensation in the East for concessions to Germany on the issues of Danzig and the Corridor, disappeared when two talks between Ribbentrop and the Polish Ambassador to Germany, Josef Lipski, ended in hostile deadlock. These talks took place on March 21 and March 26.

Colonel Beck on March 23 rejected a British proposal for a consultative pact, directed against German aggression, with Great Britain, France, the Soviet Union, and Poland as signatories. With very good reasons, as past and future events proved, Beck distrusted Soviet designs as much as German. His countersuggestion was a bilateral Anglo-Polish agreement. Chamberlain announced his willingness to accept this when he told the House of Commons on March 31:

> As the House is aware, certain consultations are now proceeding with other governments. In order to make perfectly clear the position of His Majesty's Government in the meantime, before these consultations are concluded, I now have to inform the House that during that period, in the event of any action which clearly threatened Polish independence, and which the Polish Government accordingly considered it vital to resist with their national forces, His Majesty's Government would feel themselves bound at once to lend

the Polish Government all support in their power. They have given the Polish Government an assurance to this effect.

I may add that the French Government have authorized me to make it plain that they stand in the same position in this matter as do His Majesty's Government.

So Britain and France drew a line along the irregular frontier of Poland and challenged Hitler to step over it. The weakness of this challenge was that the western powers were no more able to help Poland directly than they would have been able to help Czechoslovakia six months earlier. The veteran statesman David Lloyd George put his finger on the fragility of the guarantee when he said in Parliament after the Government's announcement:

"If war occurred tomorrow you could not send a single battalion to Poland."

Lloyd George added: "I cannot understand why, before committing ourselves to this tremendous enterprise, we did not secure the adhesion of Russia."

But this was more easily said than done. A hopeless dilemma was involved in any practical attempt to implement the guarantee to Poland. That country was not able to resist the German attack successfully with its own strength. But it was impossible to obtain Soviet aid on terms compatible with Poland's sovereignty and independence. The devious course of Soviet diplomacy, leading up to the bombshell of the Soviet-German pact, fully justified the reflections of Neville Chamberlain, expressed in a private letter of March 26:

> I must confess to the most profound distrust of Russia. I have no belief whatever in her ability to maintain an effective offensive, even if she wanted to. And I distrust her motives, which seem to me to have little connection with our idea of liberty, and to be concerned only with getting everyone else by the ears. Moreover, she is both hated and suspected by many of the smaller states, notably by Poland, Rumania and Finland.

Did American influence contribute to this British decision to take a step which, as Winston Churchill, himself a vehement critic of Munich, remarks in retrospect "meant in all human probability a major war in which we should be involved"?[11] Churchill further comments on this decisive step on the British road to war:

"Here was decision at last, taken at the worst possible moment and on the least satisfactory ground, which must surely lead to the slaughter of tens of millions of people."[12]

The evidence on the Roosevelt Administration's prewar dealings with Britain and France is by no means all available. But in the documents published in *The German White Paper* the Polish Ambassador to France, Lukasiewicz, is credited with a report of an interesting conversation with American Ambassador William C. Bullitt on March 24. Lukasiewicz expressed discontent with what he considered a trend in British policy to expose Poland to the risk of war without making adequate commitments or taking suitable preparedness measures. Said Lukasiewicz:

"It is as childish as it is criminal to hold Poland responsible for war or peace . . . a great deal of blame for this falls on England and France whose insensate or ridiculously weak policy has provoked the situation and events which are now transpiring."[13]

Bullitt, according to Lukasiewicz, was so much impressed by this reasoning that on the following day he informed the Polish diplomat that he had used his special powers to request Joseph P. Kennedy, Ambassador in London, to present these considerations to Chamberlain. Bullitt at this time was in high favor with Roosevelt and enjoyed the privilege of special access to the President by telephone. How he used his influence may be judged from records of other conversations included in the documents the Germans claimed to have found in the archives of the Polish Ministry of Foreign Affairs. The Polish Ambassador in Washington, Jerzy Potocki, is credited in these same documents with the following summary of part of a long conversation with Bullitt on January 16, 1939, when the latter was about to return to Europe.

It is the decided opinion of the President that France and Britain must put an end to any sort of compromise with the totalitarian

11. Churchill, *Gathering Storm*, 346.
12. Ibid., 347.
13. *German White Paper*, 51–53.

countries. They must not let themselves in for any discussions aiming at any kind of territorial changes.

They have the moral assurance that the United States will leave the policy of isolation and be prepared to intervene actively on the side of Britain and France in case of war. America is ready to place its whole wealth of money and raw materials at their disposal.[14]

Lukasiewicz is credited with reporting Bullitt as saying to him in February 1939:

One can foresee right from the beginning the participation of the United States in the war on the side of France and Britain, naturally after some time had elapsed after the beginning of the war.[15]

It is improbable that the expansive Bullitt concealed these opinions in his talks with French and British officials,[16] and these opinions, coming from a man known to possess the President's confidence, would naturally have carried considerable weight. We do not know whether or how far this or that step of British and French policy was influenced by representations or hints from Washington. It seems safe to say that the whole direction of Anglo-French policy would probably have been different if the occupant of the White House had been known as a firm and sincere opponent of American involvement in European wars.

The code name for the German attack on Poland was "Case White." The first direction for planning this operation, with September 1 as the suggested date, was issued by General Keitel, Hitler's Chief of Staff, on April 3, three days after the announcement of the British guarantee to Poland. A visit to London by Colonel Beck was followed by an Anglo-Polish communiqué of April 6, announcing that "the two countries were prepared to enter into an agreement of a permanent and recip-

14. Ibid., 32–33. I have been privately informed by an extremely reliable source that Potocki, now residing in South America, confirmed the accuracy of the documents, so far as he was concerned.

15. Ibid., 43–44.

16. I have been privately informed by a reliable source that an intimation, conveyed to the British Government through diplomatic sources, that Roosevelt favored the adoption of conscription exerted considerable influence on the British decision to introduce this measure in the spring of 1939.

rocal character to replace the present temporary and unilateral assurance given by HMG to the Polish Government."

The alliance foreshadowed in this statement was only drawn up in final form on August 23, the eve of the outbreak of war. There was little the British Government could have done to give reality to its guarantee. But even that little was not done. After leisurely negotiations a very modest credit of eight million pounds for the purchase of munitions and raw materials was arranged in July. Only a small part of the goods ordered under this credit ever reached Poland.

The Poles were no more fortunate in their French allies than in their British. The Polish War Minister, General Kasprzycki, arrived in Paris in May to work out the practical application of the Franco-Polish alliance. He received an assurance from General Vuillemin, commander of the French Air Force, that "the French Air Force can from the outset act vigorously with a view to relieving Poland." He also signed a protocol with the French Commander in Chief, Marshal Gamelin, promising a French offensive in force against Germany, to begin on the sixteenth day after the French mobilization.[17] Neither of these promises was kept.

Meanwhile a scheme for crushing Poland in the jaws of a totalitarian nutcracker was already in process of development. Hitler delivered a defiant speech on April 28, denouncing both the German-Polish declaration of amity of 1934 and the Anglo-German naval agreement. Still more significant in this speech was the omission of any hostile reference to the Soviet Union. The rapprochement between the Nazi and Soviet leviathans, stimulated by the British guarantee to Poland, had already begun. A further hint of this trend ensued on May 3, when Maxim Litvinov was abruptly replaced as Commissar for Foreign Affairs by V. M. Molotov.

Litvinov as Soviet spokesman in the League of Nations had identified himself for years with a crusading attitude against fascism and aggression.[18] He had argued that peace is indivisible.

17. Namier, *Diplomatic Prelude*, 457–60.
18. By a curious accidental irony, an English translation of Litvinov's speeches, entitled *Against Aggression*, appeared just as the Soviet Union had been expelled from the League of Nations for its aggressive attack on Finland.

How far the Soviet Government would have backed up Litvinov's eloquence is open to question. It was good Leninist strategy to take advantage of divisions in the camp of the "imperialist" and "capitalist" powers. If war had broken out on some such issue as Ethiopia, Spain, or Czechoslovakia, there is a strong probability that the Soviet Union would have behaved exactly as it acted when war broke out over Poland in 1939. It might have been expected to bow itself out of the conflict and look on with satisfaction while its enemies destroyed each other.

However, Litvinov was at least a symbol of antifascism. He was also a Jew. On both counts he was distasteful to the Nazis. His dismissal was an indication that an important shift in Soviet foreign policy was in the making.

As early as March 1939, Stalin had publicly intimated his willingness to come to an understanding with Germany. Addressing the Congress of the Communist party, he said:

> The fuss raised by the British, French and North American press about the Soviet Ukraine is characteristic. . . . It looks as if the object of this suspicious fuss was to raise the ire of the Soviet Union against Germany, to poison the atmosphere and provoke a conflict without any visible grounds for it.[19]

Here was a hint that Hitler could hardly misunderstand. Stalin was representing as an unworthy intrigue of the western powers the suggestion that Germany might be interested in detaching the Ukraine from Russia—a charge which had been made in the treason and sabotage trials of the Trotskyites not very long before. A deal with Germany about Eastern Europe was being offered.

And on April 17, the very day when the Soviet Government was openly proposing a triple alliance with Great Britain and France,[20] the Soviet Ambassador in Berlin, Merekalov, made a secret tentative overture for Soviet-Nazi rapprochement. Calling on the German Secretary of State, von Weizsäcker, Merekalov let drop the following very broad hints:

19. Wolfe, *Imperial Soviets*, 148.
20. Namier, *Diplomatic Prelude*, 154.

Ideological differences of opinion had hardly influenced the Russian-Italian relationship, and they did not have to prove a stumbling block with regard to Germany either. Soviet Russia had not exploited the present friction between Germany and the Western democracies against us, nor did she desire to do so. There exists for Russia no reason why she should not live with us on a normal footing. And from normal the relations might become better and better.[21]

Three clear and positive impressions emerge from study of the tangled, complex, and still incomplete diplomatic record of the months before the war. There is the tragic futility of the British and French efforts to square the circle, to obtain Soviet co-operation against Germany without sacrificing the independence of Poland and the Baltic states. There is the curious combination in Hitler of flexibility with violence, reflected in his willingness to put aside temporarily his strongest emotion, anticommunism, in order to disrupt the coalition which was being formed against him.

Finally, there is the truly Machiavellian cunning of Stalin, carrying on two sets of negotiations at the same time, an open set with Great Britain and France, a secret set with Germany. Stalin gave the western powers just enough encouragement to put pressure on Hitler to complete the coveted deal which would give the Soviet Union a share in the spoils of Eastern Europe and leave it outside the impending war.

Stalin also included Poland in his web of deception. The Soviet Deputy Commissar for Foreign Affairs, Potemkin, paid a special visit to Warsaw on May 10 and assured the Polish Government that it had nothing to fear from Russia in case of a German attack. On the contrary, Poland could count on Russian friendliness and supplies of munitions and other war materials.[22]

In retrospect there is nothing "enigmatic" or "mysterious" in Stalin's policy in 1939. It was plainly designed to achieve, and did achieve, a thoroughly logical goal from the Communist standpoint: war for the

21. *Nazi-Soviet Relations*, 2. The quotation is from a memorandum prepared by Weizsäcker on the basis of his conversation with Merekalov.
22. Raczyński, *British-Polish Alliance*, 19.

capitalist world; peace, with opportunities to expand territorially and build up militarily, for the Soviet Union.

Like Lenin, Stalin had always regarded war as a factor favorable to Communist revolution. He told the Seventeenth Congress of the Communist party, in 1934, that a new imperialist war "will surely turn loose revolution and place in jeopardy the very existence of capitalism in a number of countries, as happened in the case of the first imperialist war."[23] The inevitability of war and the close relation between war and social revolution are themes which recur over and over again in the writings and speeches of the Soviet dictator.[24]

This viewpoint does not imply that Stalin would gamble the existence of his own regime by precipitating a conflict in which the Soviet Union would be involved. But, from Stalin's standpoint, war between the democracies and the fascist states was a most desirable development. The promotion of such a war is the key to the understanding of the tortuous Soviet policy in the spring and summer of 1939.

Neville Chamberlain was as eager to preserve capitalism as Stalin was to destroy it, but he had got into a vulnerable position by his hasty and ill-considered guarantee to Poland, which was followed in April by similar unilateral guarantees to Greece and Rumania. He was constantly being prodded by critics like Churchill and Lloyd George, who pointed out the importance of Soviet military co-operation apparently without appreciating the impossible moral and political price which would have to be paid for this co-operation.

Efforts to induce the Soviet Government to join in an anti-Hitler pact continued despite Chamberlain's strong personal suspicions of Soviet motives and intentions. A Foreign Office official, Mr. William Strang, went to Moscow in June to reinforce the efforts of the British and French Ambassadors, Sir William Seeds and M. Paul Naggiar.

But Soviet methods of discussion were evasive and dilatory. The heart of the difficulty was in two Soviet demands: that the Red Army should enter Poland and that the Baltic states should be guaranteed

23. See *Pravda* for June 28, 1934.
24. For illustrative material, see the article "Stalin on Revolution," by Historicus, in *Foreign Affairs* for January 1949.

against "direct or indirect aggression," regardless of their own desires in the matter.

Whether the Soviet Union would have entered the war even if its demands had been granted is doubtful. But it was politically and morally impossible to accede to these demands. For this would have amounted to conceding to Stalin that very right of aggression against weaker neighbors which was the ostensible cause of fighting Hitler. Such glaring inconsistencies may be tolerated in war, as the records of the Teheran and Yalta conferences testify. But the coercion of friendly powers to part with sovereignty and territory was impossible in time of peace. As Chamberlain said in Parliament on June 7: "It is manifestly impossible to impose a guarantee on states which do not desire it."

The showdown with Poland occurred after the Soviet Government, continuing its cat-and-mouse tactics, had consented to open military conversations with Great Britain and France. These conversations were admirably calculated to impress on Hitler the necessity of coming to a speedy and definite agreement with Russia.

The Soviet representative in the conversations, Marshal K. E. Voroshilov, raised the question of the passage of Soviet troops across Poland on August 14. He abruptly declared that unless this was agreed on, further military negotiations would be impossible. The French put pressure on Beck to yield, but without success. Beck flatly told the French Ambassador, Léon Noël: "This is a new Partition which we are asked to sign." The Polish Premier expressed doubt whether the Soviet troops, once installed in eastern Poland, would take an effective part in the war. And on the night of August 19 Beck summed up his position with finality to Noël:

This is a question of principle for us. We neither have nor wish to have a military agreement with the Soviet Union. We concede to no one, under any form, the right to discuss the use of any part of our territory by foreign troops.[25]

On the same day, August 14, when Voroshilov presented his demand for the passage of Soviet troops across Polish territory, von Ribben-

25. Namier, *Diplomatic Prelude*, 206–9.

trop addressed to Molotov a suggestion for close German-Soviet co-operation. The nature of the imminent Soviet-German "nonaggression pact" was foreshadowed in the following sentences:

> The Reich Government is of the opinion that there is no question between the Baltic and the Black Seas which cannot be settled to the complete satisfaction of both countries. Among these are such questions as: the Baltic Sea, the Baltic area, Poland, Southeastern questions, etc.

Ribbentrop also foreshadowed the character of Nazi and Soviet propaganda for the next two years. The "capitalistic Western democracies" were represented as "the unforgiving enemies both of National Socialist Germany and of the U.S.S.R.," trying to drive the Soviet Union into war against Germany. Finally Ribbentrop proposed to come to Moscow "to set forth the Führer's views to Herr Stalin."[26]

Molotov's general reaction to this proposal was favorable, but he showed a disposition to delay the final agreement. It was apparently after Stalin intervened to speed up the procedure that Molotov on August 19 handed to the German Ambassador in Moscow, von Schulenburg, the draft of a nonaggression pact. This was to be valid only after a special protocol, "covering the points in which the high contracting parties are interested in the field of foreign policy," was signed.

Ribbentrop flew to Moscow and the sensational German-Soviet pact was signed on the night of August 23. This was an occasion of revelry for Stalin, Ribbentrop, and Molotov. Their conversation ranged over a wide variety of subjects, including Japan, Turkey, Great Britain, France, the anti-Comintern pact. Ribbentrop, still smarting from the failure of his diplomatic mission in London, remarked that England was weak and wanted to let others fight for its presumptuous claim to world domination. Stalin eagerly agreed with this sentiment, but offered the reservation that, despite its weakness, "England would wage war craftily and stubbornly." Stalin proposed the following toast to the Führer:

"I know how much the German nation loves its Führer; I should therefore like to drink his health."

Molotov raised his glass to Stalin, declaring that it had been Stalin

26. *Nazi-Soviet Relations,* 50–52.

who "through his speech in March of this year, which had been well understood in Germany, had brought about the reversal in political relations."[27]

Apart from Stalin's speech and Merekalov's overture on April 17, there was another important milestone on the road to the Soviet-Nazi pact. The Bulgarian Minister in Berlin, Dragonov, called at the Ministry of Foreign Affairs on June 15 and repeated the contents of some remarks which the Soviet chargé d'affaires, Astakhov, had made to him on the preceding day.

Astakhov, in a burst of highly calculated indiscretion, had informed Draganov that the Soviet Government was vacillating between three policies, the conclusion of a pact with Great Britain and France, a further dilatory treatment of the pact negotiations, and a rapprochement with Germany. It was this last possibility which was closest to the desires of the Soviet Union.[28] If Germany would conclude a nonaggression pact, the Soviet Union would probably refrain from concluding a treaty with England. The sincerity of the Soviet Government in inviting military conversations in Moscow later in the summer may be judged from these backdoor assurances, given in Berlin in June.

The published Soviet-German treaty bound each side not to attack

27. This is certainly an authoritative attribution of responsibility for the Soviet-Nazi pact. It proves beyond dispute that the pact was not a hasty improvisation in the face of imminent war, but a long-conceived design on Stalin's part.

It is sometimes alleged that Stalin was justified in concluding the pact because Britain and France were trying to steer Hitler into attacking the Soviet Union. But there is not a shadow of concrete proof that the men responsible for conducting British and French policy tried to put such a design into effect. They would have deserved a much higher historical rating for intelligence and farsightedness if they had endeavored to restrict war to the totalitarian part of the world. The Soviet Government has published all the incriminating documents it could lay its hands on in this connection; but its case is weak. The Dirksen Papers, for instance, merely show that a German unofficial envoy in London, Helmuth Wohltat, received from Sir Horace Wilson, Chamberlain's adviser on foreign affairs, and from Robert Hudson, of the Board of Trade, a vague outline of bases of Anglo-German friendship in the summer of 1939, and that von Dirksen, then German Ambassador, had a noncommittal talk with the British Foreign Secretary, Lord Halifax (see *Documents and Materials Relative to the Eve of the Second World War*).

28. *Nazi-Soviet Relations*, 21.

the other and not to lend support to any grouping or third power hostile to the other partner. Its specified duration was ten years. But more important than the published treaty was a "strictly secret protocol." This divided up a large part of Eastern Europe between the two signatories. Germany's share was to be Poland up to the line of the rivers San, Narew, and Vistula, together with Lithuania. The Soviet Union received a free hand in Finland, Estonia, and Latvia. And Germany declared itself disinterested in Bessarabia, which the Soviet Union claimed, as a former Russian province, from Rumania. The eastern part of Poland was also to be part of the Soviet share of the spoils. Later this division was modified. The Soviet Union took Lithuania, while Germany obtained a larger slice of Poland.

The plebeian dictators, Hitler and Stalin, had revived in more brutal form the partition and annexationist policies of their crowned predecessors, Frederick the Great and Catherine II. The executions and mass deportations of slave labor which characterized both Nazi and Soviet occupations of Poland far exceeded in cruelty and in the number of people affected anything recorded of the eighteenth-century partitions of Poland.

The announcement of the Soviet-Nazi agreement sounded like a crack of doom in London and Paris. To thoughtful observers it was clear that Poland's chances of survival, dim even when the threat was only from Germany, had almost vanished when its two mighty neighbors were leagued in what was soon to prove a pact of mutual aggression against that unfortunate country.

The British Government, however, had gone too far to back down. The Anglo-Polish Treaty was rushed to final ratification on August 25.

Hitler and Ribbentrop doubted to the end that Britain and France would stand firm. Ribbentrop's attitude was made clear at a meeting between him and Count Ciano, the Italian Foreign Minister, at Salzburg on August 11. Ribbentrop disclosed to the dismayed Ciano that war with Poland was imminent. But he insisted that Britain and France would remain neutral and backed his opinion with a bet of a suit of old armor against an old Italian painting. He never paid the bet.

Ciano, never an enthusiast for the German connection, had reluctantly signed the so-called pact of steel, an alliance between Germany and Italy, in May 1939. But Ciano received the impression from

Ribbentrop that Germany did not propose to precipitate war for several years.[29]

After wavering in a state of agonized uncertainty between such conflicting impulses as desire for loot and martial glory, fear of German wrath and realistic consciousness of Italian military weakness, Mussolini decided to stay out of the war for the time being. He informed Hitler in a letter of August 25 that "it would be better if I did not take the *initiative* in military activities in view of the *present* situation of Italian war preparations." In the spirit of "the cat who gave birth to a tiger" he plaintively reminded Hitler that war had been envisaged for after 1942 and that at that time he would have been ready on land, on sea, and in the air.

The last days of August 1939 resembled the last days of September 1938. There was the same atmosphere of imminent war. Diplomatic activity was on a twenty-four-hour basis. There were appeals for peace from Washington. There were exchanges of letters between Hitler and Chamberlain, between Hitler and Daladier. But this time the end was war, not accommodation.

Hitler, in communications to Chamberlain of August 23 and August 25, repeated his willingness to support the British Empire and repudiated any idea of westward expansion. But he insisted that the problems of Danzig and the Corridor must be solved.

When Sir Nevile Henderson saw von Ribbentrop at midnight on August 30, the latter produced a lengthy document which, according to Henderson, "he read out to me in German or rather gabbled through to me in a tone of the utmost scorn and annoyance."[30]

The document was a sixteen-point program for settling the issues of Danzig and the Corridor. Among other things the proposals called for a plebiscite of the inhabitants of the area who had lived there before World War I and for German and Polish rights of communication, regardless of the outcome of the plebiscite.

These proposals in themselves were not unreasonable, but they were presented in a fashion that indicated neither expectation nor desire for discussion on equal terms. Ribbentrop said the proposal was already

---

29. Ciano, *The Ciano Diaries*, 77–78, 84.
30. Henderson, *Failure of a Mission*, 284ff.

outdated because Poland had not immediately sent an envoy with plenipotentiary powers, as Hitler had demanded in his last communication to Henderson, on August 29.

Göring apparently made a last-minute attempt to dissuade Hitler from launching the war. Helmuth Wohltat, one of Göring's economic subordinates, had obtained in London from Sir Horace Wilson and Robert Hudson, two of Chamberlain's associates, suggestions for a plan of Anglo-German amity. Göring believed this plan was sufficiently hopeful to be worth trying out. But Ribbentrop's influence was predominant with Hitler; and Ribbentrop was bent on war. Göring was almost driven out of the Führer's presence when he presented his plea for caution and delay in the last days before the outbreak of war.[31]

The German offensive against Poland was launched in the early morning of September 1. British and French declarations of war against Germany became effective on September 3. Two sentences in Neville Chamberlain's announcement of the state of war to the House of Commons are worth recalling:

"This is a sad day for all of us, and to no one is it sadder than to me. Everything that I have worked for, everything that I have hoped for, everything that I have believed in during my public life has crumbled into ruin."

The note of melancholy was distinctly appropriate to the occasion. British and French statesmanship had been outmaneuvered by Soviet. What could easily have been a German thrust against the Soviet Union had been deflected against the West. The war would doom the Britain of economic freedom and private property in which Neville Chamberlain believed. And the maintenance of Poland's freedom and territorial integrity, the ostensible cause of fighting, would not be won, even though Hitler was to perish in the flaming ruins of his wrecked capital.

31. I learned this in personal conversations with Wohltat and one of his prewar diplomatic associates, Erich Gritzbach, in Germany in 1949.

# 4

# Debacle in the West

The British and French alliances with Poland brought only disaster and suffering to all the partners. The Polish Army, courageous but poorly trained in methods of modern warfare and scantily supplied with tanks and airplanes, was overwhelmed by the invading Germans during the first weeks of September. The defense of Poland was handicapped by the irregular frontiers of the country, by the location of important industrial centers near the borders, and by the obstinate determination of the General Staff to defend every inch of the national soil.

After knocking out the Polish Air Force in the first twenty-four hours of the offensive, the Germans developed a series of pincer movements with the armored columns. The chances of guerrilla resistance in the forests and swamps of eastern Poland disappeared when the Soviet Government, by prearrangement with Germany, struck its blow at the Polish rear. The German Ambassador to Moscow, von Schulenburg, reported on September 6, 1939, that the Soviet Government was doing everything to change the attitude of the population toward Germany.

Attacks on the conduct of Germany had ceased and anti-German literature had been removed from the bookstores. However, as the Ambassador noted in a moment of candor: "The statements of official agitators to the effect that Germany is no longer an aggressor run up against considerable doubt."[1]

Molotov on September 9 telephoned his congratulations and greetings to the German Government on the occasion of the entry of the German troops into Warsaw. (The Polish capital actually held out for some time longer.)

1. *Nazi-Soviet Relations*, 88.

The Polish Ambassador to the Soviet Union, Grzybowski, was awakened at 3:00 A.M. by a communication from Molotov stating that the Polish state and its government had ceased to exist. Since the Soviet Government could not view with indifference the fate of the Byelorussian and Ukrainian population, it was directing the High Command of the Red Army to order troops to cross the frontier and "to take under their protection the lives and property of the population of the Western Ukraine and Western Byelorussia."[2]

Stalin on September 25 proposed a revision of the division of spoils agreed on a month earlier. He suggested that Germany should take a larger part of Poland, up to the river Bug. In return the Soviet Union should get Lithuania. This was acceptable to Berlin. Ribbentrop paid a second visit to Moscow and was received with festive honors and the playing of the *Horst Wessel Lied*. The new boundary in Poland was affirmed in a treaty which rejected the interference of third powers in the settlement.

One of the most striking foreign comments on the Soviet-Nazi honeymoon was a cartoon by David Low. It was entitled "A Rendezvous in Poland" and represented Stalin addressing Hitler as "the bloody assassin of the workers, I presume," while Hitler greeted Stalin as "the scum of the earth, I believe." In the background was the corpse of murdered Poland.

The Kremlin quickly pressed on the governments of Latvia, Lithuania, and Estonia treaties providing for the establishment of Soviet naval and air bases in these countries. There was no interference with internal administration at this time.

Molotov delivered a long report on foreign affairs to the Supreme Soviet, or Soviet Parliament, on October 31. It deserves attention for two reasons. It shows how far the Soviet Government, which subsequently liked to assume the pose of being uncompromisingly "antifascist," was willing to go in collaboration with Nazi Germany. And it is a striking illustration of how swiftly a totalitarian government can reverse the course of its foreign policy.

In the past the Soviet Government had consistently professed the

2. Part of the population of eastern Poland was composed of people of Byelorussian and Ukrainian stock.

friendliest feeling for Poland and respect for Poland's independence and territorial integrity. Molotov struck a very different note:

"One swift blow to Poland," he said, "first by the German Army, and then by the Red Army, and nothing was left of this ugly offspring of the Versailles Treaty."

Litvinov at Geneva had missed no opportunity to arouse a crusading spirit against fascist aggression, which was used as a basis of Soviet nonaggression pacts with its western neighbors (all these pacts, with Poland, Finland, Latvia, Lithuania, and Estonia, were violated in 1939 and 1940). Molotov poured cold water on such ventures in international idealism.

"We know, for example," he told the docile delegates of the Supreme Soviet,

that in the past few months such concepts as "aggression" and "aggressor" have acquired a new concrete connotation, a new meaning. . . .

Everyone would understand that an ideology cannot be destroyed by force, that it cannot be eliminated by war. It is, therefore, not only senseless but criminal to wage such a war for "the destruction of Hitlerism," camouflaged as a fight for "democracy."

The war now, according to Molotov, was an imperialist war, waged against Germany by Britain and France for fear of losing world supremacy. (Hitler, seconded by Molotov, had made a peace offer on October 6. It was rejected, no doubt to the profound relief of the men in the Kremlin. An accommodation with the western powers, which would have enabled Hitler to turn his full force eastward, would have been most unwelcome news to Stalin and Molotov.)

The Baltic area was to be sovietized within less than a year. But Molotov assured his audience:

We stand for the scrupulous and punctilious observance of pacts on a basis of complete reciprocity, and we declare that all nonsense about sovietizing the Baltic countries is only to the interest of our common enemies and of all anti-Soviet provocateurs.

The next Soviet move to cash in on the spoils of the Stalin-Hitler deal was a blow at Finland. This attack was an unoriginal imitation of the German invasion of Poland, even down to such a detail as the conventional falsehood that Finland, with a population less than that of Moscow, had started an invasion of Russia. But the Finnish resistance was stubborn and, for a time, remarkably successful. Before the weight of Soviet numbers prevailed in March 1940 (the war began on November 30, 1939) almost 50,000 Red soldiers, by Molotov's own estimate, had perished. Only 737 Russians had been killed in the occupation of eastern Poland. German dead in the Polish campaign were a little over 10,000.

The heroic Finnish stand against a country with almost fifty times Finland's population elicited general admiration in the western world. In his drama, *There Shall Be No Night*, which extols the fight of free men against tyranny, Robert Sherwood laid the scene in Finland. And Winston Churchill devoted an oratorical purple patch to what he called "this splendid northern race":

> Only Finland, superb, nay sublime, in the jaws of peril—Finland shows what free men can do. The service rendered by Finland to mankind is magnificent. . . . If the light of freedom which still burns so brightly in the frozen North should be finally quenched, it might well herald a return to the Dark Ages, when every vestige of human progress during 2,000 years would be engulfed.[3]

Alas, war-born enthusiasms are fickle and fleeting. A time would soon come when Sherwood would shamefacedly transfer the locale of his play to Greece and when Churchill would help the Soviet Union to "quench the light of freedom" in Finland by hurling a declaration of war against that country.

The only French contribution to the military relief of Poland was some petty skirmishing in the Saar. During the winter all was quiet on the western front. But debacle, swift and terrifying, came in the spring and early summer.

The British mining of Norwegian waters on April 6, a breach of that country's neutrality, was immediately followed by a lightning German thrust against Denmark and Norway. Denmark was occupied with little resistance. A local "fifth column" of Nazi sympathizers, headed by Major

3. Reprinted in Churchill, *Blood, Sweat and Tears*, 215.

Vidkun Quisling, co-operated with a German sea and air invasion of Norway. Allied counteraction was fumbling and ineffective. The long Norwegian coastline, important for submarine warfare, passed under German control.

The decisive campaign in the West started on May 10, when German armies poured into the Netherlands, Belgium, and Luxemburg. Within six weeks Hitler's forces had achieved what the Kaiser's legions could not accomplish in four years. France, broken and prostrate, signed an armistice that amounted to a capitulation on June 23.

A main cause of the swift disaster was the failure of the French High Command to take adequate account of the revolutionary change in the nature of modern warfare. The possibilities of the tank and the airplane were underestimated. Too much reliance was placed on the powerful forts of the Maginot Line, built along the most exposed part of the French eastern frontier.

But the Germans did not attempt to storm the Maginot Line. They by-passed it, aiming their main blow through the rough country of the Ardennes forest. A fatally weak spot in the French line near Sedan was pierced, and German armored columns almost unopposed rolled on to the British Channel.

Meanwhile the British and some French forces, including the best armored divisions, had rashly abandoned their positions northwest of Sedan and had moved into Belgium to meet the German invasion there. Taken in the rear after the breakthrough at Sedan, their strategic position was hopeless. Most of the British and some French troops escaped in the memorable evacuation at Dunkirk, but at the price of losing their heavy equipment.

The disaster at Dunkirk would probably have been even greater if the German armored units, on direct orders from Hitler, had not been restrained from pressing home the attack on the town during the days of the evacuation. Churchill believes that Field Marshal von Rundstedt was responsible for this oversight. Von Rundstedt insists that his hands were tied by Hitler's instructions.

It may be that Hitler and his generals overestimated the power of resistance remaining in the French armies which were still covering the line of the rivers Somme and Aisne. They may have wished to avoid heavy losses of armor in anticipation of hard battles to come.

But there are indications of political motives in the slowing up of the drive against Dunkirk. At the time when the offensive against Dunkirk had been halted, on May 24, Hitler talked with von Rundstedt, army group commander, and with two key men on his staff, Sodenstern and Blumentritt. As the latter tells the story:

> He [Hitler] then astonished us by speaking with admiration of the British Empire, of the necessity for its existence, and of the civilization that Britain had brought into the world. . . . He said that all he wanted from Britain was that she should acknowledge Germany's position on the Continent. The return of Germany's lost colonies would be desirable but not essential, and he would even offer to support Britain with troops if she should be involved in any difficulties anywhere.[4]

Hitler's desire to preserve the British Empire was expressed on another occasion, and under circumstances which preclude the possibility that he was talking for propaganda effect. When the military fortunes of the western powers were at their lowest ebb, when France had appealed for an armistice, von Ribbentrop gave the following outline of Hitler's attitude toward England in a strictly private talk with the Italian Foreign Minister, Count Ciano:

> He [Ribbentrop] said that in the Führer's opinion the existence of the British Empire as an element of stability and social order in the world is very useful. In the present state of affairs it would be impossible to replace it with another, similar organization. Therefore, the Führer — as he has also recently stated in public — does not desire the destruction of the British Empire. He asks that England renounce some of its possessions and recognize the *fait accompli*. On these conditions Hitler would be prepared to come to an agreement.[5]

However, Hitler, the twentieth-century Napoleon, found in Churchill a more implacable adversary than Pitt. There had been increasing dissatisfaction with the conduct of the war by the Chamberlain Cabinet. Churchill, who had been First Lord of the Admiralty, assumed the

4. Liddell Hart, *German Generals Talk,* 135.
5. Ciano, *Ciano's Diplomatic Papers,* 373.

office of Prime Minister on May 10, the day when the German offensive was unleashed.

During the following weeks defeat was piled on defeat, disaster on disaster. Churchill never wavered in his resolution to fight on regardless of the consequences of a bitter-end war. Among these consequences would be the tremendous impoverishment of his own country, the wrecking of much of the European continent through savage bombing, the bringing of Asia to the Elbe, in Churchill's own brilliant phrase, and, most ironical of all for Churchill as a great imperialist, the dissolution of much of the British Empire.

Churchill's first concern was to keep France in the war. Even after the French armies had been hopelessly crushed, he hoped that a French government, taking refuge in one of the overseas possessions, would continue the struggle as an ally of Great Britain. But the collapse of French resistance advanced so fast that all Churchill's efforts were in vain, despite the active co-operation which he received from Roosevelt, a neutral only in name.

The French Government quit Paris and moved to Tours in an atmosphere of chaotic disorder on June 10. On the fourteenth, when the Germans entered Paris, there was a second government exodus, to Bordeaux. Only one who, like the writer, lived through those tragic weeks in France can appreciate the prevailing sense of helpless confusion, the loss of all sense of connection between the government and the people.

Bordeaux, normally a quiet, comfortable provincial town, was a bedlam, overrun with hordes of refugees, not only French, but Belgian, Dutch, and Central European fugitives from the Nazis. The spectacle of universal crumbling and disorganization must have weighed on the nerves of the harassed government leaders and tilted the scales in favor of acceptance of defeat.

Churchill shuttled back and forth by air between London and Paris and Tours, trying to infuse his own bellicose spirit into the French Cabinet. But France's military leaders, the venerable Marshal Pétain and General Maxime Weygand, who had succeeded the inept Gamelin after the fatal German breakthrough, knew they were beaten. As land soldiers, they underestimated the defensive possibilities of sea and air power. Knowing the British Army was less trained than the

French, they foresaw swift defeat for an England that would continue to fight. They saw no sense in continuing a futile slaughter, or, rather, a roundup by the Germans of enormous numbers of French prisoners. They raised their voices more and more insistently for an armistice.

The Prime Minister, Paul Reynaud, was intellectually in favor of continuing the struggle from French overseas territory. But he lacked the fanatical fervor of a Clemenceau. The war had never been popular in France. Amid the ruin and havoc of defeat the voices of those who had always considered it futile to "die for Danzig"[6] gained ground.

Just before he fled from Paris, Reynaud sent a message to Roosevelt, urging the President to state publicly that the United States would aid the western powers by all means short of an expeditionary force. In language that sounded like a pale imitation of Churchill's own Elizabethan heroics Reynaud declared:

"We shall fight in front of Paris; we shall fight behind Paris; we shall close ourselves in one of our provinces[7] to fight and if we should be driven out of it, we shall establish ourselves in North Africa to continue the fight and, if necessary, in our American possessions."

Churchill saw a chance to kill two birds with one stone: to keep France in the war and to draw the United States into the conflict. Roosevelt, in a speech at Charlottesville, Virginia, had characterized Mussolini's declaration of war on France as a stab in the back.[8] Churchill through the British Ambassador in Washington, Lord Lothian, informed the President that he was fortified by the Charlottesville speech and urged that everything must be done to keep France in the fight.

Roosevelt's reply to Reynaud on June 13 gave Churchill a thrill of encouragement. It was much more strongly worded than the American Ambassador to Great Britain, Joseph P. Kennedy, a sincere opponent of American involvement in the war, and some State Department officials considered advisable. It read as follows:

6. This phrase was first used by Marcel Déat, a French opponent of the war who was later associated with the Vichy regime and disappeared after the end of hostilities.

7. Reynaud was thinking of the Breton peninsula.

8. It is symptomatic of the bias of the Roosevelt Administration in favor of communism, as against fascism, that no such language was publicly used when the Soviet Union delivered its "stab in the back" to Poland.

Your message of June 10 has moved me very deeply. As I have already stated to you and to Mr. Churchill, this Government is doing everything in its power to make available to the Allied Governments the material they so urgently require, and our efforts to do so still more are being redoubled. This is so because of our faith in and our support of the ideals for which the Allies are fighting.

The fighting resistance of the French and British armies has profoundly impressed the American people.

I am, personally, particularly impressed by your declaration that France will continue to fight on behalf of Democracy, even if it means slow withdrawal, even to North Africa and the Atlantic. It is most important to remember that the French and British fleets continue in mastery of the Atlantic and other oceans; also to remember that vital materials from the outside world are necessary to maintain all armies.

I am also greatly heartened by what Prime Minister Churchill said a few days ago about the continued resistance of the British Empire, and that determination would seem to apply equally to the great French Empire all over the world. Naval power in world affairs still carries the lessons of history, as Admiral Darlan well knows.

Churchill saw in this message two points which were equivalent to belligerence: a promise of material aid, which implied active assistance, and a call to go on fighting, even if the Government were driven from France. The British Prime Minister rushed off a message to Reynaud suggesting that, if France would remain in the field and in the war, "we feel that the United States is committed beyond recall to take the only remaining step, namely becoming a belligerent in form as she already has constituted herself in fact."[9]

But the next day brought disillusionment. Roosevelt, apparently feeling that he had gone too far, refused to permit the publication of his communication to Reynaud and emphasized that this message was not intended to commit and did not commit the United States to military participation.

Churchill then tried to stimulate Roosevelt's willingness to take bel-

9. Churchill, *Their Finest Hour,* 185.

licose steps by painting a dark picture of what might happen if control of Britain should pass out of the hands of the present government. In that case, he warned, Britain might obtain easy terms by consenting to become a vassal state in Hitler's empire, and the United States might be confronted with a vast naval bloc, composed of the German, British, French, Italian, and Japanese fleets.

In the light of subsequent events this suggestion does not sound realistic. Although France was conquered, Hitler never made any use of the French Navy. The British Navy remained independent; the Italian Navy won few laurels, and Germany never came within measurable range of surface mastery of the oceans. Churchill's message failed to inspire any immediate action, but it furnished useful scare material for advocates of American intervention.

The attempt to keep France in the war failed. An offer, hastily worked out by Churchill's War Cabinet in consultation with the members of the French economic mission in England, Jean Monnet and René Pleven, and General de Gaulle, of an indissoluble union between Britain and France fell on deaf ears in Bordeaux. The harassed Reynaud resigned in favor of Marshal Pétain, who on June 17 pronounced the decisive words: "Il faut cesser le combat."

It was then merely a question of learning the armistice terms. These called for the occupation of the greater part of France, including the Channel and Atlantic coasts, together with demobilization and disarmament, although France was permitted to maintain an army of a hundred thousand men. The fleet was to be recalled to French ports, laid up, and dismantled under German supervision. Germany promised not to use French warships for military purposes.

After the first stunning shock of defeat, the swiftest and most complete in the long series of Franco-German wars, Frenchmen were divided among three camps. The then little-known General Charles de Gaulle, denouncing the armistice from London, had only a few followers. At the other extreme were men like Pierre Laval, who argued that the best French hope of survival lay in adopting a pro-German and anti-British orientation, and trying to win Hitler's favor.

The position of Pétain, the new chief of the French state, was between these extremes. The aged Marshal tried to save the French Empire, to alleviate the sufferings caused by the occupation and the food stringency, to substitute for the fallen Third Republic a conservative, paternalistic regime. It would be unfair to brand Pétain and the great majority of the French people who at this time accepted his leadership as traitors. As William L. Langer says: "Until November 1942, at least, the vast majority of patriotic Frenchmen felt they could serve best by staying in France."[10]

France fell; but Britain stood. Whatever may be thought of the judgment of the British Government in following policies which led to such a political disaster as the Stalin-Hitler pact and to such a military debacle in Poland and in France, the heroism of the British people deserved and excited world-wide admiration. They stood alone and lightly armed against the greatest military power the Continent had seen since the time of Napoleon.

On June 18, just after the French decision to surrender became known, Churchill pronounced the most famous of his many dramatic speeches, with the following ringing peroration:

> The whole fury and might of the enemy must very soon be turned on us. Hitler knows that he will have to break us in this Island or lose the war. If we can stand up to him, all Europe may be free and the life of the world may move forward into the broad, sunlit uplands. But if we fail, then the whole world, including the United States, including all that we have known and cared for, will sink into the abyss of a new Dark Age made more sinister, and perhaps more protracted, by the lights of perverted science. Let us therefore brace ourselves to our duties and so bear ourselves that, if the British Empire and its Commonwealth last for a thousand years, men will still say, "This was their finest hour."

Churchill was assiduous in seeking new allies to replace those who had failed. He was incessant in his appeals for more aid from the United States. He also turned to a less sympathetic and responsive source. He addressed a letter to Stalin on June 25, describing the two objects of British policy as saving Britain and freeing the rest of Europe from German domination. Churchill expressed readiness to discuss fully with the Soviet Government any of the vast problems created by Germany's

10. Langer, *Our Vichy Gamble*, 387.

present attempt to pursue in Europe a methodical process of conquest and absorption by successive stages.

This overture fell on deaf ears. Stalin made no formal reply. But his informal reaction, set forth to the new British Ambassador, Sir Stafford Cripps, was flatly negative. Stalin told Sir Stafford that he saw no danger of the hegemony of one country in Europe, still less any danger that Europe might be engulfed by Germany. He had not discovered any desire on Germany's part to engulf European countries. Stalin further expressed the opinion that German military successes did not menace the Soviet Union and its friendly relations with Germany. These relations were not based on transient circumstances, but on the basic national interests of both countries. Molotov hastened to inform the German Ambassador, von Schulenburg, of this rebuff to Britain.[11]

The Soviet dictator had no intention of coming to the aid of Britain in its extremity. On receiving the news of the French collapse, Molotov summoned the German Ambassador to his office and "expressed the warmest congratulations of the Soviet Government on the splendid success of the German armed forces."[12] The Soviet Government had already shared in the partition of Poland. Now it began to gather in the other territorial spoils of its deal with Hitler.

An ultimatum was sent to Lithuania on June 14, accusing that country and other Baltic states of military conspiracy against the Soviet Union. One or two border incidents were manufactured, and Red Army troops moved in. Similar ultimatums were sent to Latvia and Estonia on the sixteenth. Three Soviet "trouble shooters" (the term had literal as well as symbolic significance in this case) were rushed to the capitals of the occupied countries: Dekanozov to Kaunas, Vishinsky to Riga, Zhdanov to Tallin.

Elections on the familiar totalitarian pattern were held in July and led to the selection of parliaments which were entirely subservient to the Soviet will. Pre-election propaganda did not call for absorption into the Soviet Union, but only for maintaining friendly relations with that country. There was, therefore, no plebiscite, not even a plebiscite under foreign occupation, on this issue.

11. *Nazi-Soviet Relations*, 166–67.
12. Ibid., 154.

Soon after the tame parliaments assembled, they voted in favor of association with the Soviet Union. This request was quickly granted. Molotov gave a realistic account of the method by which annexation was accomplished when he reported to the Supreme Soviet:

The Soviet Government presented the demands you know of concerning changes in the governments of Lithuania, Latvia, and Estonia, and despatched additional Red Army units to those countries. You know the results of this step of the Soviet Government.

This was a time when Soviet actions were still appraised realistically in western capitals. Sumner Welles, Acting Secretary of State, summed up the American official reaction in the following statement of July 23:

During these past few days the devious processes whereunder the political independence and territorial integrity of the three small Baltic Republics—Estonia, Latvia and Lithuania—were to be deliberately annihilated by one of their powerful neighbors have been rapidly drawing to their conclusion.

From the day when the peoples of these republics first gained their independence and democratic form of government the people of the United States have watched their admirable progress in self-government with deep and sympathetic interest.

The policy of this government is universally known. The people of the United States are opposed to predatory activities, no matter whether they are carried on by force or by the threat of force. They are likewise opposed to any form of intervention on the part of one state, however powerful, in the domestic concerns of any other sovereign state, however weak.

The Soviet Government on June 26, after some behind-the-scenes diplomatic parleying with Berlin, served a twenty-four-hour ultimatum on Rumania, demanding the cession of Bessarabia and northern Bukovina. Bessarabia was a prewar Russian province with an ethnically mixed population which had been occupied by Rumania in the confusion after World War I. Bukovina, where many of the inhabitants were of Ukrainian stock, had formerly been part of the Austro-Hungarian Empire and had never belonged to Russia.

Germany had renounced interest in Bessarabia as part of the price of the Stalin-Hitler pact. Bukovina (Molotov had first demanded the entire province) was an awkward new request for Ribbentrop. However, after persuading the Kremlin to limit its claim to the northern part of the province, Berlin advised the Rumanian Government to yield. Stalin now regained the old Russian frontier on the Baltic and at the mouth of the Danube.

August and September were critical months for Britain. Hitler declared in a victory speech on July 19 that it had never been his intention to destroy or even to harm the British Empire and made a general peace offer in the following words:

> In this hour I feel it to be my duty before my conscience to appeal once more to reason and commonsense in Great Britain as much as elsewhere. I consider myself in a position to make this appeal, since I am not the vanquished, begging favors, but the victor, speaking in the name of reason.
>
> I can see no reason why this war must go on.[13]

This speech was followed by private diplomatic overtures through Sweden, the United States, and the Vatican. But Churchill was in the war with the objective, not of saving Britain from destruction and its navy from capture, but of destroying Nazi Germany and reconquering Europe. Lord Halifax, then Foreign Secretary, brushed aside what he called Hitler's "summons to capitulate at his will."

The British Government had already given two demonstrations of its intention to "stop at nothing," as Churchill puts it in his memoirs. When the French naval commander at Mers-el-Kebir, in North Africa, refused to comply with a British demand to sink his ships or proceed under British convoy to a British or American port, the British warships opened a full-scale attack and sank or disabled most of the French ships, with a loss of over one thousand lives. On the same day, July 3, the British seized French ships in British ports and interned those at Alexandria.

The British also took the initiative in one of the most savagely destructive methods of modern warfare, the indiscriminate bombing of

13. Hitler, *My New Order*, 837.

cities. This point was usually obscured by wartime passion and propaganda. But the evidence from British sources is strong. So Mr. J. M. Spaight, Principal Assistant Secretary to the Air Ministry, says in his work, *Bombing Vindicated.*

We began to bomb objectives on the German mainland before the Germans began to bomb objectives on the British mainland. That is a historical fact which has been publicly admitted. . . . Yet, because we were doubtful about the psychological effect of propagandist distortion of the truth that it was we who started the strategic offensive, we have shrunk from giving our great decision of May, 1940, the publicity which it deserved. That surely was a mistake. It was a splendid decision. It was as heroic, as self-sacrificing, as Russia's decision to adopt her policy of "scorched earth" (68, 74).[14]

A well-known British military commentator, Captain B. H. Liddell Hart, notes that the night bombing of London in September 1940 followed six successive British attacks on Berlin during the preceding fortnight and observes:

The Germans were thus strictly justified in describing this as a reprisal, especially as they had, prior to our sixth attack on Berlin, announced that they would take such action if we did not stop our night bombing of Berlin.[15]

When it became clear that the British Government would not consider his peace proposal, Hitler gave orders for the preparation of a plan of invasion, known as Operation Sea Lion. The original D-Day was September 15. The German Navy proposed to establish a narrow corridor across the Channel, wall it in with minefields and submarines, and ferry the armored forces across in successive waves. The Army leaders protested that they needed a wider range of coastline to attack than the Navy felt able to guarantee.

14. Cited in Fuller, *Second World War,* 222. General Fuller adds the tart comment: "Thus, on Mr. Spaight's evidence, it was Mr. Churchill who lit the fuse which detonated a war of devastation and terrorization unrivalled since the invasion of the Seljuks."
15. Liddell Hart, *Revolution in Warfare,* 72. Cited in Fuller, *Second World War,* 404.

Neither service was very optimistic about the prospects of Sea Lion. It was recognized that a preliminary condition of success was mastery of the air over southeastern England. This the Luftwaffe, in a series of fierce air combats during the last days of August and the first weeks of September, failed to achieve. Sea Lion was postponed several times and finally shelved indefinitely.

Hitler's inability to surmount the narrow barrier represented by the British Channel is a sufficient commentary on the charlatan quality of alarmists who before and during the war represented a German invasion of North America as a serious possibility.

Had Hitler regarded Britain as his principal enemy, he would have found other means of striking, even though the plan of direct invasion was frustrated. Gibraltar and Suez, at opposite ends of the Mediterranean, were key communication points of the British Empire. Had Hitler given up or postponed his reckoning with Russia and concentrated his war effort in the Mediterranean area, the course of hostilities and the final issue of the war might have been different. But the Führer's enthusiasm was reserved for continental land operations. As he once told his naval chief, Admiral Erich Raeder: "On land I am a hero, but at sea I am a coward."

The Gibralter operation, somewhat vaguely conceived after the fall of France, was held up and never undertaken because the Spanish ruler, General Francisco Franco, was unwilling to let the Germans pass through Spain without greater economic aid and political concessions than Hitler was willing to give him. When Hitler met Franco at Hendaye, on the Franco-Spanish border, in October 1940, the Spanish dictator proved so obstinate in demanding and so evasive in conceding that Hitler later remarked that he would rather have three or four teeth drawn than go through such an experience again.[16] Mussolini's attempt to win Franco's consent to the German demands in February 1941 was equally unsuccessful.

The German commander in North Africa, Field Marshal Erwin Rommel, was a brilliant tank specialist who ruined the reputation of several British generals. But he never received enough men or matériel to make possible a successful drive to Alexandria and Suez. After

16. Ciano, *Ciano's Diplomatic Papers*, 402.

December 1940, Hitler was committed to the realization of a design of which he had always dreamed: the smashing of Soviet Russia.

The dissolution of the Nazi-Soviet quasi alliance lies outside the limits of the debacle in the West. But it will be briefly described here, because it exercised a profound effect upon the military and political course of the war, in which America would soon be involved.

The situation which prevailed in Europe after the fall of France, with Hitler and Stalin as the masters of the Continent, recalls the period between 1807 and 1812. At that time Napoleon and Tsar Alexander I shared a similar domination in an equally uneasy and precarious alliance.

Stalin followed Alexander's example by using the period of understanding to attack Finland and to strengthen the Russian position on the Danube. Some of the effusive congratulations exchanged between Moscow and Berlin recall the Tsar's expansive remark to the French Ambassador Savary:

"What is Europe; where is it, if it is not you and we?"

A new brand of ideological cement was improvised for this strange friendship of two systems which had formerly exchanged the bitterest abuse. German propaganda stressed the idea that Russia and Germany were "young, revolutionary, proletarian countries," naturally leagued against "the old, weary, decadent plutocracies of the West." Ribbentrop seems to have believed his own propaganda to some extent. He expressed favorable views of Stalin and his regime, not only in public statements, but in private talks with Mussolini and Ciano. He believed that Stalin had become a "nationalist" (a somewhat delusive source of comfort to western statesmen in a later phase of the war) and that Jews were being eliminated from high places in the Soviet administration.

But the forces that made for rupture outweighed Ribbentrop's dream of lasting co-operation between nazism and communism. Among these forces were Hitler's emotional hatred of bolshevism, the Soviet tendency to procrastinate and drive hard bargains in diplomatic discussion, and the clash of German and Russian interests at the Dardanelles, so often a focal point of international rivalry.

The first serious rift in Berlin-Moscow harmony occurred when Germany and Italy guaranteed the new shrunken frontiers of Rumania in August 1940. Besides losing Bessarabia and northern Bukovina to the Soviet Union, Rumania, under pressure from Berlin and Rome, had ceded part of Transylvania to Hungary. Molotov grumbled that Germany had not been altogether loyal in giving this guarantee without consulting Moscow. The shrewd Rumanian Ambassador in Moscow, Grigore Gafencu, reports the following acid interchange between Molotov and von Schulenburg:

"Why have you given the guarantee? You know we had no intention to attack Rumania." "That is just why we gave the guarantee," retorted the German diplomat. "You have often told us that you have no further claim on Rumania; our guarantee, therefore, can be no source of annoyance to you." This was already a far cry from the saccharine congratulations on the German victories in Poland and France.

The definite turning point in Soviet-German relations, however, may be dated from Molotov's visit to Berlin in November. Representatives of Germany, Japan, and Italy had signed a tripartite pact in Berlin on September 27. This provided for Japanese recognition of the leadership of Germany and Italy in establishing a new order in Europe. Germany and Italy, in return, endorsed Japan's leadership in setting up a new order in "Greater East Asia." Clause 3 was perhaps the most important item in this treaty:

"Germany, Italy and Japan agree . . . to assist one another with all political, economic and military means when one of the three contracting powers is attacked by a power at present not involved in the European war or in the Chinese-Japanese conflict."

The only powers which might have fitted this definition were the United States and the Soviet Union, with the former a far more likely participant in intervention. Ribbentrop hoped that the Soviet Union could be fitted into the framework of the pact. As he told Ciano on November 4,[17] he wanted a political and economic pact, based on mutual recognition of the territorial situation, on an undertaking by each party never to give aid to the enemies of the other, and on a broad collaboration and friendship clause.

More than that, Ribbentrop wanted an agreement to direct Russian dynamism to the south (it was to be anti-British in character and to aim at safeguarding the position of Afghanistan and Persia as far as pos-

17. Ibid., 406.

sible). Italian "dynamism," in Ribbentrop's conception, was to be channeled toward Mediterranean Africa and the Red Sea, German dynamism toward Equatorial Africa. Ribbentrop did not wish to discuss Balkan questions with the Soviet Union; and on this point he reckoned without Molotov.

The Soviet Foreign Minister arrived in Berlin prepared for hard bargaining. When Hitler and Ribbentrop tried to allure him with visions of expansion in Asia, Molotov demanded a free hand in Finland and the right to give a guarantee to Bulgaria which would bring that country into the Soviet sphere of influence. He also wanted to obtain an assurance against an attack in the Black Sea through the Straits, "not only on paper, but in reality," and believed the Soviet Union could reach an agreement with Turkey on this point.

Hitler was cool to these hints of further Soviet expansion in the area of the Baltic and Black seas. He declared flatly that there must be no war in Finland and pointedly inquired whether Bulgaria had asked for the kind of guarantee Molotov suggested.

So the general atmosphere of the November meeting in Berlin was chilly and negative. Molotov received for consideration the draft of a four-power treaty to be signed with Germany, Italy, and Japan. Soviet territorial aspirations were rather vaguely defined in this document as centering "south of the national territory of the Soviet Union, in the direction of the Indian Ocean."[18]

Molotov's response to this offer was given to Schulenburg on November 26.[19] The Soviet Foreign Minister was willing to sign the four-power treaty, but at a high price. He demanded withdrawal of German troops from Finland, a mutual assistance pact with Bulgaria, a base in Bulgaria for Soviet land and naval forces within range of the Straits, Japanese surrender of coal and oil concessions in Soviet North Sakhalin. Molotov also stipulated that "the area south of Batum and Baku in the general direction of the Persian Gulf be recognized as the center of the aspirations of the Soviet Union."

To this proposal the German Government returned only evasive and noncommittal replies. The real answer was given on December 18,

18. *Nazi-Soviet Relations,* 257.
19. Ibid., 258–59.

1940, when Hitler issued a "top secret" directive for the preparation of Operation Barbarossa.[20] The nature of this directive was summarized in the first sentence:

"The German Armed Forces must be prepared to crush Soviet Russia in a quick campaign (Operation Barbarossa) even before the conclusion of the war against England."

Rumania and Finland, countries which had been despoiled of territory by the Soviet Union, were counted on as allies. The ultimate objective was to establish a defensive line against Asiatic Russia running approximately from the Volga River to Archangel. Then, in case of necessity, the last industrial area left to Russia in the Urals could be eliminated by the Luftwaffe. It was considered of decisive importance that the intention to attack should not be discovered.

The vast preparations necessary to mount an offensive against Russia, however, could not be entirely concealed. In January 1941 the American commercial attaché in Berlin, Sam E. Woods, sent a confidential report, based on information surreptitiously received from an anti-Nazi German in high position, outlining the plan of invasion. Undersecretary Welles, at the request of Secretary Hull, communicated this to the Soviet Ambassador, Constantine Oumansky.[21] With his farflung secret service Stalin probably received similar information from other sources.

German-Soviet relations remained outwardly correct during the first month of 1941. American and other foreign Communists followed the party line dictated by the Stalin-Hitler pact until the German attack actually took place. But as Germany overran the Balkans, the Soviet Government indulged in a few verbal gestures of dissatisfaction.

When Bulgaria adhered to the Tripartite Pact early in March 1941, and German troops moved into that country, Molotov expressed regret to Schulenburg that "the German Government has deemed it possible to take a course that involves injury to the security interests of the Soviet Union."[22] The Soviet Ministry of Foreign Affairs published a statement disapproving the Bulgarian action.

20. Ibid., 260.
21. Hull, *Memoirs*, 2:947–48.
22. *Nazi-Soviet Relations*, 278.

A more serious diplomatic brush occurred early in April. The Yugoslav Government which had subscribed to the Tripartite Pact had been overthrown by a revolt from within. Germany was poised for the invasion of Yugoslavia. Molotov informed Schulenburg on April 4 that the Soviet Government was signing a treaty of friendship and non-aggression with the new anti-German Yugoslav Government. The German Ambassador protested that the moment chosen for the signing of the treaty was very unfortunate. But Molotov persisted in his design and urgently requested the German Government to do everything in its power to preserve peace in the Balkans.[23]

The German reply was to launch a smashing and quickly successful offensive against Yugoslavia on April 6. The Soviet-Yugoslav pact had no influence whatever on the course of events. It merely served as an embarrassing revelation of Soviet diplomatic weakness.

From another direction, however, Stalin obtained some compensation for his failure to halt the German forward march in the Balkans. (The conquest of Yugoslavia was soon followed by the occupation of Greece.) He induced the volatile Japanese Foreign Minister, Yosuke Matsuoka, to sign a treaty of neutrality and nonaggression in Moscow on April 13. This was a first-rate disaster for the United States, just as the Soviet-Nazi pact had been a severe blow to France and Britain. Pearl Harbor was foreshadowed when Japan thus demonstratively insured itself against Soviet pressure from the north, thereby freeing its hands for expansion to the south.

Stalin was mainly concerned to assure Japanese neutrality in the event of a war with Germany. And it seems reasonable to assume that, with his belief in war as a midwife of revolution, the Soviet dictator viewed with complacent satisfaction the prospect that Japan would use up its energies against the United States and the European powers with colonial possessions in the Far East. The Rumanian Ambassador, Gafencu, sums up as follows some of the more far-reaching implications of the Soviet-Japanese pact, which was to run for five years:

Japanese action to the South would free Western Siberia from the Japanese menace, to some extent relieve China, hardly able to

23. Ibid., 317–18.

breathe in the Japanese embrace, *embark Japan in a war with the United States* that could only be fatal to Japan in the long run, reveal the weakness of the British Empire, drive the great masses of Central Asia to self-consciousness and prepare the struggle for the liberation of Asia.[24] (Italics supplied.)

A bizarre prelude to the attack on Russia was the flight to England of Rudolf Hess, one of Hitler's chief lieutenants. Hess had been aware of peace feelers which Albrecht Haushofer, son of the famous geopolitician, had tried to put out to England. But his message, when he was arrested and interrogated after his arrival in England, was little more than a restatement of Hitler's earlier offers, to an accompaniment of hallucinations and hysteria which bordered on insanity.

As the hour of danger grew nearer with the coming of summer, Stalin made desperate efforts to appease Hitler. He was punctilious in fulfilling Soviet promised deliveries of grain and raw materials to Germany, although German deliveries to Russia fell into arrears. He withdrew diplomatic privileges from the Belgian, Norwegian, and Yugoslav missions in Moscow. He recognized a short-lived pro-German rebel regime which was set up in Iraq.

Finally, when tension and suspense had reached a high point, the Soviet official news agency, Tass, on June 13, issued a very significant communiqué referring to rumors circulating in the foreign, especially in the British, press to the effect that Germany had presented territorial and economic demands to Russia, that these demands had been refused, and that both sides were mobilizing troops. Characterizing these rumors as "absurd," Tass denied that any such negotiations had taken place, professed full confidence in Germany's pacific intentions, and continued:

"The recent movement of German troops, released from the Balkan campaign toward regions to the east and northeast of Germany was

---

24. Gafencu, *Prelude to the Russian Campaign*, 156. Gafencu in the same book offers this plausible interpretation of Stalin's design in signing the pact with Hitler: "Stalin no longer fought to prevent war, but only to turn it from his own frontiers. . . . A war in the West, with every prospect of being long continued and exhausting for all the Western peoples, was to Russia a guaranty of peace at the moment and preponderance in the future."

from other motives and does not concern the relations between the Soviet Union and the Reich."

As for Russia's "summer mobilization," this, according to Tass, was nothing out of the ordinary. To suggest that it is aimed at Germany "is, of course, absurd."

The wording of this statement is an excellent example of Asiatic style in diplomacy—cunning, oblique, and full of double meaning. The communiqué was designed to intimate to Berlin that the Soviet Government knew of the large German troop transfers toward its borders and was taking mobilization measures of its own. But at the same time there was an expression of willingness to set down everything as a misunderstanding, due to British intrigue, if only Germany would not attack. It was a clear invitation for some kind of reassuring declaration from Berlin. But no such declaration came. Instead, at dawn on June 22, Ambassador Schulenburg delivered a three-line message to Molotov:

"In view of the intolerable pressure exercised by Russian troops on the lines of demarcation separating them from the German troops, the latter have received orders to advance into Soviet territory."

The war of the totalitarian giants had begun.

Hitler explained his attack in a long proclamation issued on June 22. He declared that it was only with extreme difficulty that he brought himself to send Ribbentrop to Moscow in 1939. He recalled the Soviet demand for Lithuania, contrary to the original terms of the Moscow pact, and the later Soviet demands at Berlin for a free hand in Finland, Bulgaria, and the Straits. These statements are consistent with the documentary evidence discovered after the fall of the Nazi regime.[25]

More doubtful is Hitler's assertion that the Soviet Union promised delivery to Yugoslavia of arms, aircraft, and munitions through Salonica. And the accusations of Soviet frontier violations are no more credible than the earlier German charges against Poland—or the Soviet accusations against Finland and the Baltic states.

Molotov's hard bargaining seems to have been one cause of the

25. The main outlines of Nazi-Soviet relations during the period from the spring of 1939 until Hitler's attack on Russia are convincingly presented, on the basis of documents captured in the German Foreign Office, in *Nazi-Soviet Relations*.

German attack. Hitler also emphasized the point that such powerful German forces were tied up in the East "that radical conclusion of the war in the West, particularly as regards aircraft, could no longer be vouched for by the German High Command." Other phrases in the proclamation suggest that Hitler hoped to rally a united Europe in an anti-Communist crusade.

The German invasion of the Soviet Union was the last but one of the big political developments in choosing sides for World War II. A few months later there would be Pearl Harbor and the formal belligerence of the United States against Japan, Germany, and Italy.

The origins of this war and its character must be understood if America's involvement is to be fairly judged. Several points which were overlooked at the time stand out with increasing clarity, now that more evidence is available.

First, there is no factual evidence, after close examination of all captured Nazi archives, that Hitler had prepared any plan for offensive action against the Western Hemisphere.

Second, German ambitions were directed toward the east, not toward the west. The danger, hysterically stressed in the United States by advocates of intervention, that Hitler might capture the British Navy and press it into service against the United States was nonexistent. There is no proof that Britain and France would ever have been attacked if they had not gone to war on the Polish issue. Even after the debacle on the western front, Britain at any time could have had peace on the basis of retaining its fleet and its empire. The attack on Britain was undertaken reluctantly and with inadequate means. It was quickly abandoned for the more congenial enterprise of Continental eastward expansion.

Third, no element of freedom, democracy, or morality entered into the struggle for Eastern Europe between Hitler and Stalin, two tyrants with equally bloody and obnoxious records. When a satisfactory division of prospective loot was arranged in 1939, Stalin was quite ready to pledge eternal friendship to Hitler. We now know that Russia would have formally joined the Axis if Molotov's demands for an additional cut in the spoils had not gone beyond what Hitler was prepared to concede.

Fourth, the professed war objective of the western powers, the maintenance of the independence and territorial integrity of Poland, was almost impossible to achieve. The western powers could bring no military pressure to bear directly on Eastern Europe. The Soviet Union was just as clearly committed as Germany to the extinction of Polish independence and the mutilation of Poland's frontiers. We shall see in a later chapter how feebly, half-heartedly, and unsuccessfully America and Great Britain defended the cause of Poland.

Fifth, it should not have required great perspicacity to recognize that the Soviet Union, in view of its record of aggression and bad faith, its philosophy of world revolution, and its vast assets in territory, manpower, and natural resources, would be a very difficult and dangerous ally. If the war against Hitler perhaps could not be won without Russia, it was certainly doubtful whether the peace could be won with Russia.

These considerations were certainly important. They should have been carefully weighed in the balance before the United States committed itself to a Second Crusade. That they exercised little influence on the thinking of those responsible for shaping American policy is evident from the record which will be set forth in the next three chapters.

# 5

## "Again and Again and Again"

No people has ever been led into war with so many soothing promises of peace as the Americans received from their Chief Executive in
1939 and 1940. The national mood after World War I had become one
of profound disgust and disillusionment. It had become increasingly
obvious that America's First Crusade had not made the world safe for
democracy. On the contrary, a war fought to the bitter end and a peace
based on revenge, not reconciliation or compromise, had visibly promoted the growth and spread of the twin modern creeds of violence
and dictatorship: communism and fascism.

There was an increasing sense in America of having been tricked
into the First World War on false pretenses, or for reasons which, in
retrospect, seemed inadequate to justify the expenditure of blood and
treasure. Seventy-one per cent of the people who replied to a public
opinion poll in 1937 expressed the opinion that our participation in
the First World War had been a mistake.[1]

A note of acrimony had crept into much American comment on
Europe and into much European comment on America. On the other
side of the Atlantic the United States was reproached for not joining
the League of Nations and for trying to collect the money which had
been lent to its European associates in the war. Europeans felt that
these debts should be written off as subsidies in a common cause.

But as American enthusiasm about the results of the war waned, the
attitude on the debts tended to harden. Whatever the ethics of these
two issues may have been, the German reparations and the American
war debts were uncollectable for strictly economic reasons. Since these
reasons involved complicated issues of currency exchange and transfer

1. Johnson, *Battle against Isolation*, 19.

which the average American could scarcely be expected to understand, American public opinion was inclined to interpret nonpayment of the debts as deliberate "welshing" on legal obligations. Bitterness was reflected in sour witticisms which were plentifully sprinkled in the pages of the American press. As a student of public opinion recorded:

> American newspapers said in 1921 that the only American book "supremely popular" in Europe was Uncle Sam's pocketbook; in 1923 that we had become a leading member of the "League of Donations"; in 1928 that Europe counted too much on being "Yank-ed" out of economic difficulties; in 1932 that our being expected to "succor" Europe suggested too strongly "sucker"; in 1933 that whenever an international conference met "to get at the bottom of things, one of the things is Uncle Sam's pocket."[2]

Revelations of the profits of munitions makers, popularly labeled "merchants of death," intensified the impulse to stay out of overseas wars. The immediate cause of America's involvement in the First World War had been Wilson's assertion of America's rights on the high seas against the German submarine blockade. So it was decided to forego those rights in advance, as not worth the cost of war. Neutrality legislation, passed by overwhelming majorities in both houses of Congress and adopted in finally revised form on May 1, 1937, completely repudiated Wilson's position.

The Act in its final form provided that "whenever the President shall find that there exists a state of war between or among two or more foreign states," certain measures should automatically come into effect. There was to be an embargo on the sale of arms, munitions, and implements of war to all belligerents. American citizens were forbidden to travel on belligerent ships and to buy or sell securities of warring powers. Such products as cotton, scrap iron, and oil could be sold to belligerents, but could not be transported in American ships. This was the so-called cash-and-carry arrangement.

President Roosevelt during the first years of his long Administration made no attempt to combat the prevalent mood in favor of isolating the United States from foreign wars. Addressing the New York State

2. Bailey, *Man in the Street,* 48.

Grange before his nomination, on February 2, 1932, he rejected the idea of American membership in the League of Nations for the following reasons:

American participation in the League would not serve the highest purpose of the prevention of war and a settlement of international difficulties in accordance with fundamental American ideals. Because of these facts, therefore, I do not favor American participation.[3]

Roosevelt adhered to this attitude after his election. He showed a tendency to favor economic as well as political isolationism when, in a message to the London Economic Conference in 1933, he bluntly refused to co-operate in plans for international currency stabilization, stating:

The sound internal economic system of a country is a greater factor in its well-being than the price of its currency in changing terms of the currencies of other nations.

He was lukewarm in his support of such a mild experiment in internationalism as American participation in the World Court. Neutrality and noninvolvement in foreign wars were emphasized as desirable objectives in Roosevelt's Chautauqua speech of August 14, 1936:

We shun political commitments which might entangle us in foreign wars; we avoid connection with the political activities of the League of Nations. . . . We are not isolationists, except insofar as we seek to isolate ourselves completely from war. . . . I have passed unnumbered hours, I shall pass unnumbered hours, thinking and planning how war may be kept from this nation.

The President in this speech sounded a warning against the Americans who, in a hunt for profits, would seek to "break down or evade our neutrality" in the event of an overseas war.

Roosevelt's first notable departure from his stand for neutrality and noninvolvement, except in response to an attack on the Western Hemi-

3. Roosevelt, *Public Papers,* 551ff.

sphere, occurred when he delivered his "quarantine speech" in Chicago on October 5, 1937. This speech had been prepared in the State Department. But the striking passage about quarantining aggressors was inserted by Roosevelt upon his own initiative.[4] It was phrased as follows:

> The peace, the freedom, and the security of ninety per cent of the world is being jeopardized by the remaining ten per cent, who are threatening a breakdown of international order and law. Surely the ninety per cent who want to live in peace under law and in accordance with moral standards that have received almost universal acceptance through the centuries, can and must find a way to make their will prevail. . . .
>
> It seems to be unfortunately true that the epidemic of world lawlessness is spreading. When an epidemic of physical disease starts to spread, the community approves and joins in a quarantine of the patients in order to protect the health of the community against the spread of the disease.

To reconcile the implications of this suggestion with the plain meaning and intent of the Neutrality Act would be extremely difficult. And Roosevelt offered no enlightenment as to what he had in mind in subsequent talks with the press. The speech is interesting, however, as an indication of the President's changing outlook in world affairs.

The majority of the American people in 1937 were far from approving any abandonment of the official declared policy of neutrality and nonintervention. Significant straws in the wind were the absence of any demand for war after the sinking of the American gunboat *Panay* in the Yangtze River and the strong support for the Ludlow resolution. This resolution, introduced by Representative Louis Ludlow, of Indiana, provided that there should be no declaration of war, except in case of actual attack, without the sanction of a national referendum. This resolution was defeated, but only by a narrow margin.

As war in Europe became more imminent, the Administration became increasingly committed to a policy of trying to block the designs of the Axis powers. Since lip service was paid to the Neutrality Act,

4. Hull, *Memoirs*, 2:544–45.

which was the law of the land and commanded wide popular support, there was a good deal of double talk and duplicity.

At the time of the Munich crisis, Roosevelt made two appeals for peace, the first to all the governments concerned, the second to Hitler alone. At first there was a disposition in Administration circles to claim credit for the Munich settlement. Sumner Welles, Undersecretary of State, in a radio address referred to "steps taken by the President to halt Europe's headlong plunge into the Valley of the Shadow of Death." Welles made the exaggerated claim that "Europe escaped war by a few hours, the scales being tipped toward peace by the President's appeal."

Soon afterwards, however, the course was set in the direction of opposing anything that savored of "appeasement." Hugh Wilson, American Ambassador in Germany, was instructed to seize upon every informal opportunity to instill in the minds of German Foreign Office officials the belief that further German aggression would cause the gravest repercussions in the United States. Other United States ambassadors in key posts, William C. Bullitt in Paris and Joseph P. Kennedy in London, were given the same instructions, which Bullitt probably fulfilled with enthusiasm and Kennedy with reluctant misgivings.[5]

Wilson was recalled after the nation-wide Nazi-organized anti-Jewish riots which followed the murder of a German diplomat in Paris by a Jewish refugee in November 1938. The United States remained unrepresented by an ambassador in Berlin after this. Roosevelt gave out the following statement on this occasion:

The news of the past few days from Germany has deeply shocked public opinion in the United States. Such news from any part of the world would inevitably produce a similar profound reaction among American people in every part of the nation.

I myself could scarcely believe that such things could occur in a twentieth century civilization.[6]

5. Alsop and Kintner, *American White Paper*, 23–24.
6. The reference to "twentieth century civilization" was historically not very happy. The twentieth century witnessed not only in Germany but in the Soviet Union acts of mass cruelty which not only never occurred, but would not even have been conceivable, in the nineteenth.

Roosevelt attacked the Neutrality Act by implication in his address to a joint session of Congress on January 3, 1939:

Words may be futile, but war is not the only means of commanding decent respect for the opinion of mankind. There are many methods, short of war but stronger and more effective than mere words, of bringing home to aggressor governments the sentiments of our people.

The President went on to warn that

when we deliberately try to legislate neutrality our neutrality acts may operate unevenly and unfairly, may actually give aid to an aggressor and deny it to the victim.

Shortly after the Munich Conference there were some highly secret meetings in the American Embassy in Paris. A conference of Ambassador Bullitt with French Premier Daladier and with the French Minister of Aviation, Guy La Chambre, was strongly reminiscent of the time when Anglophile Ambassador Walter Hines Page had advised the British Foreign Minister how to reply to an American note of protest, for the principal subject of discussion was the procurement of airplanes from America for France. Bullitt, who was in frequent telephonic conversation with Roosevelt, suggested a means by which the Neutrality Act, forbidding shipments of arms to belligerents, could be circumvented in the event of war. His suggestion was to set up assembly plants in Canada, apparently on the assumption that Canada would not be a formal belligerent.[7]

Ambassador Bullitt arranged for a French mission to come to the United States and purchase airplanes in the winter of 1938–39. The visit was kept under cover, and Bullitt persuaded Roosevelt to by-pass the Secretary of War, Harry Woodring, and to make Henry Morgenthau, Jr., Secretary of the Treasury, the liaison agent between the mis-

7. This information was given to me by a participant in these conferences. Another interesting sidelight on conditions in the winter of 1938–39 is that the Germans were willing to sell airplane engines to France; the proposed deal was canceled because of objections from the French Ministry of Foreign Affairs. This is another bit of circumstantial evidence indicating that Germany's military aspirations were directed toward the East, not toward the West.

sion and the government. The secret leaked out when a French aviator crashed on the West Coast. Woodring accused Morgenthau of giving the French American military secrets, although the bombers for which negotiations were going on were already outmoded.

Roosevelt then invited some members of the Senate Foreign Affairs Committee to a conference, warned them that war was imminent, and suggested that America's frontier was on the Rhine. But this talk alarmed and irritated most of the senators instead of winning them over. It hindered rather than helped the accomplishment of Roosevelt's design: the elimination of the arms embargo from the Neutrality Act. The persistent efforts of Roosevelt and Hull to obtain the removal of the embargo before the outbreak of war failed both in the House and in the Senate. The final blow was an adverse 12–11 vote in the Senate Foreign Affairs Committee in July 1939.

There is not sufficient evidence to establish with certainty how far Washington may be held directly responsible for the fateful British decision to challenge Hitler on the issue of Poland. Cordell Hull's testimony on America's prewar policy is ambiguous if not contradictory:

"Though we had repeatedly sought to encourage the democracies of Europe, the arrival of war found us with no entangling agreements that would drag us in."[8]

Obviously there were no formal treaties or commitments; these would have been impossible under the American Constitution and in the prevalent state of American public opinion. But it would have been difficult to give encouragement without holding out hope of American aid and perhaps ultimate involvement. The vehement partisanship of high Administration officials was calculated to arouse these hopes. Welles called the seizure of Prague "the first unshaded instance of open thievery," and Hull "was moved to use all his transcendent talent for picturesque profanity."[9]

If Col. Charles A. Lindbergh or one of the senators known for anti-interventionist sentiments had been President, the case for letting Hitler move eastward would have seemed much stronger in London

---

8. Hull, *Memoirs*, 1:667.

9. Alsop and Kintner, *American White Paper*, 34.

and Paris. A well-known American statesman, not connected with the Roosevelt regime, visited Neville Chamberlain in March 1938 and suggested to the British Prime Minister that it would be much better if Germany moved east, rather than west. It would be a disaster to civilization, the American remarked, if the western democracies were dragged down by a war, the end of which would be to save the cruel Russian despotism.

Chamberlain expressed agreement with these views and said they dominated his own policies. He was only concerned about the French alliance with Russia. This might induce Hitler to destroy the weaker link first. Had the views of the American visitor prevailed in the White House, Chamberlain might never have changed his policy by giving the guarantee to Poland which worked out so disastrously both for Poland and for Great Britain.[10]

The beginning of the war in Europe made it possible for the Administration to get rid of the undesired arms embargo. The President's first steps were to issue neutrality proclamations, one under general international law, the other under the Neutrality Act, prescribing an embargo on arms shipments. After starting his private correspondence with Winston Churchill, full details of which have not been revealed, Roosevelt called Congress in special session and asked for the elimination of the embargo. This request was based on the argument that repeal of the embargo was a means to keep the United States at peace. The President's exact words were:

Let no group assume the exclusive label of the "peace bloc." We all belong to it. . . . I give you my deep and unalterable conviction, based on years of experience as a worker in the field of international peace, that by the repeal of the embargo the United States will more probably remain at peace than if the law remains as it stands today. . . . Our acts must be guided by one single, hardheaded thought— keeping America out of the war.

Not everyone agreed with Roosevelt's viewpoint. Senator William E. Borah, the veteran lion of the isolationists, recalled that Secretary Hull

10. This incident was described to me by the American concerned.

had once said that the purpose of the Neutrality Act was to keep us out of war. Borah commented: "If the purpose of the Embargo Act then was to keep us out of war, what is the purpose of repealing it: to get us into war?"

Senator Robert M. La Follette, Jr., argued that "repeal can only be interpreted at home and abroad as an official act taken by our Government for the purpose of partial participation in the European war."

After the debate had gone on for several weeks, Roosevelt, in a radio broadcast of October 26, gave another of his innumerable professions of intention to keep America at peace. He characterized appeals against sending Americans to the battlefields of Europe as "a shameless and dishonest fake." "The fact of the international situation . . . is that the United States of America is neutral and does not intend to get involved in war."

The period when all was quiet on the Maginot Line passed with no appreciable change in the American position. The President made the following statement of the American attitude toward Finland at the time of the Soviet invasion:

Here is a small Republic in northern Europe, which, without any question whatsoever, wishes solely to maintain its own territorial and governmental integrity. Nobody with any pretense at common sense believes that Finland had any ulterior designs on the integrity or safety of the Soviet Union.

That American sympathy is ninety-eight per cent with the Finns in their effort to stave off invasion of their own soil is by now axiomatic.

The German military sweep in the spring and summer of 1940 took place so swiftly that American military intervention, even if it had been sanctioned by public opinion, could not have been effective. Calling for additional defense appropriations on May 16, after the German breakthrough in France, the President tried to make the nation's flesh creep by pointing out alleged possibilities of attack on American soil by air from various points in the Eastern Hemisphere. Like all arguments based upon the danger of physical invasion of the American continent, this overlooked the limitations imposed by the current range and speed of aircraft. The Ural industrial region of Russia was much closer to German advanced bases than America was to any point occupied by Hitler in 1940. But this area was never subjected to serious bombing attacks.

Roosevelt hit a high emotional note in the speech at Charlottesville, Virginia, on June 10, referred to on page 78, when the French collapse had already reached an advanced stage. He denounced Mussolini, who had just entered the war against France, in the strongest language he had yet used publicly:

"On this tenth day of June, 1940, the hand that held the dagger has struck it into the back of its neighbor."

He warned against the idea that

we of the United States can safely permit the United States to become a lone island, a lone island in a world dominated by the philosophy of force.

Such an island may be the dream of those who still talk and vote as isolationists. Such an island represents to me and to the overwhelming majority of Americans today a helpless nightmare of a people without freedom—the nightmare of a people lodged in prison, handcuffed, hungry, and fed through the bars from day to day by the contemptuous, unpitying masters of other continents.

There was also a hint of the future conception of lend-lease.

We will pursue two obvious and simultaneous courses; we will extend to the opponents of force the material resources of this nation; and, at the same time, we will harness and speed up the use of those resources in order that we ourselves in the Americas may have equipment and training equal to the task of any emergency and every defense.

When Roosevelt returned to Washington, he talked in the White House office with Adolf Berle, Assistant Secretary of State, and with his most trusted adviser, Harry Hopkins. Berle suggested that there might be a clear-cut world division, with Roosevelt as the leader of the free people facing Hitler. The President seems to have taken this suggestion seriously. "That would be a terrible responsibility," he said. It is possible that his decision to run for a third term was finally taken that night.[11]

The responsibility which Roosevelt faced was indeed terrible. The subsequent Soviet-Nazi breach could not have been foreseen with certainty at this time. On any reasonable calculation of geography, manpower, and industrial resources, it was obvious that Great Britain, no matter how much aid it might receive from America, could never singlehandedly break the German military power. Roosevelt, therefore, had to choose between a policy of western hemispheric defense and a policy of increasing commitment to a war which might be expected to take millions of American lives.

Perhaps the President disguised, even to himself, the necessity and the implications of this choice. He continued, vociferously until his election for a third term, in more muted tones after that election, to profess his intention to remain out of the conflict. But at the same time, he instituted policies and made appointments which clearly indicated that America would finally be drawn into the war.

One of the most significant of these appointments was that of Henry L. Stimson as Secretary of War. Stimson had held the same office in the Cabinet of Theodore Roosevelt and had served as Secretary of State under Herbert Hoover. Stimson had been eager for stronger action against Japan in Manchuria, but was held back by Hoover's aversion to war and by the nonbelligerent temper of American public opinion. Out of public office he had been a militant advocate of an American interventionist policy, both in Europe and in Asia.

Stimson on June 18 delivered a radio address calling for the repeal of the Neutrality Act, the opening of American ports to British and French vessels, acceleration of munitions supply to Britain and France, "sending them if necessary in our own ships and under convoy," and the adoption of universal military training. Immediately after this speech, which could fairly be described as a call to undeclared war, Stimson was invited to become Secretary of War. He asked Roosevelt over the telephone whether the latter had seen the text of his radio address and whether this would be embarrassing. The President replied that he had

11. Davis and Lindley, *How War Came*, 65.

read the speech and was in full accord with it.[12] There could hardly be a more complete acknowledgment, in advance, of the insincerity of his subsequent campaign peace assurances.

At the same time, another interventionist Republican, Frank Knox, became Secretary of the Navy. Knox soon became the most articulate and garrulous warhawk in the Cabinet. Stimson's predecessor, Harry Woodring, had favored a volunteer system of enlistment as sufficient for America's defense needs. But Roosevelt was not thinking in terms of defense and Woodring was fired.

The American Government late in June received a suggestion from the Italian Ambassador in Germany, Dino Alfieri, that peace terms acceptable to Great Britain would be offered by the Axis if Britain would request them. Hull, through Welles, communicated this offer to the British Ambassador, Lord Lothian, emphasizing the point that no recommendation of any kind was being offered. On September 5, President Aguirre Cerdo of Chile proposed to Roosevelt an initiative toward peace by all the American republics. The United States reply was delayed until October 26 and was a rejection.[13]

Committed to an all-out victory which Britain could not conceivably win by its own efforts, Winston Churchill spared no effort to draw America into the war. As he tells us in the second volume of his memoirs: "My relations with the President gradually became so close that the chief business between our two countries was virtually conducted by these personal interchanges between him and me. In this way our perfect understanding was gained."[14]

A typical budget of Churchill's requests is to be found in his first message to Roosevelt after assuming office as Prime Minister, on May 15. Churchill asks for the loan of forty or fifty of the older American destroyers, for several hundred of the latest types of aircraft, for anti-aircraft equipment and ammunition, steel and other materials. Lend-lease is foreshadowed in this sentence: "We shall go on paying dollars for as long as we can; but I should like to feel reasonably sure that when we can pay no more you will give us the stuff all the same."[15]

12. Stimson and Bundy, *On Active Service*, 324.
13. Hull, *Memoirs*, 2:844–45.
14. Churchill, *Their Finest Hour*, 23.
15. Ibid., 24–25.

Churchill also proposed that an American squadron should pay a prolonged visit to Irish ports and concludes: "I am looking to you to keep the Japs quiet in the Pacific, using Singapore in any way convenient."

If America was to be drawn into the war, the Pacific, as later events were to prove, offered even more opportunities than the Atlantic.

Roosevelt sometimes felt obliged to decline or postpone the granting of Churchill's requests. As was noted in the preceding chapter, he disappointed the Prime Minister by refusing to permit the publication of the message to Reynaud—a message which Churchill had eagerly interpreted as an American commitment to enter the war. But usually Churchill's requests were granted, after a lapse of weeks or months, if not immediately.

The British Prime Minister faced a delicate psychological problem in his dealings with Washington. He wanted to scare the American Government sufficiently to speed up aid and, if possible, to procure direct intervention. Yet the painting of too gloomy a picture might create fear in American military circles that aid to Britain out of America's then very scanty military resources might be wasted. This led to occasional inconsistencies.

So Churchill suggested, in a message of June 14–15, that a point might be reached in the struggle where the present British Ministers would no longer be in control of the situation. A pro-German government might be formed; then where would America be, the Prime Minister continued, if the British Navy were surrendered to Hitler?

On the other hand, when arrangements were made to turn over fifty American destroyers to Britain in exchange for bases in the Caribbean area, Churchill was unwilling to publish an exchange of letters between Lothian and Hull, in which the former gave assurance that the British Navy would not be scuttled or surrendered. Churchill declared:

"I think it is much more likely that the German Government will be the one to surrender or scuttle its fleet or what is left of it."

This exchange was a new milestone on America's road to war. There were several legal obstacles to the transaction. In the first place, it was a violation of the Hague Convention of 1907, which forbade neutrals to sell warships to belligerents. Moreover, Section 23, Title 18 of the U.S. Code, forbade "the fitting out, arming or procurement of any vessel with the intent that it shall be employed in the service of a foreign state to cruise or commit hostilities against any state with which the United States is at peace." And Section 3, Title 5 of the Espionage Act of June 15, 1917, provides that during a war in which the United States is neutral it shall be unlawful to send out of United States jurisdiction any war vessel "with any intent or under any agreement or contract, written or oral, that such vessel shall be delivered to a belligerent nation."

There might also have seemed to be a moral obligation to submit to the judgment of Congress a decision of such consequence for American neutrality and national defense. But such legal formalities were brushed aside. Attorney General Robert H. Jackson, displaying the flexibility which was later to stand him in good stead as prosecutor in the Nürnberg trials, furnished an opinion which released Roosevelt from the necessity of abiding by the inconvenient laws.

There had been a difference of opinion between London and Washington about how the exchange should take place. Churchill, perhaps scenting a valuable precedent for future lend-lease, wanted the destroyers as a free gift and was willing to lease bases in the same way. Hull felt that Roosevelt would be on stronger ground if he could show that he had received a tangible equivalent for the destroyers.

Green H. Hackworth, legal adviser to the State Department, proposed the formula that finally proved satisfactory to both sides. Britain leased bases in Newfoundland and Bermuda as a gift and transferred others in exchange for the destroyers.

Churchill's request for the destroyers had been made in May. It was granted in September. Looking back in retrospect to the year 1940, he could write appreciatively in his memoirs: "Across the Atlantic the great republic drew ever nearer to her duty and our aid."

Meanwhile a mighty debate was shaping up in the United States on the issue of participation in the European war. Sentiment for a declaration of war and the dispatch of troops overseas was extremely slight. Up to the very eve of Pearl Harbor no such proposal would have stood a chance of endorsement by Congress. Public-opinion polls from the fall of France to the Japanese attack showed a pretty steady proportion of 80 per cent as opposed to war.

There was also extremely little sympathy with the Axis. Some impatient advocates of immediate war tried to pin the label of "fascist" on all opponents of American intervention. But this was demonstrably unfair and inaccurate. No influential leader of the fight against involvement in the conflict wanted to emulate Hitler or set up a fascist regime in this country. The leading organization which stood for this position, the America First Committee, barred Nazis, Fascists, and Communists from membership. A familiar argument of America First speakers was that war would bring the United States the regimentation, militarization, and unlimited governmental powers which were so objectionable in European dictatorships.

"Hitler's Fifth Column" was a popular subject for sensational magazine articles. One might have imagined that the United States was flooded with Axis agents, carrying on active propaganda through press, radio, and other agencies for influencing American public opinion.

But on sober analysis this "fifth column" evaporates into the mist of overheated fantasy. No doubt there were German, Japanese, and Italian agents in this country. But they were not getting a hearing on lecture platforms or publishing articles in influential magazines.

I followed America's great debate very closely, and I can recall only one alien who took an active part on the isolationist side. This was Freda Utley (now a naturalized American), an English woman publicist. She believed that Britain was being pressed by the Roosevelt Administration to fight an unnecessary war beyond its strength, and that the probable consequences of a prolonged conflict would be chaos in Europe and the triumph of communism. Miss Utley was in no sense a sympathizer with fascism.

On the other side it would be easy to recall the names of scores of alien refugees in this country who formed a kind of interventionist Foreign Legion and devoted themselves with varying degrees of tact and finesse to the task of inducing America to take up arms.

The choosing of sides in this controversy about intervention proceeded along lines that recalled America's First Crusade in some features, but not in all. There was the same element of geographical cleavage. The East and the South were the most militant sections. Isolationist feeling was strongest in the Middle West and the Rocky Mountain area. The senators who most actively opposed the successive steps of the Administration toward war—Taft, Wheeler, La Follette, Clark,

Nye—were all from states between the Alleghenies and the Rockies. Colonel Lindbergh was the son of a congressman from Minnesota who had voted against participation in World War I. The majority of Midwestern congressmen voted against the Lend-Lease Act, a major step in the direction of involvement.

There were also occupational and group cleavages, though these were blurred and shifting by comparison with the situation which prevailed at the time of World War I. Prominent on the interventionist side, in the Second Crusade as in the First, were university and college professors, especially on Eastern campuses, writers, and other intellectuals. The interventionist cause and the activities connected with it ("Bundles for Britain," for instance) were popular in well-to-do middle-class circles. Roosevelt gained support among prowar Eastern Republicans by his attitude toward international affairs.

An amusing illustration of this point may be found in John P. Marquand's novel *So Little Time.* One of the characters, a woman who regards herself as belonging to the social elite, remarks on the eve of the 1940 election:

"Fred and I always think the same way at election time. . . . We voted for Hoover in 1932. We voted for Landon in 1936. This year for the first time we're voting for Mr. Roosevelt. . . . We're voting for Mr. Roosevelt because England wants us to have Mr. Roosevelt. That's the least we can do for England."

Americans who for ethnic or religious reasons felt special sympathy for the peoples and groups in Europe which had suffered from Nazi oppression were often inclined in favor of intervention. There was more isolationist sentiment in communities with large numbers of people of Irish, German, or Italian origin.

There were no clear-cut lines of political, economic, and religious division on the issue. Conservatives and radicals, Catholics and Protestants, representatives of business, labor, and farm groups could be found on both sides.

There were spiritual descendants of the pastors of World War I who thumped their pulpits and shouted: "God damn the Kaiser." There were more sober advocates of intervention. But there was enough pacifist and pacific sentiment in the Protestant churches to prevent the formation of anything like a united crusading front. *The Christian Century,* a nondenominational Protestant weekly, was one of the strongest and most serious champions of the anti-interventionist viewpoint.

Some Catholic prelates, such as Cardinal William O'Connell, of the Boston archdiocese, were vigorously and outspokenly opposed to involvement. Others upheld the Administration or side-stepped the issue. Here again there was no unity of viewpoint. Catholic doubts about the advisability of starting a second crusade were intensified after Russia entered the war. Dr. John A. O'Brien, of Notre Dame University, spoke for a considerable section of Catholic opinion when he said on June 24, 1941:

"The American people cannot be driven by propaganda, trickery or deceit into fighting to maintain the Christ-hating Stalin in his tyranny over 180 million enslaved people."

It was the well-to-do classes which were most enthusiastic in support of America's participation in the First World War. Opposition came mostly from the left, from Socialists, IWW's, agrarian radicals. This time there was no such clear-cut pattern. It was government planners in Washington, rather than businessmen, who saw in a booming war economy the way out of the long depression which all the contradictory remedies of the New Deal had failed to cure.

The *Saturday Evening Post,* widely read organ of the American middle class, was editorially vigorously opposed to involvement until the spring of 1941, when there was a change of editorship. Some Eastern financiers maintained the pro-British attitude which was characteristic of this group in the First World War. But a number of industrialists, especially in the Middle West, were vigorous supporters of the America First Committee. There was also division on the left. The Socialist party, which had already lost much of its strength through the secession of many of its members to the Communists, was further divided into two small groups which differed in opinion on the war issue.[16] The group which retained the party name, headed by Norman Thomas, was anti-war. The Social Democratic Federation was in favor of intervention.

The Communists, of course, could not be split. They always func-

16. These groups had separated on other grounds before the question of American involvement in war had arisen.

tioned as a disciplined unit, with Soviet interests as their dominant consideration. So they were unitedly on opposite sides of the debate, at various times. As long as the Hitler-Stalin pact was in force, the Communists denounced the idea of intervention, stirred up strikes in defense plants, coined antiwar slogans, and spawned a number of antiwar front organizations. As soon as Russia was attacked, on June 21, 1941, they turned a complete somersault and became as clamorous to get America into the war as they had been to keep it out before Hitler broke with Stalin.

The principal organization around which interventionist sentiment crystallized was the Committee to Defend America by Aiding the Allies. This was launched, with William Allen White as chairman, at a luncheon in New York on April 29, 1940. It was the successor to a group which had been formed in the previous autumn to urge revision of the Neutrality Act by permitting the sale of munitions on a cash-and-carry basis to Great Britain and France. White had been the leader of this group and stressed the limited character of the aid which he favored in a statement to the following effect:

> These European democracies are carrying our banner, fighting the American battle. . . . We need not shed our blood for them now or ever. But we should not deny them now access to our shores when they come with cash to pay for weapons of defense and with their own ships to carry arms and materials which are to protect their citizens and their soldiers fighting for our common cause.

Frederick R. Coudert gave a luncheon for White on October 20, 1939. Among those present were Clark Eichelberger, director of the League of Nations Association, Nicholas Murray Butler, president of Columbia University, Thomas Watson, of the International Business Machines Corporation, Henry L. Stimson, the future Secretary of War, and Wendell Willkie, the future Republican candidate for the presidency. Willkie said on this occasion:

"Well, if money is all Mr. White needs, let's get it for him."[17]

William Allen White was a well-known, loved, and respected Midwestern small-town editor with a national audience. It seemed good

17. Johnson, *Battle against Isolation,* 51.

strategy to the bellicose Easterners to induce him to head an interventionist organization.

It has already been shown that White was as disillusioned as the majority of his countrymen with the fruits of America's First Crusade.[18] In the face of World War II he reacted with the divided sentiment which was characteristic of the mood of many Americans. White sincerely abhorred the thought of American participation in the war. But he felt that Hitler must be defeated. He found a solution for this contradiction in the wishful thought that America could turn the tide by giving economic aid to Britain.

White was sincere in this conception of limited liability intervention. But several members of the Committee advocated a declaration of war as early as June 1940. And most of its active leaders were disposed to drift toward war at the Administration's pace, or a little faster. There was a close connection between the Administration and the Committee. As White said:

"I never did anything the President didn't ask for, and I always conferred with him on our program."[19]

The playwright Robert E. Sherwood inserted large advertisements in the newspapers of various cities under the heading: "Stop Hitler Now." The newspaper publishers George and Dorothy Backer, Henry Luce, and others subscribed twenty-five thousand dollars to pay for these. The advertisement contained the sentiments: "Will the Nazis considerately wait until we are ready to fight them? Anyone who argues that they will wait is either an imbecile or a traitor." Roosevelt took time out from assurances of his intention to keep America out of the war to describe this advertisement as "a great piece of work."[20]

By July 1, 1940, petitions with approximately two million signatures had been sent to the White House, along with thousands of telegrams, postcards, and letters to congressmen. There were nation-wide radio broadcasts and local rallies. By November the Committee had organized 750 local chapters (200 of the first 300 were in New England) and had received $230,000 in contributions from over 10,000 donors.

18. See page 20, above.
19. Johnson, *Battle against Isolation,* 91.
20. Ibid., 95–97.

The Committee promoted broadcasts by prominent military and naval figures, including General John J. Pershing. Sometimes these men of war went beyond the declared program of the organization. Admiral Harry E. Yarnell (retired) advocated a declaration of war on July 7 and was joined by Admiral Standley (subsequently Ambassador to the Soviet Union) on October 12.

The Women's Division of the Committee in New York enrolled five hundred women volunteers from each of the five boroughs as "Minute Americans," to serve at a minute's notice. Each of these received a page from a telephone directory with instructions to call the names in order to explain why aid to Great Britain was essential to national defense and to try to enlist the subscriber as a new "Minute American." By the first week of October 1940, the Minute Americans had talked with half a million New York housewives.

The trend toward advocating war measures was becoming so strong toward the end of 1940 that White felt obliged to apply a douche of cold water. In a letter published in the Scripps-Howard newspapers of December 23 he expressed sentiments which were both surprising and unpalatable to many of his associates:

> The only reason in God's world I am in this organization is to keep this country out of war. . . . The Johnson Act (prohibiting loans to countries in default on obligations to the United States) should not be repealed. It is not true even remotely that we favor repealing [the Neutrality Act] to carry contraband of war into the war zone. . . . If I were making a motto for the Committee it would be: "The Yanks Are Not Coming." . . . Any organization that is for war is certainly playing Hitler's game.

This stirred up a storm of protest and on January 2, 1941, White resigned the chairmanship of the Committee. His successor was ex-Senator Ernest Gibson, of Vermont, who was later replaced by Clark Eichelberger. As White had been left behind by his Committee, the Committee was outpaced by a group more impatient to plunge into the slaughter. This was Fight for Freedom, organized on April 19, 1941, with the Episcopal Bishop Henry W. Hobson as chairman and Francis P. Miller, Ulric Bell, Wayne Johnson, and Mrs. Calvin Coolidge among the leading members. It set forth the position that America was already at war in the following statement:

We still think in terms of keeping out of a war in which we are already engaged in every sense except armed combat. We have too long left the main burden of winning a victory to other people. Thus we are in the immoral and craven position of asking others to make the supreme sacrifice for this victory which we recognize as essential to us.

"Fight for Freedom" specialized in putting out posters calculated to make the American flesh creep. One which appeared in the *New York Times* of October 19, 1941, showed a uniformed Nazi bludgeoning an American and shouting, "Shut up, Yank; learn to speak Nazi." A poster prepared for labor groups showed a uniformed Nazi whipping workers and bore the caption: "There sits in Berchtesgaden an anemic pipsqueak who's going to change all that labor stands for. Or is he?" Another scary, if somewhat fanciful, advertisement, designed to impress church groups, represented Hitler as saying: "Repeat after me, Yank: Adolf Hitler, hallowed be thy name." This bit of psychological warfare bore the sprightly inscription: "Holy cats, look who's holy!"

The Committee to Defend America came out openly for war in late June 1941, thereby catching up with Fight for Freedom. Clark Eichelberger, chairman of the Committee, stated on October 18, 1941, that "the United States has been in the war for some time, but that fact has not yet been made clear to the world." Here was the end of a road that had begun with ardent professions of desire and intention to keep America out of war.

The largest and most representative of the antiwar organizations was the America First Committee. This organization stemmed from the initiative of a group of Yale Law School students. It was formally established in September 1940 under the chairmanship of General Robert E. Wood, Quartermaster General of the United States Army in World War I and later an executive of Sears, Roebuck & Company. Its statement of principles, published regularly in its weekly *America First Bulletin,* was as follows:

1. Our first duty is to keep America out of foreign wars. Our entry would only destroy democracy, not save it.

2. We must build a defense, for our own shores, so strong that no foreign power or combination of powers can invade our country by sea, air or land.

3. Not by acts of war, but by preserving and extending democracy at home can we aid democracy and freedom in other lands.

4. In 1917 we sent our ships into the war zone; and this led us to war. In 1941 we must keep our naval convoys and merchant vessels on this side of the Atlantic.

5. Humanitarian aid is the duty of a strong free country at peace. With proper safeguards for the distribution of supplies we should feed and clothe the suffering and needy people of the occupied countries.

6. We advocate official advisory vote by the people of the United States on the question of war and peace, so that when Congress decides this question, as the Constitution provides, it may know the opinion of the people on this gravest of all issues.

Despite the increasingly powerful government and social pressures for a prowar attitude, the America First Committee won wide popular support. Its stand in favor of adequate defense attracted a much larger membership than a pacifist body could have hoped to gain. Its exclusion of Nazis, Fascists, and Communists freed it from the taint of unpopular alien creeds. It served as a tangible rallying point for those who felt a deep-seated aversion to "foreign wars" and cherished the suspicion that a second crusade would be more costly in lives and resources and no more productive of positive results than the first had been.

Moreover, America First possessed an extremely magnetic spokesman in Charles A. Lindbergh. Invested with the glamor and prestige of his pioneer lone flight to Europe across the Atlantic, known for other achievements in aviation and science, tall, vigorous, and youthful, he became the outstanding personality of the antiwar party.

Lindbergh in 1940 foresaw with remarkable prescience the need for solidarity among the nations of the West which had become, perhaps too late, an objective of American diplomacy in 1950. He wrote:

The answer is not in war among western nations, but in sharing influence and empire among a sufficient number of their people to make sure that they control an overwhelming military strength. Then, and then only, can our civilization endure in safety and in peace—only through the cooperation of a group of western nations strong enough to act as a police force for the world.

Germany is as essential to this group as England or France, for she alone can either dam the Asiatic hordes or form the spearhead of their penetration into Europe. . . . Now Russia is pushing Europe's frontier slowly westward again, while Germany, France and England are carrying on their suicidal quarrels.[21]

About the same time Lindbergh's wife, a poet and author gifted with a sensitive imagination and a beautiful style in prose and verse, published a forecast of the shape of things to come which stands the test of being read ten years later extremely well. In an article, "Prayer for Peace," published in the *Reader's Digest* for January 1940, Mrs. Lindbergh wrote:

In a long and devastating war, how can one help but see that the British Empire, the "English way of life," the English government which we have so admired, are unlikely to survive in their present form? That the French democracy, love of freedom and spirit of sanity, so needed in the world today, will go down to something else. That there will be no winner in a prostrated Europe unless it is the disruption, mediocrity and spiritual death which are in Russia today. Who is the potential invader of Europe, the real threat to European civilization? Ask the Balkans and the Baltic states. Ask Finland; ask Rumania; ask Turkey. Against a strong and united Europe—even against a strong Germany—the hordes of Russia are no menace. But against a divided Europe, bled by wars and prostrated by devastation, her advance will be slow, inevitable and deadly—like a flow of lava.

Lindbergh was approached indirectly on behalf of the White House and offered the post of Secretary of Air (to be created in the Cabinet) if

21. *The Atlantic* (March 1940).

he would cease opposing America's entrance into the war. He rejected the offer and threw himself into the struggle against involvement.

Lindbergh in his speeches emphasized the ideas that America should stay out of European wars, that the United States was strong enough to defend the Western Hemisphere but not strong enough to impose its will upon the entire world, and that it was no service to Europe to prolong the war. In his testimony before the House Foreign Affairs Committee, opposing the Lend-Lease Act, he argued for American neutrality on the following grounds:

> I believe this is not our war. . . . We were given no opportunity to take part in the declaration of this war. I believe when we left Europe after the last war and discontinued a part in the peace that was brought about after that war, then logically we took the stand that we would not enter another war. . . .
>
> I prefer to see neither side win. I would like to see a negotiated peace. I believe a complete victory on either side would result in prostration in Europe, such as we have never seen. . . .

Asked on which side he was, the aviator replied:
"On no side, except our own."

Lindbergh accurately analyzed the stepping up of foreign requests for aid, echoed by interventionists in America, at an America First meeting in Philadelphia on May 29, 1941:

> First they said, Sell us the arms and we will win. Then it was, Lend us the arms and we will win. Now it is, Bring us the arms and we will win. Tomorrow it will be, Fight our war for us and we will win.

Lindbergh presented the following analysis of the forces which were promoting American intervention in a much-criticized speech at Des Moines on September 11, 1941. The gist of this address was in the following paragraphs:

> The three most important groups that have been pressing this country toward war are the British, the Jewish and the Roosevelt Administration. Behind these groups, but of lesser importance, are a number of capitalists, Anglophiles and intellectuals who believe that

their future and the future of the world depend upon the domination of the British Empire. Add to these the communist groups, who were opposed to intervention until a few weeks ago, and I believe I have named the major war agitators. . . .

England has devoted and will continue to devote every effort to get us into the war. . . . If we were Englishmen we would do the same. . . . The second major group mentioned is the Jewish. It is not difficult to understand why Jewish people desire the overthrow of Nazi Germany. The persecution they suffered in Germany would be sufficient to make bitter enemies of any race. No person with a sense of the dignity of mankind can condone the persecution of the Jewish race in Germany. But no person of honesty and vision can look on their pro-war policy here today without seeing the dangers involved in such a policy, both for us and for them. . . . Their greatest danger to this country lies in their large ownership and influence in our motion pictures, our press, our radio and our government. . . .

The power of the Roosevelt Administration depends upon the maintenance of a wartime emergency. The prestige of the Roosevelt Administration depends upon the success of Great Britain, to whom the President attached his political future at a time when most people thought that England and France would easily win the war. The danger of the Roosevelt Administration depends upon its subterfuge. While its members have promised us peace, they have led us to war, heedless of the platform upon which they were elected.

Senator Robert A. Taft was a vigorous opponent of intervention on conservative grounds. He declared in June 1941: "Americans don't want to go to war to beat a totalitarian system in Europe if they are to get socialism here when it is all over." And after the German attack on Russia, Taft asserted in a nation-wide broadcast that the victory of communism in the world would be far more dangerous to the United States than the victory of fascism.

Former President Hoover was a consistent opponent of involvement, although he did not associate himself with the America First Committee or any other organization. After the German attack on Russia he remarked that "collaboration between Britain and Russia will bring them military values, but it makes the whole argument of our joining the war to bring the four freedoms to mankind a Gargantuan jest." A good many people behind the postwar Soviet iron curtain would probably heartily endorse this sentiment.

Hoover, together with former Vice-President Charles G. Dawes, the former Republican presidential candidate Alfred Landon, and others issued a protest against "undeclared war" on August 5, 1941:

> Exceeding its expressed purpose, the Lend-Lease Bill has been followed by naval action, by military occupation of bases outside the Western Hemisphere, by promises of unauthorized aid to Russia and by other belligerent moves.
>
> Such warlike steps, in no case sanctioned by Congress, undermine its constitutional powers and the fundamental principles of democratic government.

The positions of the two sides in this great debate, carried on through forums, radio addresses, magazine articles, and other means of influencing public opinion, may be briefly summarized as follows: The interventionists saw a grave threat to the United States in the possible victory of Hitler. Some of them emphasized the military, others the economic, others the moral, nature of this threat. They argued that it was an imperative American national interest to "stop Hitler." They became increasingly reticent about the usual original qualification, "by methods short of war."

The isolationists took their stand on the disappointing aftermath of America's First Crusade. They maintained that there was no serious danger of an attack on the American continent, whereas an American invasion of Europe gave every prospect of being an appallingly costly operation. They foresaw dubious political results from American intervention, especially with Soviet Russia as a cobelligerent.

These opposing viewpoints were argued with varying degrees of factual knowledge and temperance. A few home-grown crackpots with extremist racial and religious views attached themselves to the isolationist cause, despite the efforts of the America First Committee to disown such undesirable and undesired camp followers.

Not all interventionists were as starry-eyed as the author of the following passage, which appeared in an article published in the *Atlantic:*

In man the refusal to fight save in self-defense may be not only profoundly immoral, but morally catastrophic. For man is a willing and
purposeful creature. He can make his world. He can lift up his eyes
to the hills and achieve the summits. Sometimes he decrees golden
domes to arise upon the flat plains of his existence. And whenever
he has done so he has been at peace with himself and approached
a little nearer to the angels. There is something, I believe, for which
Americans will fight: our souls' repose and a world made in our own
splendid image.[22]

And despite the grotesque scare posters sponsored by Bishop Hobson, most members of Fight for Freedom would not have endorsed the
peculiar conception of liberty implied in a message which was sent to
an antiwar meeting in Cincinnati:

> I am not grateful to you for sending me notice of the traitorous
> assemblage to be held on June 16. I do not care to listen to Nazi
> agents, even when [*sic*] United States Senators and their wives. If I
> had the authority, I would bomb and machine-gun your meeting. I
> am a member of the Fight for Freedom Committee.

The momentous issue of deliberate involvement in the European
war might well have been submitted to a referendum of the American people in the presidential election of 1940. The majority of the
Republicans in both houses of Congress before and after this election
systematically voted against measures calculated to bring about this
involvement.

Had Roosevelt frankly presented to the voters the program which he
actually carried out in 1941 (lend-lease, convoys, undeclared shooting
war in the Atlantic, commercial blockade of Japan) and had Roosevelt's opponent been a sincerely noninterventionist Republican, a very
interesting discussion would certainly have ensued. The verdict of the
people would then have given a clear mandate either to go into the war

22. David L. Cohn, "I Hear Australians Singing," *The Atlantic*, 167 (April 1941),
406–7. It would be interesting to hear the unexpurgated comments of soldiers in
foxholes on this lush noncombatant eulogy of the idea of fighting for "our souls'
repose."

frankly and vigorously or to stay out of it, except in the event of direct attack.

But neither of the leading candidates in the 1940 election made a candid statement of his position on the most important issue confronting the American people. A comparison of Roosevelt's words before the election and of his deeds after the election fully substantiates the tart comment of Clare Boothe Luce: "He lied the American people into war because he could not lead them into it."

And by an unfortunate accident of American politics, the Republican nomination did not go to a man who shared the viewpoint of the majority of Republican members of Congress. The candidate was Wendell Willkie, a newcomer in politics, a man who in the preceding autumn had volunteered to raise money for interventionist purposes.

The result was that the very large number of American voters who wanted to stay out of the war were, for all practical purposes, disfranchised. The campaign was an amazing exhibition of double talk. Roosevelt and Willkie vied with each other in making the most sweeping promises to keep the country at peace. The frequency and forcefulness of these pledges mounted to a crescendo as the election day approached. This was a significant straw in the wind, indicating how the majority of voters in both parties felt on the issue. There were evidently few votes to be won and many to be lost by a frank call to arms.

Both platforms contained antiwar commitments. The Democratic read: "We will not participate in foreign wars and we will not send our army, naval or air forces to fight in foreign lands outside the Americas, except in case of attack."

The equivalent Republican statement was more concise: "The Republican Party is firmly opposed to involving this nation in foreign wars."

Willkie said in Chicago on September 13: "If you elect me President, I will never send an American boy to fight in a European war."

He told his audience in Cleveland on October 2: "I am for keeping out of war. I am for peace for America."

He declared in Philadelphia on October 4: "We must stop this drift toward war," and in a radio broadcast on October 8 he asserted: "We must keep out of war at all hazards." He told the voters of Boston on

October 11: "Our boys shall stay out of European wars." On October 22 he offered the following explanation of the difference between his foreign policy and that of the Administration:

"One difference is my determination to stay out of war. I have a real fear that this Administration is heading for war, and I am against our going to war and will do all that I can to avoid it."

So Willkie, whose whole attitude after the election promoted the "drift toward war" which he condemned before the votes were counted, tried to win as the champion of peace against war. But he could not outbid Roosevelt in promises on this issue. Between October 28 and November 3 the President gave repeated assurances that he would not lead the country into any foreign wars. As his admirer, Robert E. Sherwood, says:

> That Madison Square Garden speech (on October 28) was one of the most equivocal of Roosevelt's career. . . . Here Roosevelt went to the length or depth of taking credit for the Neutrality Law and other measures which he had thoroughly disapproved and had fought to repeal and had contrived by all possible means to circumvent. While boasting of the Neutrality Law as part of the Administration record, he deliberately neglected to make any mention of his own Quarantine Speech.[23]

Two days later, in Boston, Roosevelt went even further. "Fear-of-war hysteria," in Sherwood's phrase, seemed to be growing. Telegrams poured in from Democratic leaders, urging the President to make stronger and more specific antiwar pledges. The election, according to these telegrams, hung in the balance. Henri IV thought Paris was worth a Mass. Roosevelt apparently believed that another term of power was worth promises which would soon be disregarded, which could be broken without incurring legal liability. At the urging of Sherwood[24] he decided to strengthen his pledge with the words "again and again and again." And the rich, soothing voice poured out to the audience at Boston the following reassurance:

23. Sherwood, *Roosevelt and Hopkins*, 189.
24. Ibid., 191.

While I am talking to you, mothers and fathers, I give you one more assurance.

I have said this before, but I shall say it again and again and again.

Your boys are not going to be sent into any foreign wars.

On November 2 Roosevelt promised: "Your President says this nation is not going to war."

On November 3 he added: "The first purpose of our foreign policy is to keep our country out of war."[25]

No isolationist could have offered more sweeping and categorical pledges. How these pledges were observed will be the subject of the next two chapters. Professor Thomas A. Bailey, a sympathizer with Roosevelt's foreign policy, admits that the President's tactics were disingenuous, but offers an apology in the following passage:

> Franklin Roosevelt repeatedly deceived the American people during the period before Pearl Harbor. . . . He was like the physician who must tell the patient lies for the patient's own good. . . . The country was overwhelmingly non-interventionist to the very day of Pearl Harbor, and an overt attempt to lead the people into war would have resulted in certain failure and an almost certain ousting of Roosevelt in 1940, with a consequent defeat of his ultimate aims.[26]

Professor Bailey offers the following somewhat Machiavellian conception as to how democracy should work.

> A president who cannot entrust the people with the truth betrays a certain lack of faith in the basic tenets of democracy. But because the masses are notoriously shortsighted and generally cannot see danger until it is at their throats our statesmen are forced to deceive them into an awareness of their own long run interests. This is clearly what Roosevelt had to do, and who shall say that posterity will not thank him for it?

25. For a complete survey of the antiwar professions of Roosevelt and Willkie, see Beard, *American Foreign Policy*, 265–323.
26. Bailey, *Man in the Street*, 11–13.

That Roosevelt resorted to habitual deception of the American people both before and after the election of 1940 is not open to serious question. That such deception, on an issue which was literally a matter of life and death for many American citizens, savors of personal dictatorship rather than of democracy, responsive to the popular will, also seems obvious.

Whether Roosevelt's deception was justified is open to debate. This is a question which everyone must answer on the basis of what America's Second Crusade cost, what it accomplished, what kind of world emerged from it, and how real was the danger against which it was undertaken.

# 6

# Road to War:
# The Atlantic

Roosevelt was elected President for a third term by the votes of isolationists who trusted his dozen or more specific pledges to stay out of war and of interventionists who did not believe he meant what he said. The latter had far more reason for satisfaction. Once assured of four more years in the White House, Roosevelt set the ship of state on a much more militant course. But the double talk, the carrying out of steps which logically pointed to full belligerence to an accompaniment of soothing "no war" assurances, continued almost until Pearl Harbor.

One man who was not deceived by the double talk was the former Ambassador to Great Britain, Joseph P. Kennedy. He had supported Roosevelt in the campaign. But on November 18 he indicated a change of attitude and made two significant and correct predictions in a press interview. One was that Roosevelt's policies were dragging America into war. The other was that Britain would go socialist after the war.

Immediately after the election there was a political lull. Roosevelt departed on December 2 on a Caribbean cruise with Harry Hopkins as his only guest. The President was apparently mainly concerned with rest and recreation. But on this cruise he received a very important letter from Winston Churchill. In this communication, dated December 8, one finds the final inspiration for the lend-lease idea.

Churchill emphasized two points: the serious threat of the submarine war and the approaching exhaustion of Britain's financial assets. He suggested that America should protect its shipments to Britain with warships. Realizing that this was probably too much to expect, he suggested, as an alternative, "the gift, loan or supply of a large number of American vessels of war." Another proposal, which was soon to bear fruit, was that the United States Navy should "extend its sea control of the American side of the Atlantic."

Churchill warned that the moment was approaching "when we shall no longer be able to pay cash for shipping and other supplies." After receiving this letter Roosevelt, according to Hopkins, came out one evening with the whole lend-lease scheme, the delivery of munitions and supplies free of charge to Great Britain and the other anti-Axis belligerents.

"He didn't seem to have any clear idea how it could be done legally," Hopkins observes. "But there wasn't a doubt in his mind that he would find a way to do it."

After returning to Washington, Roosevelt outlined the principle of lend-lease at a press conference. He used as an illustration the case of a man lending his garden hose to a neighbor whose house was on fire.

In the course of his "fireside" chat to the American people on December 29 the President painted a dire picture of the peril that was supposedly hanging over the Western Hemisphere.

> Never since Jamestown and Plymouth Rock has American civiliza-
> tion been in such danger as now. . . . If Great Britain goes down,
> the Axis powers will control the continents of Europe, Asia, Africa,
> Australia and the high seas — and they will be in a position to bring
> enormous military and naval resources against this hemisphere. It
> is no exaggeration to say that all of us in the Americas would be
> living at the point of a gun — a gun loaded with explosive bullets,
> economic as well as military.

Yet along with this melodramatic scare note, which was to be struck again and again and again during 1941, there were soothing assurances that the United States would not get into the war.

> There is far less chance of the United States getting into the war if
> we do all we can now to support the nations defending themselves
> against the Axis. . . . You can therefore nail any talk about sending
> armies to Europe as deliberate untruth. . . . We must be the arsenal
> of democracy.

Roosevelt outlined the plan for lend-lease aid to the anti-Axis powers in his message to Congress of January 6, 1941. This was the longest single stride on the road to war. For it is a long-recognized principle of international law that it is an act of war for a neutral government (as distinguished from private firms or agencies) to supply arms, munitions, and implements of war to a belligerent.

The United States had demanded and obtained heavy damages, by decision of a court of arbitration, from Great Britain because the British Government did not prevent the escape from a British port of the cruiser *Alabama,* built for the Confederacy, which subsequently preyed upon United States shipping. But Roosevelt brushed off objections based on international law with the off-the-cuff declaration:

"Such aid is not an act of war, even if a dictator should unilaterally proclaim it so to be."

The bill envisaged enormous and undefined expenditures and conferred vast and unprecedented discretionary powers upon the President. Its terms were to be effective "notwithstanding the provisions of any other law." But Roosevelt gave specific assurances that neither the Johnson Act, barring loans to countries in default on earlier obligations to the United States, nor the Neutrality Act, forbidding loans to belligerents, would be repealed.

Here was surely legal confusion heavily compounded. It was obvious that if the lend-lease bill should become law, the United States would have departed much farther from neutrality than Wilson had gone before America formally entered the First World War. Yet legislation enacted on the basis of America's experience in 1917, designed to keep the country out of war by foregoing neutral rights which Wilson had upheld, was left on the statute books. It was all very confusing; and confusion of public opinion was what Roosevelt needed gradually to steer America into undeclared hostilities while professing devotion to peace.

In his message to Congress of January 6, Roosevelt enunciated the Four Freedoms on which the world should be founded. These were freedom of speech and expression, freedom of worship, freedom from fear, and freedom from want. These were to prevail everywhere in the world. The Four Freedoms, together with the seven points of the Atlantic Charter, announced later in the year, were America's war aims, the equivalent of Wilson's Fourteen Points. They still furnish a mirror by which the success of the Second Crusade may be judged.

In this same speech, speaking on behalf of a country which was still technically nonbelligerent, Roosevelt banged, barred, and bolted the door to suggestions of a compromise or negotiated peace:

"We are committed to the proposition that principles of morality and considerations of our own security will not permit us to acquiesce in a peace dictated by aggressors and sponsored by appeasers."

In retrospect the adoption of the Lend-Lease Act seems to be the most decisive of the series of moves which put America into an undeclared war in the Atlantic months before Japan struck at Pearl Harbor. This measure marked the end of any pretense of neutrality. It underwrote the unconditional victory of Britain with America's industrial power and natural resources. It opened up the immediate prospect of an appeal for naval action to insure that the munitions and supplies procured under lend-lease would reach England in spite of the submarine blockade. While Congress and the American people were being officially assured that lend-lease was not a move toward war, Roosevelt's personal envoy, Harry Hopkins, was giving Churchill the following categorical pledge of all-out American aid in January 1941: "The President is determined that we shall win the war together. Make no mistake about that."[1]

Yet this fateful measure was not frankly presented and advocated as equivalent to a state of limited belligerence. If one studies the record of the debates in House and Senate, one finds supporters of the bill employing this kind of reasoning:

"The present bill is a peace measure for our people."—Representative McCormack, of Massachusetts.

"In my judgment there is nothing in this bill which will hasten or accentuate our involvement in the war."—Representative Luther Johnson, of Texas.

"We believe that this measure offers the surest method by which we can avoid participation actively in this war and at the same time help those nations which are heroically grappling with a universal enemy and preserve the doctrines of our fathers and the aspirations of our own hearts."—Senator Alben Barkley, of Kentucky.

1. Churchill, *Grand Alliance*, 23.

Leading Cabinet members and high military authorities testified on behalf of the bill and indulged in some very bad guessing. Frank Knox, Secretary of the Navy, predicted on January 17 a crisis within sixty days. On January 31 he forecast a great air blitz on Britain and the use of poison gas within sixty or ninety days. Stimson saw great danger of an air-borne invasion, and General Marshall predicted an attack on Great Britain in the spring. It is interesting to note that Churchill's authoritative memoirs do not bear out the alarmist arguments which were employed to push through the lend-lease bill. Describing the situation at the beginning of 1941, he points out in detail how British strength to resist a German invasion had immensely increased and states the following conclusion: "So long as there was no relaxation in vigilance or serious reduction in our own defense the War Cabinet and the Chiefs of Staff felt no anxiety."[2] Recurring to the situation in the spring of 1941, he observes: "I did not regard invasion as a serious danger in April, 1941, since proper preparations had been made against it."[3]

Willkie was as quick as Roosevelt to forget his antiwar pledges. He testified enthusiastically in favor of lend-lease. Reminded of his earlier statement that the Administration would put America in war by spring, he airily brushed this off as "just campaign oratory."

A powerful voice from across the Atlantic joined the chorus of those who insisted that the lend-lease bill would keep America out of war. Winston Churchill, whose private letters to Roosevelt had long been filled with pleas for American warlike action, broadcast this reassurance to the American people on February 9, 1941:

> We do not need the gallant armies which are forming throughout the American Union. We do not need them this year, nor next year, nor any year I can foresee. But we need urgently an immense and continuing supply of war materials. . . . We shall not fail or falter, we shall not weaken or tire. . . . *Give us the tools and we will do the job.* [Italics supplied.]

2. Ibid., 4–5.
3. Ibid., 238.

Viewing this broadcast in retrospect, Churchill frankly observes: "This could only be an interim pronouncement. Far more was needed. But we did our best."[4]

On any sober, realistic appraisal of British and Axis strength this was assurance which could not be fulfilled. But it was what many Americans wished to hear. Lend-lease was carried because the minority of all-out interventionists were reinforced by a larger number who hoped, and were given every assurance to this effect by Administration spokesmen, that unlimited subsidies of munitions and supplies would buy America out of active participation in the war.

There were voices of opposition. Senator Taft saw as "the important thing about this bill" that "its provisions in effect give the President power to carry on an undeclared war all over the world, in which America would do everything except actually put soldiers in the front-line trenches where the fighting is." The Senator could not see (and events would soon bear him out) how we could long conduct such a war without being in "the shooting as well as the service-of-supply end." Senator C. Wayland Brooks, of Illinois, called it a "war bill with war powers, with the deliberate intention of becoming involved in other people's wars." Colonel Lindbergh described lend-lease as "a major step to getting us into war." The veteran Socialist leader Norman Thomas foresaw as consequences of the lend-lease legislation "total war on two oceans and five continents, a war likely to result in stalemate, perhaps in such a break-up of western civilization that Stalin, with his vast armies and loyal communist followers, will be the victor."

The bill became law on March 11, 1941. The vote was 265 to 165 in the House, 60 to 31 in the Senate. These were substantial, but not overwhelming majorities. Had the measure been frankly presented as a measure of limited war, which it was, it is most improbable that it could have been passed.

While Congress was discussing lend-lease, important American and British staff talks were taking place in Washington in an atmosphere of extreme secrecy. These talks went on from the end of January until the end of March. The principal American representatives were Admirals R. L. Ghormley and Richmond Kelly Turner and Captains A. G. Kirk,

4. Ibid., 128.

C. M. Cooke, and DeWitt Ramsey, for the Navy, and Generals S. D. Embick, Sherman Miles, and L. T. Gerow, and Colonel Joseph T. Mc-Narney, for the Army. British participants were Admirals R. M. Bellairs and V. H. Danckwerts, General E. L. Morris, and Air Commodore J. C. Slessor.

General George C. Marshall, Chief of Staff of the Army, and Admiral Harold R. Stark, Chief of Naval Operations, addressed the opening session of the conference and urged the utmost secrecy, in order not to provide fuel for opponents of the lend-lease bill. The members of the British delegation wore civilian clothes and passed themselves off as technical advisers of the British Purchasing Commission.

At the very time when anxious Congressmen were being assured that the lend-lease bill was designed to avoid war, these military and naval experts were adopting a report which took American participation in the war for granted. The principal conclusions of this report were phrased as follows:

> The staff conference assumes that *when* the United States becomes involved in war with Germany it will at the same time engage in war with Italy. In these circumstances the possibility of a state of war arising between Japan and an association of the United States, the British Commonwealth and its allies, including the Netherlands East Indies, must be taken into account.
>
> Since Germany is the predominant member of the Axis powers, the Atlantic and European area is considered the decisive theatre. The principal United States effort will be exerted in that theatre, and operations in other theatres will be conducted in such a manner as to facilitate that effort.[5] [Italics supplied.]

The use of the word *when,* not *if,* was certainly suggestive of the Administration's attitude.

Typical of the furtive methods by which Roosevelt edged the country into a state of undeclared war was the noteworthy care taken to conceal these American-British talks (not only their content, but the fact that they were taking place) from the knowledge of Congress. This is made clear by Robert E. Sherwood when he writes:

5. U.S. Congress, *Hearings,* part 15, ex. 49, 50, 51.

Although the common-law alliance involved the United States in no undercover commitments, and no violation of the Constitution, the very existence of any American-British joint plans, however tentative, had to be kept utterly secret. It is an ironic fact that in all probability no great damage would have been done had the details of these plans fallen into the hands of the Germans and the Japanese, whereas, had they fallen into the hands of Congress and the press, American preparation for war might have been well nigh wrecked and ruined.[6]

There could scarcely be a more candid admission, from a source favorable to Roosevelt, that America was stealthily maneuvered into war behind the backs and without the knowledge of the elected representatives of the American people. A study of the Congressional debates and private talks with some members of that body confirm this view. Even members of the Senate and House Foreign Relations Committees were kept very much in the dark as to what the President was doing or intending to do. As Nathaniel Peffer subsequently wrote in an issue of *Harper's Magazine:*

> When, for example, the United States traded to Great Britain destroyers for bases, it was for all practical purposes entering the war. Congress had no voice in that. It was notified later by the President, but then the fact was accomplished. Similarly, when the President ordered the freezing of Japanese assets in this country in July, 1941, he was decreeing a state of war with Japan. And with respect to that act the Senate Committee on Foreign Relations had no more to say than a similar number of North Dakota wheat farmers.[7]

Like the Roman god Janus, Roosevelt in the prewar period had two faces. For the American people, for the public record, there was the face of bland assurance that his first concern was to keep the country out of war. But in more intimate surroundings the Chief Executive often assumed that America was already involved in war.

6. Sherwood, *Roosevelt and Hopkins*, 273–74.
7. Nathaniel Peffer, "The Split in Our Foreign Policy," *Harper's Magazine*, 187 (August 1943), 198.

Consider, for example, the testimony of Dr. Constantin Fotitch, the Yugoslav Ambassador in Washington. He carried away this impression of American belligerence from a talk with the President on April 3, 1941:

> The United States was still neutral, yet the President spoke to me about the organization of peace after the victory; about "common objectives, common efforts and the common enemy"; in short, as though the United States were already in the war against the Axis.[8]

The American Government certainly did everything in its power to push Yugoslavia into war. Sumner Welles on March 24 asked Fotitch to convey to his government the following communication from the President.

> In case the Yugoslav Government signs an agreement with Germany detrimental to the interests of Great Britain and Greece, who are fighting for the freedom of all, the President will be bound to freeze all Yugoslav assets and to revise entirely the American policy toward Yugoslavia.

There is a tragic parallel between British policy toward Poland in 1939 and this American policy of pushing Yugoslavia into combat. In each case a high-spirited but industrially backward people was encouraged to enter a hopelessly uneven struggle. As Britain could not help Poland, America could not help Yugoslavia. No American lend-lease arms even reached Yugoslavia prior to the country's military collapse before the swift Nazi thrust in April 1941. And when the day of victory finally dawned, the Poles and Yugoslavs who were most western-minded, who had placed their faith in Britain and the United States, were abandoned by Churchill and Roosevelt to their fate at the hands of the new Communist masters of those unfortunate countries.

The next milestone on the road to war in the Atlantic was the decision to employ American naval forces to insure the deliveries of munitions and supplies to Britain. There had been much discussion of naval convoys during the debate on the Lend-Lease Act. Roosevelt stated

8. Fotitch, *The War We Lost*, 86.

on January 21 that he had no intention of using his powers under this bill to convoy merchant ships. "Convoys," he said, "mean shooting and shooting means war."

The Lend-Lease Act as finally passed contained several amendments clearly designed to prevent the President from using it as an authorization for carrying on undeclared war. According to these amendments, nothing in the Act was to authorize convoying by United States naval vessels, the entry of any American vessel into a combat area, or the change of existing law relating to the use of the land and naval forces of the United States, "except insofar as such use relates to the manufacture, procurement and repair of defense articles, the communication of information and other noncombatant purposes enumerated in this act."

As soon as the Lend-Lease Act became law Roosevelt characteristically set out to find a means of convoying supplies which could be plausibly called by some other name. "Patrol" seemed to fill the needs of the situation.

The bellicose Secretaries of War and the Navy, Stimson and Knox, had agreed toward the end of March "that the crisis is coming very soon and that convoying is the only solution and that it must come practically at once."[9] However, the plan which Roosevelt finally approved on April 24 was less bold than the open dispatch of convoys, although it achieved much the same purpose. Under this scheme, the American Navy was assigned the responsibility of patrolling the Atlantic west of a median point represented by 25° longitude. Within this area United States warships and naval planes would search out German raiders and submarines and broadcast their position to the British Navy. Roosevelt and Hopkins drafted a cable to Churchill, outlining this scheme and suggesting that the British keep their convoys west of the new line up to the northwestern approaches.[10]

With typical indirection, Roosevelt, even in private Cabinet meetings, tried to represent this as merely a defensive move, designed to protect the Western Hemisphere against attack. The more candid Stimson recorded in his diary for April 24:

9. Stimson and Bundy, *On Active Service*, 367.
10. Sherwood, *Roosevelt and Hopkins*, 291–92.

He [Roosevelt] kept reverting to the fact that the forces in the Atlantic were merely going to be a patrol to watch for any aggression and report that to America. I answered there, with a smile on my face, saying: "But you are not going to report the presence of the German Fleet to the Americas. You are going to report it to the British Fleet." I wanted him to be honest with himself. To me it seems a clearly hostile act to the Germans, and I am prepared to take the responsibility of it. He seems to be trying to hide it into the character of a purely reconnaissance action, which it clearly is not.[11]

Even before the patrol system had been adopted, the American Navy had been stepping far beyond the bounds of hemisphere defense. The Congressional Pearl Harbor investigation turned up two interesting letters from Admiral Harold Stark, Chief of Naval Operations, to Admiral Husband E. Kimmel, commander in chief of the Pacific fleet. In the first of these, dated April 4, 1941, Stark wrote: "The question as to our entry into the war seems to be *when,* and not *whether.*" The second is more specific about military preparations on the other side of the Atlantic:

I am enclosing a memo on convoy which I drew up primarily to give the President a picture of what is now being done, what we would propose to do if we convoyed, and of our ability to do it. . . .

Our officers who have been studying the positions for bases in the British Isles have returned, and we have decided on immediate construction of 1 destroyer base and 1 seaplane base in Northern Ireland. We are also studying Scotland Iceland bases for further support of the protective force for shipping in the northward approaches to Britain.

All this did not harmonize with the President's pre-election promises that "this country is not going to war." But with no election in prospect, there was no brake on the gradual slide toward open belligerence.

Roosevelt in a press conference on May 16 referred to a subject which evidently appealed to his imagination, since he raised it on several other occasions. This was the presidential right to wage undeclared

11. Stimson and Bundy, *On Active Service,* 368–69.

war, as illustrated by such precedents as the clash with France during the Administration of John Adams and with the Barbary pirates when Jefferson was President. Roosevelt declared that the Germans were really pirates. On the same day Knox announced: "It is impossible to exaggerate the mortal danger of our country at this moment."

Stimson had already sounded a call to war in a radio address of May 6, which ended as follows:

> Today a small group of evil leaders have taught the young men of Germany that the freedom of other men and nations must be destroyed. Today those young men are ready to die for that perverted conviction. Unless we on our side are ready to sacrifice and, if need be, die for the conviction that the freedom of America must be saved, it will not be saved. Only by a readiness for the same sacrifice can that freedom be preserved.

Roosevelt himself on May 27, 1941, delivered a speech which seemed designed to scare the American people into approving warlike measures. "The war," the President said, "is approaching the brink of the Western Hemisphere itself. It is coming very close to home." He spoke of "the Nazi book of world conquest" and declared the Nazis planned to treat the Latin American countries as they were now treating the Balkans. Then, according to the President, the United States and Canada would be strangled. American labor would have to compete with slave labor, and the American farmer would get for his products exactly what Hitler wanted to give. Roosevelt outlined a very elastic and expansive conception of defense requirements.

"The attack on the United States can begin with the domination of any base which menaces our security—north or south."

Therefore:

> Old-fashioned common sense calls for the use of a strategy that will prevent such an enemy from gaining a foothold in the first place.
>
> We have, accordingly, extended our patrol in North and South Atlantic waters. We are steadily adding more and more ships and planes to that patrol. It is well known that the strength of the Atlantic Fleet has been greatly increased during the last year, and that it

is constantly being built up. . . . [12] We are thus being forewarned. We shall be on our guard against efforts to establish Nazi bases closer to our hemisphere.

The speech ended in a bellicose climax:

We in the Americas will decide for ourselves whether, and when, and where, our American interests are attacked or our security is threatened.
We are placing our armed forces in strategic military position.
We will not hesitate to use our armed forces to repel attack.

There was also a declaration of a state of "unlimited national emergency." However, there was a sense of anticlimax when Roosevelt in his press conference on the following day denied any intention to institute convoys or to press for the repeal of the Neutrality Act.

In the retrospect of years, how well founded was the sense of national mortal peril which the President, the more bellicose members of his Cabinet, and a host of individuals and organizations tried to cultivate in the American people? In the light of the ascertainable facts, which are now pretty well known, one cannot but feel that the picture was grossly exaggerated.

What was the over-all military picture in May 1941? There was no longer serious danger of a Nazi invasion of England.[13] The American and British surface fleets were enormously stronger than the combined Axis naval strength. There was, therefore, not the slightest prospect that German armies could cross the Atlantic in force.

At that time there were constant rumors of German infiltration into French North Africa. A favorite scare story was that Hitler's legions would move into Dakar (itself a long jump from North Africa) and then move across the Atlantic into Brazil. Commentators who spread these stories never took the trouble to explain how it would be possible to transport substantial forces across the ocean in the face of superior American and British naval power.

12. This fact was doubtless "well known" to the Japanese Intelligence Service and was one consideration which prompted the attack on Pearl Harbor.
13. This point is recognized by Churchill several times in *The Grand Alliance*.

And we know now that there was never any factual basis for these rumors. The reports of two American representatives on the spot, Robert D. Murphy, in North Africa, and Consul Thomas C. Wasson, in Dakar, are in agreement on this point; Murphy's reports show that there were about two hundred Germans, mostly connected with the armistice commission, in North Africa. Wasson informed the State Department that the only Germans in Dakar were a few Jewish refugees.[14]

The fall of Germany and the capture of the Nazi archives revealed no evidence of any plan for the invasion of North or South America. It is reasonable to assume that a victorious Nazi Germany would have been an uncomfortable neighbor, just as a victorious Soviet Russia is today. But there is no proof that Hitler envisaged the American continent as part of his empire.

And there is a strong element of overheated fantasy in the vision of American labor ground down by the competition of slave labor, of the American farmer condemned to take what Hitler would give. The Nazis could scarcely have made slave labor more prevalent than it is in Stalin's huge postwar empire. American labor standards have not been depressed as a result. And the level of American farm prices depends far more on the state of supply and on the willingness of American taxpayers to pay subsidies than it does on the character of foreign political regimes.

Unquestionably the war was not going well for Britain in the spring of 1941. The Germans had overrun the Balkans and had seized Crete by an air-borne operation. The reconquest of Europe from Hitler and the crushing of the Nazi regime in its own territory, the obvious war aim of Churchill and Roosevelt, gave every prospect of being a difficult, long, and costly enterprise.

But the suggestion that the Western Hemisphere was in imminent peril can fairly be dismissed as a fraudulent exaggeration. The fraud and the exaggeration are all the greater if one considers that both the American and the British governments were in possession of reliable information to the effect that Hitler's main military strength would soon be hurled against Russia. The most fevered alarmist imagination

14. Langer, *Our Vichy Gamble,* 87.

could scarcely envisage Hitler simultaneously invading Russia and mounting an offensive against the American continent.

Not all Americans were convinced by the dire forebodings of Roosevelt's "unlimited national emergency" speech. Senator Taft commented drily in a nation-wide broadcast:

> The whole argument of the war party that Hitler can conquer the United States or dominate the seas that surround us has just about faded into the discard. But the President now lays more stress on the danger to our trade. He threatens the American workman that his wages and hours would be fixed by Hitler. . . . What is Japan to do with its silk except sell it to us? We take over half Brazil's coffee. Even if the Nazis dominated the Netherlands East Indies there would be nothing to do with the rubber except sell it to us. It is utterly ridiculous to suppose that our trade with South America or Asia or even Europe will be wiped out.

Hitler's attack on Russia gave the war an entirely new character. Now there was a gigantic duel between two dictators for the mastery of a continent from which every other strong military power had been eliminated. From the standpoint of defeating Hitler, Russia was a valuable military asset. But this military advantage was offset by grave political risks. There was nothing in the Soviet political record to suggest the likelihood of respect for the Four Freedoms, or of the ideals later formulated in the Atlantic Charter.

On the contrary, there was every prospect that a victorious Soviet Union would be as ruthless in victory, as eager to expand as a victorious Germany. There was neither moral nor political advantage in substituting Stalin for Hitler.

Curiously enough, it was a man of no experience in foreign affairs who sensed the necessity for a careful handling of the Soviet Union as an associate. Senator Harry S. Truman was quoted in the *New York Times* of June 23, 1941, as saying:

> If we see Germany is winning we ought to help Russia and if we see Russia is winning we ought to help Germany, and in that way let them kill as many as possible, although I wouldn't want to see Hitler

victorious under any circumstances. Neither of them think [*sic*] anything of their pledged word.

But the official decision, in Washington as in London, was to go all-
out in aid to Stalin. There was apparently no thought of requiring, as
the price of this aid, that Stalin renounce the spoils of his pact with
Hitler and give specific binding guarantees against Soviet annexation
of foreign territory.

As soon as Churchill received the news of Hitler's attack, he went on
the air to announce all possible aid to Russia and the Russian people.

"No one," the British Prime Minister declared, "has been a more
consistent opponent of communism than I have for the last twenty-five
years. I will unsay no word that I have spoken about it. But all this fades
away before the spectacle that is now unfolding."

Sumner Welles struck a similar note as spokesman for the State Department. "Any defense against Hitlerism, any rallying of the forces
opposing Hitlerism, from whatever source these forces may spring, will
hasten the eventual downfall of the present German leaders, and will
therefore redound to the benefit of our own defense and security."

There was an exchange of notes between Welles and the Soviet Ambassador, Constantin Oumansky, on August 2. The former pledged "all
economic assistance practicable for the purpose of strengthening the
Soviet Union in its struggle against armed aggression."

Meanwhile Harry Hopkins had rushed to Moscow to press American
aid on Stalin. Hopkins was in England on one of his confidential missions in July and suggested a visit to Moscow in a cable to Roosevelt on
July 25:

> If Stalin could in any way be influenced at a critical time I think it
> would be worth doing by a direct communication from you through
> a personal envoy. I think the stakes are so great that it should be
> done. Stalin would then know in an unmistakable way that we mean
> business on a long-term supply job.[15]

Roosevelt approved the trip and Hopkins flew to Moscow with Churchill's blessing late in July. On meeting Stalin he told the Soviet dictator
that Roosevelt considered Hitler the enemy of mankind and therefore

15. Sherwood, *Roosevelt and Hopkins*, 317–18.

wished to aid the Soviet Union in its fight against Germany. Hopkins impressed upon Stalin America's determination to extend all possible aid to the Soviet Union.

Stalin took a moral tone in his reply. The Germans, he said, were a people who would sign a treaty today and break it tomorrow. Nations must fulfill their treaty obligations, or international society could not exist.[16]

Here was a moment when Hopkins might well have suggested that the Soviet Government, like the Nazi Government, had been known to break treaties and that a solemn public pledge to restore the independence and territorial integrity of Poland, Finland, and the Baltic states would be a reasonable *quid pro quo* for American aid. But neither then nor at any other time did Hopkins show any awareness of the bargaining possibilities of lend-lease aid. His whole attitude was that of one who had come to seek a favor, not to confer one. It was not a happy psychological approach to a tough-minded dictator.

Stalin outlined his military needs and gave Hopkins a sketch of Soviet military resources. He suggested that the one thing which would defeat Hitler would be an announcement that the United States was going to war with Germany. He even said that he would welcome American troops on any part of the Russian front under the complete command of the American Army.[17]

This was an indication of what a grave view Stalin took of the situation at this time when his armies were reeling back under the first shock of the German attack, and hundreds of thousands of Soviet troops were surrendering voluntarily because of hatred for the regime. Later the Soviet authorities displayed the utmost reluctance to permit even small units of the American and British air forces to operate on Soviet soil and barred Allied officers from inspecting the front with a view to determining the needs of the Red Army.

From his conferences with Stalin, Hopkins was flown back to London. Thence he proceeded to take part in the first wartime meeting

16. Ibid., 328.

17. Ibid., 343. If Stalin felt himself in such dire straits that he was willing to admit foreign troops, under foreign command, on his territory, it is most unlikely that he would have refused at this time a demand for giving up the gains of his pact with Hitler.

between Roosevelt and Churchill. This meeting, prepared in the greatest secrecy, took place on warships in the harbor of Argentia, in Newfoundland, one of the bases which the United States had acquired in exchange for its destroyers. Sumner Welles was Roosevelt's principal political adviser at this conference, which began on August 9 and ended on the twelfth. General Marshall and Admiral Stark, the leading American military and naval figures, met British officers of corresponding rank.

The principal result of this conference was the framing of the famous Atlantic Charter. This was a joint declaration of war aims, although Congress had not voted for American participation in the war. Welles and the British permanent Undersecretary for Foreign Affairs, Sir Alexander Cadogan, worked out the draft text of the document. Its final form, of course, was approved by Roosevelt and Churchill.

The full text of the Atlantic Charter is as follows:

The President of the United States of America and the Prime Minister, Mr. Churchill, representing His Majesty's Government in the United Kingdom, being met together, deem it right to make known certain common principles in the national policies of their respective countries on which they base their hopes for a better future for the world.

First, their countries seek no aggrandizement, territorial or other.

Second, they desire to see no territorial changes that do not accord with the freely expressed wishes of the peoples concerned.

Third, they respect the right of all peoples to choose the form of government under which they will live; and they wish to see sovereign rights and self-government restored to those who have been forcibly deprived of them.

Fourth, they will endeavor, with due respect for their existing obligations, to further the enjoyment of all States, great or small, victor or vanquished, of access, on equal terms, to the trade and to the raw materials of the world which are needed for their economic prosperity.

Fifth, they desire to bring about the fullest collaboration between all nations in the economic field with the object of securing for all improved labor standards, economic adjustment and social security.

Sixth, after the final destruction of the Nazi tyranny, they hope to see established a peace which will afford to all nations the means of dwelling in safety within their own boundaries, and which will afford assurance that all the men in all the lands may live out their lives in freedom from fear and want.

Seventh, such a peace should enable all men to traverse the high seas and oceans without hindrance.

Eighth, they believe that all of the nations of the world, for realistic as well as spiritual reasons, must come to the abandonment of the use of force. Since no future peace can be maintained if land, sea or air armaments continue to be employed by nations which threaten, or may threaten aggression outside of their frontiers, they believe, pending the establishment of a wider and permanent system of general security, that the disarmament of such nations is essential. They will likewise aid and encourage all other practicable measures which will lighten for peace-loving peoples the crushing burden of armaments.

Since the principles of the Atlantic Charter were repeatedly reaffirmed not only by America and Great Britain, but by the Soviet Union and other members of the United Nations coalition, it may be regarded as a morally binding statement of the ideals which should have governed the making of the peace. The first three clauses restate a familiar Wilsonian idea: the right of all peoples to choose their national allegiance and form of government.

Clause 4 is a promise of equality in commercial opportunity between nations. Other objectives of the Charter are the promotion of improved social and economic conditions, the insuring of a stable peace, the disarming of "aggressor" nations.

Churchill was later to contend that the provisions of the Charter did not apply to Germany. But this is in contradiction to the plain wording of the document. Clause 4 refers to "all states, great or small, *victor or vanquished*" (italics supplied), and Clause 6 mentions "all the men in all the lands."

There were two disagreements regarding the phrasing of the Char-

ter. The qualifying phrase "with due respect for their existing obligations" was inserted by Churchill at the insistence of Lord Beaverbrook,
a staunch champion of Empire economic preferences. Clause 6 in its
original form included the words "by effective international organization." These were struck out by Roosevelt because of fear of opposition
which might be aroused in the United States.

Another important subject at the conference was American and
British diplomatic action against Japan. Churchill pressed for a joint
threat of war. From his standpoint it would be just as well if America
got into the war in the Pacific as in the Atlantic. So the draft of the
declaration which Roosevelt was supposed to address to the Japanese
Government, as submitted by Cadogan, contained the ultimate specific threat. It read:

> 1. Any further encroachment by Japan in the Southwestern Pacific
> would produce a situation in which the United States Government
> would be compelled to take counter-measures even though these
> might lead to war between the United States and Japan.
>
> 2. If any third power becomes the object of aggression by Japan in
> consequence of such counter-measures or of their support of them,
> the President would have the intention to seek authority from Con-
> gress to give aid to such power.

However, on reflection Roosevelt considerably softened this statement. When he received Japanese Ambassador Nomura on August
17 the warning had been watered down to vaguer and more oblique
terms:

> This Government now finds it necessary to say to the Government
> of Japan that if the Japanese Government takes any further steps in
> pursuance of a policy or program of military domination by force
> or threat of force of neighboring countries the Government of the
> United States will be compelled to take immediately any and all steps
> which it may deem necessary toward safeguarding the legitimate
> rights and interests of the United States and American nationals and
> toward insuring the safety and security of the United States.

There was also an agreement during the Roosevelt-Churchill meeting that the United States should occupy the Azores Islands, while

Great Britain proposed to take over the Canary and Cape Verde Islands.[18] The Cape Verde Islands were to be transferred to American occupation later. This plan never went into effect because the rumored German move into the Iberian peninsula which inspired the design to seize the islands in the East Atlantic never took place.

In view of the agreements about a joint warning to Japan and about military action on the foreign soil of the East Atlantic islands, Roosevelt was not candid when he declared after the conference that there were no new commitments and that the country was no closer to war. To be sure, something had occurred on the last day of the conference which was calculated to impose a brake on a too-headlong interventionist course. The renewal of the Selective Service Act, enacted in 1940 for one year, squeezed through the House of Representatives by only one vote.

Churchill, however, enjoyed the satisfaction of being escorted as far as Iceland by American destroyers. He made good propaganda out of this in a broadcast:

And so we came back across the ocean waves, uplifted in spirit, forti-fied in resolve. Some American destroyers which were carrying mail to the United States Marines in Iceland happened to be going the same way too, so we made a goodly company at sea together.

Roosevelt's next move toward war in the Atlantic was the procla-mation, without consulting Congress or obtaining congressional sanc-tion, of a shoot-at-sight campaign against Axis submarines. The pretext was an exchange of shots between the *Greer,* an American destroyer bound for Iceland, and a German submarine on September 5. Roose-velt misrepresented this incident as a wanton, unprovoked attack on the American vessel.

"The attack on the *Greer,*" he declared, "was no localized military operation in the North Atlantic. . . . This was one determined step toward creating a permanent world system based on force, terror and murder. When you see a rattlesnake poised to strike you do not wait until he has struck to crush him."

18. The Azores and Cape Verde groups belong to Portugal, the Canary Islands to Spain.

The *Greer,* Roosevelt declared, was carrying American mail to Iceland and flying the American flag. Her identity as an American ship was unmistakable. She was then and there attacked by a submarine. "I tell you the blunt fact that the German submarine fired first upon this American destroyer without warning, and with deliberate design to sink her." The shoot-at-sight warning was conveyed in the following words:

> In the waters which we deem necessary for our defense, American naval vessels and American planes will no longer wait until Axis submarines lurking under water or Axis raiders on the surface of the sea strike their deadly blow first. The aggression is not ours. Ours is solely defense. But let this warning be clear. From now on, if German or Italian vessels of war enter the waters, the protection of which is necessary for American defense, they do so at their own peril.

Bismarck's editing of the Ems telegram was a masterpiece of straightforwardness compared with Roosevelt's picture of the *Greer* as the peaceful mail-carrier, wantonly set on by a hostile submarine. The Senate Naval Affairs Committee looked into the matter and obtained the following account of the incident from Admiral Stark:

At 8:40 A.M. a British airplane notified the *Greer* that a submarine was submerged ten miles ahead on the course the destroyer was following. The *Greer* put on speed and zigzagged its way to the reported location. As soon as its sound detection apparatus picked up the propeller beat of the submarine the destroyer commenced to track the submarine, broadcasting its location for the benefit of any British airplanes and destroyers which might be in the vicinity.

"This," said Admiral Stark, "was in accordance with her orders, that is to give out information, but not to attack."

At 10:32 the airplane dropped four depth charges which missed their mark and twenty minutes later withdrew from the hunt. The *Greer* continued to trail the submarine. At 12:40 the German vessel changed its course, closed in on the *Greer,* and fired a torpedo, which missed. The *Greer* counterattacked, apparently without success.

The announcement of the Presidential shooting war in the Atlantic was followed by more serious clashes. The destroyer *Kearny* was hit by a torpedo with the loss of eleven lives on October 17, and on October

30 the *Reuben James,* another destroyer, was sunk with a casualty list of 115 members of her crew.

Roosevelt struck a new high bellicose note in his Navy Day speech of October 27:

> The shooting has started. And history has recorded who fired the first shot. In the long run, however, all that will matter is who fired the last shot. . . .
>
> I say that we do not propose to take this lying down.
>
> Today, in the face of this newest and greatest challenge of them all, we Americans have cleared our decks and taken our battle stations. We stand ready in the defense of our nation and the faith of our fathers to do what God has given us the power to see as our full duty.

But the majority of the American people remained markedly indifferent to these warlike appeals. The contrast between the President's categorical pledges not to get into war in 1940 (when the danger to Britain was certainly far greater than it was after Hitler attacked Russia) and his present obvious efforts to get into hostilities at any price was too strong.

Some public-opinion polls taken during this period are not very revealing. Much depended on who was conducting them, on how questions were phrased, on which groups in the community were reached. But Congress was a pretty reliable barometer of the mood of the nation. The one-vote majority by which selective service was renewed was one signal of the aversion to the idea of a second crusade. Another unmistakable signal was given only three weeks before Pearl Harbor.

The President had asked for authority to arm American merchant ships and to send these ships into war zones. This amounted to a repeal of the Neutrality Act, which Roosevelt had done everything in his power to circumvent. This proposal was still far short of a declaration of war. But it proved extremely difficult to get legislation providing for these changes through Congress. The bill passed the Senate, 50–37, on November 7 and narrowly escaped defeat in the House, where the vote was 212–194, a week later. A change of ten votes would have given the Administration a severe setback. Very strong pressure from the White House was put on the representatives, including promises of judgeships and other federal appointments where these would do the most good.

Interventionists at this time freely admitted and deplored the reluctance of the American people to plunge into the slaughter. The Committee to Defend America by Aiding the Allies took a full-page advertisement to lament the "dreadfully narrow margin" by which the bill authorizing the arming of merchant ships had passed. Walter Lippmann wrote in September 1941 of "the low state of our war morale." Stanley High, another publicist who favored intervention, commented regretfully on Lippmann's observation in a letter published in the *New York Herald Tribune:*

"No, the whole truth about our war morale is not that it is now in a slump. Measured by what we are up against, it was never in anything else."

An investigation of the alleged attempt of the moving-picture industry to promote a war psychosis was started in the Senate in September. John T. Flynn, one of the active leaders of the America First Committee, accused film producers of "using propaganda to raise the war hysteria in this country, to inflame the people of the United States to a state of mind where they will be willing to go to war with Germany." He cited *Underground* as one of some fifty films designed to arouse feelings of hatred and vengeance.

The radio and the press, like the films, were overwhelmingly on the interventionist side by the autumn of 1941. Flynn asserted that in three days he had counted 127 interventionist broadcasts, compared with six on the other side.

And yet, with all the sparks that were being generated, the people failed to catch fire. Hundreds of chapters of the America First Committee pledged themselves to work for the defeat of congressmen who had voted to repeal the Neutrality Act. Francis P. Miller, an extreme interventionist, was defeated by a Republican in an off-year election in Fairfax County, Virginia, in November 1941. This was a district in which a Democratic victory was normally taken for granted.

The autumn of 1941 was a difficult period for Roosevelt. He was under pressure from those members of his Cabinet, Stimson and Knox and Morgenthau, who favored stronger action. He was exposed to a barrage of transatlantic pleas from Churchill. He had stretched his

Presidential powers to the limit. He had provoked shooting incidents in the Atlantic and misrepresented these incidents when they occurred. But he had not aroused much will to war in the country.

General Wood, chairman of the America First Committee, challenged Roosevelt to put the issue of a declaration of war to the test of a vote in Congress. This was a challenge which the President could not accept, in view of the close vote on the less provocative question of repealing the Neutrality Act. Robert E. Sherwood tells how gloomy the situation seemed at this time to those who wished to get America into the war:

> The truth was that, as the world situation became more desperately critical, and as the limitless peril came closer and closer to the United States, isolationist sentiment became ever more strident in expression and aggressive in action, and Roosevelt was relatively powerless to combat it. He had said everything "short of war" that could be said. He had no more tricks left. The hat from which he had pulled so many rabbits was empty.[19]

But just when the situation in the Atlantic seemed very unpromising, from the standpoint of speedy full involvement in war, rescue for the Administration came from the Pacific. The Japanese attack on Pearl Harbor, followed by Hitler's declaration of war, extricated Roosevelt from one of the most difficult dilemmas in which a statesman can find himself—the dilemma of having led his people halfway into war.

The eleven principal steps by which Roosevelt took America into undeclared war in the Atlantic may be briefly summarized as follows:

1. The repeal of the arms embargo in November 1939.
2. The trade of destroyers for bases in September 1940.
3. Enactment of the Lend-Lease Act in March 1941.
4. The secret American-British staff talks, January–March 1941.
5. The institution of "patrols" in the North Atlantic on April 24.
6. The sending of American laborers to build a naval base in Northern Ireland.
7. The blocking of German credits in the United States and the closing of consulates in the early summer of 1941.

19. Sherwood, *Roosevelt and Hopkins*, 382–83.

8. The occupation of Iceland by American troops on July 7.
9. The Atlantic Conference, August 9–12.
10. The shoot-at-sight orders given to American warships and announced on September 11.
11. Authorization for the arming of merchant ships and the sending of merchant ships into war zones in November 1941.

The first three of these steps were accompanied by loud protestations that they were designed to keep America at peace, not to get it into war. Several of the other measures were taken without consulting Congress in an atmosphere of exaggerated alarmism, secrecy, contrived confusion, and official misrepresentation of facts. The entire record may be usefully set against Roosevelt's repeated categorical assurances that his principal aim was to keep America out of war. Seldom if ever in American history was there such a gulf between appearances and realities, between Presidential words and Presidential deeds.

# 7

# Road to War:
# The Pacific

By 1941 the United States had become deeply involved in the Pacific, as well as in the Atlantic theater of World War II. The Roosevelt Administration was striving to block and discourage Japan's expansion by a variety of measures short of war: economic discrimination, aid to China, diplomatic warnings, display of naval force.

There was, to be sure, no undeclared naval war in the Pacific. Until December 7, 1941, no deadlier missiles than notes were exchanged between Washington and Tokyo. But there was an element of finality about the blow in the Pacific, when it fell at Pearl Harbor. This was all-out war. When Hitler declared war three days later, the Administration's dilemma was happily resolved. There were no longer inhibitions on the use of American manpower and resources everywhere in the global struggle.

The war cloud which burst at Pearl Harbor had begun to form ten years earlier. The Japanese military commanders in September 1931 seized Mukden, capital of the semi-independent Chinese regime in Manchuria. This action followed a series of disputes between the Japanese and Manchurian authorities about the implementation of Japan's somewhat vaguely defined economic rights in South Manchuria. Japan had replaced Russia as the dominant power in that area after the Russo-Japanese War of 1904–5. Japan's privileges in South Manchuria included the right to maintain troops and armed railway guards.

The seizure of Mukden was the beginning of a process which only ended when all Manchuria, with an area three times that of Japan proper, had been brought under Japanese control. A new state, Manchukuo, was set up. The nominal ruler was a shadowy emperor, descendant of the former Chinese dynasty. The real power was in the hands of Japanese army officers and civilian officials, many of whom were attached as "advisers" to Manchukuo ministries. Manchuria was soon covered with a network of new railways and roads. Industries were developed and expanded. The productive power of the region was greatly stimulated by the inflow of Japanese capital and technical knowledge. It is worth pointing out also that hundreds of thousands of Chinese migrated to Manchukuo during the period of Japanese control.

The American Secretary of State at that time, Henry L. Stimson, vigorously opposed the Japanese occupation of Manchuria. He could not resort to war because of the opposition of President Hoover and the distinctly nonbellicose state of American public opinion. But in a note of January 7, 1932, he committed the American Government to a policy of passive resistance, of refusing to recognize "any situation, treaty or agreement" which might be brought about by methods incompatible with the Kellogg Pact, which outlawed war.

The League of Nations, acting on the appeal of China as a member, sent the Lytton Commission to investigate the situation in Manchuria. The only effect of this intervention was Japan's withdrawal from the League. The American refusal to recognize Manchukuo, a refusal in which states belonging to the League associated themselves, also led to no practical consequences, except perhaps to discourage foreign investment which might or might not have taken place under other circumstances.

Several years of uneasy tension followed. Japan denounced the naval limitation agreement which had been concluded at Washington in 1922. This had established a 5:5:3 ratio between the navies of the United States, Great Britain, and Japan. Its abrogation left each of these powers free to build up naval strength at will. The United States adhered to the so-called Stimson Doctrine of not recognizing Manchukuo. Apart from this, its policy in the Far East during the first few years of the Roosevelt Administration was rather passive.

A new crisis arose when large-scale war between Japan and China began in the summer of 1937. By the autumn of 1938 the Japanese forces had occupied the largest Chinese cities and most of the country's limited network of railways. But the Chinese Nationalist Government held out in its new far-inland capital, Chungking. And Japanese control was not effectively consolidated far from the large centers and lines of communication.

A war waged over a large expanse of Chinese territory inevitably led to incidents affecting the security of American lives and property. American business communities were located in the larger cities, and several thousand American missionaries lived in China, some in the cities, many in smaller towns throughout the country.

The American economic stake in China was not large. American investments were about 200 million dollars, as compared with 1,200 million dollars in the case of British investments. The prospect of vast trade with China, which had encouraged America to take over the Philippines, had never materialized. Despite its huge population, China, because of its extreme poverty and economic backwardness, had never taken a large part in world trade.

China's purchases in the United States in 1936, the last prewar year, were about 55 million dollars. Japan's were more than four times that amount. For Japan, despite its smaller population, was far more advanced than China in the development of its industry, shipping, and international trade.

From a purely economic standpoint, there was no reason for America to run a risk of war with Japan by actively supporting China against Japan. But American Far Eastern policy was influenced by various non-economic motives.

There was sentimental sympathy for China as the "underdog" in the struggle against Japan. This was nourished by missionaries and other American residents of China. The "Open Door" policy for China, enunciated by Secretary of State John Hay about the turn of the century, was regarded as a sacrosanct tradition of American diplomacy and was seldom subjected to critical and realistic examination. Considerations of prestige made it difficult to surrender established rights under pressure. The groups which believed in a permanent crusade against aggression, in a policy of perpetual war for the sake of perpetual peace, were quick to mobilize American opinion against Japan. Some of the considerations which helped to shape American policy were outlined by Secretary Hull in a communication to Vice-President Garner, published on May 10, 1938:

The interest and concern of the United States in the Far Eastern situation, in the European situation and in situations on this continent are not measured by the number of American citizens residing in a particular country at a particular moment nor by the amount of investment by American citizens there nor by the volume of trade. There is a broader and more fundamental interest—which is that orderly processes in international relationships be maintained.

The situation was further complicated because the majority of the American people had no more desire to fight in the Orient than to see their young men shipped to the battlefields of Europe. Public sympathy was for China and against Japan; but there was no desire to die for the abstract slogan, "that orderly processes in international relationships be maintained."

A wistful desire to have one's cake and eat it too is reflected in the public-opinion polls of the time. A Gallup poll in the autumn of 1937 showed 59 per cent of those questioned for China, 1 per cent for Japan, and 40 per cent indifferent. But another poll, taken almost simultaneously, revealed a majority in favor of withdrawing American troops from China. (At that time small detachments of Marines were maintained in Shanghai and in the Peking-Tientsin area.) Polls in the summer of 1939 revealed 66 per cent in favor of a movement to stop buying Japanese goods, but only 6 per cent wished to fight Japan in order to protect American interests in China.

The most serious incident affecting America's relations with Japan before Pearl Harbor was the sinking of the United States gunboat *Panay* by Japanese bombers on December 12, 1937. This closely followed the capture of Nanking, the Chinese capital; and the Japanese military leaders were in an exuberant, trigger-happy mood. Four lives were lost in the bombing, one of the victims being an Italian journalist. However, the sinking of the *Panay* failed to kindle any war flames in the United States, and the Japanese Government was quick to proffer apologies and pay an indemnity of two and a quarter million dollars.

After the autumn of 1938 the war in China became a stalemate. The Japanese were baffled and held back from further large-scale operations, not so much by Chinese resistance as by the vast size and poor communications of the country. The Chinese lacked the military organization, the airplanes, the heavy artillery which would have enabled them to defeat the Japanese in the open field and retake the large cities which the invaders had captured. The war became a long endurance contest.

The march of events in Europe affected the course of this oriental war. As the attention of powers with large Far Eastern interests, Britain, France, and the Netherlands, became absorbed by the threat of German expansion, Japan saw its opportunities for conquest enhanced. At the same time, the United States cast its weight more and more into the scales, taking a sharper tone in communications and cautiously moving toward the imposition of economic sanctions on Japan. A forceful move by the United States often followed a gesture of weakness or conciliation on the part of Britain.

So, soon after the conclusion of the Munich agreement had revealed British and French weakness, the American Government, on October 6, 1938, set forth its case against Japanese expansion in China in a strongly worded note. The Japanese Government and the Chinese administrations under Japanese control were accused of various violations of American commercial rights. The note called for the elimination of discriminatory exchange control and of monopolies and preferences calculated to injure American trade and industry and the stoppage of Japanese interference with American property and other rights. The note stiffly reaffirmed American rights under the Nine Power Treaty and under the Open Door commercial policy in China.

Japan's reply, on November 18, was partly a denial of specific charges, partly a contention that the *status quo* in China was being rendered obsolete by the movement of events. The Japanese Prime Minister, Prince Fumimaro Konoye, had already described Japan's aim as the establishment of a new order, based on "the tripartite relationship of mutual aid and co-ordination between Japan, Manchukuo and China in political, economic, cultural and other fields."

Another American note, of December 31, tartly denied that "there was any need or warrant for any one power to take upon itself to prescribe what shall be the terms and conditions of a 'new order' in areas not under its sovereignty and to constitute itself the repository of authority and the agent of destiny in regard thereto."

With war imminent in Europe, the British Ambassador in Tokyo, Sir

Robert Craigie, concluded an agreement with the Japanese Foreign Office on July 24, 1939, which bordered on recognition of Japanese belligerent rights in China. Neither Japan nor China had ever formally recognized that a war was in progress. Sir Robert Craigie's step followed a period of prolonged harassment of British nationals by the Japanese military authorities in the North China port of Tientsin.

America's response to this British move of retreat was swift. Senator Vandenberg on July 18 had introduced into the Senate a resolution in favor of abrogating the United States–Japanese commercial treaty. Without waiting for action on this resolution, Secretary Hull on July 26 gave the six-months' notice required for denouncing the treaty. This opened the door for discriminatory economic measures, forbidden under the terms of the treaty.

During the next year there were no sensational developments in American-Japanese relations. The impulse to apply embargoes and other economic restraints against Japan was restrained by the outbreak of war in Europe, but the year from July 1940 to July 1941 was marked by a number of American measures which reflected rising tension in the Pacific.

President Roosevelt in July 1940 placed under license exports of machine tools, chemicals, nonferrous metals, oil products, scrap metal, and aviation gasoline outside the Western Hemisphere.

On September 25, 1940, China received a loan of 25 million dollars for currency stabilization. An embargo on all exports of scrap iron and steel, except to Britain and nations of the Western Hemisphere, was declared on September 26.

American nationals were warned to leave the Far East on October 8.

China received an additional 100 million dollars loan on November 30.

China became eligible for lend-lease aid on March 11, 1941.

On April 26, 1941, there was a monetary stabilization accord with China.

The climax, and the prelude to Pearl Harbor, occurred on July 25, 1941. On that date the President froze all Japanese assets in the United States, amounting to 130 million dollars. This was followed by similar action on the part of Great Britain and the Netherlands Indies. What this amounted to was an economic blockade of Japan, a cessation of all trade relations.

It has already been pointed out that, in the opinion of Nathaniel Peffer, an experienced student of Far Eastern affairs, "when the President ordered the freezing of the Japanese assets in this country in 1941, he was decreeing a state of war with Japan." Certainly the imposition of a commercial blockade on Japan, like many of the President's moves in the Atlantic, was not a measure calculated to keep America out of war.

Indeed, Roosevelt himself, on the very eve of the freezing order, had publicly expressed the opinion that a complete blockade of Japan would precipitate war. He was outlining the reasons for the government's decision not to cut off all oil supplies to Japan:

> It was very essential, from our own selfish point of view of defense, to prevent a war from starting in the South Pacific. So our foreign policy was trying to stop a war from breaking out down there. At the same time . . . we wanted to keep that line of supplies from Australia and New Zealand going to the Near East. . . . So it was essential for Great Britain to try to keep the peace down there in the South Pacific.
>
> All right. And now here is a nation called Japan. Whether they had at that time aggressive purposes to enlarge their empire southward, they didn't have any oil of their own up in the north. Now, if we cut the oil off, they probably would have gone down to the Netherlands East Indies[1] a year ago, *and we would have had war.* [Italics supplied.][2]

It is surprising that the war-making decision of July 25 excited slight reaction at the time, even in isolationist circles. There were several reasons for this apathetic reaction of American public opinion.

Attention was generally focussed on developments in the Atlantic, so that the likelihood that war might come in the Pacific was overlooked. There was a tendency, very marked if one studies the periodicals of

1. The only proved oil deposits of importance within the range of Japanese striking power are in the Netherlands East Indies.
2. Davis and Lindley, *How War Came,* 258.

the time, to underestimate Japanese striking power. Some publicists spread the comforting idea that Japan was so weak that it either would not dare to fight or would be crushed with little difficulty by the air and naval power available to the United States and its prospective allies in the Pacific.

There was also at that time a general disposition to overestimate the chances of peaceful coercion, to assume that Japan could be brought into line by boycotts and embargoes. This stemmed from wishful thinking, from the American desire to "stop" Japan without going to war.

Even the minority report on the Congressional Pearl Harbor investigation, signed by Senators Brewster and Ferguson, although it is severely critical of many Administration steps before Pearl Harbor, says little about the momentous decision of July 25. The seriousness of this decision was, however, understood in high military and naval circles.

The Navy's War Plans Division, in a report drafted on July 19, disapproved of the impending embargo. According to its estimate, Japan already had in stock enough oil for eighteen months of war operations. The embargo could not, therefore, exercise an immediate paralyzing effect and was rather calculated to harden Japan's determination and to precipitate war. A warning sent by General Marshall and Admiral Stark to American military and naval commanders in the Pacific when the embargo was about to be imposed, on July 25, ended as follows:

"The Chief of Naval Operations and the Army Chief of Staff do not anticipate immediate hostile reaction by the Japanese through the use of military means, but you are furnished this information in order that you may take appropriate precautionary measures against any possible eventualities."

Japan's higher councils were divided during the critical period before Pearl Harbor. There was an extremist group, composed of the more fire-eating generals and admirals and of some civilian leaders, a group which saw in Europe's difficulty Japan's opportunity to build up a vast Asiatic empire. There is no evidence that even these militarists worked out plans for invading the American continent.

There were also influential statesmen, with access to the Emperor, who disliked the idea of breaking with the West, who believed that Japan could support its fast-growing population through industrial leadership and commercial expansion, without resorting to force. The

Japanese Ambassador to the United States in 1941, Admiral Kichisa-buro Nomura, belonged to this moderate group. Hull credits Nomura with "having been honestly sincere in trying to avert war between his country and mine."[3]

Conversations between Hull and Nomura, with a view to finding a basis of settlement, began in February 1941 and continued until the eve of Pearl Harbor. There were forty or fifty meetings. Hull entered these conversations in a pessimistic mood; he did not believe there was one chance of success in a hundred.[4] And he showed little flexibility or imagination. He insisted on giving Nomura long lectures on the virtues of peace, free trade, and international morality. He showed little inter-est in the face-saving compromises and adjustments which might have made possible a substantial Japanese withdrawal from China and a gradual dissociation of Japan from its loose association with the Axis.

Early in 1941 two Catholic ecclesiastics with experience in the Far Eastern mission field, Bishop James Edward Walsh, Superior General of the Catholic Foreign Mission Society, and Father Drought, returned to the United States from Japan. They had talked with a number of highly placed Japanese, including Foreign Minister Matsuoka, who often talked publicly in bellicose language. They carried away the im-pression that there was a serious desire in Japan to reach an agreement with America on the Chinese question and to modify the Japanese commitment to the Axis.

With the consent and approval of Roosevelt and Hull, Bishop Walsh and Father Drought established contacts with some members of the Japanese Embassy in Washington and carried on informal conversa-tions, in which Postmaster General Frank Walker also took part. A Japanese draft proposal emerged from these talks and was submitted to Hull on April 9.

According to this proposal Japan would feel bound by her military obligations under the Tripartite Pact only if one of the partners was "aggressively attacked" by a power not involved in the European war. Hull objected to this on the ground that it left Japan free to interpret the somewhat elastic phrase, "aggressive action." Hull, like Roosevelt,

3. Hull, *Memoirs*, 2:987.
4. Ibid., 985.

was already anticipating American initiative in precipitating a shooting war in the Atlantic.

The terms which were proposed for peace in China were as follows. Chiang Kai-shek was to negotiate with Japan, on the basis of China's independence, withdrawal of Japanese troops in accordance with an agreement to be reached between Japan and China; no acquisition of Chinese territory and no indemnities. There was to be a fusion of the Chiang Kai-shek and Wang Ching-wei governments.[5] There was to be large-scale immigration of Japanese into China, and Chiang was to recognize Manchukuo.

It was proposed that America should sponsor these terms. If Chiang accepted, Japan would consider itself bound by these conditions and would discuss joint defense against communism and economic co-operation. To a negotiator genuinely anxious to obtain a Far Eastern settlement without war, these terms would have seemed well worth examining. They were certainly better than anything China could reasonably hope to obtain by its own armed force. But instead of examining the practical details of such a settlement, Hull replied with an enunciation of four very general abstract principles:

1. Respect for the territorial integrity and sovereignty of each and all nations.

2. Support of the principle of non-interference in the internal affairs of other countries.

3. Support of the principle of equality, including equality of commercial opportunity.

4. Non-disturbance of the *status quo* in the Pacific except as the *status quo* may be altered by peaceful means.[6]

No one can say with certainty whether the Japanese moderates, among whom the Prime Minister at that time, Prince Konoye, must be reckoned, could have checked the career of southward expansion on which the military and naval extremists had set their hearts. But obvi-

5. Wang Ching-wei was the most eminent figure in the Kuomintang who had consented to co-operate with the Japanese by setting up an administration under their sponsorship in Nanking.
6. Hull, *Memoirs*, 2:995.

ously the Japanese moderates could not hope to succeed without more co-operation from Washington than Secretary Hull's moral lectures. What is certain is that at no time during the critical months before Pearl Harbor did the American Government offer even the most modest *quid pro quo* for a reorientation of Japanese policy. The United States was not willing to commit itself even to such a small gesture as recognition of the long-accomplished fact of the existence of Manchukuo. The attitude of consistent stiff negativism in Washington was an important factor in eliminating any possibility of a peaceful settlement in the Pacific.

Even at that time it might have seemed debatable whether the United States was bound by considerations of morality or of political interest to fight Japan on the assumption that a fully independent and friendly China would emerge from the debris of a large-scale Far Eastern war. And the China that is shaping up five years after the downfall of Japan is closely dependent on the Soviet Union and bitterly hostile to the United States.

What is perhaps most surprising, as one reviews the tangled course of events in the last months before Pearl Harbor, is the inability of the Roosevelt Administration either to make a constructive move toward peace or to take effective precautions against war. The able and experienced American Ambassador to Japan, Joseph C. Grew, cabled to the State Department on January 27, 1941, a warning of a possible attack on Pearl Harbor. This was based on information from the Peruvian Minister, who stated he had heard from many sources, including a Japanese one, "that a surprise mass attack on Pearl Harbor was planned by the Japanese in the event of 'trouble' between Japan and the United States, that the attack would involve the use of all the Japanese military facilities." The State Department passed on this information to the War and Navy Departments.[7]

Given a Japanese decision to risk war with the United States, a surprise blow at the American Pacific fleet, concentrated at the great Hawaiian base, was a very probable development. Japanese military and naval teaching had always emphasized the importance of secrecy and surprise. The experience of the war in Europe showed that cer-

7. Ibid., 984.

tain operations which would not have been technically feasible in World War I could be carried out because of the increased range of air power.

But the orders and information sent by the higher military authorities in Washington to General Walter C. Short and Admiral Husband E. Kimmel, respectively commanders of the military and naval forces at Pearl Harbor, were notably lacking in precision and urgency. The commanders on the spot were encouraged to maintain a normal, "business as usual" attitude until the attack actually took place.

This was all the stranger and less excusable because United States cryptoanalysts, through an operation known as MAGIC, had cracked the code used in communications from Tokyo to members of the Japanese diplomatic corps throughout the world. This created a situation suggestive of playing poker while watching your opponent's cards in a mirror.

Why it was possible for Japan, despite this handicap, to start the war with a stunning surprise blow is one of the great mysteries of history. The Army Pearl Harbor Board which reported its findings to the Secretary of War on October 20, 1944, voiced the following criticism:

Washington was in possession of essential facts as to the enemy's intentions and proposals.

This information showed clearly that war was inevitable and late in November absolutely imminent. . . .

The messages actually sent to Hawaii by the Army and Navy gave only a small fraction of this information. It would have been possible to have sent safely, information ample for the purpose of orienting the commanders in Hawaii, or positive directives for an all-out alert. . . .

In the first days of December this information grew more critical and indicative of the approaching war. Officers in relatively minor positions who were charged with the responsibility of receiving and evaluating such information were so deeply impressed with its significance and the growing tenseness of our relations with Japan, which pointed only to war and war almost immediately, that such officers approached the Chief of the War Plans Division (General [Leonard T.] Gerow) and the secretary of the General Staff (Colonel [now Lieutenant General Walter Bedell] Smith) for the purpose of having sent to the department commanders a true picture of the war atmosphere which, at that time, pervaded the War Department and which was uppermost in the thinking of these officers in close contact with it. The efforts of these subordinates to have such information sent to the field were unsuccessful.[8]

Was this merely the carelessness of overworked men, underestimating the chances of a Japanese surprise stroke at America's main citadel in the Pacific? Or was there, on the part of the directors of American foreign policy, from the President down, a deeper and subtler motive in not demanding maximum alertness? Was there a feeling, perhaps subconscious and unavowed, that a decisive blow, marking the transition from nominal peace to outright war, might be struck in the Pacific and that this blow was more likely to be delivered if there were no vigorous preparations to ward it off?

With MAGIC supplementing other sources of intelligence, the State, War, and Navy Departments were kept in close and prompt touch with important Japanese Government decisions. The German invasion of Russia placed before the Japanese Cabinet the necessity of such a decision. Von Ribbentrop was urging the Japanese Government to invade Siberia and take advantage of the promised Soviet military collapse.

But the Japanese Cabinet decided otherwise. There was no oil in Siberia. The United States, with a tender solicitude for Soviet interests that seems strange in the retrospect of 1950, was almost threatening war in the event of a Japanese move hostile to Russia.

So the Japanese Cabinet resolution, confirmed by a solemn Imperial Council[9] on July 2, was against the Siberian adventure and in favor of a move to the south. The Army was authorized to occupy the southern part of French Indo-China. From this vantage point there was a triple

8. U.S. Army. The Army Pearl Harbor Board. *Report to the Secretary of War* (October 20, 1944). Vol. 39, Chap. 3 (pp. 103–4) of the *Hearings before the Joint Committee on the Investigation of the Pearl Harbor Attack. . . .* Since the war was still in progress, the Board was not in a position to state that the Japanese code had been cracked.

9. These Councils, held in the presence of the Emperor with the participation of the highest military and naval officers and civilian officials, were a familiar and regular mark of important Japanese state decisions.

threat, to the Philippines, to Malaya and Siam, and to the Netherlands East Indies. However, Prime Minister Konoye still hoped that war with the West could be avoided. As he says in the memoir which he wrote before committing suicide, following the end of the war:

"There was a good prospect that we might use the advance of the Japanese troops in Indo-China as the basis of a compromise in the Japanese-American talks then under way. I am confident I will be able to prevent a war."[10]

Konoye made a desperate effort, a sincere effort, in the judgment of Ambassador Grew, to reach a settlement with the United States in August and September 1941. His desire was for a personal meeting with Roosevelt, and he was willing to make the important concession of taking the initiative and going to American soil, to Alaska or Honolulu, for the conference.

There had been an informal proposal for a Konoye-Roosevelt meeting in April. Admiral Toyoda, who had succeeded the bellicose and garrulous Matsuoka as Foreign Minister after the German attack on Russia, developed this suggestion in a talk with Grew on August 18. Toyoda intimated that Japan would be willing to withdraw from Indo-China as soon as the China affair was settled and suggested that Konoye should go to Honolulu to meet Roosevelt. Admiral Nomura repeated the invitation to Roosevelt on August 23.

Roosevelt at first was favorably impressed by the prospect of the meeting. He indicated a preference for Juneau, Alaska, over Honolulu. However, he accepted Hull's suggestion that there should be no talk until there had been a preliminary agreement about the points at issue.

It was on this obstacle that the proposed meeting, which might have staved off the Pacific war, foundered. There was no willingness on Hull's part to leave any room for give-and-take, to allow some scope for negotiation after the meeting began.

As a consequence, although the Japanese proposal was never flatly rejected, it was allowed to perish from long neglect. That Konoye was eager for the meeting and was willing to take considerable risks, po-

10. See the *New York Times* of December 23, 1945, for a report of the memoir, as published in the Tokyo newspaper *Asahi*.

litical and personal,[11] in order to bring it about is evident from Grew's account of his experience in the preliminary talks in Tokyo. The United States at that time had an excellent diplomatic team in Tokyo. Grew was a veteran career diplomat of seasoned judgment and long experience. His counselor, Eugene Dooman, possessed an unusual and remarkable mastery of the difficult and complex Japanese language.

On September 6, Konoye and his secretary, Ushiba, invited Grew and Dooman to dinner at the home of a Japanese friend under circumstances of extreme privacy. Konoye professed willingness to accept Hull's four principles and said the Ministers of War and the Navy had given complete agreement to his plan. A full general and a full admiral would accompany him, so that the services would be committed to accept the results of the conference. The Vice-Chiefs of Staff of the Army and Navy would also take part.

The Japanese Prime Minister emphasized the importance of the time factor. He could not guarantee a settlement six months or a year in the future. Now he was confident of success. When Grew raised the point that Japanese words in the past had not always corresponded with Japanese actions, Konoye assured him that any commitments he (Konoye) would undertake would bear no resemblance to the irresponsible assurances of the past. The Premier added that if President Roosevelt would desire to communicate suggestions personally and confidentially he would be glad to arrange subsequent secret meetings with Grew. Konoye expressed his earnest hope that "in view of the present internal situation in Japan the projected meeting with the President could be arranged with the least possible delay."

There were later talks between Ushiba and Dooman and between Toyoda and Grew. The Japanese proposals, as set forth by Toyoda, were in substance those which Nomura had presented in the spring.

Grew strongly recommended the meeting in a report to the Secretary of State on September 29. This report may be summarized as follows:

The Ambassador, while admitting that risks will inevitably be involved, no matter what course is pursued toward Japan, offers his

11. Assassination had been the fate of many Japanese statesmen who opposed the extreme militarists.

carefully studied belief that there would be substantial hope at the very least of preventing the Far Eastern situation from becoming worse and perhaps of insuring definitely constructive results, if an agreement along the lines of the preliminary discussions were brought to a head by the proposed meeting of the heads of the two governments. . . . He raises the questions whether the United States is not now given the opportunity to halt Japan's program without war, or an immediate risk of war, and further whether through failure to use the present opportunity the United States will not face a greatly increased risk of war. The Ambassador states his firm belief in an affirmative answer to these two questions.

The Ambassador does not consider unlikely the possibility of Prince Konoye's being in a position to give President Roosevelt a more explicit and satisfactory engagement than has already been vouchsafed in the course of the preliminary conversations.

Grew further warned of the possibility of serious Japanese reaction if the preliminary discussion should drag on in the hope of obtaining clear-cut commitments. He predicted:

The logical outcome of this will be the downfall of the Konoye Cabinet and the formation of a military dictatorship which will lack either the disposition or the temperament to avoid colliding head-on with the United States.[12]

Grew notes on October 1 that a Japanese friend of high standing informed him that political circles now know of Konoye's intention, and that the proposal is generally approved, even among the military, because of the economic necessity of reaching a settlement with the United States. About the same time the Ambassador made the following comment in his diary:

For a Prime Minister of Japan thus to shatter all precedent and tradition in this land of subservience to precedent and tradition, to wish to come hat in hand, so to speak, to meet the President of the United States on American soil, is a gauge of the determination of the Government to undo the vast harm already accomplished in alienating

12. Grew, *Ten Years in Japan*, 456–62.

our powerful and progressively angry country. . . . Prince Konoye's warship is ready waiting to take him to Honolulu or Alaska or any other place designated by the President and his staff of the highest military, naval and civilian officers is chosen and rarin' to go.

But Hull was unmoved and immovable. He sometimes expressed the view that the maintenance in power of the Konoye Cabinet afforded the best prospect of keeping the peace. But he refused to give this Cabinet any diplomatic encouragement. Konoye resigned on October 16 and was succeeded by General Hideki Tojo.

From this time events began to move at a swifter pace. The blockade of Japan by America, Great Britain, and the Netherlands Indies was beginning to pinch. It became increasingly clear from the public statements of Japan's leaders and from the private messages intercepted by MAGIC that the sands of peace were running out, that the United States must choose between some kind of compromise and a strong probability of war. The suggestion of a time limit began to appear in the Japanese secret communications. So the new Japanese Foreign Minister, Shigenori Togo, sent this message to Nomura:

> Because of various circumstances, it is absolutely necessary that all arrangements for the signing of this agreement be completed by the 25th of this month. I realize that this is a difficult order, but under the circumstances it is an unavoidable one. Please understand this thoroughly and tackle the problem of saving the Japanese-American relations from falling into a chaotic condition.[13]

Another Japanese envoy, Saburo Kurusu, a career diplomat with an American wife, was rushed to Washington in mid-November, the transpacific Clipper being held for him at Hong Kong. Kurusu arrived in Washington on November 17 and was received by Roosevelt and Hull. It was later suggested that Kurusu possessed advance knowledge of the blow that was being prepared against Pearl Harbor. But it seems more probable that his coming to Washington was merely in line with the familiar Japanese practice of having more than one man responsible for action in a moment of grave crisis.

13. Hull, *Memoirs,* 2:1056–57.

Nomura's desire to avoid war was unquestionably genuine, as indicated by his intercepted message of November 19:

After exhausting our strength by four years of the China Incident, following right upon the Manchurian Incident, the present is hardly an opportune time for venturing upon another long-drawn-out war on a large scale. I think it would be better to fix up a temporary "truce" now in the spirit of "give-and-take" and make this the prelude to greater achievements later.[14]

Tokyo offered Nomura and Kurusu a slight relaxation of the original time limit on November 22. The envoys were informed that it would be satisfactory if an agreement were reached by the twenty-ninth. This communication, which, of course, was available to high American officials, ended on this ominous note:

"This time we mean it, that the deadline absolutely cannot be changed. After that things are automatically going to happen."

The background of this warning was that on November 25 a Japanese task force under the command of Admiral Isoruku Yamamoto was to take off, with Pearl Harbor as its objective. The advancement of the time limit was apparently because it was realized in Tokyo that this force could be turned back without committing any act of aggression if an agreement were reached while the expedition was in its early stages.

The Japanese Government had worked out for discussion a Plan A and a Plan B, the latter the limit in concessions. Plan B, submitted to Hull by Nomura and Kurusu on November 20, was worded as follows:

Japan and the United States to make no armed advance in any region in Southeast Asia and the Southwest Pacific area.

Japan to withdraw her troops from Indo-China when peace is restored between Japan and China or when an equitable peace is established in the Pacific area.

Japan and the United States to co-operate toward acquiring goods and commodities which the two countries need in the Netherlands East Indies.

14. See *Pearl Harbor: Intercepted Japanese Diplomatic Messages.* Joint Congressional Committee, Exhibit I, p. 158.

Japan and the United States to restore their commercial relations to those prevailing prior to the freezing of assets, and the United States to supply Japan a required quantity of oil.

The United States to refrain from such measures and actions as would prejudice endeavors for the restoration of peace between Japan and China.

These proposals met with no favor in the eyes of Secretary Hull. He did not believe the Japanese offer to withdraw from southern Indo-China was adequate compensation for the lifting of the American blockade. However, he seriously considered a counterproposal, aimed at creating a three months' *modus vivendi*. This was the only conciliatory move the American Government seems to have thought of making during the protracted negotiations with Japan in 1941, and this move was not made.

An undated memorandum in Roosevelt's handwriting seems to have contained the germ of the *modus vivendi* idea:

"US to resume economic relations . . . some oil and rice now—more later. Japan to send no more troops . . . US to introduce Japanese to Chinese, but . . . to take no part in their conversations."

Henry Morgenthau, Secretary of the Treasury, who liked to have a finger in every diplomatic pie, set his staff to work preparing a detailed blueprint of a temporary economic truce. Some features of the Treasury plan were incorporated in the scheme which was finally approved by Hull after being worked over by State Department experts.

This scheme provided for mutual American and Japanese pledges against aggressive moves in the Pacific, for Japanese withdrawal from southern Indo-China, and for limitation of Japanese forces in northern Indo-China to 25,000 men. The *quid pro quo* was to be a relaxation of the blockade, permitting Japan to export freely and to import limited supplies of cotton, oil, food, and medical supplies.

No one can say whether the influence of the Japanese moderates would have been strong enough to stop the planned attack in return for these restricted American concessions. But the offer was never made. Hull dropped his one experiment in conciliation under pressure from China and Great Britain.

Eden and Churchill, Chiang Kai-shek and his brother-in-law, T. V.

Soong, and Owen Lattimore, American adviser to Chiang,[15] all eagerly took a hand in blocking this tentative move toward peace. The *modus vivendi* had been cautiously framed with a view to offering minimum concessions. But Eden, in a message of November 25, wanted to make stiffer demands on the Japanese: complete withdrawal from Indo-China and suspension of military activities in China.

Lattimore reported from Chungking that any *modus vivendi* now arrived at with Japan would be disastrous to Chinese belief in America. Chiang Kai-shek, according to Lattimore, questioned his ability to hold the situation together "if the Chinese national trust in America is undermined by reports of Japan's escaping military defeat by diplomatic victory."

The idea that Japan faced military defeat as a result of any past, present, or prospective action by China was unrealistic, if not downright ludicrous. But in the fevered atmosphere of the time, it was a good propaganda line. Hull later declared that "Chiang has sent numerous hysterical cable messages to different Cabinet officers and high officials in the Government — other than the State Department."

As a climax Churchill introduced himself into the situation with a special message which reached Roosevelt on November 26:

> Of course it is for you to handle this business and we certainly do not want an additional war. There is only one point that disquiets us. What about Chiang? Is he not having a very thin diet? Our anxiety is about China. If they collapse our joint danger would enormously increase. We are sure that the regard of the United States for the Chinese cause will govern your action. We feel that the Japanese are most unsure of themselves.

Under this barrage of foreign criticism Hull's impulse to offer the truce arrangement wilted. As Secretary of War Stimson records in his diary for November 26: "Hull told me over the telephone this morning that he had about made up his mind not to give the proposition that Knox and I had passed on the other day to the Japanese, but to kick the whole thing over, to tell them he had no proposition at all."

15. Mr. Lattimore's appointment as adviser to Chiang is somewhat ironical, in view of his subsequent expressions of sympathy with the Chinese Communists.

On the previous day, November 25, there had been an important council at the White House, with the President, Hull, Stimson, Knox, Marshall, and Stark present. The spirit of this meeting is reflected in Stimson's comment in his diary:

"The question was how we should maneuver them [the Japanese] into firing the first shot without allowing too much danger to ourselves."

Here, perhaps, is a clue both to the abandonment of the truce proposal and to the curious absence of concern for normal precautionary measures at Pearl Harbor.

Secretary Hull certainly made a notable contribution to the end suggested by Stimson when, after discarding his compromise proposal, he handed the Japanese envoys what amounted to a demand for unconditional surrender in a set of ten proposals presented to them on November 26. One of these proposals was that Japan should withdraw its forces from Indo-China and from China. Another demanded that there should be no support of any government in China other than the National Government (Chiang Kai-shek).

There was a suggestion for a multilateral nonaggression pact among the governments principally concerned in the Pacific. Only on these terms, which amounted to relinquishment by Japan of everything it had gained on the mainland during the preceding ten years, would the United States consent to restore normal economic relations. After reading these proposals, Kurusu remarked that when they were communicated to Tokyo the Government would be likely to throw up its hands.

Technically, Hull's ten points did not constitute an ultimatum. No time limit was set, and counterproposals were not excluded. But when one considers the circumstances under which they were presented, and their completely uncompromising character, one may feel that the Army Board which investigated the Pearl Harbor attack was justified in describing Hull's communication as "the document that touched the button that started the war."

Maximum pressure, short of war, had been applied to Japan four months earlier, when the economic blockade was put into effect. Refusal to abandon or even relax this blockade except on condition that Japan surrender unconditionally on the points at issue in all probability meant war. Hull seems to have realized this when he told Stimson on November 27 that "he had broken the whole matter off." The Secretary of State added: "I have washed my hands of it and it is now in the hands of you and Knox, the Army and the Navy." It is difficult to reconcile this candid statement with Hull's later assertion that "we labored desperately during the next two weeks [after November 22] striving to the last for peace or at least more time."[16]

The Japanese attack on Pearl Harbor achieved the effect of a devastating military surprise. But there was, or should have been, no element of political surprise. After November 26 the President, the Secretary of State, the heads of the armed services had every reason to expect hostile Japanese action anywhere at almost any moment. Apart from the virtual rupture of the negotiations, there were repeated hints of impending action in the intercepted Japanese communications. Some of these pointed clearly to Pearl Harbor as a possible Japanese military objective.

For example, a message from Tokyo to Japanese agents in Honolulu on November 29, the day after which "things were automatically going to happen," read:

"We have been receiving reports from you on ship movements, but in future you will also report even when there are no movements."

Still more suggestive was a message of December 2:

In view of the present situation, the presence in port of warships, airplane carriers, and cruisers is of the utmost importance. Here-

16. Hull, *Memoirs*, 2:1074. There is a direct conflict of testimony between Stimson and Hull as to whether the Secretary of State said that he had "washed his hands" of the situation. Stimson's diary for November 27, 1941, records that Hull told Stimson that day: "I have washed my hands of it and it is now in the hands of you and Knox, the Army and the Navy" (Stimson and Bundy, *On Active Service*, 389). In his memoirs published seven years later Hull asserts: "I did not make, and could not have made in the light of what occurred, the statement later attributed to me that I had 'washed my hands' of the matter" (1080).

It seems reasonable to prefer Stimson's testimony, set down on the day when the remark is alleged to have been made, to Hull's recollection years afterwards, when he may be presumed to have desired to present his record in as pacific a light as possible. In any event, the remark which Stimson says Hull made to him represents the reality of the situation after the Secretary of State had decided to throw over the idea of offering the Japanese a standstill formula.

after to the utmost of your ability let me know day by day. Wire in each case whether or not there are any observation balloons above Pearl Harbor or if there are any indications that any will be sent up. Also advise me whether or not the warships are provided with anti-mine nets.[17]

Thanks to the deciphering of the Japanese code, the American Government did not have to wait long for an authentic Japanese reaction to Hull's ten-point message. Foreign Minister Togo informed Nomura and Kurusu on November 28 that the American proposal was humiliating, unexpected, and regrettable. The Foreign Minister continued:

The Imperial Government can by no means use it as a basis for negotiations. Therefore, with a report of the views of the Imperial Government which I will send you in two or three days, the negotiations will be *de facto* ruptured. This is inevitable. However, I do not wish you to give the impression that the negotiations are broken off. Merely say to them that you are awaiting instructions.

It was a reasonable deduction from this message that Japan was preparing a secret blow for which an outward pretense of continuing negotiations was a necessary mask. And there was strong reason to suspect that Hawaii might be the target of this blow.

There was no reason to conceal Japanese movements elsewhere. There had been diplomatic discussion of the presence of Japanese troops in Indo-China. As early as November 28 it was known in Washington that a Japanese flotilla, escorting a force of some twenty-five thousand men, was steaming down the China coast toward an unknown destination. Only the main objective of the impending offensive, Pearl Harbor, with the big warships of the Pacific fleet berthed at anchor and hundreds of airplanes on the ground, did not visibly figure in Japanese calculations. This fact alone might have been regarded as suspicious by an alert intelligence service, especially in view of the Japanese fondness for secrecy and surprise.

But the messages which were sent from Washington to General Short and Admiral Kimmel did not convey the full gravity of the situation. Nowhere was it suggested that Pearl Harbor be put on a war footing,

17. Morgenstern, *Pearl Harbor,* 249.

or that an attack might be imminent. General Marshall's message to General Short of November 27 read as follows:

Negotiations with Japan appear to be terminated to all practical purposes with only the barest possibilities that the Japanese Government might come back and offer to continue. Japanese future action unpredictable but hostile action possible at any moment. If hostilities cannot, repeat cannot, be avoided the United States desires that Japan commit the first overt act. This policy should not, repeat not, be construed as restricting you to a course of action that might jeopardize your successful defense of the Philippines. Prior to hostile Japanese action you are directed to take such reconnaissance and other measures as you deem necessary but these measures should not, repeat not, be carried out so as to alarm the civil population or disclose intent.

The Chief of Naval Operations sent a more specific warning to Kimmel, and to Admiral Hart in the Philippines.

This despatch is to be considered a war warning. Negotiations with Japan looking toward stabilization of conditions in the Pacific have ceased and an aggressive move by Japan is expected in the next few days. The number and equipment of Japanese troops and the organization of naval task forces indicate an amphibious expedition against either the Philippines, Thai, or Kra peninsula, or possibly Borneo.

This Navy warning was not so weakened by qualifications and reservations as the Army's. However, it pointed to the likelihood of Japanese action in places far away from Hawaii. As for Marshall's message to Short, the Army Board which investigated Pearl Harbor offered the following criticism:

Had a full war message, unadulterated, been despatched, or had direct orders for a full, all-out alert been sent, Hawaii could have been ready to meet the attack with what it had. What resulted was failure at both ends of the line. Responsibility lay both in Washington and in Hawaii.

Short received no further information after the message of November 27 except three communications of November 27 and 28 suggesting possible danger from sabotage. When Short, years later, was able to state his case before a congressional committee of investigation he testified:

> The impression conveyed to me by this message [of November 27] was that the avoidance of war was paramount and the greatest fear of the War Department was that some international incident might occur in Hawaii and be regarded in Washington as an overt act. . . .
>
> No mention was made of a probable attack on Hawaii since the alert message of June 18, 1940. An examination of the various military estimates prepared by G-2[18] shows that in no estimate did G-2 ever indicate an attack upon Hawaii. There was nothing in the message directing me to be prepared to meet an air raid or an all-out attack. "Hostile action at any moment" meant to me that as far as Hawaii was concerned the War Department was predicting sabotage. Sabotage is a form of hostile action.

Of course, if Short and Kimmel had been of the stature of Napoleon and Nelson, they would have taken more active defense measures on their own initiative. But the consistent failure of Washington to keep them fully informed of the intense gravity of the situation remains amazing.

It is all the more amazing because there is strong reason to believe that a direct war warning, in the form of a deciphered Japanese code message, reached the Navy Department in Washington on December 4. The Japanese signal that war with the United States had been decided on was the phrase "East Wind Rain," inserted in the daily Japanese language news broadcast. According to the testimony of Captain L. F. Safford, chief of the radio intelligence unit, Office of Naval Communications, in the Navy Department, this decisive phrase appeared in a Japanese broadcast designed for London and was picked up in Washington on the morning of December 4.

Safford's testimony was at first supported by Lieutenant Commander

18. The Army Military Intelligence.

(later Captain) Alvin D. Kramer, senior language officer for Navy communications intelligence. Subsequently Kramer changed his testimony before the Congressional investigating committee. First he said that England was the country referred to in the code message. Later he declared that "the 'winds' message was phony." There are indications that strong pressure was brought to bear from high quarters to discredit the "winds" message. Secretary of War Stimson, after receiving and temporarily suppressing the Army Board report on Pearl Harbor, started three personal investigations, directed by Major General Myron C. Cramer, Major Henry C. Clausen, and Colonel Carter W. Clarke.

When the Navy Court of Inquiry turned in its report on Pearl Harbor, Secretary James Forrestal instituted another investigation. This was headed by Admiral H. K. Hewitt; but the most active role was played by Lieutenant Commander John Sonnett. Safford testifies that Sonnett "attempted to make me reverse my testimony regarding the 'winds' message and to make me believe I was suffering from hallucinations."[19]

Safford, however, stuck to his story. He affirmed that when he could not find the "winds" message in the Navy files, he became suspicious of a conspiracy. Asked by committee counsel why he thought anyone might want to destroy the message, he replied: "Because it was the unheeded warning of war." Questioned why there was a failure to make use of the message when it came in, if it meant war, he answered: "That question has puzzled me for four years. I don't know the answer."[20]

Still another question to which there is no clear answer is the strange neglect of the final tip-off—the text of the Japanese reply to Hull's note of November 26. It was apparently the Japanese design to communicate this reply to the State Department almost simultaneously with the attack on Pearl Harbor. Of course the Japanese Foreign Office did not know that the contents of the communication would be known in advance to the highest authorities in Washington because of the cracking of the code.

The Japanese reply was sent in fourteen parts, of which the first

19. See the hearing before the Joint Congressional Committee Investigating Pearl Harbor, of February 2, 1946.

20. Morgenstern, *Pearl Harbor*, 219. This book contains an admirable summary of some of the salient points brought out in the Congressional investigation.

thirteen were available to Lieutenant Commander A. D. Kramer, in the Navy Department, early in the evening of December 6. The message was definitely unfavorable and truculent in tone. Part 13 characterized Hull's ten points as follows:

"The proposal in question ignores Japan's sacrifices in the four years of the China Affair, menaces the very existence of the Empire and disparages its honor and prestige. Therefore, viewed in its entirety, the Japanese Government regrets that it cannot accept the proposal as a basis of negotiation."

Kramer appraised this communication as so important that he brought it to the attention of the President himself. Roosevelt read it at his desk while Harry Hopkins paced the floor. Roosevelt then showed it to Hopkins, with the remark: "This means war." Hopkins observed it was too bad that we could not strike the first blow and avert a Japanese surprise attack. Roosevelt's comment was:

"No, we can't do that. We are a democracy. We are a peaceful people. We have a good record."

Under questioning by the Congressional committee neither General Marshall nor Admiral Stark could give any clear account of what he was doing on the evening of December 6. The secretary of the General Staff, Colonel (later Lieutenant General) W. Bedell Smith, seems to have made no attempt to bring the important information conveyed by the Japanese note to the attention of his chief, Marshall, who was in his quarters at Fort Myer.

The next morning there was still more definite evidence of imminent war. The fourteenth section of the Japanese communication was decoded and contained such decisive sentences as these:

Thus the earnest hope of the Japanese Government to adjust Japanese-American relations and preserve and promote the peace of the Pacific through co-operation with the American Government has finally been lost. The Japanese Government regrets . . . that in view of the attitude of the American Government it cannot but consider that it is impossible to reach an agreement through further negotiations.

Still more significant was another message from Tokyo instructing the Japanese Ambassador to present this note to the United States Government at 1 P.M. on December 7. Here was not only the date, but the hour when hostilities might be expected to commence. An alert mind might have reckoned that 1 P.M. in Washington was dawn in Honolulu, the most probable moment for an air attack.

Efforts to reach Marshall early in the morning of the seventh failed. The General had gone for a horseback ride. When he reached his office in the War Department it was already eleven, two hours before the Japanese deadline. When he realized the significance of the last section of the Japanese note, he decided to send a warning to Short in Hawaii and to MacArthur in the Philippines, worded as follows:

> Japanese are presenting at 1 P.M. eastern standard time today what amounts to an ultimatum, also they are under orders to destroy their code machine immediately. Just what significance the hour set may have we do not know, but be on alert accordingly. Inform naval authorities of this communication. Marshall.

The Chief of Staff had at his disposal a "scrambler" telephone, which makes of conversations a jumble of meaningless sounds, to be reassembled at the other end. He could have reached Short by this means in a few minutes. But, as the climax of a long series of curious blunders in Washington, Marshall chose to send this belated last warning by the slower method of cable communication. It reached Short after the raid was over.

Was the failure to order military alert in Pearl Harbor despite all the ominous information at the disposal of the Washington authorities merely the result of lack of foresight and imagination? Or was there a subtler purpose, of which one might find a hint in Stimson's expressed desire to maneuver the Japanese into the position of firing the first shot? Had there been a state of visible preparedness in Hawaii, the Japanese attack, so dependent for success on surprise, might have been scared off or reduced to the proportions of an incident.

The evidence is not decisive; a case can be made for either interpretation of the known facts. What is certain is that the Japanese, although they tipped their hand repeatedly in deciphered messages which they considered secret, achieved full surprise and complete military victory in the attack which burst on Pearl Harbor on the morning of December 7.

They killed some 2,500 American soldiers and sailors, and sank or crippled eight battleships, three cruisers, and three destroyers—all at a loss to themselves of twenty-nine aircraft, five midget submarines, and one fleet submarine.

The Japanese envoys were slow in decoding their note. They were received by Hull after two. By this time the Secretary of State not only knew the contents of the communication, but had been informed by Roosevelt of a report, still unconfirmed, that the Japanese had attacked Pearl Harbor. Naturally the reception was brief and frigid. After making an appearance of reading the note Hull glared sternly at Nomura and said:

I must say that in all my conversations with you during the last nine months I have never uttered one word of untruth. This is borne out absolutely by the record. In all my fifty years of public service I have never seen a document more crowded with infamous falsehoods and distortions—infamous falsehoods and distortions on a scale so huge that I never imagined until today that any government on this planet was capable of uttering them.

From the Japanese standpoint Pearl Harbor was worse than a crime; it was a blunder. For it plunged Japan into a war that could not be won with an enemy enormously superior in technology and industrial power and completely immune to direct Japanese attack on its munitions centers.

Politically it would have been much wiser for the Japanese to have moved against Dutch and British possessions, by-passing the Philippines. America would probably have entered the war in any case. But public opinion would have been very divided. However, Japan's military and naval leaders were conditioned to think only in strategic terms. And the prospect of knocking out the American Pacific fleet in one swift surprise action was an irresistible temptation. Perhaps some future discovery will prove or disprove the suspicion that this temptation was deliberately spread before their eyes.

The fundamental cause of the war was the clash between Japan's ambitions on the Asiatic mainland and the American determination to underwrite the cause of China. There is no evidence that the Japanese militarists in their wildest dreams thought of invading the American continent. Nor would the Philippines have been worth a war with the United States.

Such well-qualified witnesses as Roosevelt and Stimson confirm the view that the war was over China. Roosevelt, speaking at a dinner of the Foreign Policy Association in 1944, said:

"We could have compromised with Japan and bargained for a place in a Japanese-dominated Asia by selling out the heart's blood of the Chinese people. And we rejected that!"

Stimson concurs in this viewpoint in the following words:

"If at any time the United States had been willing to concede to Japan a free hand in China there would have been no war in the Pacific."[21]

The imposition of the commercial blockade of Japan in July; the failure to accept Konoye's pleas for a meeting; the dropping of the idea of a proposed *modus vivendi;* Hull's uncompromising note of November 26—these were all steppingstones to war. These measures possessed little justification except as part of a crusade for China. The necessity and wisdom of this crusade seem questionable, to put it mildly, when one considers that the principal result of the war in the Far East was the emergence in China of a regime subservient to Moscow and bitterly hostile to the United States.

Despite the shock of a severe military defeat, leading figures in the Roosevelt Administration greeted the news of Pearl Harbor with relief, if not with positive joy. The Japanese had extricated this Administration from the awkward position in which it found itself in the last months of 1941.

Every step that could be represented, however disingenuously, as short of war had been taken in the Atlantic. But the Nazi power was unbroken. Churchill was clamoring for more aid. And Congress was balking at measures far less serious than a declaration of war.

Stimson wrote in his diary on December 7:

"When the news first came that Japan had attacked us, my first feeling was of relief that indecision was over and that a crisis had come in a way which would unite all our people."

Roosevelt seems to have shared this feeling of relief. Postmaster

21. Stimson and Bundy, *On Active Service,* 256.

General Walker remarked to Frances Perkins after the Cabinet meeting on the night of December 7:

"I think the Boss really feels more relief than he has had for weeks."

Eleanor Roosevelt, recalling Pearl Harbor day in an article in the *New York Times Magazine* of October 8, 1944, observes:

"December 7 was just like any of the later D-days to us. We clustered at the radio and waited for more details—but it was far from the shock it proved to the country in general. We had expected something of the sort for a long time."

Overseas tributes to Roosevelt's skill in having "maneuvered the Japanese into the position of firing the first shot" were heartfelt and outspoken. Winston Churchill ecstatically told the House of Commons on February 15, 1942:

When I survey and compute the power of the United States and its vast resources and feel that they are now in it with us, with the British commonwealth of nations, all together, however long it may last, till death or victory, I cannot believe that there is any other fact in the whole world which can compare with that. This is what I have dreamed of, aimed at and worked for, and now it has come to pass.

And Captain Oliver Lyttleton, a British Cabinet Minister, told the American Chamber of Commerce in London on June 20, 1944: "America provoked Japan to such an extent that the Japanese were forced to attack Pearl Harbor. It is a travesty on history to say that America was forced into war."[22]

22. See AP dispatch from London in the *Chicago Tribune* of June 21, 1944.

# 8

# The Coalition
# of the Big Three

Pearl Harbor was quickly followed by declarations of war on America by Germany, Italy, and the Axis satellites. The Japanese Government invoked the Tripartite Pact on December 3[1] and called on Germany and Italy to fulfill their obligations as cosignatories.

Why Hitler kept this promise, when he broke so many others, is a question to which no positive answer can be given, in the light of available information. Perhaps he regarded it as a matter of prestige, and of revenge for the undeclared naval war in the Atlantic. The Italian Foreign Minister, Count Ciano, shrewdly appraised the significance of what was to happen at Pearl Harbor when he wrote in his diary on December 3, after the Japanese Ambassador had told Mussolini of his government's intention:

"Now that Roosevelt has succeeded in his maneuver, not being able to enter the war directly, he has succeeded by an indirect route—forcing the Japanese to attack him."[2]

It would have been a clever move for Hitler to have abstained from this declaration of war. There would have then been strong pressure of American public opinion in favor of a concentration of military effort in the Pacific. The German and Italian declarations of war completely freed the hands of the Roosevelt Administration to direct the main effort against Germany, according to the plans drawn up by American and British staff officers early in 1941.

The diplomatic as well as the military conduct of this global cru-

---

1. Ciano, *The Ciano Diaries*, 414ff.
2. Ibid.

sade against the Axis powers was in the hands of three men, Franklin Delano Roosevelt, Winston Churchill, and Josef Stalin. It was fashionable to refer to the conflict as "a people's war." But in practice the three leaders of the strongest United Nations powers took their decisions in the utmost secrecy and with a minimum of popular influence and control. It may well be said of the two meetings of the Big Three at Teheran and Yalta that seldom was so much concealed from so many by so few.

Of the three partners in the coalition, Stalin was the most clear-sighted and consistent in his political aims. And he had the most reason for satisfaction with the political landscape of the world when hostilities ended.

Stalin pursued two main objectives. The first was to realize certain old-fashioned imperialist objectives of Tsarist Russia in eastern Europe and eastern Asia. The second was to create world-wide conditions for Communist revolution. For it is not true, as is sometimes suggested, that Stalin is interested only in protecting Russian national interests, that the dream of world conquest through world Communist revolution died with Trotsky.

The disagreement between Stalin and Trotsky on this point was one of timing and tactics, not of grand strategy. Trotsky, a doctrinaire Marxist revolutionary, wished to support Communist revolutions everywhere, using Soviet Russia as a base. He was convinced that the Russian Revolution would degenerate and fail unless it were supported and stimulated by Communist upheavals in industrially more advanced countries.

Stalin, more practical, cynical, and opportunist, believed that it was necessary to build up a powerful militarized state in Russia before getting involved in foreign adventures. Hence his insistence on a frantic pace of development for war industries during the five-year plans, regardless of the cost in human suffering and deprivation for the Russian people.

Such a state could impose Soviet-sponsored political and economic changes on Russia's weaker neighbors at the first convenient opportunity. At the same time, Stalin kept a tight rein on Communist parties outside of Russia. He regarded these as useful volunteer agencies of propaganda and espionage in peacetime, as useful centers of sabotage and treason when the day of Soviet conquest should arrive.

Belief in the necessity of world revolution is repeatedly stressed in Stalin's writings. The following passage in his authoritative book, *Leninism,* is characteristic:

> The victory of socialism in one country is not an end in itself; it must be looked upon as a support, as a means for hastening the proletarian victory in every other land. For the victory of the revolution in one country (in Russia, for the present) is not only the result of the unequal development and the progressive decay of imperialism; it is likewise the beginning and the continuation of the world revolution.

One also finds in Stalin's writings repeated references to war as the generator of revolution. On occasion the Soviet dictator could speak pacifically to "bourgeois" visitors. But it is significant that his statements about the possible peaceful co-existence of communism and capitalism have never been given the wide circulation accorded to his more orthodox militant utterances.

This son of an alcoholic cobbler in a remote little Asiatic town was as shrewd, cunning, and calculating as the cleverest disciple of Talleyrand and Metternich. Stalin's diplomatic masterpiece was his promotion, through his pact with Hitler, of a war from which he hoped to remain aloof.

This attractive dream of watching the capitalist world tear itself to pieces and then stepping in to collect the fragments was shattered by Hitler's attack in June 1941. The first months of the war were marked by severe defeats for the Red Army, defeats which were as much political as military in character.[3] There were moments when Stalin most probably felt that the very existence of his regime was hanging in the balance.

3. The supposed unity of the Soviet peoples in supporting the Soviet regime was a fiction. There were mass surrenders to the Germans on a scale suggesting desertion rather than defeat. And, despite the stupid Nazi brutalities in occupied Soviet territory, the Germans succeeded in recruiting several hundred thousand Soviet citizens for their armies.

But even when Moscow was threatened and a third of European Russia was occupied by the Germans, the Soviet dictator was intent on keeping the spoils of his pact with Hitler. When the tide of the war definitely turned in the winter of 1942–43, with the Russian victory at Stalingrad and the expulsion of the Axis forces from North Africa, Stalin was in a position to resume his march toward his goal: expansion of Soviet and Communist power in Europe and in Asia.

In this march he received great and probably unexpected aid in the policy which was consistently followed by President Roosevelt and his most influential lieutenant and adviser, Harry Hopkins. A firm Anglo-American front, such as Churchill desired, would have set some bounds to Soviet expansion. But no such front was established until after the end of the war.

Churchill was a champion of British national and imperial interests. He made no secret of his desire to preserve the British Empire intact. As he said on one occasion: "I have not become His Majesty's First Minister in order to preside over the liquidation of the British Empire."

Churchill's energy, his mental resilience, his physical endurance were prodigious. But he was in the difficult position of being boxed in between two more powerful allies. The Soviet Union put in the field enormously larger land forces. The United States possessed far greater reserves of manpower, much larger natural resources, and higher industrial productivity. Churchill had to reckon not only with the historic antagonism between Russian and British interests in the Balkans and the Near East but with coolness and suspicion in regard to certain issues on Roosevelt's part.

There was a prolonged Anglo-American difference of opinion, partly military and partly political, about the time and scope and method of invading the European continent. Churchill remembered vividly the heavy price in human lives which Britain had paid in World War I. He wished to postpone the cross-Channel operation which American military leaders favored in 1942 and 1943. The British Premier was also a persistent advocate of a Balkan invasion which American military opinion was inclined to dismiss as an undesirable sideshow.

In this last dispute there was a political angle. A successful Anglo-American occupation of the Balkan countries would have tipped the political balance in this part of the world in favor of the West and against Russia. It was a relief to Stalin to find Marshall, Eisenhower, and other American generals who thought in purely military terms opposing Churchill's scheme which would have limited the extent of Soviet conquest.

Churchill was handicapped in his wartime diplomacy because Roosevelt seems to have suspected British postwar designs more than Russian. Elliott Roosevelt is certainly not the most profound and probably not the most reliable of political reporters. Yet his accounts of his talks with his father in moments of relaxation during the war are not without value and indicate persistent suspicion of Churchill's designs without any corresponding distrust of Stalin.

According to Elliott Roosevelt, the President said to him, at the time of the meeting at which the Atlantic Charter was signed:

"America won't help England in this war simply so that she will be able to ride roughshod over colonial peoples."[4]

On another occasion Roosevelt is represented as saying: "Great Britain signed the Atlantic Charter. I hope they realize the United States means to make them live up to it."[5]

There is no record that Roosevelt ever expressed an intention to "make" Stalin live up to the Atlantic Charter in his treatment of Poland, Finland, and the Baltic states. After Teheran Roosevelt is quoted as offering the following explanation of United States policy:

> The biggest thing was in making clear to Stalin that the United States and Great Britain were not allied in one common bloc against the Soviet Union. That's our big job now, and it will be our big job tomorrow, too, making sure that we continue to act as referee, as intermediary between Russia and England.[6]

Stalin, who loved to practice the old maxim Divide and Rule, could have wished nothing better.

Churchill tried to reach a satisfactory separate agreement with Stalin. As is shown in another chapter, Churchill took the initiative in

4. E. Roosevelt, *As He Saw It*, 25.
5. Ibid., 122.
6. Ibid., 206.

the dismemberment of Poland at Teheran. In an attempt to "compensate" Poland for the territory which he wished to hand over to Stalin, the British Prime Minister threw the weight of his influence behind the idea of expelling millions of Germans from the eastern part of that country. This is made clear in Churchill's statement to the House of Commons on December 15, 1944:

> This is what is proposed: the total expulsion of the Germans from the area to be acquired by Poland in the West and North. For expulsion is the method which, so far as we are able to see, will be the most satisfactory and lasting. . . . A clean sweep will be made. I am not alarmed by the prospect of the disentanglement of population, nor even by those large transferences, which are more possible in modern conditions than they ever were before.

So one of the most inhuman and politically unwise decisions of the provisional peace settlement, the expulsion of millions of Germans from lands that had been German for centuries, was approved in advance by Churchill. The betrayal of Poland, the acquiescence in creating a terrific refugee problem in Germany, the support of Tito in Yugoslavia, were all part of an attempt to strike an acceptable deal with Stalin.

For a time Churchill thought he had succeeded. He confidently told the House of Commons on October 27, 1944, that "our relations with Soviet Russia were never more close, intimate and cordial than they are at the present time." In an earlier broadcast, on November 29, 1942, he ventured the hopeful prediction that "there will be a far higher sense of comradeship around the council table than existed among the victors at Versailles."

But after the damage had been done, the wrong decisions taken, the dishonorable departure from Atlantic Charter principles accepted, the British Prime Minister experienced a very substantial change of opinion. In the introduction to the first volume of his war memoirs, written in March 1948, one finds this striking admission:

"The human tragedy reaches its climax in the fact that after all the exertions and sacrifices of hundreds of millions of people and of the victories of the Righteous Cause, we have still not found Peace or Security, *and that we lie in the grip of even worse perils than those we have sur-mounted.*[7] (Italics supplied.)

Churchill was one of the leading promoters of Britain's and of America's participation in the Second Crusade. Yet the sharpest critic could scarcely pronounce a more devastating judgment upon its result. The British statesman was in a still gloomier mood in October 1948. He then told a Conservative party organization that "nothing stands between Europe today and complete subjugation to Communist tyranny but the atomic bomb in American possession."[8]

Roosevelt's role in the war, because of the vast preponderance of American military power, was even more significant than Churchill's. But there was no political purpose to give America's voice at the council table a weight of authority corresponding to American military power. Roosevelt bears complete and undivided responsibility for the development of American foreign policy during the war. The Secretary of State was the elderly and ailing Cordell Hull, who was obliged by illness to resign in November 1944. Hull did not even attend the Big Three conferences at Teheran and Yalta and exerted little if any influence on what went on there.

Hull's successor, Edward R. Stettinius, was surely one of the most naive and inexperienced men in the field of foreign affairs who ever occupied that office. A witty former colleague remarked that Stettinius could not distinguish the Ukraine from a musical instrument. It required a battery of promoters at the San Francisco conference which inaugurated the United Nations to keep Stettinius from continually muffing his lines and making his country appear ridiculous.

Hull himself was of extremely mediocre caliber as a diplomat. He was equally deficient in first-hand knowledge of foreign lands and foreign languages. An able career diplomat who served under him complained that it was impossible to induce him to make decisions of the greatest urgency within a reasonable length of time or to keep his ambassadors reasonably familiar with the development of Administration policy.

Hull was a popular figure because of his reputation for rugged in-

7. Churchill, *Gathering Storm,* iv–v.
8. *The New York Times,* October 10, 1948.

tegrity and because of a Lincolnesque boyhood. The future Secretary of State educated himself while working at farming and logging in the rough hill country of western Tennessee. He had a fund of homely mountaineer stories which he was fond of telling on all occasions.

But, however attractive Hull might have been as a personality, he was not well qualified to conduct America's foreign relations. He was too much inclined to regard the enunciation of a series of pompous platitudes as a major achievement in statesmanship. From one irrepressible Washington hostess he earned a revealing nickname: "The hillbilly Polonius."

Even if Hull and Stettinius had been more effective diplomats, it was not in Roosevelt's power-loving and secretive nature to let the threads of foreign policy slip out of his hands. The aims of his highly personal policy may be briefly summarized as follows:

Appeasement of Stalin at any cost.

Complete military, political, and economic smashing of Germany and Japan.

Evolution of the military coalition known as the United Nations into a world association, capable of preserving the peace.

A rather vaguely conceived new deal in colonial relations, with trusteeship arrangements replacing old-fashioned imperialist rule.

A postwar effort to promote the relief and reconstruction of the "peace-loving nations,"[9] that is, the members of the United Nations coalition, with a liberal use of United States funds.

Roosevelt's admirers may dispute the word "appeasement" as descriptive of his Russian policy. Yet this word appears in one of the most authoritative discussions of this policy, published by Forrest Davis in two articles which appeared in the *Saturday Evening Post* of May 13 and May 20, 1944. These articles were read and approved by Roosevelt in advance of publication. After stating that Roosevelt's objectives call for "finesse, a skillful statecraft that cannot always be exposed to view" and emphasizing that the President voided the slightest cause of offense to the Kremlin, Davis continues:

9. By a ludicrously ironical decision taken at Yalta only nations which declared war against Germany by a certain date were adjudged "peace-loving" and hence eligible for membership in the United Nations.

The core of his policy has been the reassurance of Stalin. That was so, as we have seen, at Teheran. It has been so throughout the difficult diplomacy since Stalingrad. Our failure to renew our offer of good offices in the Russo-Polish controversies must be read in that light. Likewise our support, seconding Britain, of Tito, the Croatian Communist partisan leader in Yugoslavia. So it is also the President's immediate and generous response to Stalin's demand for a share in the surrendered Italian fleet or its equivalent. Our bluntly reiterated advice to the Finns to quit the war at once without reference to Soviet terms falls under the same tactical heading.

Suppose that Stalin, in spite of all concessions, should prove *unappeasable.* . . . [Italics supplied.]

Roosevelt, gambling for stakes as enormous as any statesman ever played for, has been betting that the Soviet Union needs peace and is willing to pay for it by collaborating with the West.

A similar picture is conveyed by William C. Bullitt, former Ambassador to the Soviet Union and to France, and for a time one of Roosevelt's favored advisers. Writing in the magazine *Life* in the autumn of 1948, Bullitt asserts that Roosevelt, acting on the advice of Hopkins, hoped to convert Stalin from imperialism to democratic collaboration by following these methods:

1. To give Stalin without stint or limit everything he asked for the prosecution of the war and to refrain from asking Stalin for anything in return.
2. To persuade Stalin to adhere to statements of general aims, like the Atlantic Charter.
3. To let Stalin know that the influence of the White House was being used to encourage American public opinion to take a favorable view of the Soviet Union.
4. To meet Stalin face to face and persuade him into an acceptance of Christian ways and democratic principles.

This is certainly an accurate nutshell summary of Roosevelt's Russian policy during the war. At the President's request, Bullitt prepared a memorandum, setting forth the reasons for believing that such a policy would fail. After a discussion of this memorandum lasting three hours, the President said to Bullitt, according to the latter's testimony:

> Bill, I don't dispute your facts; they are accurate. I don't dispute the logic of your reasoning. I just have a hunch that Stalin is not that kind of a man. Harry [Hopkins] says he's not and that he doesn't want anything but security for his country. And I think that if I give him everything I possibly can and ask for nothing from him in return, noblesse oblige, he won't try to annex anything and will work with me for a world of democracy and peace.

So, on the "hunch" of a man even less acquainted than he was with Russian history and Communist philosophy, Roosevelt set out on a course which was predestined to end in diplomatic bankruptcy. In view of the President's shrewdness in domestic politics, his naïveté and downright ignorance of Soviet politics and economics are surprising. The Soviet political system had moved toward increasingly unrestrained dictatorship. The Soviet economic system had become one of isolationist autarchy. Yet Roosevelt cheerfully remarked to Frances Perkins, after his return from Teheran:

"I really think the Russians will go along with me about having no spheres of influence and about agreements for free ports all over the world. That is, ports which can be used freely at all times by all the allies. I think that is going to be the answer."[10]

Perhaps Roosevelt's most realistic remark, also to Frances Perkins, was, "I don't understand the Russians. I don't know what makes them tick."

Roosevelt framed his policy of "charming" Stalin into good will and good behavior with the close co-operation of Harry Hopkins. The latter was, after the President, the most powerful man in America during the war.

An ex–social worker with a passion for night life and gambling on horse races, Hopkins was never so happy as when he was living off or spending other people's money. He enjoyed abundant opportunity to satisfy this urge as administrator of WPA and later as dispenser of lend-

10. Perkins, *The Roosevelt I Knew,* 86.

lease aid. Another worker in the New Deal vineyard, Harold Ickes, paid the following tributes to Hopkins as a spender in articles published in the *Saturday Evening Post* of June 12 and June 19, 1948:

> Hopkins had been a social worker. The funds that he had handled as such were in the nature of handouts. He has been acclaimed as the best of spenders. And he was a good spender. If the idea was for the money to be got rid of rapidly, Harry performed in a most competent manner. . . .
>
> If he did not give even the vaguest idea what the money was to be spent for, or where, neither did he ever present any reports as to where it had been spent and in what amounts.

Hopkins had been a prominent figure throughout the New Deal. During the war years he rose to a status of unique power as the President's chief confidential adviser. His influence with Roosevelt probably exceeded that of Colonel E. M. House with Wilson, if only because the President's infirmity made him more dependent on a companion who would sit with him in periods of relaxation.

A person familiar with the Roosevelt household believes that the beginning of Hopkins's role as supreme court favorite may be traced to the physical collapse of the President's secretary, Marguerite Le Hand, who had previously filled the role of companion. Hopkins came to dinner at the White House, became ill (he was afflicted with chronic stomach trouble), and stayed on indefinitely. Mrs. Roosevelt once observed in her column that it had been a great sacrifice for Hopkins to live in the White House.

Anyone who stands on the dizzy pinnacle of power and responsibility occupied by a wartime president is apt to feel the need of relaxed confidential companionship. Hopkins supplied this requirement. His personal devotion to Roosevelt was absolute. He became the President's other self, able to anticipate how Roosevelt's mind would react to a given situation. Working without a definite post, he was able to take a mass of responsibility off the President's shoulders.

Despite his lack of higher education, Hopkins possessed a naturally keen and vigorous mind. Churchill, who could always clothe flattering appreciation in an attractive phrase, humorously proposed to give him a title: Lord Root of the Matter. His services in cutting through red tape and concentrating on essentials at important conferences are attested by such American and British military leaders as General Marshall and Sir John Dill. Hopkins did not spare himself and often took trips and exposed himself to exertions which imposed a severe strain on a feeble constitution.

But his defects in the very high and responsible position which he held far outweighed his merits. He was profoundly ignorant in the field of foreign affairs. The very eulogistic biography of Robert E. Sherwood does not reveal in Hopkins any serious knowledge of such subjects as history, politics, and diplomacy.

Hopkins was not a Communist or a fellow traveler. In fact, he seems to have held no political or economic philosophy of any kind except a belief, at once naive and cynical, that Franklin D. Roosevelt should be kept in office indefinitely by a liberal expenditure of public funds. It has been disputed whether Hopkins made the statement:

"We will tax and tax, spend and spend, elect and elect."

That this represented his working philosophy can scarcely be doubted. Hopkins's constant advocacy of appeasing the Soviet Union, of giving everything to Stalin and asking nothing in return, was not a result of fanatical devotion to Marxist and Leninist dogmas. It was rather a case of following the line of least resistance. After all, the entire theory on which the Second Crusade was based, especially the insistence on the complete crushing of Germany and Japan, made logical sense only on the assumption that Stalin would turn out to be a peace-loving democrat at heart.

Neither Roosevelt nor Hopkins possessed a profoundly reflective type of mind. Yet both must have given at least occasional passing thought to the situation America would face in the postwar world. What that situation would be if Stalin should live up to his own past record of aggression and bad faith, to his own profession of faith in world revolution, was too painful a prospect to face squarely and realistically. So the President and his confidential aide piled appeasement on appeasement and proved their capacity to "get along" with Stalin by the simple and easy method of giving the Soviet dictator everything he wanted and asking nothing in return.

Because Hopkins was a man ignorant in foreign affairs, he was amazingly gullible. Stalin could tell him the most obvious untruths without

exciting contradiction or even surprise, because Hopkins was too unfamiliar with the historical facts concerned.

For example, Stalin informed Hopkins, on the occasion of the latter's
visit to Moscow in the summer of 1945, that in the course of twenty-five
years the Germans had twice invaded Russia by way of Poland and that
Germany had been able to do this because "Poland had been regarded
as a part of the *cordon sanitaire* around the Soviet Union."[11]

Now at the time of the First World War, Poland did not exist as an
independent state. Most of Poland's ethnic territory was a part of the
Russian Empire. And at the time of the second German invasion, in
1941, Poland's independence had again been destroyed—as a result of
the Stalin-Hitler pact. So Stalin's assertion that Russia had twice been
invaded by Germany because of the existence of a hostile Poland was
sheer fantasy. Yet Hopkins seems to have accepted it without question.

Stalin followed this up with a declaration that "there was no intention on the part of the Soviet Union to interfere in Poland's internal
affairs." This, it may be noted, was after the imposition on Poland of
a made-in-Moscow government, after the treacherous arrest by Russian soldiers of the Polish underground leaders, after the infiltration
of the Polish Army and the Polish police with Russian "advisers," after
the stamping out with ruthless terror of independent Polish nationalist
movements. Again Hopkins swallowed this obvious falsehood without
gagging. Very probably he believed it.

There is small reason for surprise that, as Ambassador Harriman
noted: "Stalin in greeting Hopkins at Teheran showed more open and
warm cordiality than he had been known to show to any foreigner."
Such a naive and trusting benefactor in such an influential position was
well worth a demonstration of cordiality to the Soviet dictator.

It is interesting to note how consistently American policy, in small
things as in large, was keyed to the objective of pleasing and "getting
along" with Stalin. Roosevelt in 1943 remarked to the Polish Ambassador, Ciechanowski, "Harry gets along like a house afire with Stalin—in
fact they seem to have become buddies."[12] Who was gaining from this

11. Sherwood, *Roosevelt and Hopkins,* 899.
12. Ciechanowski, *Defeat in Victory,* 231.

fraternization, the Soviet Union or the United States, was a consideration that seems never to have disturbed Roosevelt's mind.

But this question did give considerable concern to General John R. Deane, head of the American military mission in Moscow. The Russians were in the habit of requesting large shipments of military items, such as Diesel engines, which were in short supply in the United States and were needed on American fronts. Deane felt that in such cases there should be some explanation of the reality and nature of the Russian need.

But, as Deane found to his disappointment, Soviet military cooperation stopped with unloading the ships which brought some eleven billion dollars' worth of lend-lease supplies. Supplementary information was withheld.

Deane discussed this matter with Anastasius Mikoyan, Soviet Commissar of Foreign Trade. He received no satisfaction.

> He [Mikoyan] argued that it should not be necessary to go behind a request made by the Soviet Government, since it was axiomatic that such a request would not be made unless the need was great. He also implied that his Purchasing Commission in Washington would have no trouble obtaining approval of the Russian requests, regardless of what action I might take. The hell of it was, when I reflected on the attitude of the President, I was afraid he was right.[13]

Mikoyan was indeed soon to be proved right. General Deane sent a telegram to the Chiefs of Staff in Washington on January 16, 1944, suggesting that allocations of material in short supply in the United States should be made only on the recommendation of the American Military Mission in Moscow. General Marshall approved this suggestion. But, as Deane reports:

> Unfortunately Harriman, in reply to a telegram he had sent along the same lines to Harry Hopkins, received what amounted to instructions to attach no strings to our aid to Russia. The Russians on this occasion, as Mikoyan had predicted, received the extra supplies they had requested.[14]

13. Deane, *The Strange Alliance,* 97–98.
14. Ibid., 98.

A letter from Deane to Marshall, dated December 2, 1944, reflects the atmosphere of one-sided appeasement which dominated American-Soviet relations until the end of the war:

> After the banquets we send the Soviets another thousand airplanes and they approve a visa that has been hanging fire for months. We then scratch our heads to see what other gifts we can send and they scratch theirs to see what they can ask for. . . .
>
> In our dealings with the Soviet authorities the United States Military Mission has made every approach that has been made. Our files are bulging with letters to the Soviets and devoid of letters from them. This situation may be reversed in Washington, but I doubt it. In short we are in the position of being at the same time the givers and the supplicants. This is neither dignified nor healthy for United States prestige.[15]

The first meeting of the Big Three took place in Teheran, capital of Iran, then under joint Soviet-British occupation, and lasted from November 26 until December 1, 1943. There had already been several Anglo-American, Anglo-Russian, and American-Russian contacts.

Churchill came to America after Pearl Harbor, late in December 1941, and the secret informal British-American understanding which had existed for many months before the Japanese attack assumed more concrete form. A co-ordinating organ, the Joint Chiefs of Staff, with three American and three British representatives, was set up.

The Soviet Commissar of Foreign Affairs, Vyacheslav Molotov, visited Washington in June 1942 and pressed for the creation of a second front on the European continent. An ambiguous communiqué was issued on June 11 stating that "full understanding was reached with regard to the urgent tasks of creating a second front in Europe in 1942." This the Soviet leaders chose to interpret as a pledge of action, although the state of American and British preparations would have made a large-scale landing in France in 1942 an extremely risky enterprise.

It was left to Churchill, on a visit to Moscow in August, to break the news to Stalin that there would be no second front in Europe in 1942. Stalin showed anger to the point of becoming insulting. If the British

15. Ibid., 84–85.

infantry would only fight the Germans as the Russians had done, said the Soviet dictator, it would not be frightened of them. Churchill adroitly retorted: "I pardon that remark only on account of the bravery of the Russian troops."

Both Stimson and Marshall were in favor of launching the cross-Channel invasion, first known under the code name BOLERO, in 1943. But Churchill, never enthusiastic over the project, won Roosevelt's approval for the North African expedition in November 1942 and for the idea of limiting operations in 1943 to the Mediterranean area.

Roosevelt, Churchill, the Canadian Prime Minister Mackenzie King, and other American, British, and Canadian civilian and military notables met in conference at Quebec in August 1943. Stalin had been invited to the conference but refused to come. This was the fourth time he had rejected Roosevelt's persistent overtures for a personal meeting. The Soviet dictator gave the impression of being in a sour mood in the summer of 1943. He recalled his relatively western-minded ambassadors, Litvinov and Maisky, from Washington and London and replaced them with less prominent, grimmer, and less communicative successors, Gromyko and Gusev.

The year 1943 buzzed with rumors of secret Soviet-German peace discussions. American Army Intelligence reported negotiations between German and Soviet representatives in the neighborhood of Stockholm late in June. Apparently the stumbling block in these talks was German unwillingness to evacuate the Ukraine unconditionally.[16] There were some meetings between a German representative in Stockholm named Kleist and Alexandrov, a member of the European division of the Soviet Ministry of Foreign Affairs. The talks led to no positive results, partly because Hitler conceived the suspicion that Alexandrov was a Jew, partly because Hitler and the German Foreign Office suspected that Stalin was putting on the negotiations mainly for the purpose of frightening Roosevelt and Churchill.[17]

The Japanese Government was anxious to promote a Soviet-German peace, so that the full military power of the Axis could be employed

16. See article by Donald B. Sanders in the *American Mercury* for November 1947.

17. This information is based on a well-informed private source.

against America and Great Britain. Josef Goebbels, in his diary for April 22, 1943, notes that "the Japanese have always tried hard to end the conflict between the Reich and the Soviet Union in one way or another. If this were possible in some way the war would assume a totally different aspect. Of course I don't believe that such a possibility will arise in the foreseeable future."[18]

The skepticism of Goebbels was vindicated. But the fear of a separate peace between Germany and the Soviet Union seems to have exerted a paralyzing influence upon Anglo-American diplomacy vis-à-vis Stalin. This fear was apparently stimulated by hints which the Soviet Government deliberately dropped from time to time. The Soviet chargé d'affaires, Andrei Gromyko, informed Hull on September 16, 1943, that Russia had rejected a Japanese overture designed to promote a separate peace between Russia and Japan.[19]

This could be construed as a veiled intimation of what might happen if the United States and Great Britain should fail to acquiesce in Stalin's desires for expansion in Eastern Europe. There is every reason to believe that pressure of this kind represented nothing but bluff. Stalin had far more to lose than the United States from a breakup of the wartime coalition. But the bluff was apparently not without effect.

Hopkins brought with him to the Quebec conference a curious and significant document, entitled "Russia's Position." It was attributed to "a very high level United States military strategic estimate." In all probability it was endorsed by General Marshall. Its salient passages were as follows:

> Russia's postwar position in Europe will be a dominant one. With Germany crushed, there is no power in Europe to oppose her tremendous military forces. It is true that Great Britain is building up a position in the Mediterranean vis-à-vis Russia that she may find useful in balancing power in Europe. However, even here she may not be able to oppose Russia unless she is otherwise supported.
>
> The conclusions from the foregoing are obvious. Since Russia is the decisive factor in the war, she must be given every assistance and every effort must be made to obtain her friendship. Likewise,

18. Goebbels, *The Goebbels Diaries*, 340.
19. Hull, *Memoirs*, 2:1263–64.

since without question she will dominate Europe on the defeat of the Axis, it is even more essential to develop and maintain the most friendly relations with Russia.

Finally, the most important factor the United States has to consider in relation to Russia is the prosecution of the war in the Pacific. With Russia as an ally in the war against Japan, the war can be terminated in less time and at less expense in life and resources than if the reverse were the case. Should the war in the Pacific have to be carried on with an unfriendly or a negative attitude on the part of Russia, the difficulties will be immeasurably increased and operations might become abortive.[20]

The political naïveté of this judgment, emanating from a high military source, is breathtaking. The Soviet Union was to be permitted and even encouraged to establish over Europe the totalitarian domination which America was fighting Hitler to prevent. And every effort was to be made to enlist the Soviet Union as an ally against Japan without even passing consideration of the probability that Soviet domination of East Asia would be no less harmful to American interests than Japanese.

Whoever prepared this document rendered a very bad service to his country. For, as Sherwood says, "this estimate was obviously of great importance as indicating the policy which guided the making of decisions at Teheran and, much later, at Yalta."

The foreign ministers of America, Great Britain, and the Soviet Union met for the first time in Moscow in October 1943. Up to that time Secretary Hull had been a bulwark against appeasement in Washington. He had squelched a British maneuver to accept Soviet demands for the annexation of Eastern Poland and the Baltic states in the spring of 1942.

But Stalin and Molotov made unusual attempts to conciliate and placate Hull in Moscow. By the time the conference was over, the venerable Tennessean had reached the conclusion that the Soviet leaders were pretty good fellows, after all. Any intention he may have cherished before going to Moscow of pressing for a showdown on the Polish question on the basis of the Atlantic Charter had evaporated.

20. Sherwood, *Roosevelt and Hopkins*, 748–49.

Several considerations probably contributed to the marked weakening of Hull's stand, in practice, for the moral principles which he was so fond of proclaiming in diplomatic communications. He possessed one characteristic of a man unsure of himself. He was abnormally sensitive to criticism. A number of American left-wing organs had been conducting a violent campaign against Hull as an anti-Soviet reactionary.[21]

Hull was desperately anxious to refute this criticism by proving that he could get along with the Soviet leaders. Stalin and Molotov seem to have taken his measure very quickly. They cheered the old man to the echo when he called for "a drumhead court-martial of Hitler and Mussolini and Tojo and their arch-accomplices" and for the hanging of all "instigators of the war."

Stalin astonished and delighted Hull by assuring him that after the Allies succeeded in defeating Germany the Soviet Union would join in defeating Japan. After saying good-bye to Hull and walking away a few steps, Stalin walked back and shook hands again. This gesture seems to have made a considerable impression upon the Secretary. "I thought to myself," he writes in retrospect, "that any American having Stalin's personality and approach might well reach high public office in my own country."[22]

Hull at Moscow on a smaller scale repeated the experience of Wilson at Paris. He had become obsessed with the idea that the setting up of a postwar United Nations organization, garnished with suitable moral principles, was the key to world peace. As Wilson offered up his fourteen points, one by one, as sacrifices on the altar of the Covenant of the League of Nations, Hull and Roosevelt scrapped the Atlantic Charter and the Four Freedoms in order to woo Stalin's adhesion to the United Nations.

The one sacrifice was as futile as the other. America never joined the

21. These same publications attacked the temporary deal with Admiral Darlan which was of great military value in North Africa, called for a blockade of Spain, and were enraged over the policy of dealing with the Badoglio regime in Italy. They turned a blind eye to the far more serious threat of Soviet imperialist expansion.

22. Hull, *Memoirs*, 2:1311.

League. And the United Nations has given America no security whatever beyond what it enjoys through its military and industrial power.

Hull, as he tells us, was "truly thrilled" by the signature of the Four
Nation Declaration which emerged from the Moscow conference. This
Declaration was phrased in broad general terms. It contained no reference to the treatment of Poland, acid test of Soviet willingness to abide
by the principles of the Atlantic Charter. Its most positive statement of
intention was Article 4, worded as follows:

"They[23] recognize the necessity of establishing at the earliest practicable date a general international organization, based on the principle of the sovereign equality of all peace-loving States, and open to
membership by all such States, large and small, for the maintenance of
international peace and security."

This Moscow conference was a curtain-raiser for the first meeting of
the Big Three in Teheran later in the year. Roosevelt had not wished to
go so far as Teheran, which was difficult to reach by plane because of
surrounding high mountains. A constitutional question was involved,
whether the President could receive and return legislation passed by
Congress within the prescribed limit of ten days. But Stalin was ada-
mant. It was Teheran or no meeting, so far as he was concerned. After
pleading in vain for Basra, in southern Iran, Roosevelt, as usual in his
dealings with the Soviet dictator, gave way.

Before Roosevelt and Churchill went to Teheran, they held a conference on Far Eastern questions in Cairo, with the participation of
Chiang Kai-shek. No very binding or important military decisions were
taken. The unconditional surrender was affirmed in regard to Japan.
War aims in the Orient were stated as follows:

That Japan shall be stripped of all the islands in the Pacific which she
has seized or occupied since the beginning of the First World War in
1914, and that all the territories Japan has stolen from the Chinese,
such as Manchuria, Formosa and the Pescadores, shall be restored
to the Republic of China. Japan will also be expelled from all other

23. The four signatories, Hull, Molotov, Eden, and the Chinese Ambassador
Foo Ping-sheung. Hull regarded it as a great victory that China was included as a
signatory. This point might well seem more debatable in 1950.

territories which she has taken by violence and greed. The aforesaid three great powers, mindful of the enslavement of the people of Korea, are determined that in due course Korea shall become free and independent.

It is not known who deserves the dubious credit of composing this piece of self-righteous moralizing. It may be ranked among the unhappy exhibits of crusading diplomacy, along with the "unconditional surrender" slogan and the Morgenthau Plan. Other powers besides Japan have certainly acquired territory by what might fairly be called violence and greed, and even theft. Japanese aggression, like the aggression which contributed to the building up of the European colonial empires or the aggression that gave the United States a vast area formerly belonging to Mexico, is morally reprehensible. There is an element of rather smug hypocrisy in singling it out for special reprobation and punishment. The cooping up of Japan's growing population of almost eighty million people within an area smaller than the state of California and their exclusion from the mainland of Asia have not worked out happily from the standpoint of American and British interests, especially in the light of what has happened in China.

From Cairo Roosevelt flew to Teheran, where his long-sought and long-evaded meeting with Stalin took place on November 28. It is noteworthy that the Soviet Government never took the initiative in bringing about wartime conferences with its allies. Stalin was keenly conscious of the psychological advantage of being the wooed, not the wooer, in international relations. So was at least one American observer, the candid and perceptive General Deane.

"No single event of the war," he wrote, "irritated me more than seeing the President of the United States lifted from wheelchair to automobile, to ship, to shore and to aircraft in order to go halfway around the world as the only possible means of meeting J. V. Stalin."[24]

Had Roosevelt matched Stalin in cool-headed aloofness, the monstrous unbalance of power in postwar Europe and Asia could have been averted, or at least mitigated. The President might well have let Stalin ask for lend-lease, instead of sending Harry Hopkins to Moscow to press this aid on the Soviet ruler with both hands. Before America was

24. Deane, *The Strange Alliance,* 160.

involved in the war, lend-lease aid could have been made conditional on a specific recognition of the Soviet frontiers of 1939, on a disgorging of the spoils of the Stalin-Hitler pact.

But a gambler is often exposed to the temptation of constantly doubling his stakes. Roosevelt was gambling on the assumption that Stalin was a potential good neighbor who could be appeased. Teheran and its concessions were a natural outgrowth of the policy of constantly making overtures to the Kremlin. Yalta and its still greater concessions followed Teheran as a logical sequel.

After Roosevelt arrived in the Iranian capital, he accepted Stalin's invitation to move from the American Embassy to a villa in the Soviet compound. The invitation was motivated by a conveniently discovered alleged plot against the President's security, details of which were never revealed. The attendants in the President's new quarters were poorly camouflaged Soviet secret service operatives, who were able to keep Roosevelt's every movement under watchful surveillance.

The President was quick to live up to his role as the constant and cheerful giver. He suggested in his first talk with Stalin that after the war, surplus American and British ships should be handed over to the Soviet Union. Stalin saw nothing to object to in this suggestion. Every big issue at the conference was settled according to Stalin's wishes. He found allies in the American military representatives in resisting Churchill's suggestion for Anglo-American operations in the Balkans. OVERLORD, the American-British cross-Channel invasion, was definitely set for the spring or early summer of 1944. Stalin sharply brushed off what he mistakenly regarded as an attempt to raise the question of the independence of the Baltic states. And he learned that Churchill would co-operate in his scheme for annexing almost half of Poland, and that Roosevelt would offer no opposition.[25]

Roosevelt, still in the role of the cheerful giver, suggested that the Soviet Union should have access to the port of Dairen, main outlet of Manchuria. Stalin himself suggested a doubt. The Chinese, he thought, would object. But Roosevelt was sure the Chinese would agree to a plan for Dairen as a free port under international guarantee. This arrangement was actually confirmed at Yalta and written into the Soviet-

25. This subject is treated in more detail in Chapter 11.

Chinese treaty of August 1945. But years have passed, and Dairen remains under complete Soviet control and as far removed from the status of a free port as could well be imagined.

The shrewd and wily Stalin must have derived a certain grim satisfaction from watching Roosevelt try to conciliate him by resorting to horseplay at the expense of Churchill. Finding that his charm was not melting Stalin's reserve as rapidly as he had hoped, Roosevelt at one of the conferences ostentatiously whispered to Stalin, through an interpreter: "Winston is cranky this morning; he got up on the wrong side of the bed." The President went on teasing Churchill about his Britishness, about John Bull, about his cigars, and his habits.[26] Churchill glowered and Stalin finally gave satisfaction with a guffaw of laughter. Then Roosevelt, always obsessed with the idea that diplomacy was a matter of hail-fellow-well-met personal relations, felt the day was won.

There was another incident at one of the numerous banquets. Stalin proposed a toast to the execution of 50,000 German officers. Churchill objected to putting anyone to death without trial. Roosevelt tried to pour oil on troubled waters by suggesting a compromise: the execution of 49,000.

In more serious moments Yugoslavia's fate, as well as Poland's, was settled at Teheran. It was agreed that "the Partisans in Yugoslavia should be supported by supplies and equipment to the greatest possible extent and also by commando operations." In Yugoslavia, as in Poland, there were two movements of resistance to the Germans. One, headed by General Drazha Mihailovic, had started as soon as the Germans overran Yugoslavia. It was nationalistic, anti-Communist, and looked to the western powers for support.

The so-called Partisan movement was led by the Moscow-trained Communist Josip Broz Tito. It was Communist in leadership and aims and set as its goal the destruction of Mihailovic and the conservative nationalists. Just as in Poland, although more speedily, the American and British governments decided to throw over their friends and support their enemies.[27]

26. Perkins, *The Roosevelt I Knew*, 84.

27. Tito broke with Moscow in 1948, and this led to a gradual relaxation of tension between his dictatorship and the western powers. This does not affect the fact that during the war and immediate postwar years Tito was blatantly pro-

For this blunder Churchill bears a large share of responsibility. He allowed himself to be deceived by observers, including his own son, Randolph, and Brigadier Fitzroy Maclean, who played down Tito's communism and Moscow affiliations and presented him as a purely nationalist leader. In the same speech in the House of Commons in which Churchill announced his support for Stalin's annexationist demands on Poland (February 22, 1944) Churchill declared:

"In Yugoslavia we give our aid to Tito. . . . Every effort in our power will be made to aid and sustain Marshal Tito and his gallant band."

Later, on May 24, he asserted:

"Marshal Tito has largely sunk his communist aspect in his character as a Yugoslav patriot leader. . . . In one place [Greece] we support a king, in another a Communist—there is no attempt by us to enforce particular ideologies."

Churchill treated the Yugoslav government-in-exile in the most brusque and cavalier fashion. He put the strongest pressure on young King Peter to discard Mihailovic and endorse Tito. For several months the King and his Prime Minister, Dr. Puric, resisted Churchill's more and more insistent demands that Mihailovic, War Minister of the government, be dismissed. Finally Churchill threatened that if the King did not yield he would publicly accuse Mihailovic of collaboration with the enemy and treat the King and his government accordingly. In his dealings with Yugoslavia, the conservative British Prime Minister almost accepted Stalin's standard. Anyone opposed to communism was a "fascist."[28]

The young monarch sent a pathetic letter to Roosevelt, who inspired more hopes in the anti-Communist forces of Eastern Europe than he was willing or perhaps able to satisfy.[29] The government, King Peter

---

Moscow and anti-Western, and that the abandonment of Mihailovic reflects little credit either on the honor or the judgment of Roosevelt and Churchill.

28. In the savage and confused civil war in Yugoslavia the hatred between the forces of Mihailovic and Tito was greater than the hatred of either for the Germans and Italians. There were cases of technical collaboration, especially with the Italians, on the part of some of Mihailovic's subordinate commanders. Mihailovic himself, however, had a price set on his head by the Germans and remained a consistent, anti-Communist Yugoslav patriot to the end.

29. Fotitch, *The War We Lost*, 247–49.

pleaded, could not abandon Mihailovic without betraying the people. "I would become a traitor to my people and to my army in Yugoslavia." The King's message continued:

> We cannot believe that anything could have been decided either at Moscow or at Teheran concerning the future of Yugoslavia without consulting us. If so, why do we have to commit suicide? Even if I should be forced into betrayal, or worse, be capable of it, why provoke one of the greatest scandals in history by libelling as "traitors" our valiant people who are fighting alone without anyone's help? We have been told that there will not be any landing in the Balkans. If such a fatal decision was taken, I implore you to change it. . . . The case of Tito is not of exclusive Yugoslav concern. It is a test case for all of Central Europe and if successful it will lead to much more, with no end in sight.

Roosevelt brushed off Peter much as he brushed off the similar pleas of the Polish democratic leader Mikolajczyk.[30] He advised the young sovereign to do pretty much what Churchill told him to do. Peter finally yielded and appointed a Croat politician, Ivan Subasic, as Prime Minister in a cabinet designed to pave the way for Tito's assumption of power. Churchill's high-handed methods with the government-in-exile found striking illustration in his handling of the cabinet change on May 24, 1944. Puric had refused to resign, and the King had not dismissed him. Churchill made the announcement of the change of cabinet as if Puric's resignation had already been tendered.[31]

No one gained much advantage from these unsavory proceedings. Peter lost his throne. Subasic lost his liberty; he soon found that no one could "do business" with Tito. And Churchill soon learned that Britain had lost its last shreds of influence in Yugoslavia.

Teheran set the pattern of appeasing Soviet demands, which is responsible for the disturbed and chaotic condition of postwar Europe and for the Communist conquest of China. But Roosevelt does not seem to have realized, at least until the eve of his death, what a defeat he had sustained. Had he not induced Stalin to unbend to the point

30. In this connection see Chapter 11.
31. Fotitch, *The War We Lost*, 252.

of emitting a guffaw of laughter? According to Sherwood,[32] Roosevelt then felt sure that Stalin was, to use his own word, "getatable," "despite his bludgeoning tactics and his attitude of cynicism toward such matters as the rights of small nations."

Indeed, after the President returned to the United States, he expressed no reservations about the prospect of friendly co-operation with the Soviet dictator. Roosevelt announced in a broadcast on December 24, 1943:

> To use an American and ungrammatical colloquialism, I may say that I got along fine with Marshal Stalin. . . . I believe that we are going to get on well with him and the Russian people, very well indeed. . . . The rights of every nation, large and small, must be respected and guarded as jealously as are the rights of every individual in our republic. The doctrine that the strong shall dominate the weak is the doctrine of our enemies, and we reject it.

There was the same note of cheery unalloyed optimism in the communiqué issued under the signatures of the Big Three after the Teheran meeting:

"Emerging from these cordial conferences, we look with confidence to the day when all peoples of the world may live free lives, untouched by tyranny, and according to their varying desires and their own consciences."

Poles, Yugoslavs, Latvians, Lithuanians, Estonians, and other peoples of Eastern Europe, apart from the small minorities of Communist sympathizers, probably felt skeptical about these glowing assurances. But their voices were not heard in the carefully guarded meetings where the Big Three enjoyed the intoxicating sense of settling the destinies of the world.

The horrors of Soviet mass deportations from eastern Poland and the Baltic states during the period of the Stalin-Hitler pact were well known to responsible American officials. But the details of the packed fetid trains, with human beings treated worse than cattle, of mass deaths, separation of members of families, slave labor in concentra-

32. Sherwood, *Roosevelt and Hopkins,* 798–99.

tion camps were carefully concealed from the American people. It was considered broad-minded to forget the misery which Soviet rule had brought to millions of people and to view with sympathy Stalin's professed desire to assure Soviet "security" by annexing or dominating all Russia's neighboring states.

When the venerable Hull returned from Moscow, still feeling the warm pressure of Stalin's repeated handshakes, he told a joint session of Congress on November 18, 1943, that he found in Marshal Stalin "a remarkable personality, one of the great statesmen and leaders of this age." He also ventured the following optimistic but almost amusingly inaccurate prediction:

> As the provisions of the Four Nations Declaration are carried into effect, there will no longer be need for spheres of influence, for alliances, for balance of power, or any other of the special arrangements through which, in the unhappy past, the nations strove to safeguard their security or to promote their interests.

Hull soon learned that Churchill was seeking very energetically to safeguard British interests by coming to an agreement with Stalin about spheres of influence. The British Ambassador in Washington, Lord Halifax, inquired of the Secretary of State on May 20 how the American Government would feel about an arrangement which would give Russia a controlling influence in Rumania and Britain a controlling influence in Greece.[33] Hull's reaction was critical. Churchill then telegraphed directly to Roosevelt, urging his sanction for the arrangement. The British Government had proposed such an agreement earlier; the Soviet Government had replied expressing general agreement with the idea, but withholding final assurance until the United States attitude was known.

Churchill followed this up with another message on June 8, arguing that someone must "play the hand" and that events moved very rapidly in the Balkans. Roosevelt, at Hull's advice, replied with an expression of preference for consultative arrangements in the Balkans. This elicited from Churchill a more urgent communication, of June 11, suggesting that a consultative committee would be slow and obstructive

33. Hull, *Memoirs*, 2:1451.

and asking a three-months' trial for the arrangement he had proposed. Roosevelt accepted this suggestion without notifying Hull.

When Churchill and Eden went to Moscow in October 1944, they extended the arrangement further. According to reports from the American embassies in Moscow and Ankara, it was agreed that Russia would have a 75:25 or 80:20 predominance in Bulgaria, Hungary, and Rumania. Influence in Yugoslavia was to be split 50:50.[34] There was never any serious attempt to implement these mathematical divisions. Soviet influence was absolute in all the mentioned countries until Tito rebelled against Moscow in 1948.

It was in the autumn of 1944 that Churchill's comments on Anglo-Soviet relations were most optimistic. He would soon learn that no agreement for "sharing influence" in countries run by satellite Communist parties was worth anything.

The Soviet weight in the balance of forces among the three principal allies steadily increased during 1944. The German eastern front was crumbling. The Red Army swept up to the line of the Vistula in Poland and paused deliberately while the Germans crushed the revolt of the Polish nationalists in Warsaw. Rumania and Bulgaria followed the Balkan tradition of deserting the losing for the winning side. Rumania was quickly occupied by the advancing Red Army.

What happened in Bulgaria was characteristic of Soviet speed and initiative, as contrasted with the slow and fumbling methods of the western powers. Agents of the Bulgarian Government were negotiating with American and British representatives in Cairo in August and September 1944. Instead of rushing the armistice discussions to a swift conclusion and sending an Anglo-American army of occupation into Bulgaria, the talks in Cairo were allowed to drag, and Moscow was dutifully informed of all the details.

Since Bulgaria was not at war with Russia, the first negotiations were confined to the United States and Great Britain. But on September 8 the Soviet Government hurled a declaration of war at Bulgaria and carried out a lightning occupation of that country, thereby excluding Anglo-American troops. A sanguinary purge, repeated at intervals up to the present time, disposed not only of Bulgarian conservatives,

34. Ibid., 1458.

but of liberals, socialists, and dissident Communists and brought that country firmly into the Soviet orbit. Missions of the western powers, when they were finally allowed to enter Bulgaria, were treated with calculated and ostentatious discourtesy.

Meanwhile, Soviet armies, benefiting from the ever increasing American flow of trucks, telephone equipment, canned food, and other lend-lease supplies, were streaming westward. They left behind them a trail of murder, rape, and pillage worthy of the hordes of Genghis Khan. And they were carving out for Stalin a mightier empire than any Tsar had ever ruled. The Red Star was very much in the ascendant when the second meeting of the Big Three took place, very appropriately, on Soviet soil, in the Crimean resort of Yalta.

# 9

---

# The Munich Called Yalta:
# War's End

The second conference of the Big Three, held at Yalta in February 1945, represented the high point of Soviet diplomatic success and correspondingly the low point of American appeasement. This conference took place under circumstances which were very disadvantageous to the western powers.

Roosevelt's mental and physical condition had disquieted Stimson at the time when the Morgenthau Plan was being approved.[1] It certainly did not improve as a result of the strenuous presidential campaign and the long trip to the Crimean resort.

There has been no authoritative uninhibited analysis of the state of the President's health during the war. But there is a good deal of reliable testimony of serious deterioration, especially during the last year of Mr. Roosevelt's life. And it was during this year that decisions of the most vital moral and political importance had to be taken.

Among the symptoms of the President's bad health were liability to severe debilitating colds, extreme haggardness of appearance, occasional blackouts of memory, and loss of capacity for mental concentration. An extremely high authority who may not be identified described Roosevelt's condition at three of the principal conferences as follows:

"The President looked physically tired at Casablanca; but his mind worked well. At Teheran there were signs of loss of memory. At Yalta he could neither think consecutively nor express himself coherently."

An official who was in frequent contact with Roosevelt during the last months of his life gave me the following account of getting essential state papers considered:

---

1. See Chapter 12.

I would go to the President with perhaps a dozen documents requiring his approval or signature. By talking fast as soon as I opened the door of his study I could get action, perhaps, on three or four. Then the President would begin to talk about irrelevant matters, repeating stories and anecdotes I had often heard from him before and falling behind in his schedule of appointments. It was difficult and embarrassing to get away from him.

A similar impression was carried away by General Joseph Stilwell, who talked with Roosevelt after the Cairo and Teheran conferences and asked what American policy he should communicate to Chiang Kai-shek after returning to China. The reply was a long rambling monologue. The President told how his grandfather made a couple of million dollars out of China in the 1830's and "all through the Civil War." He expounded a plan for taking fifty or one hundred million American dollars and buying up Chinese paper money on the black market so as to check inflation. He talked about postwar airplanes and how much the Chinese should pay American engineers. And Stilwell never got his direction as to policy.

It is certainly no exaggeration to say that Roosevelt was physically and mentally far less fit than Churchill and Stalin during the period when American military power was at its height, and the supreme decisions which confronted the national leaders in the last phase of the war had to be taken. Had Roosevelt been able to delegate power, and had there been a strong and capable Secretary of State, some of the unfortunate consequences of the President's incapacitation might have been averted and softened.

But Roosevelt clung to power with hands that were too weak to use it effectively. After his death it required much searching of files and ransacking of the memories of the participants to reconstruct what had occurred and to find out just what the President had or had not agreed to.

When Hull laid down his office on account of bad health in November 1944, his successor was Edward Stettinius. The ignorance and naïveté of the latter in foreign affairs soon became a byword to his associates in government service and to foreign diplomats. Stettinius was much better qualified to be master of ceremonies at the high jinks of some fraternal organization than to direct American foreign policy at a critical period.

Stettinius shared Roosevelt's harmful delusion that successful diplomacy was largely a matter of establishing friendly personal contacts. At the Dumbarton Oaks conference which shaped the preliminary draft of the United Nations charter, Stettinius made himself ridiculous by cheerfully shouting "Hi, Alex" and "Hiya, Andrei" at his partners in the negotiations, the correct and pained Sir Alexander Cadogan and the sullen and bored Andrei Gromyko.

The appointment of Stettinius was due to the influence of Hopkins. The latter's star as court favorite, after a temporary eclipse, was again in the ascendant at the time of the Yalta Conference. Hopkins was a very sick man and had to spend most of his time at Yalta in bed.

Roosevelt went to Yalta with no prepared agenda and no clearly defined purpose, except to get along with Stalin at any price. He had been provided with a very complete file of studies and recommendations, drawn up by the State Department, before he boarded the heavy cruiser *Quincy*, which took him to Malta, where there was a break in the journey to the Crimea. But these were never looked at. The President suffered from a cold and from sinus trouble, and his appearance "disturbed" James F. Byrnes, who accompanied him on this trip.[2]

The conference at Yalta lasted a week, from February 4 until February 11, 1945. The principal subjects discussed were Poland, German boundaries and reparations, the occupation regime for Germany, the conditions of Soviet participation in the war against Japan, procedure and voting rights in the future United Nations organization.

At the price of a few promises which were soon to prove worthless in practice, Stalin got what he wanted in Poland: a frontier that assigned to the Soviet Union almost half of Poland's prewar territory and the abandonment by America and Great Britain of the Polish government-in-exile in London. Roosevelt made a feeble plea that Lwów and the adjacent oil fields be included in Poland. Churchill appealed to Stalin's sense of generosity. Neither achieved any success.

On the German question, Churchill took a stand for moderation. Stalin recommended that the western frontier of Poland should be

2. Byrnes, *Speaking Frankly*, 22–23.

extended to the Neisse River, bringing large tracts of ethnic German territory under Polish rule. Churchill suggested that it would be a pity to stuff the Polish goose so full of German food that he would die of indigestion.

The British Premier privately estimated to Byrnes that nine million Germans would be displaced by giving Poland a frontier on the Neisse River and that such a number could never be absorbed. It is the Neisse River that marks the Polish-German frontier in 1950, although the Yalta communiqué merely stated that "Poland must receive substantial accessions of territory in the North and West."

There was agreement in principle that Germany should be broken up into separate states. However, no positive decision was adopted. The matter was referred to the European Advisory Commission, composed of American, British, and Soviet representatives sitting in London. Here it died a natural death. The dismemberment of Germany was not discussed at the next major conference, at Potsdam.

The Soviet representatives at Yalta had large and fairly precise ideas as to what they wished to take from Germany as reparations. They wanted to remove physically 80 per cent of Germany's heavy industries and also to receive deliveries in kind for ten years. Churchill recalled the unsuccessful experience with reparations after the last war and spoke of "the spectre of an absolutely starving Germany." Ivan Maisky, Soviet spokesman on this question, proposed that reparations be fixed at the figure of twenty billion dollars, with the Soviet Union to receive at least half of this sum.

Roosevelt had little to suggest on this subject, except to remark that the United States would have no money to send into Germany for food, clothing, and housing. It was finally decided to leave the details to a reparations commission. There was no firm promise on America's part to support a Soviet claim for ten billion dollars in reparations, although the Soviet Government, with its usual tendency to lose nothing for want of asking for it, later tried to represent that there had been such a commitment.

If one considers the value of the territory lost by Germany in the East, the prodigious looting, organized and unorganized, carried out by the Red Army, and the system in the Soviet zone of occupation under which a large share of German industrial output is siphoned off for Soviet use, it is probable that Germany was stripped of assets considerably in excess of ten billion dollars in value.

The protocol on reparations mentioned "the use of labor" as a possible source of reparations. Roosevelt observed that "the United States cannot take man power as the Soviet Republic can." This gave implied American sanction to the large-scale exploitation of German war prisoners as slave labor in Britain and France, as well as in Russia, after the end of the war. The Morgenthau Plan, which Roosevelt and Churchill had approved at Quebec, recommended "forced German labor outside Germany" as a form of reparations.

Procedure in the United Nations was discussed at some length. The records show that Roosevelt and Churchill were as unwilling as Stalin to forego the right of veto in serious disputes, where the use of armed force was under discussion. There was a dispute, not settled at Yalta, as to whether the right of veto should apply to discussion of controversial matters. The Russians insisted that it should, the western representatives contended that it should not. Stalin conceded this minor point when Harry Hopkins visited Moscow in June 1945.

The Soviet Government received Roosevelt's consent to its proposal that Byelorussia and the Ukraine, two of the affiliated Soviet republics, should be granted individual votes in the United Nations Assembly. When Byrnes learned of this he raised vigorous objection, reminding Roosevelt that some of the opposition to America's entrance into the League of Nations was based on the argument that Britain would have five votes, one for each member of the Commonwealth. Roosevelt then asked for and obtained Stalin's consent to an arrangement which would give the United States three votes in the Assembly. This compensation was never pressed for and did not go into effect.

In reason and logic there was no case for giving separate votes to the Ukraine and Byelorussia. If the Soviet Union was a loose federation of independent states, like the British Commonwealth, each of its sixteen constituent republics should have been entitled to a vote. If it was a centralized unitary state, it should have received only one vote. No one with an elementary knowledge of Soviet political realities could doubt that the Soviet Union belongs in the second category. It would cause no special shock or surprise to see Canada, South Africa, Australia, or India voting in opposition to Britain on some issues. It would be unthinkable for the Ukraine or Byelorussia to oppose the Soviet Union.

So far as the Assembly is concerned, Moscow's three votes have thus far been of little practical importance. The Assembly possesses little power, and the Soviet satellites are in the minority. But, as Byrnes was to discover later during the arduous negotiation of the peace treaties with Italy, Hungary, Bulgaria, Rumania, and Finland, it was an advantage for the Soviet Union to start with three of the twenty-one votes of the participating nations in its pocket.

Contempt for the rights of smaller and weaker nations was conspicuous in the Soviet attitude at Yalta. At the first dinner Vishinsky declared that the Soviet Union would never agree to the right of the small nations to judge the acts of the great powers. Charles E. Bohlen, American State Department expert on Russia,[3] replied that the American people were not likely to approve of any denial of the small nations' right. Vishinsky's comment was that the American people should "learn to obey their leaders."[4]

Churchill, discussing the same subject with Stalin, quoted the proverb: "The eagle should permit the small birds to sing and not care wherefore they sang." Stalin's low opinion of France, as a country that had been knocked out early in the war, was reflected in his remark: "I cannot forget that in this war France opened the gates to the enemy."

What Stalin did forget, and what no one reminded him of, was that while France was fighting the Germans, the Soviet Government was enthusiastically collaborating with the Nazi dictatorship, sending messages of congratulation after every new victory of the Wehrmacht. French Communists, acting under Stalin's orders, certainly contributed more than other Frenchmen to "opening the gates to the enemy."

Stalin was only willing to grant France a zone of occupation on condition that this should be carved out of territory assigned to the United States and Great Britain. For a time he held out against giving France a place on the Allied Control Council for Germany. In the end he yielded to Roosevelt on this point. The President's attitude toward General de

3. Bohlen, an excellent Russian linguist with experience as a member of the Embassy staff in Moscow, had risen rapidly in influence during the later phase of the war. He was not only an interpreter, but a policy adviser at Yalta.

4. Sherwood, *Roosevelt and Hopkins*, 852.

Gaulle had always been strained and chilly. But, in Hopkins's words, "Winston and Anthony [Eden] fought like tigers" for France. They enlisted the aid of Hopkins, who persuaded Roosevelt to use his influence, in this case successfully, with Stalin.

On the subject of Iran there was complete disagreement. That country had been jointly occupied by Russia and Britain since 1942. There had been an agreement at Teheran that all foreign troops should be withdrawn six months after the end of the war, but the Soviet Government was already displaying the balkiness about implementing this agreement which was to lead to a serious international crisis in 1946. The brief text of the final discussion at the meeting of foreign ministers on February 10 is worth quoting as a foretaste of Molotov's methods in negotiation:

> Mr. Eden inquired whether Mr. Molotov had considered the British document on Iran.
>
> Mr. Molotov stated that he had nothing to add to what he had said several days ago on the subject.
>
> Mr. Eden inquired whether it would not be advisable to issue a communiqué on Iran.
>
> Mr. Molotov stated that this would be inadvisable.
>
> Mr. Stettinius urged that some reference be made that Iranian problems had been discussed and clarified during the Crimean Conference.
>
> Mr. Molotov stated that he opposed this idea.
>
> Mr. Eden suggested that it be stated that the declaration on Iran had been reaffirmed and re-examined during the present meeting.
>
> Mr. Molotov opposed this suggestion.[5]

In Yugoslavia, as in Poland, the Yalta Agreement provided a screen of fair words behind which the friends of the West were ruthlessly liquidated. It was decided to recommend that a new government be formed on the basis of agreement between Tito and Subasic.[6] The antifascist Assembly of National Liberation (an organization of Tito's predominantly Communist followers) was to be enlarged by the addition of

5. Ibid., 865.
6. See p. 208, above.

members of the last Yugoslav parliament who "had not compromised themselves by collaboration with the enemy." Legislative acts passed by the Assembly were to be subject to ratification by a constituent assembly.

All this sounded fair enough. What is meant in practice was that two non-Communists, Subasic and Grol, joined Tito's regime, the former as Foreign Minister, the latter as Vice-Premier. But their tenure of office was precarious and brief. Grol's newspaper was suppressed, and he resigned from the government in August 1945, accusing the regime of a long series of violations of elementary political and civil liberties. Subasic followed his example soon afterwards and was placed under house arrest.

And Tito's constituent assembly was chosen under an electoral law "which rendered the very appearance of a candidate's name on the opposition list a danger to that candidate's life."[7] The "new democracy," so very like the old fascism in psychology and methods, marched on to further victories. Yalta put the seal on the process which had begun at Teheran of betraying the East Europeans who preferred free institutions to communism. All that followed, or could follow, was a long series of futile diplomatic protests from Washington and London.

Another country was offered up as a sacrifice on the altar of appeasement at Yalta. This was China. Stalin had told Hull at Moscow and Roosevelt at Teheran that he would be on the side of the United States and Great Britain against Japan after the end of the war with Germany. At Yalta, with German military collapse clearly impending, the Soviet dictator set a price for his intervention in the Far East. The price was stiff. And it included items which it was not morally justifiable for the United States to accept. The Big Three agreed that

the former rights of Russia, violated by the treacherous attack of Japan in 1904,[8] shall be restored, viz.:

7. Fotitch, *The War We Lost*, 311.
8. This was not an objective picture of the origins of the Russo-Japanese War, nor did it correspond with the general American sympathy with Japan in the course of this war.

(a) The southern part of Sakhalin as well as the islands adjacent to it shall be returned to the Soviet Union.

(b) The commercial port of Dairen shall be internationalized, the pre-eminent interest of the Soviet Union in this port being safe-guarded and the lease of Port Arthur as a naval base of the Soviet Union restored.

(c) The Chinese Eastern Railway and the South Manchuria Rail-way, which provide an outlet to Dairen, shall be jointly operated by the establishment of a joint Soviet-Chinese company, it being understood that the pre-eminent interests of the Soviet Union shall be safeguarded and that China shall retain full sovereignty in Man-churia.

The Kurile Islands, a long chain of barren, volcanic islands extend-ing into the North Pacific northeast of Japan proper, were to be handed over to the Soviet Union. The *status quo* was to be preserved in Outer Mongolia, a huge, sparsely populated, arid region which the Soviet Union took over without formal annexation in 1924.

South Sakhalin (which had belonged to Russia until 1905) and the Kurile Islands might be regarded as war booty, to be taken from Japan. And China had no prospect of upsetting *de facto* Soviet rule of Outer Mongolia by its own strength. But the concessions which Roosevelt and Churchill made to Stalin in Manchuria were of fateful importance for China's independence and territorial integrity.

Manchuria, because of its natural wealth in coal, iron, soya beans, and other resources, and because of the large investment of Japanese capital and technical skill, intensified after 1931, was the most indus-trially developed part of China. To give a strong foreign power control over its railways, a predominant interest in its chief port, Dairen, and a naval base at Port Arthur was to sign away China's sovereignty in Man-churia.

And this was done not only without consulting China but without informing China. The Chinese Government was prevented from even discussing Soviet claims in the future. For, at Stalin's insistence, the agreement to satisfy his annexationist claims was put in writing and contained this decisive assurance:

"The Heads of the three Great Powers have agreed that these claims of the Soviet Union shall be unquestioningly fulfilled after Japan has been defeated."

In the opinion of former Ambassador William C. Bullitt "no more unnecessary, disgraceful and potentially disastrous document has ever been signed by a President of the United States."[9]

Severe as this judgment sounds, it has been borne out by the course of subsequent events. The Soviet intervention in the Far Eastern war was of no military benefit to the United States, because it took place only a few days before Japan surrendered. Politically this intervention was an unmitigated disaster.

During the Soviet occupation of Manchuria industrial equipment of an estimated value of two billion dollars was looted and carried off to Russia. This delayed for a long time any prospect of Chinese industrial self-sufficiency. As soon as Soviet troops occupied Manchuria, Chinese Communist forces, as if by a mysterious signal, began to converge on that area.

The Soviet military commanders shrewdly avoided direct, ostentatious co-operation with the Communists. After all, the Soviet Government had signed a treaty of friendship and alliance with the Nationalist Government of China on August 14, 1945. One clause of this treaty prescribed that "the Soviet Government is ready to render China moral support and assistance with military equipment and other material resources, this support and assistance to be given fully to the National Government as the central government of China."

This treaty was to prove about as valuable to the cosignatory as the nonaggression pacts which the Soviet Government concluded with Poland, Finland, Latvia, Lithuania, and Estonia. There is no indication that the Soviet Government gave the slightest "moral" or material support to the Chinese Nationalist Government. But Manchuria became an arsenal for the Chinese Communists, who were able to equip themselves with Japanese arms, obligingly stacked up for them by the Soviet occupation forces.

Soviet control of Dairen was used to block the use of this important port by Nationalist troops. Manchuria became the base from which the

9. See Mr. Bullitt's article in *Life* for October 13, 1947.

Chinese Communists could launch a campaign that led to the overrunning of almost all China.

Roosevelt's concessions at Yalta represented an abandonment of the historic policy of the United States in the Far East. This policy was in favor of the "open door," of equal commercial opportunity for all foreign nations, together with respect for Chinese independence. The American State Department had always been opposed to the "closed door" methods of Imperial Russia.

But at Yalta the "open door" was abandoned in a document that repeatedly referred to "the pre-eminent interests of the Soviet Union" in Manchuria. Those interests have now become pre-eminent in China. And the surrender of Manchuria to Stalin is not the least of the reasons for this development.

The Yalta concessions were a violation of the American pledge at Cairo that Manchuria should be restored to China. If New York State had been occupied by an enemy and was then handed back to the United States on condition that another alien power should have joint control of its railway systems, a predominant voice in the Port of New York Authority, and the right to maintain a naval base on Staten Island, most Americans would not feel that American sovereignty had been respected.

Whether considered from the standpoint of consistency with professed war aims or from the standpoint of serving American national interests, the record of Yalta is profoundly depressing. The large-scale alienation of Polish territory to the Soviet Union, of German territory to Poland, constituted an obvious and flagrant violation of the self-determination clauses of the Atlantic Charter. An offensive note of hypocrisy was added by inserting into the Yalta communiqué repeated professions of adherence to the Atlantic Charter.

The hopes of tens of millions of East Europeans for national independence and personal liberty were betrayed. The leaders of the Axis could scarcely have surpassed the cynicism of Roosevelt and Churchill in throwing over allies like Poland and China. The unwarranted concessions to Stalin in the Far East opened a Pandora's Box of troubles for the United States, the end of which has not yet been seen.

There was not one positive, worth-while contribution to European revival and stability in the sordid deals of Yalta, only imperialist power politics at its worst. The vindictive peace settlement, far worse than that of Versailles, which was being prepared promised little for European reconstruction. Roosevelt not long before had piously declared that "the German people are not going to be enslaved, because the United Nations do not traffic in human slavery."[10] But at Yalta he sanctioned the use of the slave labor of German war prisoners, a throwback to one of the most barbarous practices of antiquity.

The agreements, published and secret, concluded at Yalta are defended mainly on two grounds.[11] It is contended that military necessity forced the President to comply with Stalin's demands in Eastern Europe and East Asia. It is also argued that the source of difficulties in postwar Europe is to be found, not in the Yalta agreements, but in the Soviet failure to abide by these agreements.

Neither of these justifications stands up under serious examination. America in February 1945 was close to the peak of its military power. The atomic bomb still lay a few months in the future. But the United States possessed the most powerful navy in the world, the greatest aircraft production in quantity and quality, an army that, with its British and other allies, had swept the Germans from North Africa, France, Belgium, and much of Italy.

The lumbering Soviet offensive in the East was dependent in no small degree on lend-lease American trucks and communication equipment. There was, therefore, no good reason for approaching Stalin with an inferiority complex or for consenting to a Polish settlement which sacrificed the friends of the West in that country and paved the way for the establishment of a Soviet puppet regime.

No doubt Stalin could have imposed such a regime by force. Only the Red Army in February 1945 was in a position to occupy Poland. How much better the outlook would have been if Churchill's repeated

10. Roosevelt could scarcely have been altogether ignorant of the vast network of slave labor camps in the Soviet Union.

11. The three main sources of information about the Yalta conference are James F. Byrnes's *Speaking Frankly*, Robert E. Sherwood's *Roosevelt and Hopkins,* and Edward R. Stettinius's *Roosevelt and the Russians.* Sherwood's account is the liveliest, that of Stettinius the most detailed. All these authors have a defensive, apologetic attitude toward the conference.

prodding for action in the Balkans had been heeded, if the Polish Army of General Anders, battle-hardened in Italy, had been able to reach Poland ahead of the Red Army!

But there would have been a great difference between a Soviet stooge regime set up by the naked force of the Red Army and one strengthened by the acquiescence and endorsement of the western powers. The former would have enjoyed no shred of moral authority. As it was, nationalist guerrilla resistance to the made-in-Moscow government was prolonged and embittered. Many thousands of lives were lost on both sides before the satellite regime, with a good deal of Russian military and police aid, clamped down its rule more or less effectively over the entire country. How much stronger this resistance would have been if the United States and Great Britain had continued to recognize the government-in-exile and insisted on adequate guarantees of free and fair elections!

There was equally little reason to give in to Stalin's Far Eastern demands. The desire to draw the Soviet Union into this war was fatuous, from the standpoint of America's interest in a truly independent China. Apparently Roosevelt was the victim of some extremely bad intelligence work. He was given to understand that the Kwantung Army, the Japanese occupation force in Manchuria, was a formidable fighting machine, which might be used to resist the American invasion of the Japanese home islands which was planned for the autumn.

But the Kwantung Army offered no serious resistance to the Soviet invasion in August. It had evidently been heavily depleted in numbers and lowered in fighting quality.

Apologists for the Yalta concessions maintain that Japan in February 1945 presented the aspect of a formidable, unbeaten enemy. Therefore, so the argument runs, Roosevelt was justified in paying a price for Soviet intervention, in the interest of ending the war quickly and saving American lives.

But Japanese resistance to American air and naval attacks on its own coasts was already negligible. American warships were able to cruise along the shores of Japan, bombarding at will. According to an account later published by Arthur Krock, of the *New York Times*, an Air Force general presented a report at Yalta pointing to the complete undermining of the Japanese capacity to resist. But the mistaken and misleading view that Japan still possessed powerful military and naval force prevailed.

Acceptance of this view by Roosevelt was especially unwarranted, because two days before he left for Yalta Roosevelt received from General MacArthur a forty-page message outlining five unofficial Japanese peace overtures which amounted to an acceptance of unconditional surrender, with the sole reservation that the Emperor should be preserved. The other terms offered by the Japanese, who were responsible men, in touch with Emperor Hirohito, may be summarized as follows:

1. Complete surrender of all Japanese forces.
2. Surrender of all arms and munitions.
3. Occupation of the Japanese homeland and island possessions by Allied troops under American direction.
4. Japanese relinquishment of Manchuria, Korea, and Formosa, as well as all territory seized during the war.
5. Regulation of Japanese industry to halt present and future production of implements of war.
6. Turning over of any Japanese the United States might designate as war criminals.
7. Immediate release of all prisoners of war and internees in Japan and areas under Japanese control.

MacArthur recommended negotiations on the basis of the Japanese overtures. But Roosevelt brushed off this suggestion with the remark: "MacArthur is our greatest general and our poorest politician."

That the President, after receiving such a clear indication that Japan was on the verge of military collapse, should have felt it necessary to bribe Stalin into entering the Far Eastern war must surely be reckoned a major error of judgment, most charitably explained by Roosevelt's failing mental and physical powers.[12]

12. The story of the Japanese peace overtures is told in a dispatch from Washington by Walter Trohan, correspondent of the *Chicago Tribune* and the *Washington Times-Herald*. It appeared in these two newspapers on August 19, 1945. Previous publication had been withheld because of wartime censorship regulations. Mr. Trohan personally gave me the source of his information, a man of unimpeachable integrity, very high in the inner circle of Roosevelt's wartime advisers.

Captain Ellis M. Zacharias, Navy expert on Japan whose broadcasts in fluent Japanese hastened the surrender, asserts that intelligence reports indicating Japanese impending willingness to surrender were available at the time of the Yalta Conference.

One such report, communicated in the utmost secrecy to an American intelligence officer in a neutral capital, predicted the resignation of General Koiso as Premier in favor of the pacific Admiral Suzuki. The Admiral, in turn, according to the report, would turn over power to the Imperial Prince Higashi Kuni, who would possess sufficient authority and prestige, backed by a command from the Emperor, to arrange the surrender.

I am convinced that had this document, later proven to be correct in every detail, been brought to the attention of President Roosevelt and his military advisers, the war might have been viewed in a different light, both Iwo Jima and Okinawa might have been avoided, and different decisions could have been reached at Yalta.[13]

Zacharias also believes that if the Japanese had been given a precise definition of what America understood by unconditional surrender as late as June, or even at the end of July 1945, both Soviet intervention and the dropping of atomic bombs on Hiroshima and Nagasaki could have been averted.[14]

Certainly there was a hopeful alternative to the policy, so disastrous in its results, of encouraging and bribing the Soviet Union to enter the Far Eastern picture. This was to aim at a quick peace with Japan, before the Soviet armies could have been transferred from the West to the East. There is every reason to believe that such a peace was attainable, if the Japanese had been assured of the right to keep the Emperor and perhaps given some assurance that their commercial interests in Manchuria and Korea would not be entirely wiped out.

There is little weight in the contention that the Yalta agreements, in themselves, were excellent, if the Soviet Government had only lived up to them. These agreements grossly violated the Atlantic Charter by assigning Polish territory to the Soviet Union and German territory to

13. Zacharias, *Secret Missions,* 335.
14. Ibid., 367–68.

Poland without plebiscites. They violated the most elementary rules of humanity and civilized warfare by sanctioning slave labor as "reparations." And the whole historic basis of American foreign policy in the Far East was upset by the virtual invitation to Stalin to take over Japan's former exclusive and dominant role in Manchuria.

There was certainly no reason for self-congratulation on the part of any of the western representatives at Yalta. But human capacity for self-deception is strong. According to Robert E. Sherwood, "the mood of the American delegates, including Roosevelt and Hopkins, could be described as one of supreme exultation as they left Yalta."[15] And Hopkins later told Sherwood:

> We really believed in our hearts that this was the dawn of the new day we had all been praying for and talking about for so many years. We were absolutely certain that we had won the first great victory of the peace—and by "we," I mean *all* of us, the whole civilized human race. The Russians had proved that they could be reasonable and farseeing and there wasn't any doubt in the minds of the President or any of us that we could live with them and get along with them peacefully for as far into the future as any of us could imagine.[16]

A chorus of hallelujahs went up from the less perspicacious politicians and publicists in the United States. Raymond Gram Swing perhaps took first prize for unqualified enthusiasm. He said: "No more appropriate news could be conceived to celebrate the birthday of Abraham Lincoln." William L. Shirer saw in Yalta "a landmark in human history." Senator Alben Barkley pronounced it "one of the most important steps ever taken to promote peace and happiness in the world." In the face of such authoritative declarations the suicides of scores of "unknown Polish soldiers" in Italy, desperate over the betrayal of their country, received little attention.

However, the honeymoon mood inspired by the first news of Yalta did not last long. The ink on the agreements was scarcely dry when there were two serious and flagrant violations: one in Rumania, one in Poland. It had been formally agreed at Yalta that the three big powers

15. Sherwood, *Roosevelt and Hopkins,* 869.
16. Ibid., 870.

should "concert their policies in assisting the peoples liberated from the domination of Nazi Germany and the peoples of the former Axis satellite states to solve by democratic means their pressing political and economic problems." The three governments were "to jointly assist the peoples in these states in such matters as establishing conditions of internal peace and forming interim governmental authorities." And there was to be immediate consultation on "the measures necessary to discharge the joint responsibilities set forth in this declaration."

The Kremlin decided to get rid of the government of General Radescu, set up after Rumania had turned against Germany, and to replace it with a regime subservient to Moscow. Rejecting and ignoring repeated American proposals for three-power consultation on the question, the Soviet Government sent Deputy Foreign Minister Andrei Vishinsky to Bucharest on February 27. Vishinsky stormed and bullied until the young Rumanian King Michael dismissed Radescu and appointed the Soviet-designated Prime Minister, Petru Groza. The Soviet envoy's methods of persuasion varied from slamming a door in the royal palace so hard that the plaster cracked to threatening the King that it would be impossible to guarantee the further existence of Rumania as an independent state if Groza were not appointed.

The King yielded, and Rumania was started on the road to complete Communist dictatorship. When the American Ambassador in Moscow, Averell Harriman, proposed that a three-power committee be set up in Bucharest to implement the Yalta resolution on consultation, Molotov's rejection was prompt and blunt. This was typical of the Soviet attitude not only in Rumania, but in all countries under Red Army occupation.

Meanwhile the Soviet Government was delaying and sabotaging the creation of a new government in Poland. Stalin and Molotov interpreted the Yalta agreement on this point (the phrasing was loose and elastic) to mean that no Pole distasteful to the Provisional Government (made up of handpicked Soviet candidates) should be eligible for membership in the new government.

And the Provisional Government authorities, backed up by Soviet military and police power, were rapidly making the Yalta promise of "free unfettered elections" an empty mockery. There were numerous arbitrary arrests. Freedom of the press was nonexistent. The historic

Polish parties were dissolved and replaced by pro-Communist groups which stole their names. In order to conceal the reign of terror that was going on, foreigners were systematically excluded from Poland. There was long delay even in admitting representatives of UNRRA, interested in working out a program to meet the country's urgent need for food, clothing, and other relief supplies.[17]

Toward the end of March, Churchill warned Roosevelt that the Yalta agreement on Poland was clearly breaking down. The President on March 27 informed Churchill that he too "had been watching with anxiety and concern the development of the Soviet attitude since Yalta."[18] Along with this message he sent the draft of a proposed communication to Stalin.

This communication, sent to Moscow on April 1, was phrased in sharper terms than Roosevelt had been accustomed to use in exchanges with the Soviet dictator. Perhaps by this time the President had realized that personal charm and an avoidance of unpleasant subjects do not constitute an unfailing formula for diplomatic success.

Roosevelt in this telegram expressed concern over the development of events. He regretted the "lack of progress made in the carrying out, which the world expects, of the political decisions which we reached at Yalta, particularly those relating to the Polish question." The President emphasized that "any solution which would result in a thinly disguised continuation of the present government would be entirely unacceptable and would cause our people to regard the Yalta agreement as a failure."

Roosevelt urged that American and British representatives be permitted to visit Poland. If there was no successful co-operation in solving the Polish question, he warned, "all the difficulties and dangers to Allied unity will face us in an even more acute form." The President also referred to Rumania, suggesting that developments there fell within the terms of the Yalta declaration on liberated areas and requesting Stalin to examine personally the diplomatic exchanges which had taken place on this subject.[19]

17. Further details of the disregard of the Yalta assurances on Poland are contained in Chapter 11.
18. Byrnes, *Speaking Frankly*, 54.
19. Ibid., 54–55.

Stalin's reply, dispatched on April 7, offered no satisfaction. It contested Roosevelt's interpretation of Yalta and flatly refused to permit the sending of American and British observers to Poland—on the ground that the Poles would consider this an insult to their national dignity! Apparently Stalin felt no corresponding squeamish fear of insulting Polish national dignity by filling high posts in the Polish Army and police with Russian agents, some of whom could not even speak Polish.

Roosevelt and Churchill decided to send a new joint message to Stalin. While this was in preparation Roosevelt died. News of the treacherous arrest of fifteen Polish underground leaders could scarcely have strengthened his confidence in Stalin's good faith and good will. And even before the sharp exchanges on the Polish question, this confidence had been shaken by another incident.

About the middle of March, there was a preliminary meeting in Berne of American, British, and German military representatives to arrange for the surrender of the German armies in Italy, under the command of Marshal Kesselring. The Soviet Government had been informed of this development, and Molotov had expressed a desire to send Red Army officers to take part in the discussions. The Chiefs of Staff informed Molotov that nothing would be done at Berne, except to make preparations for a further meeting at Allied headquarters in Caserta, in Italy. This elicited from Moscow a sharp reply, refusing to send military representatives and "insisting" that the "negotiations" be stopped.

Roosevelt personally assured Stalin that no negotiations had taken place and that the Soviet Government would be kept fully informed of further developments. Then Stalin sent a message which Roosevelt took to heart very deeply as an insult to his integrity and loyalty to the alliance. Stalin declared that Roosevelt had been misinformed by his military advisers. According to Red Army intelligence reports, Stalin continued, a deal had been struck with Kesselring. The front would be opened to the American Army, and Germany would be granted easier peace terms in exchange.

These allegations are devoid of any shadow of probability. American policy toward Germany had been based on rigid adherence to the unconditional surrender formula and avoidance of any step that would have remotely suggested separate dealing with Germany.

Roosevelt's hurt feelings found reflection in a reply which expressed "deep resentment" over "the vile misrepresentations of Stalin's informers." The President intimated that these informers wished to destroy the friendly relations between the two countries.

The friction over the Polish and Rumanian issues and over Stalin's insinuations of American bad faith were shrouded in secrecy at the time. This friction is now a matter of record and seems to dispose of a favorite thesis of Soviet sympathizers. This is that American-Soviet relations were invariably smooth and friendly during Roosevelt's lifetime and only began to deteriorate after his death. The evidence indicates that this is not the case, that Roosevelt was hurt and offended by what he regarded as a betrayal of the Yalta assurances, and had he lived, he would quite probably have shifted America's policy more quickly than Truman felt able to do.

Two well-known American journalists who saw Roosevelt separately in the last weeks of his life agree that he was both discouraged and indignant over what he regarded as breach of faith and lack of cooperative spirit on the Soviet side. He was considering, according to their reports, a fundamental re-examination of American policy toward the Soviet Union.

What Roosevelt would have done, had he lived longer, is a matter of conjecture. He left an unhappy legacy in foreign relations to his successor, who was without personal knowledge and experience in this field. So secretive and personal had been Roosevelt's diplomacy that for some time it was impossible for the new Chief Executive to get a clear picture of what assurances had been given to foreign governments, of what diplomatic IOU's were outstanding.

Mr. Truman was not predisposed in favor of appeasement and cherished no sentimental sympathy with communism. He gradually eliminated from his Administration extreme New Dealers and fellow travelers. But in the first months of office his hands were tied, partly by inexperience, partly because of reluctance to give the impression that Roosevelt's friendly policy was being reversed. If a frank public statement setting forth the points at issue had been made, American public opinion would have been better prepared to support the government in a firmer attitude toward Moscow. But the feeling that nothing should disturb the outward show of harmony prevailed. Only an initiated few knew how sharp was the tone of the communications which had been passing between Washington and London and Moscow.

After Roosevelt's death Churchill tried his hand at winning Stalin by a personal appeal. He sent a letter on April 29, in the last days of the war in Europe, addressing the Soviet Premier as "my friend" and begging him "not to underrate the divergences which are opening about matters which you may think are small, but which are symbolic of the way the English-speaking democracies look at life."[20]

In this letter Churchill declared that "we in Great Britain will not work for or tolerate a Polish government unfriendly to Russia," but added:

Neither could we recognize a Polish Government that did not truly correspond to the description in our joint declaration at Yalta, with proper regard for the rights of the individual as we understand these matters in the western world. . . .

There is not much comfort in looking into a future where you and the countries you dominate, plus the Communist parties in many other States, are all drawn up on one side, and those who rallied to the English-speaking nations and their associates or dominions are on the other. It is quite obvious that their quarrel would tear the world to pieces, and all of us, leading men on either side, who had anything to do with that would be shamed before history.

But neither this letter nor Roosevelt's earlier note moved Stalin one iota from his grand design of conquering as much of Europe as he could by the device of setting up not friendly, but vassal governments, run by obedient local Communists. The desire to keep up the pretense of friendship and co-operation with the Soviet Union caused the American and British Governments to neglect valuable political opportunities in the last weeks of the war. Churchill emphasized this point with regret in a speech of October 9, 1948.

The gulf which was opening between Asiatic Communist Russia and the western democracies, large and small, was already brutally obvious to the victorious War Cabinet of the national coalition

20. Churchill made the contents of this letter public in Parliament on December 10, 1948. See *The* (London) *Times*, December 11, 1948, p. 2.

even before Hitler was destroyed and the Germans laid down their arms. . . .

It would have been wiser and more prudent to have allowed the British Army to enter Berlin, as it could have done, and for the United States armored divisions to have entered Prague, which was a matter almost of hours.

Churchill was not speaking with the insight of hindsight. He had pressed for action of this kind when it was feasible. After the western armies had crossed the Rhine and enveloped the Ruhr Basin in March 1945, Eisenhower worked out a plan for the final blow at the collapsing German resistance and communicated this plan to Stalin. The Soviet Generalissimo was doubtless pleased. For Eisenhower left Berlin to the Russians and proposed to advance across central Germany, with flanking moves to the north, to cut off Denmark, and to the south, aimed at Austria.

Churchill, according to Eisenhower,[21] was disturbed and disappointed because the plan did not call for a rapid sweep to Berlin ahead of the Russians by the British army on the left wing, under command of Field Marshal Montgomery. Churchill also felt that Eisenhower's message to Stalin exceeded his authority to communicate with the Soviet ruler only on military matters.

Eisenhower was profoundly innocent in high politics. He probably did not know what a serious cleavage had developed since Yalta. So, when Marshall communicated Churchill's criticisms to him, he replied with complete disregard of political considerations:

"May I point out that Berlin itself is no longer a particularly important objective. Its usefulness to the German has been largely destroyed and even his government is preparing to move to another area."[22]

Eisenhower argues in his memoirs that the capture of Berlin or any other advance beyond the agreed line of demarcation with the Soviet forces was immaterial, because the American and British forces would have to be pulled back anyway. A demarcation line very unfavorable to the western powers and agreed on in the European Advisory Commis-

21. Churchill, *Crusade in Europe*, 399.
22. Ibid., 401.

sion, where America was ineptly represented by Ambassador John G. Winant, had been ratified at Yalta. Almost half of Germany was assigned to Soviet occupation.

Eisenhower is convinced in retrospect that the western allies could probably have obtained an agreement to occupy more of Germany.[23] Despite his refusal to press for Berlin, despite his acceptance of an urgent Soviet request not to let American troops move on to Prague, western troops were far to the east of the agreed demarcation line when the fighting stopped with the German surrender on May 8. A considerable area in Saxony and Thuringia was evacuated and handed over to the Russians.

Eisenhower's view that the United States Government should stand by its bargain,[24] even though it proved to be a bad one on the demarcation line, would have been quite reasonable if the Soviet Government had carried out its obligations. But this important condition was not fulfilled. In the short interval of time between the Yalta Conference and the German surrender, there had been repeated Soviet violations of the Yalta agreements.

There would, therefore, have been full moral and political justification for checking Stalin's designs. Berlin and Prague would have been invaluable pawns for this purpose.

Suppose American and British troops had occupied both these cities and the intervening German and Czechoslovak territory. Suppose that the American and British Governments had then dispatched a joint note to the Kremlin, intimating that these troops would be withdrawn when, and only when, "free and unfettered elections" had been held in Poland and other violations of the Yalta agreement had been made good.

It is most improbable that Stalin would have risked a new war against the comparatively fresh American and British armies, backed as these were by the enormous productive power of American industry. He would have been forced to choose between loosening his grip on Poland and seeing almost all Germany and the capital of Czechoslo-

23. Ibid., 474.
24. It was not merely a question of Eisenhower's personal view. The President and the War and State departments seem to have concurred.

vakia, most industrialized of the East European states, pass under western influence and control. Whichever horn of the dilemma he might have chosen, the western position in the impending cold war would have been immensely strengthened.

But this precious opportunity, enhanced because the Germans were eager to surrender to the western powers, rather than to the Russians, was allowed to slip by unused. Churchill might have possessed the vision and audacity to seize it. But Churchill's voice was not decisive. The men who were in the seats of authority in Washington were still prisoners of the disastrous illusions which had dominated Roosevelt's wartime policy toward Russia. So the Soviet Union was able to overrun Germany up to the Elbe and, in places, beyond the Elbe. Czechoslovakia was made ripe for the Communist coup d'état of February 1948, for the disillusioned death of Beneš and the pathetic suicide (or murder) of Jan Masaryk, after both had done their utmost to get along with the Kremlin.

There was a feeble attempt to use the American occupation of territory beyond the agreed demarcation line as a bargaining counter for satisfactory conditions of joint occupation in Berlin, located deep in the Soviet zone. There was an exchange of communications between Truman and Stalin on this subject on June 14 and 16. Truman stated that the American troops would be withdrawn to the agreed line when the military commanders had reached a satisfactory agreement, assuring road, rail, and air access to Berlin to the western powers.

An agreement was worked out on June 29. But the ability of the Soviet military authorities to impose a blockade upon the western sectors of Berlin in 1948 shows that it could scarcely be considered satisfactory. There were provisions for an air corridor for western planes and for a single railway line and a highway from Magdeburg to Berlin to be placed at the disposal of the non-Russian occupation powers.

It was characteristic of Winant's woolgathering methods in negotiation that he never raised in the European Advisory Commission the question of providing a corridor, under western military control, to insure rail and road communications with Berlin. General Lucius D. Clay, Eisenhower's deputy, tried to get a corridor stipulation written into the final military agreement. But Soviet Marshal Zhukov flatly refused. The subsequent necessity of resorting to the expensive airlift in order to thwart the Soviet blockade was part of the price of this excessive confidence in the goodness of Soviet intentions.

Stalin got his way on every important European postwar issue, with one exception. This was the disposition of the port of Trieste. Some of Tito's Partisans forced their way into that city together with a New Zealand unit which belonged to the Allied forces in Italy, under the command of Marshal Sir Harold Alexander. The Partisans created a reign of terror. Thousands of Trieste citizens who were obnoxious to them disappeared, to be seen no more. But they were not allowed to take over the city. Marshal Alexander gave out this challenging statement:

> Our policy, publicly proclaimed, is that territorial changes should be made only after thorough study and after full consultation and deliberation between the various governments concerned.
>
> It is, however, Marshal Tito's apparent intention to establish his claims by force of arms and military occupation. Action of this kind would be all too reminiscent of Hitler, Mussolini and Japan. It is to prevent such action that we have been fighting this war.

The American and British Governments backed up Alexander, and Tito finally withdrew his forces. Trieste, with its 70 per cent Italian population, was preserved as one of the outposts of the West in a Europe that was becoming increasingly divided by the line of the iron curtain.

Roosevelt in the last weeks of his life was certainly shaken, if not altogether disillusioned, in his great expectations of Stalin's co-operation. But Harry Hopkins seems to have remained naive and self-deluded to the bitter end. On this point we have the testimony of a sketchy memorandum which he wrote in August 1945, shortly before his death.

> We know or believe that Russia's interests, so far as we can anticipate them, do not afford an opportunity for a major difference with us in foreign affairs. We believe we are mutually dependent upon each other for economic reasons. We find the Russians as individuals easy to deal with.[25] The Russians undoubtedly like the American people. They like the United States. . . .

25. This was emphatically not the impression of General Deane and of the great majority of other Americans who had to deal with Soviet officials.

The Soviet Union is made up of 180 million hardworking proud people. They are not an uncivilized people. They are a tenacious, determined people, who think just like [*sic*] you and I do.[26]

The secretary of some branch of the Council of American-Soviet Friendship could scarcely have pronounced a judgment more dismally lacking in intelligent anticipation of the shape of things to come. And this man, as ignorant of foreign languages as of history and political and economic theory, was, after Roosevelt, the main architect of America's disastrous foreign policy.

There were trained and experienced foreign service officials who saw the situation far more realistically. Joseph C. Grew, Undersecretary of State during the first months of 1945, wrote his views on the growing Russian danger in a remarkably prescient memorandum in May 1945. Arthur Bliss Lane fought gallantly and consistently for justice to Poland. Loy Henderson and George Kennan never succumbed to the trend in favor of blindly trusting Stalin and appeasing him at any cost.

Unfortunately the judgments and recommendations of these trained experts were often brushed aside. Roosevelt preferred the opinions of his court favorites, inexperienced amateurs, dilettantes, wishful thinkers. It is, after all, not difficult to be a wishful thinker on a subject of which one has no real knowledge.

The war ended with the unconditional surrender of the Axis powers. But the realization of this vainglorious Casablanca slogan did not usher in the reign of assured peace, international justice, and all the humane virtues which the more imaginative evangelists of intervention had so confidently prophesied. What followed the world's worst war was the world's most dismal inability to achieve any kind of peace settlement. Indeed, five years after the end of the fighting, there was no formal peace at all, only the shadow of another war. There is the measure of the failure of America's Second Crusade.

26. Sherwood, *Roosevelt and Hopkins*, 922–23.

# 10

## Wartime Illusions and Delusions

One might have supposed that an alert public opinion would have warded off some of the moral inconsistencies and political blunders which have been described in preceding chapters. Of course, complete freedom of speech is never maintained in time of war. Father Coughlin's magazine, *Social Justice*, for example, was harassed into extinction. There were a few convictions for sedition, notably of some members of a Trotskyite group in Minneapolis and of a few obscure and politically illiterate anti-Semitic fanatics.

But there was fair latitude for discussion during the war. Critics and skeptics were not handled as ruthlessly as they were under the Espionage Act in World War I. What was lacking in most molders of public opinion was not the physical ability to speak out, but the perception and the moral courage to take advantage of the freedom which existed.

America's wartime intellectual climate was a depressing compound of profound factual ignorance, naïveté, wishful thinking, and emotional hysteria. All this played into the hands of a small number of individuals who consciously placed loyalty to the Kremlin above all other considerations.

That the aims of the Soviet Government were above suspicion and reproach, that Russia had been wronged by the democracies in the past, that Soviet communism was just another form of democracy—these and similar ideas were constantly proclaimed under the most respectable auspices. They became the stock-in-trade of influential lecturers and radio commentators. Governors, judges, clergymen, and other eminent citizens joined Communist-front organizations.

Rapprochement with Russia, without raising any inconvenient questions, was the "party line" of the Roosevelt Administration. Under these circumstances infiltration of strategic government agencies by fanatical Soviet sympathizers encountered no difficulty. They were welcomed as fellow laborers in the vineyard.[1]

Some of this American wartime psychology was a product of sympathy for the achievements of the Red Army in fighting off the Wehrmacht. But its full scope and intensity are only understandable if one remembers that sympathy with communism had long been an occupational disease of many American intellectuals, not of the majority, of course, but of a very active and articulate minority.

One heard much before and during the war of Hitler's fifth column in America. But when there were attempts to expose this supposedly formidable threat to American national unity, one got only the names of a few obscure crackpots of whom the vast majority of Americans had never heard. It would have been impossible for an avowed Nazi sympathizer to have published an article in a magazine of national circulation or to have delivered regular radio broadcasts.

The rejection of nazism and fascism by educated Americans was prompt, vigorous, and very nearly unanimous. Unfortunately this was not true with respect to communism. Ever since I left Moscow in 1934, with what seemed to me natural and human reactions to the slave-labor system, the liquidation of the kulaks, the man-made famine, the routine regime of espionage and terror, I have been surprised and dismayed by the curious double standard of morals which some Americans who regard themselves as liberals or radicals practice in regard to Soviet communism. Denunciation of Nazi and Fascist acts of cruelty and oppression was vigorous and justified in these circles. There was a laudable desire to cure imperfections and injustices in the American social order.

But when it was a question of feeling the normal reactions of civilized human beings to Soviet atrocities, these American Leftists simply flunked the most elementary moral tests. They either ignored indisputable evidence of these atrocities or swallowed the crudest propaganda

1. The best and most vivid picture of this side of America's wartime life is to be found in a novel, *The Grand Design*, by John Dos Passos. No future historian of the period can afford to overlook this revealing book.

apologetics, the kind of apologetics which they would have been the first to ridicule if the source had been Nazi or Fascist.

One had the spectacle, at once pitiful and ridiculous, of intellectuals bowing before the shrine of a dictatorship that had stripped the intellectual in Russia of his last shred of independence and self-respect, that enforced conformity by the most inquisitorial means. Individuals who quivered with indignation over occasional violations of civil liberties in the United States sang the praises of a regime which recognized no civil liberties whatever.

Some ministers of religions prostrated themselves in genuflections before a system which was not only dogmatically atheistic, but which was profoundly immoral in theory, and still more so in practice. Artists, playwrights, writers, musicians, whose knowledge of Russian language and history and Communist theory and practice was usually limited, to say the least—such people developed a habit of tossing off cocksure blanket endorsements of the wholesale death sentences meted out in Soviet political trials. "Hooray for Murder" is the appropriate phrase of Eugene Lyons.[2]

These tireless signers of Stalinite manifestoes experienced one letdown that might well have cured them of the habit. An initiating committee of ten persons, Corliss Lamont, Dorothy Brewster, Dashiell Hammett, George Marshall,[3] Professor Walter Rautenstrauch, Vincent Sheean, Donald Ogden Stewart, Maxwell Stewart, Rebecca Timbers, and Mary Van Kleeck, persuaded some four hundred individuals of more or less distinction in the intellectual world to sign an open letter. This document denied "the fantastic falsehood" that Russia could have anything in common with Germany. "The Soviet Union," which the signers confidently affirmed, "continues as always to be a consistent bulwark against war and aggression," suddenly marched into Poland, Finland, and the Baltic states. Stalin and Molotov began to exchange greetings and toasts with Hitler and Ribbentrop.

This produced temporary demoralization in the fellow-traveler camp

2. Lyons's book, *The Red Decade,* in which this phrase occurs, contains massive documentation on the extent of Communist influence in American intellectual circles during the decade before the war.

3. Not the famous general of the same name.

and worked a few permanent cures. But the ground lost by Soviet propaganda during the period of Nazi-Soviet collaboration was more than made up when Hitler invaded Russia. People of all shades of thought, from hundred per cent Communist addicts to individuals who knew little or nothing about the subject, joined the chorus hailing the Soviet Union as a gallant ally whose good faith and good intentions were not to be questioned.

A leading exponent of the "Russia can do no wrong" theory was Henry A. Wallace, Vice-President of the United States during Roosevelt's third term. Wallace also headed two alphabetical wartime agencies, SPAB and BEW (Supply, Priorities and Allocations Board and Board of Economic Warfare). In the turgid writings and hysterical oratory of Henry Wallace one can find all the characteristic illusions of America's Second Crusade. There is the naive assurance that the struggle is between absolute good and absolute evil. There is the confident assumption that Soviet imperialism and international communism would present no difficulties after the end of the war. There is the vague, comforting, inane belief that the common man, whoever he may be, is on the march, that a better life is somehow being born out of an orgy of ruin and destruction.

Wallace's ideology and his peculiar English style have been amusingly and accurately analyzed as follows:

Wallaceland is the mental habitat of Henry Wallace, plus a few hundred thousand regular readers of the *New Republic,* the *Nation* and *PM.* It is a region of perpetual fogs, caused by the warm winds of the liberal Gulf Stream coming into contact with the Soviet glacier. Its natives speak Wallese, a debased provincial dialect.

Wallese is as rigidly formalized as Mandarin Chinese. The Good people are described by ritualistic adjectives, "forward-looking," "freedom-loving," "clear-thinking" and, of course, "democratic" and "progressive." The Bad people are always "reactionaries" or "Red-baiters"; there are surprisingly few of them, considering the power they wield, and they are perversely wicked, since their *real* interests would best be served by the Progressive and Realistic policies favored by the Good people.[4]

4. MacDonald, *Henry Wallace,* 48.

Wallace is a man of many interests. He discovered a resistant type of hybrid corn and won a more dubious notoriety as the reputed author of the "Guru" letters. These letters, signed HAW, H. A. Wallace, Galahad, and also with a cabalistic sign, were addressed to Nicholas Roerich. The latter was a Russian painter, explorer, and dabbler in occult beliefs, with whom Wallace was intimately acquainted.

The letters refer to President Roosevelt as The Flaming One and to Cordell Hull as The Sour One.[5] Churchill is The Roaring Lion, and Russia The Tiger. This is a sample of the intellectual content of these strange epistles:

"I have been thinking of you holding the casket, the sacred, most precious casket. And I have thought of the new country going forth to meet the seven stars under the sign of the three stars. And I have thought of the admonition: 'Await the stone.'"[6]

Wallace has never specifically claimed or repudiated the authorship of the Guru letters. But there is no question that he delivered his "quart of milk" speech at a meeting of the Free World Association in New York on May 8, 1942. In this speech one can find every illusion and delusion of America's Second Crusade, flamboyantly packaged in evangelical, mystical oratory:

"This is a fight between a free world and a slave world," Wallace began, conveniently forgetting about the millions of slaves in Soviet concentration camps. "The peoples," he continued, "are on the march toward even fuller freedom than the most fortunate peoples of the world have hitherto enjoyed." This could hardly be considered an accurate forecast of postwar conditions behind the Iron Curtain. Then the orator, intoxicated with his flights of fantasy, proceeded to utter perhaps the crowning absurdity of the speech:

"The object of this war is to make sure that everybody in the world has the privilege of drinking a quart of milk a day."

So, out of a war of unprecedented destruction, certain to lower, not

---

5. As one learns from his *Memoirs*, Hull was frequently irritated by the interference of Wallace's Board of Economic Warfare with what the Secretary regarded as the proper functions of the State Department.

6. Wallace's Cabinet colleague, Henry Morgenthau, Jr., reports in a magazine article that Wallace got the Great Pyramid printed on the currency of the United States in the belief that it possessed some mystical value.

raise the living standards of the vanquished and of many of the victors as well, there was to gush, by some miracle, an endless stream of free milk. Wallace insisted that the peace must mean a better standard of living not only in the Allied countries, but in Germany, Japan, and Italy.

This aspiration was generous and humane, if heavily tinged with wishful thinking. But Wallace never uttered a word of audible protest against the Morgenthau Plan and other destructionist schemes which made a mockery and an hypocrisy of the Atlantic Charter promises of a higher all-round standard of living. And when American policy toward Germany became saner and more constructive, Wallace's was one of the loudest voices raised in opposition.

The mental level of the "quart of milk" speech may be judged from the following excerpts:

> Satan is turned loose upon the world. . . . Through the leaders of the Nazi revolution Satan now is trying to lead the common man of the whole world back into slavery and darkness. . . . Satan has turned loose upon us the insane. . . . The Goetterdaemmerung has come for Odin and his crew. . . . We shall cleanse the plague spot of Europe, which is Hitler's Germany, and with it the hell-hole of Asia—Japan. No compromise with Satan is possible.

This hysterical outburst elevated Wallace to the status of a major prophet in America's Second Crusade. He stumped the world like a modern Peter the Hermit. He visited eastern Siberia, where the percentage of slave labor is highest in the world,[7] and told the gaping citizens of Irkutsk that only free men could live in these free open spaces. He gave the benefit of his mystical lore to Chiang Kai-shek in Chungking. He dashed down to Latin America and lectured perplexed statesmen on the necessity of developing close relations with the Soviet Union and ushering in the century of the common man.

It is reasonable to assume that Communists and Communist sympathizers found a hearty welcome in any agency where Wallace was influ-

---

7. One finds abundant and detailed proof of this statement in *Soviet Gold,* by Vladimir Petrov, a Russian who escaped from the Soviet Union after serving a sentence of several years in the slave-labor camps of eastern Siberia.

ential, for he pronounced the judgment on one occasion that the "few Communists" he knew had been very good Americans.

If Wallace was a major prophet, Wendell Willkie may be considered a minor prophet of the wartime era. After a swift flight around the globe and brief visits to Russia, China, and countries of the Near and Middle East, the former Republican candidate published a quickly written political travelogue entitled *One World*.

Willkie found that the war was, "in Mr. Stalin's phrase, a war of liberation." Russia, he assured his readers, would neither eat us nor seduce us. Without benefit of knowledge of the Russian language, he brought back the news that Russians exchange ideas in private conversation almost as freely as we do. And he offered the following blueprint for peace:

> To win the peace three things seem to me necessary. First, we must plan for peace now on a world basis; second, the world must be free, politically and economically, for nations and men, that peace may exist in it; third, America must play an active, constructive part in freeing it and keeping its peace.[8]

These were resounding generalities. But they meant little unless there was some spelling out in terms of frontier settlements and definitions of freedom. But all Willkie and most other wartime writers and speakers could offer in this connection was more, and vaguer, generalities. The following passage in *One World* is a good example:

> When I say that peace must be planned on a world basis, I mean quite literally that it must embrace the earth. Continents and oceans are plainly only parts of a whole, seen, as I have seen them, from the air. England and America are parts. Russia and China, Egypt, Syria and Turkey, Iraq and Iran are also parts and it is inescapable that there can be no peace for any part of the world unless the foundations of peace are made secure through all parts of the world.[9]

What Willkie and other "one-worlders" never perceived through the fog of platitudes in which they liked to envelop themselves was the tre-

8. Willkie, *One World*, 176.
9. Ibid.

mendous, fundamental cleavage which western civilization sustained as a result of the emergence of totalitarianism after World War I. Technologically, to be sure, conditions for closer world unity had been created.

But political and cultural barriers had risen faster than the speed of airplanes had increased. There was far more opportunity for unhampered travel, although by slower means of communication, before the First World War than one found either before or after the Second. There were infinitely more possibilities of cultural communion between Russian, German, Polish, British, French, and American scholars and intellectuals before the chilly blasts of totalitarian thought control blew over the European continent.

There was probably less preaching of primitive hatred during the Second Crusade than during the First. Americans were a little ashamed in retrospect of such emotional indulgences as "goddamning" the Kaiser, banning Beethoven, and likening "Huns" to snakes. There were lapses, to be sure. Admiral William ("Bull") Halsey let out enough bloodthirsty yawps to have earned himself a prime rating as a "war criminal" if his country had been on the losing side. *Collier's* produced this racist masterpiece:

> Suppose the ape race should suddenly find itself armed with all the modern appliances of human war—tanks, planes, machine-guns, etc. and should become imbued with a hatred for the human race. We could expect a fight like the fight now being waged on us under the tutelage of the Nazis. . . . This is a war between humans and subhumans for the mastery of the earth.
>
> PS. The above remarks are made with apologies to the apes.

This is an exhibit of intellectual war profiteering which is just as familiar and just as obnoxious as the financial type. Writers of mediocre detective stories and specialists in literary criticism transformed themselves overnight into "authorities" on German and Japanese history, politics, economics, and psychology. The ranks of the intellectual war profiteers were swelled by eccentric poets, would-be philosophical moralists, ex–sports writers who professed to know all the answers in European politics, and some college professors.

Emerging blinking from their ivory towers of specialized knowledge, these men of learning often proved the most naive, gullible, and confused of commentators on the world tragedy that was being played before their eyes. The Stork Club was a familiar rendezvous where hymns of hate were intoned to an accompaniment of popping corks. And some suburban noncombatant readers of the *New York Herald Tribune* developed extreme bloodthirstiness in their letters to that newspaper.

However, the besetting weakness of most educated Americans who discussed war issues was not vindictiveness, but rather a kind of straw-chopping futility. Scores of individuals and many groups under the auspices of churches and universities worked out unimpeachable schemes for "just and durable peace," based on the ideals of the Atlantic Charter.

But when the Atlantic Charter pledges of self-determination and equality of economic opportunity were most obviously and crudely violated, voices of protest were few and timid. The Yalta agreement and the Morgenthau Plan and the Potsdam agreement were complete repudiations of the Atlantic Charter. Yet, despite all the well-meant efforts to lay the bases of "just and durable peace," there was little public criticism.

The typical American planner of the postwar international order lived in a curious dual world. He was prolific in schemes for human improvement, full of high-sounding if vague idealistic phraseology. But this seldom led him to take a clear stand against schemes of indiscriminate vengeance and unprincipled annexation.

An appalling amount of ignorant misinformation about Russia was circulated in America during the war. Apart from deliberate Communist propaganda, there was much hasty writing and speaking on the basis of imperfect or inaccurate knowledge. A widely syndicated journalist, for instance, gave the following picture of Stalin's childhood environment:

"He was born in a tribal society in the remote Caucasian mountains. . . . His tribe was ruled by feudal princes. . . . In his childhood the masses of the people of Greater Russia were serfs who could be beaten by their masters and even sold from one landowner to another."

This was a pure flight of fictional fancy. Stalin was born not in some remote mountain fastness where tribal customs prevailed, but in the town of Gori. He owed no allegiance to any "feudal prince." And serfdom was abolished in the Russian Empire in 1861, eighteen years before Stalin was born. The same columnist endorsed the declaration of Brendan Bracken, British Minister of Information, that "Soviet Russia has never broken its word." Yet the breach of nonaggression pacts with Poland, Finland, Latvia, Lithuania, and Estonia was surely a matter of public record.

One finds a medley of grotesque errors in Emil Ludwig's wartime book *Stalin*, of which the following sentence is a sample:

"One half of all arable land—some people estimated it at 70%— belonged to a few hundred great lords, the Tsar and the Church; the rest was divided among sixteen million peasant families, owning an average of six to eight acres."

As a matter of factual record the nonpeasant land-owning class in prewar Russia was composed of some 200,000 country gentry, not of "a few hundred great lords." The Russian nobility in 1914 owned less than a quarter of the amount of land in possession of the peasants. The average size of the peasant holding in 1905 was 28 acres.

Similar examples of gross inaccuracy could be multiplied indefinitely. I made a collection of a few dozen which appeared in print over a short period of time. A research bureau could have filled a book with specimens of factual blunders in writing about Russia. Some of this was the result of ignorance, carelessness, and the American national vice of writing too much too quickly.

But there was a vast amount of deliberate slanting of American public opinion in a pro-Soviet direction. One publisher suggested that all books containing criticisms of any of the United Nations should be combed out of publishing lists and destroyed. Fortunately this proposal, which would have eclipsed the Nazi book-burnings, was not put into effect.

But an unwritten censorship operated against the publication of books containing material which might be offensive to the Soviet Government. Trotsky's biography of Stalin was held back after review copies had been sent out. There was a vast hue and cry, sponsored by trade unions and other organizations where Communist influence was strong, against the publication of a novel, *The Fifth Seal*, by the Russian émigré writer Mark Aldanov. This essentially nonpolitical novel, dealing with the lives of Russians outside the Soviet Union, had been selected by the Book-of-the-Month Club.

Christopher Morley found an ingenious device for discrediting the clamor. He wrote to one of the most vociferous critics suggesting that perhaps his objection could be met by eliminating a passage in which a "Georgian renegade" ridicules Stalin. The reply was prompt and uncompromising:

"Other passages just as objectionable as the ones you mention."

Here was convincing evidence that the objector had not even read the book before joining in the party-line demand for its suppression. For there was no "Georgian renegade" among its characters.

Pro-Soviet hysteria perhaps reached its highest point in connection with the publication of William L. White's *Report on the Russians* in the spring of 1945. The author is a well-known journalist and writer who accompanied Eric Johnston, then president of the United States Chamber of Commerce, on a trip to the Soviet Union which included a visit to Siberia and Turkestan. The book was not and did not pretend to be a profound study of the Soviet Union. It was an excellent reporting job, vivid, clear-cut, and well balanced.

Far from being a one-sided tirade of abuse, as might have been imagined from some of the reviews, the book recognized every important fact that could fairly be cited in favor of the Soviet regime. White found the Russians superb artists and good farmers. He had high praise for the absence of discrimination against non-Russian nationalities. Stalin, in his opinion, was a great man.

White was enthusiastically in favor of the ideal of co-operation with the Soviet Union, in peace as in war. He leaned over backward to be fair, even favorable, in his estimate of Soviet foreign policy. He expressed the view, much more optimistic than the facts warranted, that the Roosevelt Administration had "done an excellent job" of dealing with Russia "on a basis of delicately balanced firmness and friendliness." It would have required a very powerful microscope to discover any element of firmness in the Roosevelt-Hopkins technique of "getting along" with Stalin.

But what aroused the fury of many reviewers of the book was the author's frank, unsparing description of such negative sides of Soviet life as police terror, widespread employment of slave labor, gross discrepancy in the living standards of the higher bureaucrats and the masses of the people, and general poverty and backwardness. All these allegations were supported by a mass of corroborating evidence.

But the feeling that Russia could do no wrong, that any criticism of Stalin's dictatorship was akin to treason, had taken a strong grip on the American wartime mind. Leader of the chorus of vituperation was David Zaslavsky, professional literary executioner of the Soviet newspaper *Pravda*. Zaslavsky's standard reaction to any foreign critic of Russia, however mild, was to call him a fascist, with a choice assortment of gutter adjectives.

As soon as a summary of the book appeared in the *Reader's Digest*, Zaslavsky pronounced his elegant and scholarly verdict: "The standard stew from the fascist kitchen, with all its aroma of calumnies, unpardonable ignorance and undisguised malice."

This was routine Soviet literary controversial style. But what seems surprising and disgraceful, in retrospect, is that many American reviewers echoed Zaslavsky's sentiments, in slightly more sophisticated language.

Sixteen American writers and journalists who were or had been in the Soviet Union signed on the dotted line an abusive denunciation of the book which was forwarded to Moscow by the National Council of American-Soviet Friendship. This organization at the time was headed by Corliss Lamont, an untiring signer of pro-Soviet manifestoes. Subsequently it was placed on the Attorney-General's list of subversive organizations. But in 1945 it boasted as members a number of governors, judges, professors, clergymen, and other well-meaning individuals who were ignorant of its true purposes: to spread adulatory propaganda about the Soviet Union and to engage in defamatory enterprises like the attack on William L. White's book.

Reviewers in the United States, with a few honorable exceptions, followed the example of the sixteen correspondents[10] and chimed in with the abuse of Zaslavsky and the Council of American-Soviet Friendship.

10. The hackneyed expression "poetic justice" seems applicable to the fact that at least one of the sixteen was subsequently expelled from the Soviet Union, charged with being an American spy, and that several others were refused entrance visas.

Many proceeded on the assumption that there was a moral imperative to lie about Russia by publishing nothing unfavorable and nothing that might ruffle Stalin's supposedly tender susceptibilities.

One of the curious features of the campaign against White's book was that almost every reviewer started out with professions of high devotion to the ideal of individual freedom. Then there was a process of working up to a state of indignation with White for supplying specific evidence that a free society is preferable to a totalitarian one. An executive of the firm which published *Report on the Russians* offered the following illuminating comment on the American war mind:

"I have never known a case where a publisher came in for so many brickbats and so much name-calling, merely because we stand for the principle of free speech. Many of those who were loud in condemnation of the Nazis for burning books were equally loud in screaming to us: burn this one."

I have dwelt at some length on this incident because it furnishes such clear proof of the mental subservience of many American intellectuals during the war to a foreign power, and to a totalitarian dictatorship at that. A muddled philosophy that might be called totalitarian liberalism came into fashion, with the *Nation,* the *New Republic,* and the newspaper *PM* as its main exponents. There was a tremendous revival of the prewar double standard of morals in judging those twin phenomena, communism and fascism.

The totalitarian liberal justified or apologized for many things in Russia which he found execrable and unjustifiable in Germany, Japan, or Italy. Measures that were abominable crimes if committed by fascists became acts of stern but necessary self-preservation if carried out by the Soviet Union. The *New Republic* on one occasion artlessly remarked: "Soviet policy is no more imperialistic than is our good-neighbor policy."

But there was no indication of when and where the United States, even before the inauguration of the good-neighbor policy, had deported from their homes and sent to forced labor vast numbers of Latin Americans, thereby matching the Soviet record in the occupation of Eastern Poland and the Baltic states.

The creed of totalitarian liberalism found expression in an article which the editor of the *New Republic* devoted to "The Hang-Back Boys" of the war. In this category he placed all who refused to interpret the war on a more realistic plane than one would find in OWI handouts and refused to see the Soviet Union through the roseate lenses of Hollywood war movies and the fairy tales of the Dean of Canterbury.

These "hang-back boys," in the opinion of the editor, "have deliberately cut themselves off from the two great centers of dynamic energy in the world today. With all its faults, one of these is the Roosevelt Administration; and, with all its faults, the other is Russia."

Here was the totalitarian liberal's dream: a kind of amalgam of the New Deal with Soviet communism. And if one reviews the wartime writings, speeches, and actions of some extreme proponents of this viewpoint, one may well wonder in which war they were more concerned, Roosevelt's war or Stalin's war.

The movies, in the Second Crusade as in the First, were a potent source of emotional propaganda. Germans and Japanese provided natural villains in many run-of-the-mill war films. Hollywood also made its contribution to pro-Soviet propaganda.

Two films, *North Star* (with the participation of one of the most indefatigable joiners of fellow-traveler organizations, Lillian Hellman) and *Song of Russia,* showed a Russia that no more resembled Soviet realities than a fanciful sketch of Shangri-la. Peculiarly ludicrous were the collective-farm scenes in *Song of Russia.* Neither of these films could have been safely shown in Russia; there would have been too much spontaneous laughter.

Another film which enjoyed tremendous promotion was *Mission to Moscow,* a distorted version of a highly superficial book by the former American Ambassador to the Soviet Union Joseph E. Davies. The occasional notes of criticism which could be found in the book were carefully eliminated in the film.

Besides being a thoroughly misleading picture of Soviet life, *Mission to Moscow* was full of absurd anachronisms and historical errors. Davies was shown talking with Paderewski, represented as a high Polish official, at least fifteen years after the famous pianist had completely retired from Polish political life. Marshal M. N. Tukhachevsky, one of the numerous victims of the purges of the thirties, was shown confessing his guilt in open court — something which never occurred. Ribbentrop was depicted as a visitor to Russia, although the Nazi Foreign Minister first set foot in the Soviet Union in August 1939, long after the Davies mission was ended.

Characteristic of the spirit of the time was the comment in an article in the *Nation*, "Hollywood Goes to War."

"While this picture [*Mission to Moscow*] was criticized for the dramatic license it took with certain facts, it was an extremely useful film in that it gave a fundamentally sympathetic portrayal of our Soviet allies."

In other words, any lie was good in such a good propaganda cause.

The pro-Soviet cult during the war was not the result of any marked growth of popularity for avowed Communist organs. The important factor was the willingness, amazing in retrospect, of some well-known established magazines to take an uncritical pro-Soviet line.

There was the strange case of the *Atlantic Monthly*. The very name conveys an aroma of the great days of New England literary creation. Its long list of distinguished contributors includes Longfellow and Lowell, Whittier and Hawthorne, William Dean Howells and William James. It was one of the least likely places where one would normally have expected to find pro-Soviet bias.

But from the middle of 1942 until the end of 1945 nothing appeared in the *Atlantic Monthly* that could not have passed a severe Soviet censorship. During that period it published five articles on Russia and the closely related subject of Poland. Three of these were by Anna Louise Strong, who made no secret of her passionate emotional sympathy with communism. One was by Raymond Gram Swing, whose role will be discussed later. The other was by Max Lerner, leading editorial writer on *PM*, whose familiar practice was to cry down any criticism of Soviet actions as a sinister plot to start another world war.

The same bias extended to all departments of the magazine. The author of its anonymous "European Report" devised a few pat formulas which added up to the proposition "Heads Russia wins, tails the West loses." Acts which were denounced as outrageous aggression if committed by other powers were transformed into "vigorous security measures" if they bore a made-in-Moscow brand.

"Russia identifies fascism as the enemy and means it," wrote the author of the Report, who had apparently never heard of the Stalin-Hitler pact. He was quick to hand out bad character certificates to any peoples who showed a misguided desire to preserve their independence against Soviet encroachments. Whether these peoples were Poles or Greeks, Turks or Finns, they were quickly tagged as "slippery," "feudal," "reactionary," and what not in the pages of the *Atlantic Monthly*. Precisely the same kind of bias, in favor of Chinese and Japanese Communists, against the groups in those countries which were more naturally friendly to America, was perceptible in the "Far Eastern Report."

Censorship of everything that might hurt Stalin's feelings was pushed to the point of rejecting a satirical review of the absurd movie *Mission to Moscow*, by Edmund Wilson. The climax of the *Atlantic Monthly's* strange role as unswerving champion of Stalin's foreign policy was reached when it selected Anna Louise Strong as the contributor of two articles on Poland—a subject which it had hitherto avoided.

Miss Strong's subsequent expulsion from Russia on the familiar charge of being an American spy cannot obscure the fact that for a quarter of a century she was an energetic and uncritical spokesman for the "party line." Her two articles on Poland could have easily appeared in *Pravda* or any other Soviet newspaper. They were full of demonstrable factual errors and misstatements, all designed to support the thesis that the Soviet puppet regime in Poland was a high form of popular democracy. Poles who objected to the reduction of their country to the status of a Soviet vassal state were traduced as "fascists," criminals, and German sympathizers.

Publication of these articles elicited a good many letters of criticism. The magazine printed two of these with an editorial note to the effect that "it is the Atlantic tradition to hear from both sides of a bitterly contested issue." There was no explanation as to why nothing on the Polish nationalist side had ever appeared. And the commendable principle of "hearing from both sides" was to receive very peculiar application in practice.

The editor of the *Atlantic Monthly* invited a well-known American expert on Poland, Raymond Leslie Buell, to write an article on the subject. When this article was submitted, it was rejected—on the ground of insufficient objectivity. So, by implication, the ecstatic Communist sympathizer Anna Louise Strong was "objective." The scholarly expert Buell was not. Absurdity could go no further. But this incident and the whole record of the *Atlantic Monthly* illustrate vividly the dream world in which many Americans who were not Communists and probably did not even think of themselves as Communist sympathizers lived during the war years.

Two men who enjoyed great influence in forming public opinion during the Second Crusade were Walter Lippmann, through his widely syndicated column, and Raymond Gram Swing, through his nationwide radio broadcasts. Both failed to recognize the moral and political implications of the betrayal of Poland. Both failed to sound a badly needed warning against the danger to American interest of an indiscriminately vindictive peace. Both failed to show any anticipation of the kind of world which would exist after the war. Both failed to prepare American public opinion for the necessity of organizing some kind of defensive dike against Soviet expansion. Lippmann in 1944 offered the following argument in favor of the permanence of the wartime coalition:

> It is easy to say, but it is not true, that the Allies of today may be the enemies of tomorrow. . . . Our present alliance against Germany is no temporary contraption. It is an alignment of nations which, despite many disputes, much suspicion and even short and local wars, like the Crimean, have for more than a century been natural allies.
>
> It is not a coincidence that Britain and Russia have found themselves allied ever since the rise of German imperial aggression; that the United States and Russia, under the Tsars and under the Soviets, have always in vital matters been on the same side. . . .

This is an example of bad reasoning, supported by bad history. For it is quite inaccurate to assert that the United States, Great Britain, Russia, and China behaved toward each other like natural allies for more than a century. Great Britain was repeatedly involved in conflict with China and was long regarded by Chinese nationalists as the spearhead of western imperialist aggression. Russia pushed into Chinese territory in Manchuria and Outer Mongolia.

The Crimean War was only the extreme expression of the attitude of hostile distrust which dominated Russo-British relations from the end of the Napoleonic Wars to the eve of World War I. And at no time were British-Soviet relations enthusiastically cordial.

The United States and Russia have not always been on the same side in vital matters. American diplomatic support and sympathy were for Japan, not for Russia, at the time of the Russo-Japanese War. America repeatedly clashed with Russia on the Open Door issue in Manchuria.

This distorted history was used to back up a weak case. And the fundamental weakness of this case was the overlooking of a principle of political relations as old as the Greek city-states. This is that coalitions are formed against strength, not against weakness. As soon as Germany no longer threatened any of the United Nations, the bond uniting these nations might reasonably be expected to disappear.

Moreover, it was extremely short-sighted to assume that Soviet behavior after all checks and balances in Europe and Asia had been removed by the smashing of Germany and Japan would be the same as Soviet behavior when confronted by a preponderance of anti-Communist power.

Lippmann occasionally recognized that communism was a disturbing element in international relations. In his *U.S. War Aims* (Boston: Little, 1944) he suggests wistfully that it would be nice if the Soviet regime would begin to carry out the democratic promises of its constitution. As he had never spent any appreciable amount of time in Russia, he could perhaps not be expected to understand the extreme unlikelihood, or rather, impossibility, of such a development.

Raymond Gram Swing lived in a cloud cuckoo land of illusion. Over and over again he returned to the idea that all would be well with the world if Americans would only overcome their distrust of Soviet intentions. He was so obsessed with this theory that he gave every impression of seriously believing that what troubled the course of American-Soviet relations was not Soviet acts of aggression and bad faith in Poland and elsewhere, but American recognition of these acts for what they were. In a speech which was reprinted as an article in the *Atlantic Monthly* in 1945 he said: "We in this country can choose whether to work with the Soviet Union as partner or whether to surrender to memories and fears."

The plain implication of these words was that all responsibility for friction was on the American side, that Soviet foreign policy was above reproach. In this article, as in his broadcasts, Swing consistently fol-

lowed the methods of Dr. Coué, disposing of unpalatable facts by pre-
tending they did not exist. He was always eager to take Soviet words
at face value while ignoring the more convincing evidence of Soviet
deeds.

So in this speech-article the concrete issues which were already
clear—Poland, the validity of the Soviet pledges at Yalta—are not even
mentioned. But there is a gushing reference to "Stalin's great speech,
dedicating Soviet foreign policy to co-operation and to the establishment of a world society for the maintenance of peace and justice." The
mental attitude of supine appeasement of the Kremlin which Swing
tried to cultivate in his radio audience recalls a pertinent passage in
Arthur Koestler's work *The Yogi and the Commissar* (New York: Macmillan, 1945):

> The attitude of the Left and Liberal press in the Russian-Polish
> conflict was an uncanny replica of the Conservative attitude in the
> German-Czech conflict of 1939. The same flimsy arguments about
> ethnic minorities (Sudeten-Germans in the first, Ukrainians and
> Belorussians in the second case[11]) were invoked to soften an act
> of conquest by terror and military might; there was the same im-
> patience with the annoying victim who refuses to be murdered in
> silence and the same desire not to antagonize the aggressor. . . .

The same pro-Soviet influence that affected American public opinion was noticeable in the activity of some war agencies. A surprising
number of individuals who worked in these agencies seem to have
cherished divided loyalties. Sometimes their devotion was obviously to
the Kremlin.

The manipulation of public opinion at home and abroad in time of
war is a necessary but delicate task. It should be entrusted only to individuals of proved patriotism. But the OWI (Office of War Information)
was riddled with fellow travelers, many of them persons of foreign birth
with political pasts strongly suggestive of Communist sympathies and

11. I do not think this parallel is altogether accurate. The Sudeten Germans
had always disliked Czech rule and felt some attraction to Germany. There is not
the least evidence that any considerable number of Ukrainians and Byelorussians
wished to be absorbed into the Soviet Union.

affiliations. As the Polish Ambassador to the United States during the war, Jan Ciechanowski, writes:

> Some of the new war agencies actively conducted what could only be termed pro-Soviet propaganda.
>
> So-called American propaganda broadcasts to occupied Poland were outstanding proofs of this tendency. Notorious pro-Soviet propagandists and obscure foreign communists and fellow travelers were entrusted with these broadcasts.[12]

Ciechanowski's protests to the State Department elicited only an explanation that the Department could not control the OWI. Three of the prominent employees of the Polish branch of that agency, Herz, Arsky, and a woman named Balinska, after the war appeared in the service of Communist-dominated Poland. Their place would seem to have been on Stalin's payroll, not on Uncle Sam's. The head of the Polish desk was a Pole who had lived in France and was well known for his Communist affiliations.

Other departments were little if any better than the Polish. The Yugoslav branch was quick to hang up a portrait of Marshal Tito. An OWI alumna was Annabelle Bucar, a woman of Croat origin who renounced her American citizenship in Moscow after the war and wrote or signed her name to a scurrilous book, attacking State Department and Embassy personnel.

The OWI was not supposed to exercise domestic censorship. But a suggestion from one of its offices caused the editor of a popular magazine to make changes, without the author's knowledge, in an accepted article. The changes were designed to justify Soviet annexation of the Baltic states.

A personal experience throws some light on the prevalent spirit in the OWI. The New York office of that organization suggested that I broadcast to the Netherlands East Indies about the successes of Soviet industrialization and collective farming. It seemed to me inappropriate to use American broadcasting facilities to ballyhoo the achievements of a foreign dictatorship. Moreover, the subject seemed entirely irrele-

12. Ciechanowski, *Defeat in Victory,* 130–31.

vant to the war effort in the Far East. After I made it clear that I would consider it necessary to emphasize the heavy cost of these experiments in suffering and human lives, the offer was dropped.

Again and again, in the years after the war, I have noticed articles critical of American and favorable to Soviet policy, signed by former employees of the OWI. Certainly the obvious concentration of Soviet sympathizers in that key agency suggests grave negligence, if not design, in the matter of personnel selection.

OWI was not unique. The State Department, the OSS, and other agencies had their quotas of "bad security risks." Even before the war Soviet agents were able to obtain a large number of confidential State Department documents. This was proved by microfilm copies of these documents which Whittaker Chambers, a repentant ex–Communist agent, produced from his pumpkin hiding place.

Alger Hiss, a high State Department official, who accompanied Roosevelt to Yalta and was secretary of the United States delegation at the San Francisco conference, was indicted for perjury after denying the repeated assertions of Chambers that he had been a Communist underground worker and a main source of the stolen documents. Julian Henry Wadleigh, another former State Department employee named by Chambers in the same connection, confessed his guilt.

The first trial of Alger Hiss ended with a deadlocked jury, eight for conviction and four for acquittal. After a second trial Hiss was found guilty of all charges made against him and was sentenced to five years in prison. More corroborative evidence about the friendly relations between Hiss and his accuser, Chambers, was produced at the second trial. And a Vienna-born self-confessed former Communist underground worker, Mrs. Hede Massing, testified that she knew Hiss as the leader of an underground Communist organization in 1935. Mrs. Massing stated that she had disputed with Hiss about whether Noel Field, another State Department Communist sympathizer, should belong to her group or to his. Field, his wife, and his brother disappeared mysteriously behind the Iron Curtain in 1949.

Other officials in the Roosevelt wartime Administration were named as sources of information for Communist spy rings by Chambers and by Elizabeth Bentley, self-confessed Communist spy courier, in testimony before the House Committee on Un-American Activities. Perhaps the most important of these officials was Harry Dexter White, high Treasury official and principal author of the Morgenthau Plan.

Had this scheme, with its inevitable consequence, the death by starvation of millions of Germans, been put into operation, it would have been a political godsend to Stalin. In such a case Germany would most probably have turned to communism in sheer despair. So it is possible that other motives besides the desire to inflict vengeance on the German people for Nazi crimes helped to inspire this blueprint for destruction.

One is often impressed by the shocking carelessness which seems to have been shown in appointing individuals of dubious loyalty to responsible wartime posts. Consider the case of one Nathan Gregory Silvermaster, who, like many others mentioned by Whittaker Chambers and Elizabeth Bentley, refused to answer questions "for fear of self-incrimination." Naval Intelligence protested against his employment early in the war. The Civil Service Commission in 1942 reported:

"There is considerable testimony in the file indicating that about 1920 Mr. Silvermaster was an underground agent of the Communist Party. From that time until the present, according to the testimony of witnesses, he has been everything from a 'fellow traveler' to an agent of the OGPU [Soviet political police]." Yet Silvermaster, protected in some high quarters, went from one confidential appointment to another.

An attitude of strong distrust of Mr. Henry A. Wallace, the Vice-President of the United States during the war years, is reflected in an interview which General Leslie Groves, director of the Manhattan project, gave to the Associated Press. This interview went as follows:

Q. Did you withhold secret reports on atomic developments from Mr. Wallace?

A. Yes. I didn't show them to him after showing him one in the fall of 1943.

Q. Would they normally have been shown to Mr. Wallace in his position as a member of the President's Special Committee on Atomic Energy?

A. Normally they would have gone to him, but they didn't.

Q. Was there any special reason for not showing them to him?

A. I preferred not to.

Q. Would you consider this a deliberate withholding of information to Mr. Wallace?

A. Some people might think so.

Q. Was there any special reason for not showing Mr. Wallace the secret reports?

A. We took a number of deliberate risks on security matters in an effort to bring the war to a quicker end, *but we took no unnecessary recognizable risks.*[13] [Italics supplied.]

This is probably the first time since the days of Aaron Burr when a Vice-President of the United States has been stigmatized as a "poor security risk."

Much graver was the exposure and conviction as a Soviet spy of Dr. Klaus Fuchs, German refugee scientist in the service of the British Government. Fuchs had access to the most confidential information about atomic research, in the United States as well as in Great Britain. His motives in betraying the country where he had found asylum, as stated in his testimony, were confused, childish, and naive. He was obviously a man whose brain had developed in his specialized field at the expense of his mind. A Philadelphia scientist, Dr. Harry Gold, was arrested on the charge of having served as contact man between Fuchs and Soviet espionage agents. Gold's arrest was a sequel to FBI questioning of Fuchs in his prison in Great Britain.

There were strong fellow-traveler influences at work in shaping American policy in the Far East. This important fact should not be obscured by the obvious exaggerations which may be found in the charges of Senator Joseph McCarthy about Communist infiltration of the State Department.

The Institute of Pacific Relations became a focal point of American thinking on the Far East and during the war acquired almost semiofficial status. Many of its members were utilized on part-time and full-time government assignment. A study of the editorial policy of such Institute publications as *Pacific Affairs* and *Far Eastern Survey* reveals, with

13. See the *New York Times* for December 9, 1949.

negligible exceptions, a pro-Soviet, pro-Chinese Communist, anti-Japanese, anti-Kuomintang bias.

As I know from a personal experience, *Pacific Affairs* was committed to the policy of printing nothing which might offend the Soviet Institute of Pacific Relations—a sort of premature UN veto arrangement. It editorially supported the official Kremlin version that the Soviet purges during the thirties were aimed at "fascist fifth columnists."

Outstanding figure in the Institute and for some time editor of *Pacific Affairs* was Owen Lattimore, author of many books and articles on Far Eastern problems and a principal figure in McCarthy's charges. Whatever may be thought of McCarthy's allegation that Lattimore is a "top Soviet spy," a study of Lattimore's writings would scarcely support the idea that he is or ever has been an anti-Communist. This is how the Soviet Union appears to neighboring Asiatic peoples, according to Mr. Lattimore:

"The Soviet Union stands for strategic security, economic prosperity, technological progress, miraculous medicine, free education, equality of opportunity, and democracy: a powerful combination."[14]

The publisher's jacket on this book sums up its essential message as follows: "He shows that all the Asiatic peoples are more interested in actual democratic practices, such as the ones they can see in action across the Russian border, than they are in the fine theories of Anglo-Saxon democracies which come coupled with ruthless imperialism."

One may reasonably feel that if Mr. Lattimore is really an anti-Communist, he has been very successful in concealing this fact in his published writings. Indeed there has been a remarkable, if accidental, parallelism between his recommendations on American policy in the Far East and the aims of the Kremlin. The principal points in a memorandum which Lattimore presented to the State Department in the autumn of 1949 may be summarized as follows:

1. The United States should withdraw from Korea.
2. It should disregard Japan as a potential major ally in the Orient.
3. It should speed up recognition and trade with Communist China.

14. Lattimore, *Solution in Asia*, 139.

4. It should avoid "local entanglement," meaning presumably aid to forces resisting communism, which might annoy the Soviet Union.

Stalin might welcome more anti-Communists of this kind. Lattimore's views carried considerable weight with the Far Eastern Division of the State Department, especially with its former head, John Carter Vincent. The elimination in the summer of 1945 of two able and experienced advisers on Japan, former Ambassador Joseph C. Grew and former Counsellor of Embassy Eugene Dooman, helped to leave a free field for those who regarded the Nationalist regime of Chiang Kai-shek as an embarrassing nuisance in China and were inclined to practice economic vivisection experiments in Japan. The result of the postwar American policy in the Far East has been to leave this country at a very low ebb in prestige and influence.

Suggestive of the influences at work in the field of Far Eastern policy was the strange case of the magazine *Amerasia*. Edited by a businessman, Philip Jaffe, and Kate Mitchell, a former associate of the Institute of Pacific Relations, *Amerasia* went further than *Pacific Affairs* in echoing the Soviet viewpoint on Far Eastern matters. The FBI announced on June 7, 1945, that it had discovered large numbers of confidential documents from the State, War, and Navy Departments and from other government agencies in the office of *Amerasia*. Jaffe and Kate Mitchell, Navy Lieutenant Andrew Roth, John S. Service and E. S. Larsen, of the Far Eastern Division of the State Department, and Mark Gayn, a Manchuria-born journalist, were arrested on charge of being implicated in the theft of confidential government papers.

Jaffe pleaded guilty and got off with a fine of twenty-five hundred dollars. Larsen entered a plea of *nolo contendere* and paid a fine of five hundred dollars. The charges against the others were dropped. The FBI has maintained a good record of not making arrests without strong supporting evidence. The quashing of the charges in the *Amerasia* case led to suggestions by Representative Dondero and others that the case was deliberately not pressed as it could have been on the basis of available evidence.

When Jaffe was brought to trial, the government prosecutor made no attempt to prove his long record of association with pro-Communist organizations, although this might well have been a motive for his un-authorized collecting of government papers. According to Senator Bourke Hickenlooper, of Iowa, a member of the subcommittee which investigated the *Amerasia* case, some of the stolen documents were of the highest importance, including the location of American sub-marines in the Pacific at that time and a highly confidential message from Roosevelt to Chiang Kai-shek.[15]

We do not know, and perhaps never shall know, how much outright treason was mingled with stupidity, opportunism, emotional fellow-traveler admiration of the Soviet regime, and sheer ignorance in shaping American wartime attitudes and activities. The pattern of Soviet espionage in Canada was revealed clearly and sharply because a Soviet cipher clerk, Igor Gouzenko, who knew all the essential names and facts, risked his life by turning over this information to the Canadian authorities. No Soviet agent who knew as much as Gouzenko turned state's evidence in the United States. Consequently, revelations of Soviet espionage and American treason came out in haphazard, piecemeal fashion. It is sometimes impossible to know with certainty whether a man crossed the dangerously narrow no man's land between emotional enthusiasm for communism and willingness to be a spy in the service of a foreign power.

Moreover, there has been continuity in the political character of the Administration. There has been no great desire in high Washington quarters to press home investigations which might be damaging to the character, or at least to the judgment, of men prominently identified with the New Deal and the Roosevelt wartime Administration.

On the basis of what is known beyond reasonable doubt, however, it may be said that in no previous war was the United States so plagued with infiltration of government agencies and warping of policies in the interest of a foreign power. A number of factors combined to produce this undesirable result.

There was the old intellectual occupational disease of fellow-traveler sympathy. There was the cult of totalitarian liberalism. There was the illusion, obstinately although most illogically cherished by the most fa-natical anti-Hitler crusaders, that appeasement would work with Stalin.

15. See the *New York Herald Tribune* for May 31, 1950.

There was the significant and unfortunate fact that no one with intimate first-hand knowledge of Soviet communism in theory and practice enjoyed much confidence or influence in the White House.

All this created an atmosphere in which public opinion placed no effective brake on mistaken Administration policies, in which Soviet agents and propagandists, native and foreign, found it very easy to operate.

# 11

## Poland:
## The Great Betrayal

The questions are not: Shall Poland's eastern border be shifted westward? Shall she lose her eastern territories or, losing them, acquire in their place western territories at the expense of Germany?

"The question is: Shall Poland exist?

"Beyond this there is another question: Shall Europe exist—the Europe we have known, and hope to know again, the Europe for which the War is being fought, the Europe which alone gives the War any meaning, a Europe that is neither anarchy, nor servitude, the Europe that is a balanced and integral whole, . . . the Europe that is so much more than a geographical expression, Europe the stronghold of the Graeco-Roman and Christian heritage? That is *the* question."[1]

One wonders what would have happened if the British Government, when offering its guarantee against aggression to the Polish Government in the spring of 1939, had said:

"You must understand that this guarantee applies only against Germany. If the Soviet Union proposes to take almost half of your territory and impose on what is left of Poland a Communist-dominated government, you cannot count on our help. On the contrary, we will make no serious effort to prevent the Soviet Government from accomplishing these designs and will even support its case against yours."

Suppose that, while the Yugoslav Government was being pushed and prodded by the Roosevelt Administration into entering an un-

1. F. A. Voigt, "Poland," *The Nineteenth Century and After,* 35 (February 1944), 63.

equal struggle against Germany, some candid and far-sighted American diplomat had offered the following prophetic warning:

"You will experience all the sufferings of foreign occupation. More than that, your country will be devastated by a savage social civil war. In this war the Moscow-trained Communist Josip Broz Tito will enjoy the support not only of the Soviet Union, but of Great Britain and the United States. You, and other non-Communist Yugoslav patriots, will be lucky if you save your lives in exile or in obscurity at home."

Suppose some authoritative voice had warned the American people before Pearl Harbor:

"Our policy of giving unconditional support to Chiang Kai-shek's regime in China will lead to war with Japan. This war will be fought to the complete ruin of Japan. However, we will not worry about Soviet and Communist aggression in China. In fact, we will bribe Stalin, at China's expense, so as to draw him into our grand crusade against Japan. The end of this will be that China will fall into the grip of Chinese Communists, devoted disciples of Moscow, bitter enemies of the United States. These Communists will inflict upon American diplomatic representatives insults unheard of since the Boxer uprising."

Would our crusade have made much sense if its consequences in Eastern Europe and East Asia had been accurately foreseen?

The betrayals of those groups in Poland and Yugoslavia and China which looked to America and Britain for sympathy and support were also acts of profound stupidity, from the cold-blooded standpoint of national interest. Can any American or Briton believe in retrospect that a great outlay of blood and treasure was vindicated by the emergence of a Moscow-trained clique as rulers of Poland, of Tito as dictator of Yugoslavia, of Mao Tse-tung as the Communist overlord of China?

The betrayal of Poland was the crudest and most flagrant of the three, if only because Poland was the pretense for the whole crusade. Therefore this betrayal will be examined in detail, as a symbol of what went wrong with a war that was being waged ostensibly for national self-determination and against aggression.

During the period 1939–41, when Poland was partitioned between the Nazi and Soviet regimes, both these dictatorships did everything in their power to stamp out Polish national consciousness. The Nazis expelled Poles from cities like Gdynia and Poznan and from some regions which were marked for German colonization. They closed universities and higher schools. They were ruthless in dealing with every sign of resistance and sent large numbers of Poles to concentration camps, where many perished. Especially terrible was the planned extermination of the Jews. Most of the large Jewish population of Poland had been destroyed by the end of the war.

The Soviet masters of Eastern Poland did not resort to this maniacal policy of exterminating a whole ethnic group. But on every other count they equalled and sometimes exceeded the brutalities of the Nazis. They systematically arrested and in some cases killed individuals who were associated with political activity: leaders of Polish, Ukrainian, and Jewish organizations, members of the Diet, judges, intellectuals. They carried off about 1,200,000 persons in mass deportations to Russia. Most of the deportees were sent to slave-labor camps.

The deportations were carried out with revolting cruelty. Villages were surrounded by soldiers and police. People were rounded up and thrown like cattle into unheated freight cars. On the long trips, there was an appalling lack of food, water, and sanitary facilities. When Polish representatives were able to carry out investigations in Russia, it was found that about one-fourth of the deportees had perished as a result of hardships on the trips and maltreatment in concentration camps.[2]

A principal aim of the deportations was to diminish the number of people of ethnic Polish stock in the eastern provinces, which were annexed to the Ukrainian and Byelorussian Soviet Republics. These annexations occurred after typically farcical totalitarian "elections," held without the most elementary safeguards of freedom of speech, freedom of the press, and secrecy of voting.

It was often suggested in later discussions of the Soviet-Polish issue that there was some valid Soviet claim to Polish territory east of the so-

2. For details of the Soviet reign of terror in Eastern Poland, see Elma Dangerfield, *Behind the Urals;* Ann Su Cardwell, *Poland and Russia; Dark Side of the Moon,* a collection of narratives of Polish deportees; and Jerzy Gliksman, *Tell the West.* The barbarous character of Soviet rule places an especially dark blot on all transfers of territory to Soviet possession.

called Curzon Line. It was suggested that this line was a final impartial award on Poland's eastern frontier, which the Poles willfully transgressed.[3] It was also argued that the population of eastern Poland was mainly Russian and that the Soviet Union needed this region for reasons of strategic security.

These contentions are without any basis in fact. The Curzon Line (with the fixing of which Lord Curzon had little to do) was never thought of as a final frontier settlement. It was proposed as a temporary demarcation line by the Supreme Allied Council in Paris on December 8, 1919. Later Lord Curzon, as British Foreign Secretary, proposed that this should be the provisional frontier at a time when the Red Army held the military advantage over the Poles in the Soviet-Polish war of 1920. But the Soviet leaders at that time were bent on sovietizing all Poland. They refused to halt their armies at the Curzon Line. The Soviet Government even stated officially that the line was unjust to Poland; it was willing to grant a more favorable boundary to a Communist Poland.

The Soviet-Polish frontier, as finally established by the Treaty of Riga, in March 1921, was almost identical with the boundary imposed on Poland at the time of that country's second partition at the hands of Russia, Austria, and Prussia in 1791. Only about 150,000 Russians were on the Polish side of this frontier, while about 1,500,000 Poles were left in the Soviet Union.

To be sure, the population of eastern Poland is ethnically mixed. This is equally true of many parts of the Soviet Union and most countries of Eastern and Central Europe. According to the Polish census of 1931, the territory seized by the Soviet Union in 1939 was inhabited by 4,794,000 Poles, 4,139,000 Ukrainians, 1,045,000 Jews, 993,000 Byelorussians, 120,000 Russians, 76,000 Lithuanians, and 845,000 others. All these figures had somewhat increased in 1939. The two principal cities of eastern Poland, Wilno and Lwów, were Polish by the tests of population, language, architecture, and long historical association. Lwów had never belonged to Russia.

3. Raymond Gram Swing was especially zealous in giving this misrepresentation wide publicity through his radio broadcasts.

There was a nationalist movement among the Ukrainians of eastern Poland. But a large majority of these Ukrainians, as subsequent events[4] showed, were bitterly anti-Communist. Their aim was an independent Ukrainian state, not absorption into the Soviet Union.

As for the security argument, it is disposed of by simple and indisputable historical facts. Russia was twice invaded by Germany when the former was in possession of eastern Poland. It was never thus invaded while this region was in the possession of an independent Poland.

The Soviet Government accepted the boundary fixed by the Treaty of Riga in free negotiation. It gave a new voluntary endorsement of this frontier by concluding a nonaggression and neutrality pact with Poland in 1932. In short, there is nothing to distinguish the Soviet seizure of eastern Poland from any of the acts of predatory aggression which were supposed to warrant a global crusade against Hitler and the Japanese militarists.

Molotov had gleefully exclaimed in October 1939 that nothing remained of Poland, "that ugly offspring of the Versailles Treaty." But the Polish Government continued to function abroad, first in France, later in London. Polish aviators played a heroic and brilliant part in the Battle of Britain. Polish armed forces increased in numbers after it was possible to recruit soldiers among the war prisoners and deportees in Russia. By 1944, 140,000 Poles were fighting on land, on sea, and in the air, and there were substantial Polish units on the Italian and western fronts.

The Polish Government in London was composed of representatives of the four principal Polish political parties: the National Democratic, the Peasant, the Socialist, and the Christian Labor parties. It was in close touch with one of the most daring and active underground movements in Europe.

Communism had never been strong in Poland, even among the industrial workers. It was closely linked in the people's memory with

4. Many of these Polish Ukrainians fought with the Germans in the hope of achieving a free Ukrainian state. Disillusioned with the Germans, Ukrainian nationalists carried on a two-front war, both against the Nazis and against the Soviet Communists. There are authentic reports of guerrilla activity in Ukrainian regions long after the end of the war.

the hated Russian rule. The Polish Communist party was so weak and so torn by factional strife that it was dissolved by the Communist International in 1937.

The Union of Polish Patriots[5] which evolved into the Lublin Committee and furnished the nucleus of the government which was forced on Poland by Soviet armed force, was a highly synthetic creation. It possessed a hard core of fanatical Communists who were willing to play the role of Red Quislings, reinforced more and more by opportunists who realized that the western powers would not protect Poland against Stalin's designs.

Hitler's attack on Russia marked the beginning of a new phase in Soviet-Polish relations. Stalin's spoils from the pact of August 1939, eastern Poland and the Baltic states, were rapidly overrun by the Germans, uprisings against Soviet rule in Lithuania and eastern Galicia hastening the process. Always astute and flexible, Stalin saw the advantage of reaching a temporary agreement with the Polish Government. This government, then headed by General Wladyslaw Sikorski, was willing to forget the painful experience of Soviet occupation of eastern Poland in the interest of the common struggle against Nazi Germany. So the British-Soviet agreement of July 12, 1941, pledging the two powers to support each other and not to conclude a separate peace or armistice, was followed by the Soviet-Polish agreement of July 30. The Soviet Government recognized that the Soviet-German treaties of 1939 dealing with territorial changes in Poland had lost their validity. There were assurances of mutual support, and it was agreed that a Polish army should be raised in the Soviet Union and that there should be an amnesty for Poles detained in Russia.

There were significant omissions in this instrument. There was no specific Soviet recognition of the 1939 Polish frontier. Sikorski tried hard to obtain this, but in vain. Several members of his cabinet felt so strongly on this subject that they resigned. There was strong British pressure to get the agreement signed, and Foreign Secretary Eden, in a note of July 30, assured Sikorski that "His Majesty's Government do not recognize any territorial changes which have been effected in

5. This was a small group of Poles who acted as a mouthpiece for Soviet policy. It is doubtful whether the word "patriot" was ever so conspicuously misused.

Poland since August 1939." This was to prove a very brittle and short-lived assurance.

Sikorski went to Russia at the beginning of December 1941. Stalin gave him a hospitable reception. After discussing the common war effort and the details of forming the Polish Army in Russia, Stalin raised the question of the Polish eastern boundary. He suggested that he would be satisfied with "very slight" alterations. Sikorski flatly refused to discuss any change and the subject was dropped.

But the Soviet Government was already seeking to undermine Polish claims to sovereignty in its eastern provinces. In a note of December 1, 1941, the Soviet Government asserted the right to conscript for the Red Army Polish citizens of Ukrainian, Byelorussian, and Jewish origin who formerly lived in eastern Poland, described in the note as western Ukraine and western Byelorussia. The note contained the statement that "the question of the frontier between the Soviet Union and Poland has not been settled and is subject to settlement in the future."[6]

Stalin, who had tried to soothe Sikorski with assurances that he wanted only "slight" alterations in the Soviet-Polish frontier, showed his true intentions plainly when Anthony Eden, British Foreign Minister, visited the Soviet Union in December 1941. The Soviet dictator demanded the restoration of the Soviet borders as they were before Hitler's attack. He intimated that the conclusion of the Anglo-Soviet treaty which was under discussion would depend on British willingness to concede this point.[7]

Both Churchill and Eden, quickly forgetting the British official assurance that no territorial changes in Poland were recognized, were inclined to yield to Stalin's demand. But this was one of the very few occasions when the United States Government took a strong line in defense of the Atlantic Charter. A State Department memorandum, prepared by James C. Dunn and Ray Atherton, and approved by Secretary Hull, flatly rejected the proposed Soviet annexation of Polish territory. To yield to the Soviet demand, so stated the memorandum, "would affect the integrity of the Atlantic Charter."

The British Cabinet continued to waver. Eden, despite his reputa-

6. For the text of this note, see *Polish-Soviet Relations*, 165–66.
7. Hull, *Memoirs*, 2:1166–67.

tion as an upholder of international morality, was willing to buy Stalin's precarious friendship by turning over millions of people in Eastern Europe to the rule of the Soviet political police. But Roosevelt backed up the State Department. He assured General Sikorski in March that the American Government had not forgotten the Atlantic Charter.[8] The affair came to a head in May, when Molotov went to London for a final discussion of the terms of the Anglo-Soviet treaty. He pressed strongly for recognition of the Soviet claim to eastern Poland, the Baltic states, and part of Finland.

The British might well have given way if the State Department had not interposed an attitude of uncompromising opposition. Hull suggested that if the treaty contained the proposed territorial provisions, the United States might issue a separate statement of repudiation. The British then altered their viewpoint. The treaty, a twenty-year alliance, was signed on May 26 without territorial commitments.

The subsequent political history of the war might have been different if Roosevelt and Hull had maintained this firm attitude. This they conspicuously failed to do. But the American position, as stated by the President and the Secretary of State at this time, is the most decisive condemnation of the subsequent surrenders at Teheran and Yalta. Obviously Soviet demands which were considered inadmissible and inconsistent with the Atlantic Charter in 1942, did not become more justified with the passing of years.

But the American attitude steadily weakened, curiously enough, as American military power increased. Both in Washington and in London there was fear that Stalin might make a separate peace with Hitler. This fear was unwarranted, because Stalin's interest in smashing German military power was far greater than America's. The United States was safe from any danger of overseas invasion as soon as it had built up its wartime air and naval power. Had Stalin made a separate peace with Hitler and thereby broken his alliance with the West, he would have exposed himself to another devastating onslaught from the German war machine.

However, fear of a Soviet separate peace weakened western opposition to Soviet annexationist schemes almost to the point of paralysis.

8. Ciechanowski, *Defeat in Victory*, 100.

This fear was cunningly stimulated by petulant Soviet gestures, such as complaints about the failure to invade France in 1942 or 1943 and the recall of the Soviet ambassadors in Washington and London, Litvinov and Maisky, in 1943. Another factor which predisposed the American Government to a policy of appeasing the Soviet Union was the artificial building up of pro-Soviet sentiment by government agencies.[9] This sentiment became a Frankenstein's monster, hard to control.

So there was little reaction to the secret killing by the Soviet police of two prominent Polish Jewish Socialist leaders, Henryk Ehrlich and Viktor Alter. These men, arrested during the Soviet invasion of Poland in 1939, were released under the amnesty for Polish citizens in the summer of 1941. They were engaged in organizing an international Jewish antifascist committee when both disappeared in Kuibyshev, the temporary Soviet capital, in December 1941. Inquiries about their fate remained unanswered until Litvinov in December 1942 informed William Green, President of the AFL, that they had been shot by order of a Soviet tribunal "for collaboration with the Nazis and for their work among the Red Army and among the Soviet population on behalf of Hitler."

This defamatory and wildly improbable charge (both as Jews and as Socialists, Ehrlich and Alter were irreconcilable enemies of nazism) was vigorously denied by the Polish Government in a note of March 8, 1943.[10] The contrasted experience of Ehrlich and Alter under Soviet and under Polish rule is an instructive commentary on the familiar apologetic argument that Soviet rule, with all its faults, was an improvement on the "feudal" and "reactionary" conditions which were supposed to exist in prewar Poland.

The Polish Government in the years before the war was authoritarian. Anti-Semitism existed in Poland. Yet Ehrlich and Alter sat in the Polish parliament, attended international socialist congresses, carried on fairly free political activity. The Soviet Union, professing to bring

9. The Polish Ambassador in Washington was a shrewd, well-informed diplomat, with many good contacts in Washington. Describing the Quebec conference of 1943, he writes: "According to the President, pro-Soviet sentiment in America was superficial and, as a matter of fact, it had to be artificially fed" (*Defeat in Victory*, 201).

10. *Polish-Soviet Relations*, 178–79.

liberation to eastern Poland, shot them without public trial and on a fantastically improbable accusation.

Strengthened by the victory at Stalingrad, conscious that little serious opposition was to be feared in Washington and London, the Soviet leaders pushed ahead with their plans for the territorial mutilation and political subjugation of Poland.

The plight of the million or more Poles who had been deported to Russia was desperate. Almost all were destitute of food and clothing. Many were in the last stages of exhaustion and disease. In December 1941 the Polish Government, by agreement with the Soviet Government, tried to furnish relief through agencies which were set up in various Soviet cities. But in the summer of 1942 these agencies were closed and many of their personnel were arrested.

A further step in the same direction was taken on January 16, 1943, when the Soviet Government extended its earlier ruling that Ukrainians, Byelorussians, and Jews born in the eastern provinces of Poland were Soviet citizens, to include people of Polish ethnic origin. All these provocations were hushed up by the Polish embassies abroad under strong pressure from the American and British governments.

The final blow fell on April 25, 1943, when the Soviet Government cynically used the discovery of a crime, almost certainly committed by its own agents, as an excuse for breaking off relations with the Polish Government. This action followed a German statement that thousands of bodies of Polish officers, killed by shots in the back of the head, had been discovered in the Katyn Forest, near the town of Smolensk in western Russia.

The Polish Government, in a declaration of April 17, asked for an International Red Cross investigation of the affair. This declaration emphasized that the Germans themselves had committed many atrocities and denied the right of the Germans "to pose as the defenders of Christianity and western civilization."

The appeal for a Red Cross investigation was used by the Soviet Government as an excuse for breaking off diplomatic relations. This cleared the way for building up a puppet government for Poland, recruited from refugee Communists and other Poles willing to accept Soviet dictation.

Behind the Polish request for an investigation lay almost two years of unsuccessful effort to penetrate a very sinister mystery. There were about one hundred eighty thousand prisoners of war in Russia in 1939, including some ten thousand officers. Only a few hundred of these officers were found among the masses of Poles who were released after Hitler's invasion of Russia. Many thousands had vanished without a trace.

Prime Minister Sikorski, General Anders, commander of the Polish Army which was raised in Russia and later transferred to the Near East, and Ambassador Kot all raised the question of the fate of these officers in talks with Stalin. They received only evasive, noncommittal replies, varied with suggestions that were merely ridiculous, such as that the officers might have escaped to Manchuria. Stalin talked with Kot on November 14, 1941, and called up the headquarters of the NKVD to inquire what had become of the officers. He put down the receiver after receiving a reply, and changed the subject.

There were many Polish official inquiries. There was no Soviet official reply to the effect that the officers had been left in a prison camp, abandoned at the time of the German invasion. This version was only thought of when the corpses were discovered.

There were apparently no survivors of the massacre. The Germans held an inquiry, attended by medical experts from a number of European countries. They reached the conclusion, on the basis of letters, newspapers, and diaries found on the bodies and other circumstantial evidence, that the killings took place in March and April 1940. After the Red Army retook the area, there was a Soviet investigation which ended in the conclusion that the slaughter occurred in the autumn of 1941.

Neither the German nor the Soviet investigation could be regarded as impartial. With one exception[11] the members of the German commission were citizens of countries associated with Germany in the war or occupied by Germany. The witnesses in the Soviet inquiry were obvi-

---

11. The exception was Professor François Naville, of the University of Geneva. He has maintained his conviction that the Russians were responsible for the Katyn massacre. The International Tribunal at Nürnberg showed a rather undignified inclination to run away from the danger of discovering the truth about Katyn. It refused to call Professor Naville or General Anders as witnesses and failed to find the Germans guilty of this crime or to indicate who was guilty.

ously under the strongest pressure to testify as the Soviet Government desired. There is, however, an overwhelming weight of circumstantial evidence pointing to Soviet guilt for the Katyn massacre.[12] The following points would seem to be decisive:

1. The Soviet Government never took the opportunity to place responsibility for the fate of the officers on the Germans by stating that the prison camp had been abandoned until the bodies were discovered. Soviet replies to repeated Polish inquiries were invariably evasive.
2. All letters from the imprisoned officers to their families ceased not in 1941, but in the spring of 1940.
3. Neither the Soviet Government nor the Communist-dominated regime in Poland made any attempt to establish German responsibility for this crime after the end of the war.
4. It is most improbable, if not impossible, that all the Polish officers would have waited passively to be captured by the Germans if the camp had been abandoned, according to the Soviet version. The completeness of the massacre suggests that there was no confusion, no opportunity for some of the victims to escape.

General Sikorski lost his life in an airplane accident in July 1943. He was succeeded as Prime Minister by Stanislaw Mikolajczyk, leader of the Peasant party.

The tendency in Washington and London to sacrifice Poland's territorial integrity and national independence proceeded at an accelerated pace during 1943 and 1944. Eduard Beneš, leader of the Czechoslovak government-in-exile found the United States Government ready to throw over Poland as early as May 1943. As he wrote in retrospect:

From Roosevelt's remarks and even more from Harry Hopkins's I saw that the United States had already made a decision. In principle it accepted the Soviet stand on changes in Poland's former Eastern

12. I have never found a Pole who did not believe that the Soviet Government was responsible for the Katyn slaughter. And I have discussed the question with many Poles who were bitter in their resentment over German cruelties and certainly would have felt no desire to whitewash any Nazi atrocity.

frontier and agreed that an accord must be reached between Poland and the Soviet Union. I was convinced that the London Poles' expectation of receiving support from the United States for their claims against the Soviet Union was sheer wishful thinking. (Undersecretary of State Sumner Welles expressed this view to me the next day.)[13]

Beneš himself displayed great energy in getting his country accepted as the first Soviet satellite. He broke off discussions with Poland about a Central European federation because this would displease Stalin. He was the first representative of an East European state who signed a special treaty of friendship and alliance with the Soviet Union. He lived long enough to realize the value of this treaty, especially of the clause which stressed the principle of mutual noninterference in internal affairs. The first Soviet satellite enjoyed only the dubious privilege of being the last to be devoured.

Early in 1943 Sumner Welles asked Ciechanowski whether the Polish Government was determined not to yield an inch of its eastern territory. The British Ambassador in Washington, Lord Halifax, asked him whether the acceptance by the Polish Government of the Curzon Line as a frontier "would really be such a hardship."[14]

Sensing the attitude of weakness on the part of the western powers, the Soviet Government became more and more truculent in its diplomatic manners and methods. America and Britain on August 11, 1943, submitted a joint proposal to Moscow. They suggested a resumption of Soviet-Polish diplomatic relations and such elementary humanitarian measures as the evacuation of Polish refugees to the Near East, recognition of the Polish nationality of ethnic Poles, and permission for other Polish refugees to opt for Polish or Soviet citizenship.

The Soviet reply was delayed until September 27 and was aggressively un-co-operative in tone. The Soviet note alleged that the American and British proposals

13. See the part of Beneš's abridged memoirs published in the *Nation* of July 17, 1948, p. 70.

14. One wonders whether Halifax was naive or cynical in this inquiry. Acceptance of the Curzon Line meant for Poland the loss of almost half its territory, of rich agricultural areas, and of its only domestic source of oil.

almost coincide with the pretensions of the Polish Government, which refer in demagogic fashion to the necessity of liberating and evacuating unfortunate Polish citizens from the Soviet Union. A statement of this type is lacking in any foundation whatever and cannot be considered in any other way than as an insulting attack against the Soviet Union, to which the Soviet Government does not consider it necessary to react.[15]

A stoppage or suggestive slowing down of lend-lease shipments would probably have produced more courteous language and a more accommodating attitude. But this, as Hull tells us, was a suggestion which neither he nor the President entertained for a moment. The psychology of the rabbit vis-à-vis the boa constrictor continued to prevail. The more Stalin insulted the western leaders, the more they endeavored to placate him.

Hull gave Ciechanowski some encouragement before he left for the Moscow Conference of Foreign Ministers, but very little after he returned. And there was a still more significant occurrence. When Sikorski visited Washington in March 1943, plans had been worked out for parachuting munitions and supplies to the Polish patriot underground army. After the Moscow conference, these plans were canceled. Stalin might be displeased. The Poles, who had been fighting when Stalin and Ribbentrop had been exchanging toasts of friendship and cooperation against the "decadent democracies," were left defenseless at the moment when their unequal struggle against two totalitarian oppressors was reaching its climax.

There is still no full and authoritative account of the highly secret Teheran conference, although it is fair to assume that much that was put in written form at Yalta was predetermined at Teheran. However, Churchill, in speeches before the House of Commons, has given a frank, realistic picture of the roles which he and Roosevelt played in the betrayal of Poland. Churchill apparently took the initiative in proposing to give away Polish territory. He told the House on February

15. This language is omitted in Hull's account of the incident (*Memoirs*, 2:1271), but it is included in a report which Arthur Bliss Lane submitted to the State Department on June 1, 1945. Mr. Lane placed a copy of this report at my disposal.

22, 1944: "I took occasion to raise personally with Marshal Stalin the question of the future of Poland."

According to an American participant in this conference, Churchill shifted match sticks about to show how Poland's frontiers were to be shifted from east to west. Churchill let more light into the dark places of Teheran when he informed the House on December 15, 1944, that Poland would gain in the west and north territories more important and highly developed than what would be lost in the east.

That many millions of persons, Poles in eastern Poland, Germans in the ethnically German regions of Silesia, East Prussia, and other areas east of the Oder-Neisse boundary line, would be driven from their homes under conditions of terrible misery did not disturb Mr. Churchill.

"After all," he said, "six or seven million Germans have been killed already in this frightful war. . . . [16] Moreover we must expect that many more Germans will be killed in the fighting which will occupy the spring and summer."

"These ideals," said Churchill, "arose at the Teheran conference." And in the same speech, the British Prime Minister gave a clear characterization of the President's silent complicity in this colossal repudiation of the Atlantic Charter, to which Roosevelt, Churchill, and Stalin continued to pay lip service.

> The President is aware of everything that has passed and of all that is in the minds both of the Russians and of the British. . . . I am particularly careful not ever to speak in the name of any other power unless so directed beforehand, and I hope the House will make allowance for the care with which I pick my words upon this point. All I can say is that I have received no formal disagreement in all these long months upon the way in which the future of Poland is shaping itself, — or being shaped.

Here is a clear indication of the distribution of roles. Churchill was the outright executioner of Poland's territorial integrity and political independence. Roosevelt was the Pontius Pilate who tried to wash his hands of the whole affair. The President avoided any blunt statement

16. This estimate was considerably exaggerated.

or direct commitment that might have alienated the important Polish-American vote in the United States. But the spirit of 1942, when there was outspoken and successful American opposition to the recognition of Soviet annexationist claims, was gone.

The venerable Hull hopefully told a joint session of Congress on November 18, 1943, after his return from Moscow: "There will no longer be need for spheres of influence, for alliances, for balance of power, or any other of the special arrangements through which, in the unhappy past, the nations strove to safeguard their security or to promote their interests."

But a shrewder student of diplomacy, Eduard Beneš, noted in his memoirs[17] that at the Teheran Conference, where Hull was not present, "the first attempts were made to establish military and political spheres of influence for the Eastern and Western powers." The Soviet Union, without encountering American and British opposition, put in a claim for a zone including northeastern Germany, Poland, Czechoslovakia, Hungary, and Rumania. Beneš found that because of this zonal arrangement it was difficult to get American and British help during the uprising against German occupation in Slovakia in the autumn of 1944.

The kind of settlement for Poland envisaged at Teheran became clear on January 22, 1944, when Churchill and Eden proposed a five-point solution to the Polish Government. The five points were: acceptance of the Curzon Line frontier; assignment to Poland of East Prussia, Danzig, and Upper Silesia as far as the Oder River; removal of the entire German population from the newly annexed territory; return to Poland of Poles living east of the new frontier; American-British-Soviet approval of the new boundaries.

Prime Minister Mikolajczyk found it impossible to accept these proposals. More than territorial dismemberment was at stake. For when the United States Government, on January 19, 1944, offered mediation with a view to restoring Soviet-Polish diplomatic relations, the Soviet reply, which rejected mediation, offered the following insidious suggestion:

"The exclusion of all profascist imperialist elements and the in-

17. See *The Nation,* July 24, 1948.

clusion in the Polish Government of democratic elements would be a fundamental improvement and would create a favorable basis for the re-establishment of Soviet-Polish relations and the settlement of the border question." In Soviet terminology, later to find illustration not only in Poland, but in many other countries, "profascist imperialists" were men who stood for the independence of their countries. "Democratic elements" were either Communists or individuals who were willing to accept Communist dictation. The Soviet reply was a veiled demand that Poland accept the status of a vassal state.

Mikolajczyk placed his hopes in American support. During the first months of 1944 the American attitude was vague and noncommittal. Expressions of abstract sympathy with Poland's cause were not accompanied by any steps calculated to check the trend which had set in since Teheran.

When Mikolajczyk, after some delays, was invited to America in June 1944, Roosevelt received him very graciously and talked with him five times in ten days. The President promised to use his influence with Stalin in favor of leaving the important city of Lwów and the economically valuable Galician oil wells to Poland. He thought possibly Wilno might also be saved. Mikolajczyk was soon to learn the value of these assurances.

The Red Army advanced deep into Poland during the first half of 1944. Polish underground forces harassed the Germans and rendered considerable help in the capture of Lwów and Wilno. At first the leaders of these units were thanked, praised, and sometimes decorated by the Red Army commanders. Later they were usually arrested, deported, shot, or hanged. There was a vast and ruthless purge of all known enemies of communism.

Late in July the Red Army was within a few miles of Warsaw. A considerable detachment of the Home Army (the Polish underground force) was in the Polish capital under the command of General T. Bor-Komorowski. His radio picked up on July 30 a Polish-language broadcast from Moscow ending with the names of Molotov and Edward Osubka-Morawski, a leading figure in the Moscow-organized Polish Committee of National Liberation. The broadcast was a call to immediate revolt:

"Poles, the time of liberation is at hand! Poles, to arms! Make every

Polish home a stronghold against the invader! There is not a moment to lose!"[18]

On the following day London picked up a similar appeal, broadcast from Moscow. At the same time it was announced from London that Mikolajczyk was going to Moscow to see Stalin. Believing that Soviet military aid was certain and that the signal for action had been given, Bor gave the order for revolt.

What followed was one of the most heroic and tragic episodes of the war. For two months this guerrilla army, with the enthusiastic support of the Warsaw population, without tanks, airplanes, or heavy artillery, fought against strong and well-equipped German units. The city of Warsaw was completely demolished in the process.

During the first two weeks, the insurgents won remarkable success and held a considerable part of the city. But the Soviet advance abruptly stopped. During the decisive days of the struggle for Warsaw the Soviet Government refused even to allow American and British airplanes to use near-by Soviet bases in order to drop desperately needed munitions and supplies to the insurgents.

Stalin had promised Mikolajczyk that he would do all in his power to help the Home Army. At the same time the Soviet dictator tried to extort from Mikolajczyk acceptance of the loss of East Poland and consent to be prime minister in a cabinet in which four of eighteen members would be Communists or Communist sympathizers.[19]

Mikolajczyk refused this offer and left Moscow for London on August 9, still hoping that Soviet military aid would be forthcoming for Warsaw. He dispatched another plea for this aid to Stalin. But Tass, the official Soviet news agency, issued a statement on August 14 which revealed the true design of the Soviet Government with brutal frankness:

Tass is in possession of information which shows that the Polish circles in London responsible for the Warsaw uprising made no attempt to co-ordinate this action with the Soviet High Command. In

18. See "The Unconquerables," by General T. Bor-Komorowski, in *Reader's Digest* for February 1946.

19. Mikolajczyk, *The Rape of Poland*, 77.

these circumstances the only people responsible for the results of the events in Warsaw are the émigré circles in London.

There was, of course, no mention of the Moscow broadcasts which had encouraged the revolt or of Stalin's promise to Mikolajczyk to aid the uprising. When Averell Harriman, American Ambassador to the Soviet Union, pleaded with Molotov on August 14 for permission to use Soviet shuttle bases for American bombers, the Soviet Foreign Minister flatly refused, calling the uprising a "purely adventurous affair," to which the Soviet Government could not lend a hand. In a later discussion, on the night of August 16, Molotov admitted to Harriman that Stalin had promised Mikolajczyk aid to Warsaw. However, the Soviet Government could not countenance association with the insurrection, because it was evident from newspaper and radio statements emanating from the Polish Government in London that the movement was inspired by men antagonistic to the Soviet Union.[20]

When the revolt was almost completely crushed, the Soviet Government permitted one shuttle flight, on September 18, and the Red Army dropped some supplies from its own airplanes. By this time it was too late for such assistance to be of any value. By first provoking, then abandoning the insurrection, the Soviet Government had procured the exposure and destruction of a large part of the Home Army. It was in line with the deportations of 1939–40, designed to eliminate or greatly reduce the Polish ethnic population east of the Curzon Line, and with the Katyn massacre, which deprived Poland of patriotic trained officers.

With the endorsement of his Cabinet in London, Mikolajczyk offered counterproposals to Stalin's inacceptable suggestions in Moscow. Some modification of the eastern frontier, without giving up Lwów and Wilno, was admitted. It was also proposed to admit three representatives of the Communist party, along with three delegates from each of the four main political parties, into a Polish provisional government. The British approved this scheme; and there was a last attempt to

20. All this information, based on State Department documents, is to be found in the report of Arthur Bliss Lane, submitted on June 1, 1945.

reach agreement with Stalin in October. Churchill and Eden took part in the negotiations, along with Mikolajczyk, Stalin, Molotov, and the American Ambassador Harriman.

The emptiness of Roosevelt's assurances to Mikolajczyk during the latter's visit to Washington was dramatically exposed. When the Polish Prime Minister argued that Poland deserved a better eastern frontier than the Curzon Line, Molotov suddenly broke in:

"But all this was settled at Teheran. We all agreed at Teheran that the Curzon Line must divide Poland. You will recall that President Roosevelt agreed to this solution and strongly endorsed the line."

According to Mikolajczyk's account, he looked at Churchill and Harriman, hoping for a denial. But Harriman looked silently at the rug and Churchill replied:

"I confirm this."[21]

Later Churchill bullied Mikolajczyk almost as ruthlessly as Hitler had bullied the Czechoslovak President Hacha on the eve of his march into Prague. A painful and extraordinary scene occurred. The Polish representative held out as best he could for his country's independence and territorial integrity—the very issue for which the war was ostensibly being fought. Churchill tried to impose the deal he thought he had made with Stalin by threats and abuse.

The climax was reached when Churchill told Mikolajczyk that he would personally guarantee freedom from Russian interference for what was left of Poland. This was too much for the normally patient and rather phlegmatic Pole. He bluntly retorted that he would rather die fighting with the underground than "be hanged later in full view of your British Ambassador."

This was what almost literally happened later to Nikola Petkov, leader of the Bulgarian opposition. Mikolajczyk most probably escaped a similar fate only by a timely and successful flight from Poland.

The Polish Prime Minister on October 27 addressed an appeal to Roosevelt, recalling the hopes the President had held out to him in June and asking the latter to address a personal appeal to Stalin for the retention of Lwów and the Galician oil fields by Poland. Roosevelt's

21. Mikolajczyk, *The Rape of Poland,* 96ff.

reply of November 17[22] evaded the points raised in the appeal. It coldly intimated that America would raise no objection if an agreement on frontier changes were reached between the Polish, Soviet, and British governments.

Harriman met Mikolajczyk in London and offered to intercede with Stalin for Lwów. In view of the Soviet dictator's unbending attitude, there was little prospect that such intercession would succeed. A break between Mikolajczyk and the majority of his Cabinet occurred on the question of whether to use Harriman's good offices. The majority argued that this would constitute a recognition of the Curzon Line as the frontier, except in the Lwów area and was, therefore, unacceptable. Mikolajczyk, impressed by the absence of American and British support and fearing the complete isolation of Poland, was in favor of making greater concessions.

The desertion of the western powers placed Poland's patriots before an agonizing dilemma. Honorable difference of opinion was possible because of the unpromising nature of the two alternatives between which a choice had to be made. An attitude of refusing to yield an inch of the prewar frontier was logical and consistent. Poland's moral case was unanswerable. But, with the visible American and British willingness to try to appease Stalin at Poland's expense, an uncompromising policy meant, in all probability, that the government-in-exile would never be able to return to Poland.

On the other hand, given the Soviet record, the deportations, the Katyn massacre, the incitation and betrayal of the Warsaw uprising, the growing support for a puppet communist regime, there was little chance that Poland's independence could be saved by the sacrifice of its eastern provinces. However, Mikolajczyk and some of his political associates in the Peasant party believed that the chance, however slight, must be grasped, that they should return to Poland at any price.

Despite pleas for delay from Roosevelt, Stalin recognized his own creation, the Polish Committee of National Liberation, as the provisional government of Poland on January 5, 1945. From this time the Soviet Government took the position that this regime, which was com-

22. The American reply was probably deliberately held back until after the election, in which Roosevelt was elected President for the fourth time.

pletely dependent on Moscow for its support and its very existence, was the legitimate government of Poland.

The Polish issue figured prominently in the discussions at the Yalta Conference of the Big Three. This conference is described in more detail in Chapter 10. The agreement on Poland conceded the substance of Stalin's demands, while it contained a few face-saving phrases, designed to win the approval of western public opinion. The text of this agreement was as follows:

A new situation has been created in Poland as a result of her complete liberation by the Red Army. This calls for the establishment of a Polish Provisional Government which can be more broadly based than was possible before the recent liberation of the Western part of Poland. The Provisional Government which is now functioning in Poland should therefore be reorganized on a broader democratic basis with the inclusion of democratic leaders from Poland itself and from Poles abroad. This new government should then be called the Polish Provisional Government of National Unity.

M. Molotov, Mr. Harriman and Sir A. Clark Kerr are authorized as a commission to consult in the first instance in Moscow with members of the present Provisional Government and with other Polish democratic leaders from within Poland and from abroad, with a view to the reorganization of the present Government along the above lines. The Polish Provisional Government of National Unity shall be pledged to the holding of free and unfettered elections as soon as possible on the basis of universal suffrage and secret ballot. In these elections all democratic and anti-Nazi parties shall have the right to take part and to put forward candidates.

When a Polish Provisional Government of National Unity has been properly formed in conformity with the above, the Government of the USSR, which now maintains diplomatic relations with the present Provisional Government of Poland, and the Government of the United Kingdom and the Government of the USA will establish diplomatic relations with the new Polish Provisional Government of National Unity, and will exchange Ambassadors by whose reports the respective Governments will be kept informed about the situation in Poland.

The three Heads of Government consider that the Eastern frontier of Poland should follow the Curzon Line with digressions from it in some regions of five to eight kilometers in favour of Poland. They recognize that Poland must receive substantial accessions of territory in the North and West. They feel that the opinion of the new Polish Provisional Government of National Unity should be sought in due course on the extent of these accessions and that the final delimitation on the Western frontier of Poland should therefore await the Peace Conference.

Signed: WINSTON S. CHURCHILL,
FRANKLIN D. ROOSEVELT, J. V. STALIN

One of the most striking features of this agreement, which dealt with the most vital problems of Poland's future, is that no Pole had a word to say about it. The Big Three proceeded to carve up Poland, to take away land that was historically and ethnically Polish, to assign to Poland land that was historically and ethnically German, without even listening to any representative of the Polish people. No conquered enemy nation could have received more contemptuous treatment.

The tragic drama of Munich was re-enacted at Yalta with startling fidelity. Only the personalities changed; the atmosphere of appeasement was the same. For Czechoslovakia substitute Poland. For Hitler read Stalin. Roosevelt and Churchill played the parts of Chamberlain and Daladier. One difference, however, may be noted, American and British moral obligations to Poland, in view of that country's war sufferings, were far greater than British and French obligations to Czechoslovakia.

The phrases about free and unfettered elections, universal suffrage, and secret ballot looked well on paper. But with the Red Army in military occupation of Poland and Soviet secret police operatives all over that country, there was only one chance of assuring that these phrases would bear any relation to realities. This would have been the presence of numerous American and British observers. But every effort was made to exclude such observers during the decisive period when the new regime was consolidating its power.

The meetings of the commission composed of Molotov, Harriman, and Clark Kerr ended in deadlock. The American and British members argued that representatives of the three groups mentioned in the Yalta Declaration (the Soviet-sponsored provisional government, democratic Poles in Poland, and Poles abroad) should be included in the new government. But Molotov insisted that the existing puppet regime should be the nucleus of the new government and refused to accept any names not approved by this regime. It was a preview of how the Soviet veto would work in the United Nations. Molotov also rejected a proposal that American and British observers should be permitted to visit Poland on the ground that this would "sting the national pride of the Poles to the quick."

There was soon to be a dramatic illustration of the Soviet attitude toward "democratic Poles in Poland." Sixteen prominent Polish underground leaders, relying on the "word of honor" of a Soviet police officer, Colonel Pimenov, who assured them safe conduct, came out of hiding for consultation with the Soviet authorities. They were promptly arrested and taken to Moscow for trial on charges of having carried on diversionist activities in the rear of the Red Army.

This incident gives the impression of having been contrived as a deliberate insult to the western powers, as a sign that the Soviet authorities were able to do as they pleased in Poland. It was a patent contradiction of the spirit of the Yalta Agreement. Inquiries from Washington and London about the fate of the Poles were left unanswered for weeks.

But the American and British appetite for appeasement was still insatiable. The arrests were casually announced by Molotov at the San Francisco conference for the organization of the United Nations. There was a mild protest from Anthony Eden, who might well have felt some personal responsibility for the fate of the Poles, since the British Government had advised them to reveal their whereabouts. There was a feebler statement from the American Secretary of State, Stettinius, who probably did not know what it was all about.

And the man who, after Roosevelt, was most responsible for the policy of giving in to Stalin on every disputed point, Harry Hopkins, was sent to Moscow to straighten things out. Hopkins fulfilled this mission in his usual fashion, by accepting all Stalin's assurances at face value and giving the Soviet dictator everything he wanted.

Hopkins did not even make the release of the treacherously arrested

Polish underground leaders a condition of American recognition of the new Polish Government. And he went far beyond the Yalta concessions by assuring Stalin that "as far as the United States was concerned, we had no interest in seeing anyone connected with the present Polish Government in London involved in the new Provisional Government of Poland."[23]

The result was that Mikolajczyk and a few Poles from abroad were given minor posts in the new government. Hopkins brushed off the reproach of a friend for having consented to such an unfair arrangement with the remark: "After all, what does it matter? The Poles are like the Irish. They are never satisfied with anything anyhow."[24] Polish independence had been murdered, and there was a general desire in Administration circles to get the corpse buried with as little unseemly fuss as possible.

As a State Department official said to Ambassador Ciechanowski: "The Polish problem had to be settled because it had become an impossible headache." And on July 5, 1945, the great betrayal was finally consummated. The United States Government withdrew its recognition of the Polish Government in London and formally recognized Stalin's regime in Warsaw.

The rest of the story could easily be anticipated. The new Polish government used every police-state method to discourage, break, and finally outlaw political opposition. The Yalta promises of free, unfettered elections and democratic procedures were turned into a sorry joke.[25]

The United States sent to Poland as ambassador an able career diplomat, Arthur Bliss Lane. But he was handicapped by a timid and wavering policy in Washington. By extending recognition before the new government had held an election or possessed any mandate from the Polish people, the western powers had lost any means of pressing for the observance of the Yalta assurances.

The men who held key positions in the new regime, Bierut, Berman,

23. Sherwood, *Roosevelt and Hopkins*, 907.
24. Ciechanowski, *Defeat in Victory*, 382–83.
25. Full details of repression and fraud are described in Lane, *I Saw Poland Betrayed*, and Mikolajczyk, *The Rape of Poland*.

Radkiewicz, were politically unknown in Poland before the war. They were Moscow-trained Communists. The armed forces and the security police, headed by Radkiewicz, were heavily infiltrated with Russians. Complete Soviet control of the new state was emphasized in 1949 when the Soviet Marshal Constantine Rokossovsky, a Pole by origin, but a Soviet citizen for thirty years, was appointed head of Poland's defense forces.

Despite the abandonment of Poland by the western powers, there was a prolonged guerrilla struggle during 1946 and 1947, with substantial losses on both sides. Several Polish underground organizations kept up the fight during these years, and Ukrainian partisans were active in southeastern Poland. This guerrilla movement later subsided because of the impossibility of getting arms from abroad.

The "free, unfettered elections" promised at Yalta took place on January 19, 1947, after two years of terrorist repression which became intensified as the day of voting approached. The main issue was between a bloc of government parties, dominated by the Communists, and Mikolajczyk's Peasant party. The American Government on January 5, 1947, sent the following note to the Soviet and British Governments, as cosignatories of the Yalta Agreement. Its indictment of the bankruptcy of this agreement was worded as follows:

The methods used by the [Polish] Government in its efforts to eliminate the participation of the Polish Peasant Party in the election include political arrests and murders, compulsory enrolment of Polish Peasant Party members in the "bloc" political parties, dismissal of PPP members from their employment, searches of homes, attacks by secret police and members of the Communist Party on PPP premises and party congresses, suspension and restriction by government authorities of PPP meetings and suspension of party activities in twenty-eight districts, suppression of the party press and limitation of circulation of party newspapers, and arrest of the editorial staff of the party bulletin and of the *Gazeta Ludova*.

The crusade for Polish independence and territorial integrity which began with a bang ended in a pitiful whimper. Ambassador Lane reported after his arrival in Poland:

Despite the sufferings which the Poles had endured under the Nazi occupation and especially in Warsaw, many of the Poles with whom we spoke amazingly admitted that they preferred Nazi occupation to their present plight.[26]

Legal opposition of any kind became virtually impossible after the fraudulent election of 1947. Mikolajczyk escaped from Poland in October. In all probability he narrowly escaped the fate he had foreseen in his argument with Churchill three years earlier. Poland, so far as its government could achieve this purpose, became a thoroughly anti-western country. Its delegates in the United Nations voted invariably as the Kremlin dictated. Its human and material resources were at Stalin's disposal.

Was all this inevitable? Were Roosevelt and Churchill, in their step-by-step abandonment first of Poland's territorial integrity, then of Poland's independence, obeying the dictates of inescapable historical necessity? This is what their apologists contend in representing Teheran and Yalta as the products of sheer military necessity.[27]

I do not believe the weight of evidence supports this view. Naturally Stalin's aggression knew no bounds when it met with co-operation or only the feeblest opposition in Washington and London. But suppose the American and British Governments from the outset had taken a clear, uncompromising stand for Poland's rights under the Atlantic Charter. Suppose they had exacted specific pledges of renunciation of the spoils of the pact with Hitler when the Soviet Union was hard pressed in 1941. Suppose they had made it clear, not only by unequivocal words, but by deeds, by slowing down lend-lease shipments, for instance, that the restoration of an independent Poland within the boundaries of 1939 was a war aim which would not be compromised.

Who can say with certainty that Stalin would not have respected this attitude and pursued a more conciliatory policy, looking to the establishment in Poland of a regime that would be on good terms with Russia without being a subservient vassal? And if Stalin had overrun Poland with military force, the situation would surely have been better

26. Lane, *I Saw Poland Betrayed*, 160.
27. This line of argument is heavily overworked in the concluding chapters of Stettinius, *Roosevelt and the Russians*.

if the western powers had refused to recognize the legitimacy of this action. What was perhaps most demoralizing to the Polish people was the positive co-operation of America and Britain with the Soviet Union in according full recognition to a Soviet puppet regime.

The same pattern was repeated, with minor variations, in Yugoslavia and in Albania. With almost incredible blindness, Roosevelt and Churchill helped to build up Stalin's Eurasian empire, abandoning their natural friends in Eastern Europe. And the whole political sense and purpose of the war in the Far East were lost when Roosevelt handed Stalin the key to China at Yalta.

It is not true that Roosevelt and Churchill had no alternative to appease Stalin by sacrificing Poland and on other issues. But if this hypothesis were accepted as valid, what a revealing light is shed upon the futility and hypocrisy of the whole crusade, supposedly for freedom and international righteousness!

Was it really worth while to fight a destructive war so that Poland might be the victim not of Hitler but of Stalin, so that there might be a Soviet empire, not a German empire, in Eastern Europe, so that we should face not Japan but Stalin's henchman, Mao Tse-tung, in the Orient? War and postwar emotionalism have inhibited a frank facing of these questions. But the tragic factual record of what happened to Poland, set down in this chapter, surely suggests that there is a case for a negative answer.

# 12

## Germany Must Be Destroyed

Roosevelt's policy toward Germany found its main expression in two decisions. One was negative, the other ferociously destructionist. The first was the "unconditional surrender" slogan, proclaimed at Casablanca in January 1943. The second was the Morgenthau Plan, sanctioned at Quebec in September 1944.

Both of these decisions were grist for the Nazi propaganda mill. Both were calculated to prolong the war and to make postwar reconstruction more difficult by impelling the Germans to fight as long as any physical means of resistance were left. Both were calculated to serve Stalin's interest in making Communist political capital out of ruin and despair.

The President's creative political thinking suffered an eclipse after the enunciation of the Four Freedoms and the Atlantic Charter in 1941. One is impressed by the paucity both in content and in originality of his utterances about the nature of the peace after America entered the war. This is most probably attributable in part to his absorption in the military side of the war, in part to his failing mental and physical powers.

A negative, destructionist attitude toward Germany was closely, if unconsciously, bound up with approval of, or acquiescence in, Soviet ambitions for domination of Europe. These attitudes were two sides of the same coin. If the expansion of the Soviet empire in Europe and in Asia far beyond Russia's proper enthnographic frontiers was a cause for indifference, even for satisfaction, then and only then could a policy of pulverizing Germany and Japan, reducing these countries to complete economic and military impotence, be considered consistent with American national interest. But if unlimited Soviet expansion was not

desirable, the maintenance of some counterweight in Central Europe
and in East Asia was imperatively necessary.[1]

Roosevelt first publicly used the phrase "unconditional surrender"
at a press conference in Casablanca on January 23, 1943. It was apparently a product of scrambled history and very questionable political
strategy. General Ulysses S. Grant during the Civil War won national
fame by demanding "immediate and unconditional surrender" from
the Confederate commander who was defending Fort Donelson. This
was a localized military operation.

Roosevelt mistakenly associated the phrase with Lee's surrender at
Appomattox. The President also recalled Grant's willingness to allow
the Confederate officers to keep their horses after the surrender. When
he announced the decision at Casablanca, however, Lee and the horses
were forgotten.

The authorship of "unconditional surrender" was unquestionably
Roosevelt's. According to Elliott Roosevelt,[2] who was present at Casablanca, the President first pronounced the words at a luncheon on
January 23. Harry Hopkins immediately expressed strong approval.
Churchill, according to this version, frowned, thought, grinned, and
said: "Perfect, and I can just see how Goebbels and the rest of 'em will
squeal." Roosevelt suggested that Stalin would be pleased:

"Of course it's just the thing for the Russians. They couldn't want
anything better. Unconditional Surrender, Uncle Joe might have made
it up himself."[3]

The phrase was discussed during a debate in the House of Commons
on July 21, 1949. Foreign Secretary Ernest Bevin, who was a member
of the British War Cabinet, blamed this slogan for the difficulties of
occupation policy in Germany:

1. A shrewd Swiss observer once remarked to me: "You Americans are a
strange people. You want to check the Soviet Union after you have systematically
destroyed the two powers, Germany and Japan, which might have done this successfully."

2. E. Roosevelt, *As He Saw It*, 117ff.

3. "Uncle Joe," as later events would indicate, was happy to have "unconditional surrender" sponsored by the western powers, not by himself.

It began with the declaration of unconditional surrender at Casablanca, on which neither the British Cabinet nor any other Cabinet had a chance to say a word. It was just said, and in the middle of a war. But it left us with a Germany without law, without a constitution, without a single person with whom we could deal, without a single institution to grapple with the situation, and we have had to build absolutely from the bottom with nothing at all.[4]

Churchill then offered the following explanation of his position at Casablanca:

The statement was made by President Roosevelt without consultation with me. I was there on the spot, and I had very rapidly to consider whether the state of our position in the world was such as would justify me in not giving support to it. . . . I have not the slightest doubt that if the British Cabinet had considered that phrase it is possible that they would have advised against it, but, working with a great alliance and with great, loyal and powerful friends from across the ocean, we had to accommodate ourselves.

Later, on November 17, 1949, Churchill modified his earlier statement after consulting the records of the Casablanca Conference. The words "unconditional surrender," he told the House of Commons in this second statement, had been mentioned "probably in informal talk, I think at meal times" on January 19, 1943. Mr. Churchill sent a cable to the British Cabinet informing them of the intention to issue an unconditional surrender demand which should not apply to Italy. The Cabinet's response, according to Churchill, "was not against unconditional surrender." "They only disapproved with it not being applied to Italy as well." However, the phrase does not appear in the official communiqué of the Casablanca Conference. Its exclusive use by Roosevelt at a press conference suggests that its origin was his.

Roosevelt, according to Sherwood,[5] represented the phrase as a sudden improvisation. There had been great difficulty in persuading the rival French leaders, De Gaulle and Giraud, to meet and strike an

4. *The* (London) *Times* for July 22 contains a full account of this debate.
5. Sherwood, *Roosevelt and Hopkins*, 696.

amicable pose at Casablanca. Roosevelt, according to his recollection, thought of the difficulty of bringing about a meeting between Grant and Lee, recalled that Grant was known as Old Unconditional Surrender, and the slogan was born.

It may be doubted whether it was as unrehearsed as this version would indicate. A foreign diplomat stationed in Washington during the war has informed me that Roosevelt tried out the phrase on him some weeks before the Casablanca conference took place. Apparently the President was enormously proud of his creation. He refused to qualify, moderate, or even explain it despite the repeated efforts of General Eisenhower to obtain authorization for some message which would make the Germans more willing to lay down their arms.[6]

Eisenhower, in May 1943 on the eve of the invasion of Sicily, reported to the Combined Chiefs of Staff that he did not have the right kind of ammunition for psychological warfare with Italy. As his aide, Captain Harry C. Butcher, reports,

There have been discussions with him [Roosevelt] as to the meaning of "unconditional surrender" as applied to Germany. Any military person knows that there are conditions to every surrender. There is a feeling that at Casablanca the President and the Prime Minister, more likely the former, seized on Grant's famous term without realizing the full implications to the enemy. Goebbels has made great capital with it to strengthen the morale of the German army and people. Our psychological experts believe we would be wiser if we created a mood of acceptance of surrender in the German army which would make possible a collapse of resistance similar to that which took place in Tunisia. They think if a proper mood is created in the German General Staff there might even be a German Badoglio.[7]

There was a slight concession when Roosevelt and Churchill on July 16 used "honorable capitulation" in a message to the Italian people.

---

6. A good account of the President's unyielding resistance on this point may be found in Carroll, *Persuade or Perish*, 307–37. Mr. Carroll served in the OWI and was therefore intimately concerned with the problems of psychological warfare.

7. Butcher, *My Three Years with Eisenhower*, 443.

But they soon returned to strict insistence on the Casablanca formula. Discussion of the meaning of "unconditional surrender" with Marshal Pietro Badoglio, head of the Italian Government after the displacement of Mussolini, went on from the end of July 1943 until the beginning of September. This made it easier for the Germans to take over most of Italy. General J. F. C. Fuller caustically sums up as follows the balance sheet of "unconditional surrender" in Italy:

"Unconditional Surrender transformed the 'soft underbelly' (Churchill's phrase about Italy) into a crocodile's back; prolonged the war; wrecked Italy; and wasted thousands of American and British lives."[8]

Stalin did not fall in with the "unconditional surrender" slogan. The Soviet dictator pursued a much wilier and more intelligent political strategy. He made two public statements in 1943 which could easily be construed as invitations to the Germans to conclude a separate peace, with the understanding that their national integrity and military force would be spared. Stalin declared on February 23, 1943:

Occasionally the foreign press engages in prattle to the effect that the Red Army's aim is to exterminate the German people and destroy the German state. This is, of course, a stupid lie and senseless slander against the Red Army. . . . It would be ridiculous to identify Hitler's clique with the German people and the German state. History shows that the Hitlers come and go, but the German people and the German state remain.

This declaration was made after the great German defeat at Stalingrad. The German armies were still deep in Soviet territory, in occupation of most of the Ukraine and a large area in western Russia. But the German prospect of winning the war in the East had disappeared.

Stalin made another bid, on November 6, 1943, this time to elements in the German Army which might be willing to rebel against the Nazi party. By this time the Germans were in full retreat and had withdrawn beyond the line of the Dnieper River.

It is not our aim to destroy Germany, for it is impossible to destroy Germany, just as it is impossible to destroy Russia. But the Hitler

8. Fuller, *The Second World War,* 265.

state can and should be destroyed. It is not our aim to destroy all organized military force in Germany, for every literate person will understand that this is not only impossible in regard to Germany, as it is in regard to Russia, but it is also inadmissible from the viewpoint of the victor.

A National Committee of Free Germans was organized in Moscow in July 1943. Captured German officers of high rank were encouraged to broadcast messages to the German Army and to the German people. These messages were not filled with Communist propaganda. They were appeals to Germans, especially to those in the armed forces, to end a hopeless war in the interest of national self-preservation.

Stalin questioned the expediency of the "unconditional surrender" formula at the Teheran Conference. He felt that it merely served to unite the German people. The announcement of specific terms, however harsh, in Stalin's opinion would hasten the German capitulation.[9]

But Roosevelt clung to his pet phrase with an obstinacy worthy of a better cause. His vanity and prestige were deeply involved. Churchill saw in "unconditional surrender" a means of liquidating the inconvenient restraints of the Atlantic Charter. He told the House of Commons on May 24, 1944:

The principle of Unconditional Surrender will be adhered to so far as Nazi Germany and Japan are concerned, and that principle itself wipes away the danger of anything like Mr. Wilson's Fourteen Points being brought up by the Germans after their defeat, claiming that they surrendered in consideration of them. . . . There is no question of Germany enjoying any guaranty that she will not undergo territorial changes, if it should seem that the making of such changes renders more secure and more lasting the peace of Europe.

It apparently did not occur to Churchill that the real cause for criticism was not the Fourteen Points, but the failure to embody these points honestly in the peace settlements. It is certainly arguable that if the statesmen in Paris in 1919 had been as reasonable and cool-headed as

9. Sherwood, *Roosevelt and Hopkins*, 782–83.

their predecessors in Vienna a century earlier and worked out a peace of moderation, the Hitlerite madness would never have possessed the German people. In that event, of course, the history of Europe would have been very different and infinitely happier.

There were a number of efforts by generals, by psychological warfare experts, by the British, to obtain a definition of what "unconditional surrender" meant. All foundered on the rock of Roosevelt's stubborn opposition. The United States Joint Chiefs of Staff set up a committee of intelligence officers to study the subject.

This committee on March 16, 1944, recommended the issue of an American-British-Soviet statement reaffirming the principle of "unconditional surrender," but clarifying its meaning. The proposed statement would announce that, while the Allies proposed to prevent future German aggression, they would not wipe out Germany as a nation. There would be punishment for war criminals, but no indiscriminate penalization of the German masses. Germany's co-operation would be needed in the future peace.

Roosevelt's reply on April 1 was an uncompromising negative. He was unwilling to say that the Allies did not intend to destroy the German nation. "As long as the word Reich exists in Germany as expressing a nationhood," he declared, "it will forever be associated with the present form of nationhood. If we admit that, we must seek to eliminate the word Reich and all that it stands for today."[10]

Equally unavailing were attempts by Eisenhower to obtain some definition of "unconditional surrender" before the invasion of France. Churchill was inclined to relent on this point. But the only concrete explanation of what would follow unconditional surrender was the President's public approval of the Morgenthau Plan. This was scarcely an inducement to surrender.

Goebbels made the most of "unconditional surrender" and the Morgenthau Plan in his propaganda for last-ditch resistance. Typical of his broadcasts and writings was a speech which he delivered in the Rhineland in October 1944:

It is a matter of complete indifference whether, in the course of executing their plans of destruction, the Americans wish to destroy our

10. Carroll, *Persuade or Perish*, 320.

tools, machinery and factories, or whether the Bolsheviks want to take them, along with our workers, to Siberia. From neither enemy can we expect any mercy or protection whatsoever if we deliver ourselves up to them.[11]

The British General Fuller, a keen and caustic critic of the failures and inconsistencies of American and British war policies,[12] pronounces the following verdict on Roosevelt's favorite idea, almost the only idea he originated after America entered the war:

These two words [unconditional surrender] were to hang like a putrifying albatross around the necks of America and Britain. . . . Once victory had been won the balance of power within Europe and between European nations would be irrevocably smashed. Russia would be left the greatest military power in Europe and, therefore, would dominate Europe. Consequently the peace these words predicted was the replacement of Nazi tyranny by an even more barbaric despotism.[13]

The judgment of an experienced British statesman, Lord Hankey, on the "unconditional surrender" slogan and its corollary, the war-crimes trials, is summed up as follows:

It embittered the war, rendered inevitable a fight to the finish, banged the door to any possibility of either side offering terms or opening up negotiations, gave the Germans and the Japanese the courage of despair, strengthened Hitler's position as Germany's 'only hope,' aided Goebbels's propaganda, and made inevitable the Normandy landing and the subsequent terribly exhausting and destructive advance through North France, Belgium, Luxemburg, Holland and Germany. The lengthening of the war enabled Stalin to occupy the whole of eastern Europe, to ring down the iron curtain and so to realize at one swoop a large instalment of his avowed aims against so-called capitalism, in which he includes social democracy. By disposing of all the more competent administrators in Germany and

11. Ibid., 324.
12. General Fuller was a pioneer in recognizing the possibilities of the tank in World War I.
13. Fuller, *The Second World War,* 258–59.

Japan this policy rendered treaty-making impossible after the war and retarded recovery and reconstruction, not only in Germany and Japan, but everywhere else. It may also prove to have poisoned our future relations with ex-enemy countries. Not only the enemy countries, but nearly all countries were bled white by this policy, which has left us all, except the United States of America, impoverished and in dire straits. Unfortunately also, these policies, so contrary to the spirit of the Sermon on the Mount, did nothing to strengthen the moral position of the Allies.[14]

It is difficult to recognize a single desirable war or peace objective that was advanced by the Casablanca slogan. And it is easy to discern several unfortunate by-products of this shoddy substitute for intelligent political warfare.

First, the diplomatic position of the western powers was seriously worsened vis-à-vis the Soviet Union. Stalin did not associate himself with the phrase until the later phases of the war. He certainly did what he could in 1943 to induce the German military leaders to rebel and conclude a separate peace.

It was not due to any diplomatic skill or finesse on Roosevelt's part that America and Britain were not faced with the political catastrophe of a separate peace between the Soviet Union and Germany. And Stalin would certainly have been more amenable to western diplomatic pressure on Poland and other disputed issues if he had been made to feel that a negotiated peace between the western powers and a non-Nazi Germany was not out of the question.

Second, by supplying the powerful motive of fear to Nazi propagandists, the slogan prolonged the war and made it more savage and costly. Tens of thousands of American and British lives were sacrificed on the altar of this vainglorious phrase. "Unconditional surrender" was also a fearful stumbling block in winding up the war with Japan. Had it been amplified by reasonable explanations, two most undesirable developments, the Soviet occupation of Manchuria and the dropping of the atomic bomb, would almost certainly have been avoided.

14. Hankey, *Politics, Trials and Errors*, 125–26.

Third, the slogan was psychologically calculated to bind the Germans more closely to the Nazi regime. The official thesis in Washington during the war was that almost all Germans were tainted with nazism. There was a persistent refusal to act on the assumption that there was an anti-Nazi underground movement which represented a wide cross-section of German society and deserved, on political and moral grounds, encouragement which it did not receive in Washington and London.

The leading figures in the German underground were Colonel General Ludwig Beck, Chief of Staff of the Army until the summer of 1938, and Karl Friedrich Goerdeler, a former mayor of Leipzig. Closely associated with them were the former Ambassador to Italy, Ulrich von Hassell, the former Prussian Finance Minister, Johannes Popitz, a number of generals, officers, and officials, and some labor and socialist leaders, among whom Julius Leber and Wilhelm Leuschner were the most prominent.

A special opposition group was composed of the members of the so-called Kreisau circle, headed by Helmuth von Moltke, descendant of a famous aristocratic family, known for his radical social ideals, which inclined toward a kind of Christian socialism. Other members of this group were Peter Yorck von Wartenburg, a descendant of the General Yorck who led one of the first moves in the German war of liberation against Napoleon, and Adam von Trott zu Solz, a widely traveled and highly educated young German who had studied in England as a Rhodes scholar. It is interesting and significant that many of the leaders of the anti-Hitler movement had either family or cultural connections with the western countries.

The Kreisau circle favored nationalization of heavy industry, banks, and insurance companies, and labor representation in the management of industry. In the international field its program called for a federation of Europe, abolition of the German Army, and a trial of war criminals before an international tribunal to be composed of judges from the victorious, neutral, and defeated nations.

The underground was not a mass movement. There could be no such movement under a regime where spies were everywhere and individuals were forced by terror to act as informers on their neighbors.

But the underground was more than a group of a few individuals of no political consequence. It had members and sympathizers in high military and political posts, notably in the *Abwehr*, or Counterintelligence. Moreover, although the Nazi regime had crushed open political opposition, there were actual and potential sympathizers with any resistance movement among former members of the democratic political parties and the trade unions and among disillusioned conservatives. There was an abortive plot in the higher command of the Reichswehr on the eve of the Munich agreement in 1938. The ground was cut from beneath the feet of the conspirators because the western powers yielded to Hitler's demands.

A young officer, a lawyer in civilian life, Fabian von Schlabrendorff, placed a bomb, disguised as a bottle of cognac, in Hitler's plane on the eastern front in February 1943. This attempt failed because the percussion cap failed to go off.

Some members of the underground possessed sufficient influence to obtain passports for travel in foreign lands. They tried to establish contacts in official circles, to make known the existence and aims of an anti-Nazi movement. Von Trott talked with high officials in the State Department in the autumn of 1939. He suggested American moral support for the idea of a fair peace settlement with a regime which would succeed the Nazis, including an assurance of Germany's 1933 frontiers.

At first Roosevelt was interested in this information about the existence of an anti-Nazi underground. Later, however, he discouraged further contacts. Von Trott was even denounced as a Nazi. He returned to Germany by way of Japan and continued to work for the overthrow of Hitler until he was arrested and executed after the July 20 plot.[15]

This attitude of not wishing even to know about the existence of an anti-Nazi movement in Germany, much less to have any dealings with it, is illustrated by another incident that occurred after America had entered the war.

Louis P. Lochner, head of the Berlin office of the Associated Press, was taken to a private movement of oppositionists in Berlin in Novem-

15. For a detailed account of von Trott's activity see the article by Alexander B. Maley in *Human Events* for February 27, 1946.

ber 1941. Among those present were representatives of the pre-Nazi trade unions, of the Confessional Church,[16] of the political parties which existed under the Weimar Republic, and of the Army. There was a general feeling among those present that America would soon enter the war.

Lochner was asked to get in touch with President Roosevelt after his return to the United States, to inform him of the existence of an underground movement and to learn from him what kind of political regime in Germany would be acceptable after Hitler's downfall. Lochner was given a code in which messages could be conveyed from America to Germany.

When Lochner reached the United States after a period of internment in Germany, he made several unsuccessful attempts to see the President. Finally he explained the purpose of his request in writing. This elicited a negative reply from the President's office, suggesting that he desist because his request was "most embarrassing."[17]

It is not easy to determine on the basis of available evidence which individuals were most responsible for this consistent attitude of overlooking opportunities to drive a wedge between the Nazi regime and the German people. That Henry Morgenthau, Secretary of the Treasury, who liked to meddle with affairs outside his own department, exercised a most deleterious influence is obvious from the plan which bears his name and which he sponsored most vehemently.

German political emigrants in the United States fell into three main categories. There were men, ranging from conservatives to Social Democrats, who hated nazism but wished to see Germany exist as an independent country with reasonable frontiers and a viable economy after the war. There were bitter destructionists, individuals who wished to revenge indiscriminately on the entire German people what they or their friends and relatives had suffered at the hands of the Third Reich. And there were Communists and fellow travelers.

It was the emigrants in the last two categories who found the most sympathetic hearing in Washington during the war. Indeed, when one

16. In the Confessional Church were those pastors of the Evangelical Church who opposed racism and other Nazi teachings as un-Christian.
17. Rothfels, *The German Opposition to Hitler*, 140.

recalls the extreme laxity (to use no stronger term) of the OWI in re-sisting Communist infiltration,[18] one suspects that Gerhard Eisler, later exposed as a leading Communist agent in this country, might have been put in charge of propaganda for Germany, if he had thought of applying for the job.

One of the several attempts of the anti-Nazi Germans to establish foreign contacts[19] was the meeting between the Bishop of Chichester and two German pastors, Hans Schönfeld and Dietrich Bonhoeffer, in Stockholm in May 1942. Bonhoeffer was especially vehement in his antipathy to Hitler. At a secret church meeting in Geneva in 1941 he had said:

"I pray for the defeat of my nation. Only in defeat can we atone for the terrible crimes we have committed against Europe and the world."

Bonhoeffer was murdered in a concentration camp shortly before the end of the war. When the two pastors met the Bishop in Stockholm they pressed for a reply to a question which was of vital interest to active and passive opponents of Hitler's regime. Would the attitude of the Allies toward a Germany purged of Hitler differ from the attitude toward a Nazi Germany? They asked either for a public official decla-ration or for a private statement to an authorized representative of the underground.

The Bishop submitted a memorandum on his conversations to For-eign Secretary Anthony Eden. He was informed on July 17 that no action could be taken.[20]

It could be argued that there were two reasons for caution in dealing with the German opposition. First, so long as Hitler seemed to be win-ning the war, there was little if any prospect that his government could be overthrown. Second, the strength of the underground was doubtful and uncertain.

18. See Chapter 10, pp. 257–59.

19. Ulrich von Hassell, an ex-diplomat who was closely associated with the underground, had several meetings with an unnamed representative of Lord Halifax, British Foreign Secretary, in Switzerland in 1940. See Hassell, *The Von Hassell Diaries*, 115ff, 132–34.

20. See "The Background of the Hitler Plot," by the Bishop of Chichester, *The Contemporary Review* for September, 1945, pp. 203–8.

The first reason lost validity after the tide of the war turned with the defeat of the Germans at Stalingrad,[21] the rout of Rommel's army in Egypt, and the successful landing in North Africa. After these developments every intelligent German who was not a Nazi fanatic realized that the war was lost, even though German armies were still far outside Germany's frontiers. Pessimism and defeatism were especially prevalent in higher military circles. This is why so many prominent generals, both in Germany and on the western front, took part in the plot of July 20.

Certainly there were the strongest reasons, military and political, for encouraging the anti-Hitler forces by giving some kind of constructive peace assurance along the lines of the Four Freedoms and the Atlantic Charter. But the blank wall of negation set up by "unconditional surrender" blocked any kind of effective political warfare during 1943 and 1944, when it might well have yielded success.

The United States Government was aware of the existence and strength of the German underground at that time. The German vice-consul in Zürich, Hans Bernd Gisevius, a member of the underground, was in close touch with Allen W. Dulles, head of the OSS (Office of Strategic Services) in Switzerland. Dulles was informed in advance of the plot that was to break out on July 20. He urged that the United States Government should issue a statement urging the German people to overthrow Hitler's regime.

But, as he says, "nothing of this nature was done."[22] And, as he observes in another connection: "It sometimes seemed that those who determine policy in America and England were making the military task as difficult as possible by uniting all Germans to resist to the bitter end."[23]

Despite the complete lack of encouragement from the West, the German underground made its last desperate effort on July 20, 1944. The Gestapo was already closing in. Von Moltke and Leber had been arrested and Goerdeler was in hiding. A leader among the conspira-

21. Some German military experts believe the war was lost in 1941, when the Wehrmacht was driven back from Moscow.
22. Dulles, *Germany's Underground*, 141.
23. Ibid., 173.

tors, Col. Klaus von Stauffenberg, who had access to Hitler's headquarters in East Prussia, proposed to assassinate the dictator with a time bomb.

As soon as Hitler was killed, the generals who were involved in the conspiracy were to arrest Nazi and SS[24] leaders. The head of the Berlin police, Count Helldorff, was prepared to co-operate. In the plot, besides a number of officers and officials in Berlin, were Field Marshal von Kluge, Commander in Chief on the western front, Field Marshal Rommel, the famous tank commander of North Africa, and General Heinrich von Stülpnagel, military governor of France.

General Beck, coleader, with Goerdeler, of the underground, was to announce over the radio that he was chief of state, that General von Witzleben was in command of the armed forces, and that there would be a three-day state of emergency. During this time a cabinet would be formed and Nazi resistance would be liquidated.

Goerdeler was to become chancellor and had prepared a manifesto announcing a state based on the Christian traditions of western civilization. The Social Democrat Leuschner was designated as vice-chancellor. The Foreign Minister was to be either von Hassell or the former Ambassador to the Soviet Union, von Schulenburg, depending on whether peace contacts were first established with the West or with the East.

Stauffenberg placed the bomb, concealed in his briefcase, in close proximity to Hitler and made an excuse to leave the room. He heard a loud explosion and flew in a waiting plane to Berlin, convinced that the Führer was dead and that the conspiracy could go ahead at full speed. However, Hitler had changed his position after Stauffenberg left. Consequently he was only stunned, not seriously injured, by the explosion, which killed four other persons. According to General Heussinger, who was present when the explosion took place, two factors saved Hitler's life. The bomb was designed for use in an air raid shelter, where the explosion would have been confined. At the last moment the staff meeting was moved to a light building or tent. Moreover, the briefcase containing the bomb was placed under a heavy oak table which deflected the force of the explosion.

24. The SS represented a kind of terrorist elite within the Nazi party.

As a result, the conspiracy, which implicated a large number of the finest spirits in Germany, failed. It proved impossible to persuade the majority of officers in strategic posts to rebel when they realized that Hitler was still alive. Very few of the participants escaped the savage vengeance of the Gestapo.

Beck shot himself; Goerdeler was captured and executed; Kluge took poison; Rommel committed suicide by order. Moltke and Yorck, Leuschner and Leber, the radical noblemen and the broadminded socialists, and Ulrich von Hassell, whose memoirs show him as a superb representative of old European culture and civilization, all perished, along with thousands of others who were rightly or wrongly suspected of complicity in the plot. Some of the last words of these martyrs of freedom were historic and heroic. Moltke wrote to his wife shortly before his execution:

"I stood before Freisler,[25] not as a Protestant, not as a great landowner, not as a noble, not as a Prussian, not even as a German. . . . No, I stood there as a Christian and nothing else."[26]

And Yorck, in his final testimony, denounced "the totalitarian claim of the state on the individual which forces him to renounce his moral and religious obligations to God."

This effort of a minority of idealistic Germans to rid themselves of Hitler's tyranny received little understanding or sympathy in the United States. Typical was the comment of the *New York Herald Tribune* of August 9: "The American people as a whole will not feel sorry that the bomb spared Hitler for the liquidation of his generals."

What was never widely understood in America is that Hitlerism developed from roots quite different from those of the "Prussian militarism," which served as the propaganda scapegoat of World War I. The dangerous strength of nazism lay in its demagogic character, in its appeal to the masses. Hitlerism was really Henry Wallace's "common man" run mad. It was plebeian democracy without checks and balances and frozen into totalitarian forms. Its methods and practices were very similar to those of Soviet communism.

25. Freisler was the chief judge of the People's Court which dealt with political cases.

26. Rothfels, *German Opposition to Hitler*, 127.

Josef Goebbels, the mouthpiece of the Nazi regime, was just as scornful of monarchical and aristocratic tradition as Lenin or Trotsky would have been. This is very clear from his diaries. Hitler himself hated and despised the old-fashioned type of German officer or aristocrat who preserved ideals and standards of conduct which were quite alien to Nazi doctrine.

For a time, to be sure, there was a working alliance between the Nazis and the conservative German nationalists. But this was always an uneasy alliance. A high proportion of those who died in the effort to overthrow Hitler belonged to the civilian and military upper class of the Kaiser's time.

Encouragement from the West in the form of public or private specific assurances that a non-Nazi Germany could expect a moderate peace might have influenced some of the waverers in high places and tipped the scales in favor of the success of the July 20 conspiracy. But from America and Britain the German underground, which wanted to expiate the blood-guilt of the Nazi regime in association with the civilized forces of the West, received nothing but the "unconditional surrender" slogan, the Morgenthau Plan, and the indiscriminate bombing of German cities.

Bombing of railway and road transport and of war industries was an indispensable and valuable aid to military victory. But this cannot be said as regards the wholesale destruction of residential areas. On the basis of detailed reports from inside Germany during the war, Allen W. Dulles came to the following conclusion:

> The wholesale bombing of cities where civilian objectives were primarily affected, I believe, did little to shorten the war. In World War I a disillusioned but unbombed German population recognized the inevitability of defeat and helped to hasten the surrender. In World War II the bombed-out population turned to the state for shelter, food and transportation away from the devastated areas. If anything, these men and women were more inclined than before to work for and support the state, since they were dependent, homeless and destitute.[27]

27. Dulles, *Germany's Underground,* 168–69.

The destructionist attitude toward Germany found its climactic expression in the detailed plan of economic annihilation sponsored and advocated by Secretary of the Treasury Henry Morgenthau, Jr.

Roosevelt's thinking about the postwar treatment of Germany had been of a very sketchy character. Before Hull went to Moscow in 1943 Roosevelt referred to the question during a discussion with Hull, Admiral Leahy, and some State Department experts.[28] The President favored the partition of Germany into three or more states. All military activities should be forbidden, and East Prussia should be detached from Germany. Reparations should be exacted in manpower and equipment.

Hull was opposed to partition. At first Roosevelt overbore objections, remarking that he had studied and traveled in Germany and thought he knew more about Germany than any of the others present. Later he revised his self-estimate downward. In an unusual mood of diffidence, he observed that it was, after all, many years since he had become acquainted with Germany, and perhaps he didn't know as much about the subject as he thought.

The division of territorial studies in the State Department had worked out a plan for the postwar treatment of Germany. This provided that East Prussia and Upper Silesia be ceded to Poland. These changes were without ethnic justification, but were considerably more moderate than the amputation which was actually performed. The State Department plan provided for denazification on a reasonable scale and for payment of reparations out of current production. The Army had worked out a standard plan for military occupation.

Hull outlined the State Department scheme at the Moscow Conference of Foreign Ministers and found the Russians in substantial agreement. Roosevelt proposed much more drastic procedure at Teheran. He proposed a scheme for the complete dissolution of Germany. There were to be five autonomous states as follows: a reduced Prussia; Hanover and the Northwest; Saxony and "the Leipzig area";[29] Hesse-

28. Hull, *Memoirs*, 2:1265–66.

29. Leipzig for many generations has been located in Saxony, a fact with which Roosevelt was apparently unfamiliar. There is no area in Germany which could be accurately described as "south of the Rhine," as that river rises in Switzerland.

Darmstadt, Hesse-Kassel, and the area "south of the Rhine"; Bavaria, Baden, and Württemberg. Hamburg, the Kiel Canal, and the Ruhr and Saar areas were to be placed under the control of the United Nations.

Churchill talked of "separating Prussia from the rest" and uniting the southern states of Germany with a Danubian confederation. Stalin was lukewarm toward both suggestions, but indicated a preference for Roosevelt's. There was no positive decision and the matter was referred to the European Advisory Commission. Dismemberment was proposed at Yalta, but was again referred to the EAC and died a natural death there. The final decision was to administer Germany as a political and economic unit, divided into four zones of occupation.

Morgenthau began to play a decisive part in shaping American policy toward Germany in 1944. An old friend of Roosevelt, he had always been inclined to take a very broad view of his proper functions as Secretary of the Treasury. This is evident from his description of the situation in 1940 in *Collier's* for October 11, 1947:

"With the State Department wedded to the methods of old-fashioned diplomacy, with the War Department demoralized by dissension, Roosevelt was forced to turn a good deal to the Treasury to implement his antiaggressor program."

Hull often found Morgenthau a thorn in his side, as is evident from the following passage in his *Memoirs:*

Emotionally upset by Hitler's rise and his persecution of the Jews, he [Morgenthau] often sought to induce the President to anticipate the State Department or act contrary to our better judgment. We sometimes found him conducting negotiations with foreign governments which were the function of the State Department. . . . Morgenthau's interference at times misled some portions of the public and seriously impeded the orderly conduct of our foreign policy.[30]

As examples of Morgenthau's extracurricular activities Hull mentions his effort to get control over exports and imports vested in the Treasury, not in the State Department; his draft of a proposed settlement with Japan in November 1941; his proposal, blocked with diffi-

30. Hull, *Memoirs,* 1:207–8.

culty by Hull, to freeze Argentine funds in the United States; and his desire to have a Treasury representative at the Dumbarton Oaks conference on the United Nations. According to Hull, Morgenthau and Ickes tried to defame a State Department official by calling the latter a fascist without offering specific supporting proof.[31]

Morgenthau went to England in 1944, doing his best to win recruits for a policy of ruthless vengeance against Germany. He found some British statesmen skeptical when he suggested that, in his own words, "we could divide Germany up into a number of small agricultural provinces, stop all major industrial production and convert them into small agricultural landholders." However, he seems to have found a sympathizer in Anthony Eden, who "stressed the fact over a pleasant luncheon at his country estate that a soft peace would only arouse Russian suspicions."

Morgenthau told part of the story of his European odyssey in a series of articles in the *New York Post* in the winter of 1947–48. He quotes General Eisenhower as characterizing "the whole German population" as "a synthetic paranoid."[32] Eisenhower also, according to Morgenthau, made the far from prescient remark that, while Russia's present strength was fantastic, "Russia now had all she could digest and her present problems would keep her busy until long after we were dead."

Eisenhower confirms the fact of Morgenthau's visit[33] and recalls a general discussion on the future of Germany. The Supreme Commander favored the trial and punishment of prominent Nazis, certain industrialists, and members of the General Staff. He opposed as "silly and criminal," according to his own account, the flooding of the Ruhr mines—a pet idea of Morgenthau's.

During this trip, according to credible reports, Morgenthau or one of his aides became incensed over an Army handbook which prescribed

31. This was a favorite indoor sport of left-wingers in and out of the government service during the war years.

32. If Morgenthau's recollection is correct, Eisenhower seems to have been believing too readily everything he read in wartime magazines. Pseudoscientific indictments of the whole German people as sufferers from collective paranoia were a popular editorial fad for a time.

33. Eisenhower, *Crusade in Europe,* 287.

normal civilized occupation methods. Morgenthau brought this to the attention of Roosevelt and apparently induced him to share the indignation.

After returning to America Morgenthau, by whose authorization is not clear, set up a Treasury committee, composed of Harry Dexter White, John Pehle, and Ansel Luxford, to draft an economic plan for Germany. This was the origin of the notorious Morgenthau Plan. White was its main architect. But Morgenthau, because of his access to the President, was able to push it through to acceptance.

It is sometimes suggested that the Morgenthau Plan has been exaggerated or misrepresented. There is no excuse for misunderstanding, however, because Morgenthau himself has published the full text of the plan in a book which contains elaborate suggestions about why and how it should be put into effect.[34] The main features are as follows:

Territorially Germany was to lose East Prussia and Silesia as far west as Liegnitz. France was to get the Saar and a considerable area on the left bank of the Rhine, including the cities of Mainz and Treves. The rest of Germany was to be partitioned into North and South German states and an International Zone. The last, with its southern extremity at Frankfurt, was to include the Ruhr and the Lower Rhine Valley, together with stretches of coast on the North and Baltic seas and the cities of Bremen, Wilhelmshaven, and Kiel.

The section dealing with the International Zone contains the following key paragraphs:

(a) within a short period, if possible not longer than six months after the conclusion of hostilities, all industrial plants and equipment not destroyed by military action shall be completely dismantled and transported to allied nations as restitution. All equipment shall be removed from the mines *and the mines closed.* [Italics supplied.]

Forms of restitution and reparation proposed under the Morgenthau Plan include transfer of plant and equipment, "forced German labor outside Germany," and "confiscation of all German assets of any character whatsoever outside of Germany."

34. Morgenthau, *Germany Is Our Problem.* The complete text of the Morgenthau Plan is published in the first four pages of this book.

The Allied Military Government was not to

take any measures designed to maintain or strengthen the German economy, except those which are essential to military operations. The responsibility for sustaining the German economy and peoples rests with the German people *with such facilities as may be available under the circumstances.* [Italics supplied.]

There were to be controls over foreign trade and tight restrictions on capital imports. These were designed to prevent the establishment of key industries in the new German states.

There is a very interesting last provision of the plan. Had it been put into effect, it would have excluded America and Great Britain from any share in the occupation of Germany. This would obviously have meant Soviet domination of that country. The precise wording of this provision is as follows:

The primary responsibility for the policing of Germany and for civil administration in Germany should be assumed by the military forces of Germany's continental neighbors. Specifically these should include Russian, French, Polish, Czech, Greek, Yugoslav, Norwegian, Dutch and Belgian soldiers.

Under this program United States troops could be withdrawn within a relatively short time.

What inspired this proposal, which would have condemned the United States to defeat in the cold war? Was there some ulterior purpose of Harry Dexter White, mentioned by Whittaker Chambers and Elizabeth Bentley as a source of information to Soviet Communist spy rings? Or was it merely a case of a scheme prepared by men so blinded by desire for vengeance that they failed to recognize either the looming Soviet peril or the terrific blow to American national interest which would be represented by Soviet control of Germany?

Morgenthau apparently felt that American soldiers would not be ruthless enough for the kind of policing job he wished to see in Germany. As he wrote:

It is no aspersion on the American soldier to adjudge him too inexperienced in the ways of international banditry to serve as a guard in the German reformatory. The misfortunes of Europe have put its soldiers through the cruel and bitter course of training which fits them to serve most efficiently in the surveillance of Germany.[35]

When the Secretary of the Treasury realized that his proposal to destroy the Ruhr mines was too extreme to be accepted, he produced a substitute. He suggested that all Germans should be evicted from the Ruhr, their places being taken by "French, Belgian, Dutch and other workers."[36] Where the Germans would or could go was not suggested.

It is no exaggeration to say that the Morgenthau Plan, if applied in its full rigor, would have been an undiscriminating sentence of death for millions of Germans. The area in which it was proposed to forbid all heavy industries and mining is one of the most urbanized and thickly settled in Europe. It would have been impossible to turn millions of city dwellers, accustomed to earning their living in factories, offices, and shops, into self-supporting farmers, even if land had been available.

And here was the fatal weakness of the scheme, if it was to be discussed as a serious proposal of economic reorganization, not as a device for inflicting concentration-camp conditions on the entire German people. The avowed purpose of the Morgenthau Plan was to turn Germany into a predominantly agricultural and pastoral country. But there were no unused reserves of land for this purpose in thickly settled, industrial Germany. Indeed some of the more agricultural sections of the country were being transferred to Poland, and all Germans were being driven out of this area.

The Morgenthau Plan was a propaganda godsend to the Nazis, giving them the strongest of arguments to persuade the Germans to go on fighting. After the fall of Hitler it was a boon to the Communists, and would have been of still greater value if it had not been overmatched by the mass atrocities which accompanied the Soviet invasion of eastern Germany.

How did this fantastic scheme originate? A Cabinet committee, composed of Hull, Stimson, and Morgenthau, was set up to consider the postwar treatment of Germany. Of the three, Morgenthau took the

35. Ibid., 200.
36. Ibid., 23.

most extreme position, Stimson was the most moderate, and Hull, in the beginning, occupied a middle position, although later inclining more to agreement with Stimson.

Roosevelt himself favored strongly punitive measures. In a communication to Stimson on August 26, 1944, he echoed Morgenthau's complaint about the handbook which had been prepared for the guidance of Military Government officials:

> It is of the utmost importance that every person in Germany should realize that this time Germany is a defeated nation. I do not want them to starve to death, but, as an example, if they need food to keep body and soul together, beyond what they have, they should be fed three times a day with soup from Army soup kitchens.

During the first days of September the three Secretaries argued their cases before the President, whose physical and mental condition was giving increasing cause for concern. Stimson, as he tells us, "was not happy about the President's state of body and mind." He noted in his diary for September 11 after Roosevelt left for Quebec for a conference with Churchill:

> I have been much troubled by the President's physical condition. He was distinctly not himself Saturday [September 9]. He had a cold and seemed tired out. I rather fear for the effects of this hard conference upon him. I am particularly troubled . . . that he is going up there without any real preparation for the solution of the underlying and fundamental problem of how to treat Germany.[37]

Stimson's concern was well founded. Roosevelt had departed for Quebec without committing himself to any decision. But Morgenthau stole a march on his opponents. He went to Quebec while they remained in Washington. And Hull and Stimson received one of the severest shocks of their official careers when they received the following memorandum, initialed by Roosevelt and Churchill on September 15:

> At a conference between the President and the Prime Minister upon the best measures to prevent renewed rearmament by Germany it

37. Stimson and Bundy, *On Active Service*, 575.

was felt that an essential feature was the future disposition of the Ruhr and the Saar.

The ease with which the metallurgical, chemical and electrical industries in Germany can be converted from peace to war has already been impressed upon us by bitter experience. It must also be remembered that the Germans have devastated a large portion of the industries of Russia and of other neighboring Allies, and it is only in accordance with justice that these injured countries should be entitled to remove the machinery they require in order to repair the losses they have suffered. The industries referred to in the Ruhr and in the Saar would therefore necessarily be put out of action and closed down. It was felt that the two districts should be put under some body under the world organization which would supervise the dismantling of these industries and make sure that they were not started up again by some subterfuge.

This program for eliminating the warmaking industries in the Ruhr and in the Saar is looking forward to converting Germany into a country primarily agricultural and pastoral in its character.

The Prime Minister and the President were in agreement on this program.

Why Churchill signed this document, sanctioning the essence of the Morgenthau Plan, is not altogether clear, for both at Teheran and at Yalta his attitude on the German question was more moderate than Roosevelt's or Stalin's. One explanation may be that he was attracted by the argument, put forward by the Treasury, that the destruction of the Ruhr industries would wipe out a dangerous competitor for Britain.

But there was a more obvious inducement. Simultaneously with the communiqué which endorsed the destructionist spirit of the Morgenthau Plan there was significant agreement on the status of lend-lease after the defeat of Germany and before the surrender of Japan. It was agreed that during this interim period Britain should receive lend-lease munitions to a value of three and a half billion dollars and civilian supplies to the amount of three billion dollars.

Churchill was becoming increasingly alarmed over the bleak British economic prospect after the end of the war. Morgenthau held the purse strings. The British Prime Minister may well have felt that, as Paris was worth a Mass to Henri IV, a subsidy of 6.5 billion dollars was worth his signature to a scheme so extravagant that it might never be realized.

Hull and Stimson rallied from their defeat. The latter lunched with Roosevelt and pressed home the issue as few men would have dared to do with a President who did not bear contradiction gladly. Roosevelt in typical fashion began to twist and dodge, protested that he had no intention of turning Germany into an agrarian state, that all he wanted was to save a portion of the proceeds of the Ruhr for Great Britain, which was "broke."

Stimson brought him to the point by reading the precise words of the communiqué which had been issued in his name and Churchill's. When the Secretary read the words about "converting Germany into a country primarily agricultural and pastoral" Roosevelt seemed dumbfounded.

"He was frankly staggered by this and said he had no idea how he could have initialed this: *that he had evidently done it without much thought.*"[38] [Italics supplied.]

There have been few more damaging confessions of mental incompetence or complete irresponsibility. Here was a decision of first importance, affecting the lives and livelihood of millions of people, calculated to shape the course of European history, and the President could not recall how or why he had made it, or even that it had been made at all.

One of Stimson's assistants, John J. McCloy (now American High Commissioner in Germany), composed a searching and strongly reasoned criticism of the Morgenthau Plan:

> It would be just such a crime as the Germans themselves hoped to perpetrate upon their victims—it would be a crime against civilization itself. . . . Such an operation would naturally and necessarily involve a chaotic upheaval in the people's lives which would inevitably be productive of the deepest resentment and bitterness towards the authorities which had inflicted such revolutionary changes upon them. Physically, considering the fact that their present enlarged population has been developed and supported under an entirely different geography and economy, it would doubtless cause tremen-

38. Ibid., 581.

dous suffering, involving virtual starvation and death for many, and migration and changes for others.

Referring to the Treasury suggestion that Britain would benefit from the elimination of German competition, McCloy drily commented: "The total elimination of a competitor (who is also a potential purchaser) is rarely a satisfactory solution of a commercial problem."

However, the pressure from the White House for a vindictive treatment of Germany was so strong that McCloy, with Stimson's approval, composed the extremely harsh JCS 1067.[39] This instructed the American Military Governor "to take no steps (a) looking toward the economic rehabilitation of Germany or (b) designed to maintain or strengthen the Germany economy." These expressions are taken almost literally from the original text of the Morgenthau Plan.

Treasury agents, determined to exact the last pound of flesh, flooded Germany in the first years of the occupation and badgered and harassed those Military Government officials who were trying to carry out a constructive policy. Some adherents of the Morgenthau school of thought, referred to as the "Chaos Boys," infiltrated the Military Government.

A fanatical left-wing newspaper in New York screamed abuse of the mildest measures for restoring normal economic conditions in Germany. Caught between rigid ruthless orders and fear of being pilloried as "soft peace advocates" in this newspaper and similar organs, American administrators in Germany were inclined to see safety in being as negative as possible.

The full political ferocity and economic insanity of the Morgenthau Plan were never visited on Germany or on Europe. But the evil spirit of this scheme lived on after it had been formally discarded and wrought vast harm to American political and economic interests in Germany. As an American senior statesman of wide experience predicted on one occasion:

"The difference between governing Germany according to the Old Testament and according to the New Testament will be about a billion dollars a year for the American taxpayer."

39. On rereading JCS 1067 two years later, Stimson found it "a painfully negative document" (ibid., 582).

# 13

---

# No War, But No Peace

In the fifth year after the end of the war, there still was no peace with the two principal belligerents, Germany and Japan. The Congress of Vienna made, by and large, a good peace, with amazingly little in the way of vengeful reprisals against France for Napoleon's wars of aggression. With all its faults, it was a settlement that saved Europe for a century from the catastrophe of another war involving all the great powers. The Congress of Versailles made a bad peace, but it at least created some kind of settlement. Potsdam (the nearest approach to a peace conference that occurred after World War II) and other meetings of representatives of the Big Three powers resulted in nothing more than a continuation of the war on a different basis. They did not lead to peace.

If, however, one compares the provisional terms sketched at Potsdam with the treaties which have been concluded after other great wars, the judgment "world's worst peace" is not exaggerated. From the first line to the last Potsdam was a conspicuous, cynical, and flagrant violation of the professed war aims of the United Nations, as set forth in the Atlantic Charter.

The first three clauses of the Charter assert in the most positive and sweeping terms the right of all peoples to self-determination. The Potsdam Agreement handed over to Soviet-Polish control a large territory east of the Oder and Neisse rivers, inhabited by about nine and a half million people, an area which included one fourth of Germany's arable land. Almost all these people were of German stock. It is safe to say that a plebiscite would not have yielded even an appreciable minority of votes for transfer to Polish rule.

The Potsdam Conference was in session from July 17 until August 2, 1945. It was the last meeting of the chief executives of the United

States, the Soviet Union, and Great Britain. America was represented by President Truman and Secretary of State Byrnes, the Soviet Union by Stalin and Molotov, Great Britain at first by Churchill and Eden, later by the new Labor Premier and the new Foreign Minister, Clement Attlee and Ernest Bevin.

The conference accepted the transfer of the city of Königsberg and an adjacent area of East Prussia to Soviet sovereignty. America and Great Britain pledged their support of this claim "at the forthcoming peace conference," which, in 1950, had still not been held.

The agreement about the allocation of East German territory to Poland was less specific. It was stated that "the final delimitation of the western frontier of Poland should await the peace conference." However, prejudgment in Poland's favor was indicated by an agreement that the area in question should be under the administration of the Polish state and should not be considered part of the Soviet zone of occupation. The Potsdam declaration includes the following paragraph:

> The three governments, having considered the question in all its aspects, recognize that the transfer to Germany of German populations or elements thereof, remaining in Poland, Czechoslovakia and Hungary, will have to be undertaken. They agree that any transfers that take place should be effected in an orderly and humane manner.

Behind the deceptive benevolence of the last sentence was concealed the sanction by the western powers of one of the most barbarous actions in European history. This was the expulsion from their homes, with the confiscation of virtually all their property, of some fourteen million Germans or people of German origin. This figure includes 9,500,000 inhabitants of the East German provinces, about 1,100,000 from Danzig and Poland, 3,000,000 Sudeten Germans, who had lived for centuries in the border areas of Czechoslovakia, and some 450,000 Hungarians of German origin.

There was a strong flavor of hypocrisy in the suggestion that the transfer should be orderly and humane. Even under the most favorable and normal conditions, the driving of such a multitude of people from their homes and their resettlement elsewhere would have involved immense hardship and suffering. And conditions in Germany after the war were most unfavorable and abnormal. It was physically impossible for a thickly populated, devastated, and bomb-wrecked country, split into four zones of occupation, to absorb economically and provide for this vast horde of penniless, uprooted people.

Most of the expulsions were carried out with indiscriminate brutality. When I was in Munich in 1946 I received in semiconspirative fashion from the German Red Cross[1] a thick dossier of affidavits from Sudeten refugees who had been dumped across the border into Bavaria. These affidavits told a sickening story, as bad as most of the atrocities charged to the Nazis during the war, of torture, rape, confinement in concentration camps at heavy labor with starvation rations. Many succumbed to this treatment; the more fortunate found themselves beggared refugees in Germany, without homes, property, or means of earning a living.

The circumstances of expulsion from Poland were no better. Of course the Nazi cruelties in Poland and Czechoslovakia were notorious and outrageous. But the expulsions were without any discrimination. They were not restricted to active Nazis or to individuals guilty of acts of cruelty and oppression. They applied even to those Sudeten Germans who had risked life and liberty by opposing the Nazis.

If one examines the records of previous settlements after great European conflicts, one nowhere finds a parallel for the ruthless cruelty of these mass expulsions. The Peace of Westphalia was concluded in 1648 after all the horrors and bitter memories of the Thirty Years War, but it established the right of free migration, with property, of Catholics who wished to leave Protestant states and of Protestants who wished to depart from Catholic states.

Some of the arrangements decreed by the Congress of Vienna were not in line with modern ideas of ethnic self-determination. But one finds no case of mass spoliation, or the driving of millions of people

1. At that time Germans were forbidden, under severe penalties, to criticize any action of any of the United Nations, no matter how outrageous or how notorious the outrage might have been. These restrictions disappeared, at least so far as the Soviet Union and its satellites were concerned, in later years of the occupation.

from their homes. The Treaty of Versailles is open to criticism on many grounds, but it did not authorize mass deportations. A number of Germans were forced out of Alsace-Lorraine and out of the territory allotted to Poland, but the means of pressure were milder, and the number of persons affected was much smaller.

A census of German deportees in 1946 revealed a figure of about ten million. There were a little more than three million in the British zone, a little fewer than three million in the American zone, about four million in the Soviet zone, and a mere handful, about fifty thousand, in the French zone. There is a suggestive and ominous gap between the fourteen million who were subject to deportation and the ten million who were identified.

Perhaps half of the missing four million could be accounted for. The expulsion, although very sweeping, was not one hundred per cent complete. There were a number of individuals of mixed blood in the German-Polish border area. Some of these, by passing as Poles, succeeded in remaining. A number of German skilled workers were kept in the Sudetenland. There were also war prisoners and some civilians who were held for forced labor.

However, when every allowance has been made for persons in these categories, it seems probable that some two million people perished in this vast uprooting. Some were massacred outright; more died of hunger, cold, and disease.[2]

The Potsdam Declaration proclaimed: "It is not the intention of the Allies to destroy or enslave the German people." But this declaration of intent was not borne out by events during the first years of the occupation.

It had been the practice of civilized states in the past to release war prisoners within a reasonable time after the end of hostilities. The crusaders for righteousness in World War II set other precedents. For several years after the surrender between six and seven hundred thousand German war prisoners were kept as slave laborers in France, about four

2. One of the best factual accounts of the position of the German refugees, supplied with many official figures, is to be found in *Deutschland-Jahrbuch—1949*, published by Dr. Klaus Mehnert and Dr. Heinrich Schulte, West-Verlag, Essen. The subject has been almost completely ignored in American publications.

hundred thousand in Great Britain, and a larger number, perhaps two or three million, in Russia.

The United States did not exploit its war prisoners in this manner. But it turned over to the British and French some of the German prisoners who had been in camps in the United States and a good many who were captured in Europe.

The treatment of these prisoners varied. Reasonably humane conditions were maintained in Britain, where there were voices of protest and some uneasy scruples about the ethics of the whole procedure. There were ugly reports of near starvation of German prisoners in France in 1945, supported by the testimony of such a responsible French newspaper as *Figaro*. Subsequently, conditions improved.

Except for a minority selected for Communist indoctrination and for technicians whose services were desired, the treatment of war prisoners in Russia, which never accepted Red Cross conventions on this subject, was atrociously bad. Most of the Italian prisoners died of cold and hunger. Many of the Germans were released only when they had become physical wrecks, incapable of further work.

Forced labor is forced labor, regardless of whether it is performed under good, bad, or indifferent conditions. The German prisoners who were separated from their families and forced to work in foreign lands for years after the end of the war were not serving sentences as war criminals. There was no discrimination among those who were and those who were not Nazis.

The survivors of Napoleon's legions were not pressed into slave labor after France was defeated in 1814 and 1815. To find a precedent for this large-scale exploitation of military prisoners as slave labor after the conclusion of hostilities, one would have to go back to the wars of antiquity, when slavery was the customary fate of the vanquished. This is not a precedent that is in harmony with the Four Freedoms and the Atlantic Charter.

Potsdam set another very undesirable precedent, the mutilation and distortion of the economy of a defeated nation. By taking away a fourth of Germany's arable land and forcing at least ten million refugees into the shrunken frontiers of Germany, the victorious powers created a staggering problem of population pressure. The only solution for this problem, the only means by which Germany could hope to support its population, even on a low standard of living, was large-scale development of industry and foreign trade.

The problem was aggravated because the Soviet zone, which is more agricultural than highly industrialized West Germany, was cut off from normal economic contact with the rest of the country and milked dry of surplus food for the needs of the large Soviet army of occupation. So the western powers had to reckon with the needs of an area which was about as thickly populated as Great Britain and just as incapable of feeding its people with home-grown food.

But the Potsdam Declaration contained many provisions calculated to block German industrial recovery. One of its most important economic decisions is worded as follows:

> In order to eliminate Germany's war potential, the production of arms, ammunition and implements of war, as well as all types of aircraft and seagoing ships, shall be prohibited and prevented. Production of metals, chemicals, machinery and other items that are directly necessary to a war economy shall be rigidly controlled and restricted to Germany's approved postwar peacetime needs to meet the objectives stated in Paragraph 15. *Productive capacity not needed for permitted production shall be removed in accordance with the reparations plans recommended by the Allied commission on reparations and approved by the governments concerned, or, if not removed, shall be destroyed.* [Italics supplied.]

This last sentence reeks with the destructionist spirit of the Morgenthau Plan. It furnished the authorization for the dismantling of many nonmilitary German factories.

Paragraph 15 provides that Allied controls shall be imposed upon the German economy but "only" for the following purposes: to carry out programs of industrial disarmament and demilitarization, of reparations, and of approved exports and imports; to assure sufficient output to maintain the occupying forces and DP's[3] in Germany and to

3. The DP's (displaced persons) were citizens of various East European countries—many of whom had been brought to Germany under various degrees of compulsion during the war as slave laborers—who were stranded in Germany after the end of the war.

maintain in Germany average living standards not exceeding those of European countries, excluding Great Britain and the Soviet Union; to insure the equitable distribution of essential commodities between the several zones; to control German industry and *all* (italics supplied) economic and financial international transactions, including exports and imports; to control all German public or private scientific bodies, research and experimental institutions, laboratories, etc., connected with economic activities.

All this added up to a crippling strait jacket in which no national economy could hope to function with efficiency. It is not surprising that Western Germany remained a helpless derelict, dependent on outside aid for a subnormal standard of living, until these Potsdam decisions were scrapped or greatly relaxed.

The destructive restrictions on German industry foreshadowed at Potsdam were spelled out in more detail in an agreement about the level of German industry which was concluded between the occupation powers in March 1946. This called for the prohibition of aircraft and shipbuilding and for the complete elimination from Germany of fourteen other industries, including heavy tractors, heavy machine tools of various types, and primary aluminum. It limited German steel output to 5,800,000 tons a year, little more than the capacity of Belgium, which has about one-sixth of West Germany's population. Only the older and less efficient steel plants were to be left in Germany.

The machine-tool industry was limited to 11.4 per cent of 1938 capacity, heavy engineering to 38 per cent, other mechanical engineering to 50 per cent. No new locomotives were to be built until 1949. Output in a number of other branches was drastically limited. The industries which were left free from restriction were of minor importance: furniture and woodwork, glass, ceramics, bicycles, potash. The "level of industry plan" was designed to reduce German output to 50 or 55 per cent of the 1938 figure.

This would have been equivalent to keeping Germany permanently on the level of 1932, a year of deep economic depression and mass unemployment. It was the widespread distress of 1932 that contributed much to Hitler's rise to power.

A third basic document, besides the Potsdam Declaration and the Level of Industry Agreement, in shaping American policy during the first years after the end of the war was Occupation Directive 1067, issued on April 26, 1945. The spirit of this order is illustrated by the following excerpts:

Germany will not be occupied for the purpose of liberation but as a defeated enemy nation. . . . You will strongly discourage fraternization with the German officials and population.

No action will be taken, in execution of the reparations program or otherwise, which would tend to support basic living conditions in Germany or in your zone on a higher level than that existing in any of the neighboring United Nations. . . .[4]

You will take no steps (a) looking toward the economic rehabilitation of Germany or (b) designed to maintain or strengthen the German economy.

You will take all practicable economic and police measures to assure that German resources are fully utilized and consumption held to a minimum in order that imports may be strictly limited and that *surpluses may be made available for the occupying forces and displaced persons and United Nations prisoners of war and for reparations.*[5] [Italics supplied.]

The purposes set forth in the Potsdam Declaration are highly confused and contradictory. Along with unprecedentedly harsh and brutal punitive provisions, calculated, if not designed, to destroy any possibility of a decent standard of living in Germany even in the distant future, one finds the statement:

It is the intention of the Allies that the German people be given the opportunity to prepare for the eventual reconstruction of their life on a democratic and peaceful basis.

4. Some of the neighboring United Nations, notably Poland, Czechoslovakia, and Yugoslavia, had always possessed a much lower standard of living than Germany. Strictly interpreted, this passage in the directive would have authorized the tearing out of bathtubs and telephones, the destruction of good roads and communication facilities, so as to level down the German standard.

5. The idea that there would be food "surpluses" in a wrecked and extremely overcrowded country seems fantastic, yet this is the authentic language of the directive.

The provisions for the destruction and drastic limitation of German industries certainly excluded any possibility that Germany could develop a surplus of exports over imports which might be used for reparations. Yet Potsdam set forth a reparations plan. Soviet claims were to be met by removals of plants and equipment from the Soviet zone and from "appropriate German external assets." Moreover the Soviet Union was to get 15 per cent of the plants and equipment scheduled for removal from the western zones in exchange for products of the Soviet zone, and an additional 10 per cent without payment. At the same time Paragraph 194 of the Potsdam Declaration, one of the few passages in that document which shows a canny sense of economic realities, reads as follows:

> Payment of reparations should leave enough resources to enable the German people to subsist without external assistance. In working out the economic balance of Germany the necessary means must be provided to pay for imports approved by the Control Council in Germany.[6] The proceeds of exports from current production and stocks shall be available in the first place for payment for such imports.

This clause was not applicable to the 25 per cent share of equipment from the western zones which was assured to the Soviet Union.

In its outline of reparations procedure, as in its boundary and limitation of industry provisions, Potsdam deserves the characterization: Europe's worst peace. The wrong lessons were drawn from the experience of the past.

The Napoleonic armies had committed considerable ravages and were responsible for a good deal of looting during the first years of the nineteenth century, but no heavy burden of indemnity was laid on France by the Congress of Vienna.

The indemnity of one billion dollars which Germany imposed upon France after the Franco-Prussian War was considered a severe exaction,

---

6. This body, which never functioned effectively and ceased to function at all after the quarrel over Berlin became acute in 1948, was composed of representatives of the United States, the Soviet Union, Great Britain, and France.

but there was no tearing up of French factories, no suggestion of limiting France's ability to produce and trade. And the indemnity was paid off more quickly than Bismarck had thought possible.

Indeed there is little evidence that the indemnities which were sometimes collected from defeated states in European conflicts before World War I had any adverse effects on the economy of the Continent. The figures were kept within moderate bounds, and the charges could be and were paid like ordinary commercial obligations.

It was after World War I that reparations and the closely related subject of war debts began to bedevil international economic and financial relations. This was because the sums involved were so huge that impossible transfer problems arose. Under the bleak winds of economic crisis during the period 1929–33 the whole house-of-cards structure of agreed reparations and war-debts payments collapsed. Roosevelt, Churchill, and Stalin apparently realized from this experience that the collection of huge sums in money from a defeated enemy country with limited natural resources is not feasible.

But from this sound premise they drew the wrong conclusion. They decided to exact their pound of flesh from a Germany which had been thoroughly shattered in the very process of defeat in the most wasteful fashion imaginable. This was by impressing Germans for slave labor and by transferring the equipment of German factories to other countries. It is probably a moderate estimate that 80 per cent of the productive value of a plant is lost when it is plucked up by the roots and transferred elsewhere.[7]

Reparations could have been obtained by requiring certain German factories to work for reparations accounts and supplying these factories with necessary raw materials. No one seems to have suggested such a sensible arrangement at the wartime conferences, although the Russians began to practice it on a huge scale in their own zone after

7. During a visit to Germany in 1949 I saw the following example of the conspicuous economic waste involved in dismantling. The Krupp Borbeck steel works, in the Ruhr, was assigned to the Soviet Union. Original value of this plant was 125 million marks. The cost of dismantling was 25 million marks. The assessed value of what was finally turned over to the Russians (a curious expression, incidentally, of the policy of containing communism) was —10 million marks.

they learned from experience that the removal of German machinery brought little positive benefit to their own economy.

No doubt some of the inconsistencies and contradictions in the Potsdam Declaration were due to uncertainty in the minds of the victors as to whether they wished to ruin Germany forever as an industrial power or whether they wished to collect reparations. These two objectives were, of course, incompatible. Other discrepancies may be ascribed to differences of opinion and objective among the victors. These differences became more evident at Potsdam than they had been at Yalta.

James F. Byrnes, then Secretary of State, in his account of the Potsdam Conference,[8] says the American delegation wished to reach agreement on four major issues. These were the machinery and procedures for the earliest possible drafting of the peace treaties; the political and economic principles which should govern the occupation of Germany; plans for carrying out the Yalta Declaration in liberated Europe; a new approach to the reparations issue.

No success was achieved on any of these points. All that was gained as regards the implementation of the Yalta promises was a meaningless repetition of assurances which were being disregarded in practice every day. The machinery for turning the countries of Eastern Europe into Soviet vassal states ground on relentlessly.

Five years after Potsdam the world was still waiting for peace treaties with Germany and Japan. In view of the subsequent continual bickering between the Soviet Union and the western powers and the frequent divergences of opinion between the United States and France, with Great Britain occupying a middle position, no basis for a generally acceptable policy toward Germany was found.

Nor was there any satisfactory agreement on reparations. The Soviet Union seized what it liked in its own zone and refused to give any account of the value of what it carried off as official and unofficial loot and what it exacted in reparations from current production. It acquired an economic stranglehold on other East European countries by claiming extensive industrial properties as German assets. It completely ignored

8. Byrnes, *Speaking Frankly*, 67–87.

in practice two provisions of the Potsdam Agreement: that Germany should be treated as an economic unit and that payment of reparations should leave enough to enable the Germans to exist without external assistance.

According to Byrnes, the American delegation took a strong stand for the proposition that the question of Poland's western frontier was still open. Bevin, the new British Foreign Minister, strongly criticized these new frontiers. Stalin stated: "The western frontier question is still open and the Soviet Union is not bound."[9] But subsequent Soviet declarations have been to the effect that the frontier must be considered finally settled. And the American and British representatives certainly weakened their case by assenting to the mass deportation of Germans from the area in dispute. The distinguished journalist Anne O'Hare McCormick calls this "the most inhuman decision ever made by governments dedicated to the defense of human rights."

Molotov persisted in returning to the Yalta proposal for a reparations figure of twenty billion dollars, of which half should go to the Soviet Union. No definite figure, however, was included in the text of the Potsdam Agreement. New evidence of human capacity for self-deception is to be found in Byrnes's comment on Potsdam:

"We considered the conference a success. We firmly believed that the agreements reached would provide a basis for the early restoration of stability to Europe."[10]

A much sounder and more far-sighted judgment was expressed in an editorial which appeared at this time in the *Economist,* of London:

> The Potsdam Declaration will not last ten years, and when it breaks down there will be nothing but the razor-edge balance of international anarchy between civilization and the atomic bomb. . . . It has in it not a single constructive idea, not a single hopeful perspective for the postwar world. At the end of a mighty war fought to defeat Hitlerism the Allies are making a Hitlerian peace. This is the real measure of their failure.

9. Ibid., 80.
10. Ibid., 87.

Pope Pius XII expressed a similar thought when he declared, in his Christmas message to the College of Cardinals in 1946:

One thing is beyond all doubt. The fruits and the repercussions of victory have been, up to the present, not only of indescribable bitterness for the defeated; but for the victors, too, they have proved to be a source of untold anxiety and danger.

One may quote still another judgment on the spirit and fruits of Potsdam. This was pronounced by Lord (formerly Sir William) Beveridge after a visit to Germany in 1946:

In a black moment of anger and confusion at Potsdam in July, 1945, we abandoned the Atlantic Charter of 1941, which had named as our goals: For all nations improved labor standards, economic advancement and social security; for all states, victor and vanquished, access to the trade and to the raw materials of the world, which are needed for their economic prosperity. From Potsdam instead we set out on a program of lowering the standard of life in Germany, of destroying industry, of depriving her of trade. The actions of the Allies for the last fifteen months make the Atlantic Charter an hypocrisy.

How suitable is this word hypocrisy for all the lofty moral professions of the Second Crusade! How suitable is evident from the fact that, with one exception, every war crime committed by the Nazis was matched in some way by one or more of the United Nations. The exception is the savage, maniacal extermination of several million European Jews.

But if one calls the roll of the other crimes which are often represented as peculiar to the Nazis, or to the Germans and Japanese as peoples, one soon finds, after impartial investigation, that there are other guilty parties. Victors as well as vanquished must answer for grave offenses against international law and common humanity.

Forcible annexation of alien territory? But what of the arbitrary allotment of 104,000 square miles of historic Polish territory, with the Polish cities of Lwów and Wilno, to the Soviet Union? What is the justification, apart from naked force, for giving to the Soviet Union and Poland cities that have been German for centuries: Königsberg, Danzig, Stettin, Breslau; for assigning 61,000 square miles of ethnically

German land to Poland? What of Soviet annexation of Latvia, Lithuania, Estonia, to an accompaniment of mass arrests, deportations, and
flight of a considerable part of the population of these unfortunate
Baltic states? What of the seizure of one-tenth of Finland, with the
inhabitants, almost to the last man, leaving their homes and property
rather than live under Soviet rule?

Deportation and uprooting of people to make room for German
settlement? It is an old and true saying that two wrongs do not make a
right. The fate of the fourteen million human beings driven from their
homes in East Germany, Czechoslovakia, Poland, and other East European countries was no happier than that of Poles who were expelled
from their homes to make way for Germans.

Conscription for forced labor? This was considered such a serious crime when committed by the Nazis that its chief organizer, Fritz
Sauckel, was hanged. Many other Germans were sentenced to prison
for alleged criminal complicity. But was anyone punished in Russia, or
in France, or in Britain, for the exploitation of German war prisoners
as slave labor long after the end of hostilities?

Rape and looting? The scenes that took place in Berlin, Vienna,
Budapest, and other cities captured by the Red Army were probably
never equalled in European warfare as orgies of lust and pillage. A
vivid account of the sack of Berlin, written by an anti-Nazi German who
was an eyewitness, estimates that about half the women in the city were
violated. An ecclesiastical authority in Vienna told me that about sixty
thousand women were raped by Soviet soldiers; a Social Democratic
editor put the figure at one hundred thousand.

As for pillage, the clumsy, barbaric monuments which the Russians
have put up all over eastern Europe to "the unknown Russian soldier"
have been privately rededicated to "the unknown Russian looter."
Every capital occupied by the Red Army has its special crop of jokes
about the Russian soldier's habit of holding up individuals and taking
their watches and other valuables, with or without rape and assault and
battery thrown in.

The Soviet armies left behind them a trail of murder, rape, and looting that has not been surpassed since the Mongol invasion of Europe
in the thirteenth century. The behavior of the western troops was more
civilized, as the east-west flight of millions of Germans proves, although

there was a good deal of pillaging by the French, and the discipline of American troops left something to be desired.[11] The British troops, according to the general testimony of the Germans, were the best behaved.

There was nothing in the western zones to equal the carrying off of an enormous variety of items, from feather-bed mattresses to turbines, in the Soviet zone. But there was a good deal of indirect looting. The French, for instance, lived off the land in the area of southwestern Germany which they occupied. This region, which was never self-sufficient in food, had to support not only an army of occupation but a horde of officials, with their families and relatives. Small wonder that the food situation in the French zone (until the general economic revival in 1948) was desperately bad, with the ration sometimes falling below the starvation level of 1,000 calories.

The extreme hunger which prevailed in Germany in the first years of the occupation made it easy for military and civilian members of the military governments to buy up porcelain, silver, and other valuables for nominal prices in cigarettes and imported food. There was also sweeping requisitioning of houses for the needs of officers and officials of the military government. They were given accommodations which were luxurious by American or British standards, still more so against the background of terrific destruction and inhuman overcrowding in the German cities.

Undernourishment of the populations in occupied countries was held to be one of the Nazi war crimes. This condition certainly prevailed for a large part of the city population in all Germany until 1948, when there was a substantial change for the better in the western zones as a result of the currency reform and the inflow of Marshall Plan aid. Even then much distress could still be found among groups unable to earn their living and among the Germans who had been driven from the East.

11. A spectacular piece of American banditry was the effort of a WAC captain, one Kathleen B. Nash Durant, and a few accomplices to make off with the jewels of the state of Hesse, which were located in a castle where she was stationed. There were other Americans besides the too enterprising WAC captain who must have given the Germans a rather dubious "re-education" in the virtue supposedly associated with democracy.

The following manifesto, issued by the municipal government of Hamburg in the summer of 1946, describes accurately a situation which could be found not only in Hamburg, but in many of the large industrial towns of West Germany in the first years of the occupation:[12]

> Tuberculosis, hunger swelling, incapacity for work because of undernourishment, increase from day to day. The supply of gas and electricity is endangered because the workers, in spite of heavy rations for extra labor, collapse in front of the furnaces for lack of strength. In the factories and in the offices the falling out of workers because of complete exhaustion increases every day. For months expert observers have pointed to the coming famine with all its signs and consequences. Now it is here.

The British official in charge of food supply gave me detailed information about the Hamburg rations at this time. The main items were a little over half a pound of bread and a little less than a pound of potatoes a day. Beyond this, allotments were so small as to be negligible. The weekly ration included four ounces of meat, seven ounces of fish, three ounces of sugar, four ounces of jam, half an ounce of cheese, and a little over a pint of skimmed milk. This was far below a subsistence diet. Equally bad conditions sometimes provoked hunger strikes and demonstrations in the Ruhr.

Genocide is usually thought of as a crime peculiar to the Nazis. However, the death rate in the United States sector of Berlin in the first quarter of 1947 was almost three times the birth rate, 28.5 per thousand per annum as against 10.7 per thousand. Infant mortality was 116.2 per thousand. Comparative figures for New York in 1946 were as follows: death rate, 10.1 per thousand; birth rate, 19.6 per thousand; infant mortality, 27.8 per thousand.[13] And the American sector of Berlin was by no means the worst area under occupation.

12. I was in Hamburg at the time when this manifesto was issued. I can confirm from personal observation that it did not exaggerate the conditions of near starvation that prevailed.

13. See Stolper, *German Realities*, 33. This is far and away the most thorough analysis of postwar German social and economic conditions available in the English language.

Of course it is difficult to draw a clear line of distinction between the consequences of the lost war and vindictive, destructionist occupation policies. Even if the Potsdam decisions had been wiser and more humane, the whole German people, Nazis and non-Nazis, guilty and innocent, would have been required to pay a heavy price for Hitler's crimes. They would have been forced to wrestle with the social problems involved in wrecked factories, devastated cities, disrupted families, and hopelessly inflated currency.

Had Germany, under a government of its own choice, been left free to struggle out of the debris of defeat by its own efforts, no special moral responsibility would have attached to the victorious powers. But when these powers decided to occupy every square foot of German territory, to abolish German sovereignty, to regulate every detail of German life, they incurred a share of responsibility for the appalling physical misery and social demoralization which are only slowly being alleviated years after the end of the war.

The ghastly hunger of Hamburg, for instance, cannot be dissociated from the prohibition of all German ocean-going shipping, since it was shipping and shipbuilding that gave this large port much of its livelihood. The high mortality rates in Berlin were certainly due, at least in part, to the attempt to administer this city under a system of perpetual squabbling among the four controlling powers. The frustrating and often contradictory economic regulations imposed by the various occupation authorities certainly increased the misery by denying the Germans a reasonable opportunity to earn their own living.

There were two other characteristics of the occupation regime in Germany for which there is no parallel in other European peace settlements. These were denazification and the trials of so-called war criminals.

Denazification was an inquisitional purge, directed against all Germans who had been members of the National Socialist party or its affiliated organizations. This party was a very large mass organization which individuals joined for all sorts of reasons. Along with a hard core of fanatical believers in Hitler's teachings there was a much larger number who joined for reasons of expediency, or even of personal safety. It was almost compulsory for public officials and individuals who held high positions in industry, trade, and the professions to be party members. It was extremely difficult to study in universities or to practice any profession without joining a Nazi-dominated organization.

Newspapermen, for instance, were automatically registered in the *Reichspressekammer.* There were similar organizations for writers, musicians, teachers, doctors, radio commentators, and others.

A reasonable approach to the denazification problem would have been to exclude from public office those Nazis who were high enough in party rank to be fairly regarded as responsible policy makers, to prosecute those against whom there was evidence of specific criminal acts, and to leave the great mass who had merely gone along with the tide undisturbed.

If, as Burke said, it is impossible to indict a nation, it is surely inadvisable and impolitic to punish such a high proportion of individuals as to create a large class of embittered pariahs. Yet this is what American denazification set out to do. Every adult German in the American zone was required under criminal penalties to fill out an incredibly complex questionnaire with 131 questions. These pried into every detail of personal life, from religion to income.

In conscious or unconscious imitation of the Nazis, with their inquiries about ethnic origin, the questionnaire called for a list of titles of nobility which the individual, his wife, or any of his four grandparents might have held. There was a still more sinister imitation of Nazi methods. Persons who filled out the questionnaire were required to denounce any relatives who had held rank or office in any of over fifty organizations.

On the basis of this inquisition penalties ranging from imprisonment to fines and exclusion from the right of holding office or practicing a profession were imposed on large numbers of people. At first this was done by arbitrary action of the Military Government. Later it was turned over to the Germans; but they were required to act on the basis of a law approved by the Military Government.

The sheer physical impossibility of judging millions of people in this way forced a retreat from the more extreme methods. But the wholesale indiscriminating and arbitrary conduct of denazification led to much injustice and completely defeated its purpose. When the net was cast so wide and caught so many individuals who were personally guilty of no crime except a lack of the high moral courage required to defy a dictatorship, the inevitable result was to create sympathy, not aversion, for the people who suffered.

The same consideration holds good for the so-called war-crimes trials.[14] The largest and most spectacular of these was held at Nürnberg, where the surviving leaders of the Nazi regime were arraigned before a tribunal composed of representatives of America, the Soviet Union, Great Britain, and France. There were twelve other war-crimes trials in the American zone, held before American courts. Over 1,500 persons were found guilty in these trials, and 444 were sentenced to death.

The number of trials and convictions in the British zone was smaller. There is little official information about what happened in the Soviet zone. On the basis of reliable reports, it seems certain that more people were put to death and sent to concentration camps there than in the other zones. But there has also been more rehabilitation and utilization of ex-Nazis who were regarded as useful for the Communist cause.

Supreme Court Justice Robert H. Jackson, American prosecutor in the Nürnberg trial, ex–Secretary of War Henry L. Stimson, and others hailed the war crimes trials as a new and higher development in international law. It seems improbable that this will be the verdict of impartial history. For both the underlying conception of the trials (that victors are qualified to be impartial judges of vanquished) and many of the methods employed in conducting prosecutions and extracting confessions run counter to all established principles of western justice and international law.

No reasonable person will deny that some of the defendants in these trials were guilty of horrible crimes and that comparatively few are entitled to sympathy on the basis of their personalities and records. The real case against "victors' justice" is not the punishment that was

14. I talked with the wife of one of the men convicted in one of the most dubious of the "war crimes" trials, the prosecution of officials in the Nazi Ministry of Foreign Affairs. She told me that she gained in popularity and esteem with her neighbors when it became known that she was the wife of a "war criminal." In this trial some of the defendants, notably the former Undersecretary von Weizsäcker, were convicted for not stopping atrocities which they had no means of checking. There was no proof that they incited or approved these atrocities.

meted out to over fifteen hundred Germans, but the serious injury
which the trials inflicted upon civilized standards of impartial judicial
procedure and moral consistency. This injury may be found in the following points.

1. There was no pretense of enforcing equal responsibility before
the law. Only Germans were punished, in many cases for actions which
were also committed by soldiers and citizens of one or all of the victorious powers. But one of the clearest distinctions between a true court
of law and a lynching mob is that the court judges all without discrimination.

2. The very important principle that judges and juries should have
no personal interest or prejudice in the cases with which they are concerned was not and could not be upheld in trials of defeated enemies
by their conquerors.

3. This defect of the trials was aggravated because a considerable
number of American citizens of recent origin, political or racial refugees from Nazi Germany, took part in the investigations and police
actions which accompanied the prosecutions. The desire of some of
these individuals for vengeance was human and understandable. But
this desire should not have been satisfied through American courts.

4. The evidence on which some of the verdicts were based was
tainted by the use of brutality and chicanery in extorting confessions.

5. The trials set a dangerous precedent in violation of the well-known
principles of national and international law. One of these is that there
should be no ex post facto punishment. The other is that military officers and civilian officials should not be held responsible for carrying
out orders received from high authorities. Under this last precedent,
every military and naval officer who takes part in working out war plans
could be indicted and executed as a "promoter of aggressive war," if his
country should be defeated.

6. The proscription of the vanquished by the victors is unpleasantly
reminiscent of the practices of twenty centuries ago, when captured
rulers were strangled after being led in Roman triumphs. The war-
crimes trials were hailed and justified as war deterrents. But it seems
far more probable that the only effect will be to turn future wars into
bitter-end struggles of mutual extermination. There has never been

a war in history in which the victors did not consider the vanquished "guilty."

One of the counts in the Nürnberg indictment was the planning and waging of wars of aggression. It is now a matter of public historical record, and it was a fact well known to the Nürnberg prosecutors and judges, that the Soviet Union was an active partner in Hitler's scheme for attacking and partitioning Poland, to say nothing of its acts of aggression against the Baltic states and Finland. So, if the punishment of aggressive war was the purpose of the trials, the place of the Soviet representatives was in the dock with the accused, not on the bench with the judges. In view of the different treatment meted out to Nazi aggression and to Soviet aggression, the assumption seems justified that the Germans were punished not because they waged aggressive war, but because they waged it unsuccessfully.

Other blemishes on the Nürnberg record, from the standpoint of pure justice, were the hasty insertion and shamefaced withdrawal of charges about German responsibility for the Katyn massacre[15] and the curious reasoning employed in the indictment of Admiral Dönitz. The tribunal ruled that Dönitz was not sentenced on the ground of his breaches of international law in the conduct of submarine warfare, because American and British naval leaders had committed similar breaches. He was, however, held liable to prosecution for other offenses.

This principle was questionable in itself. But it was not consistently observed, for, as has already been shown, the Germans were by no means alone in committing such crimes against humanity and international law as launching of aggressive war, forcible annexation of foreign territory, carrying out mass deportations, exploiting the slave labor of war prisoners, committing rape, looting, and other outrages against civilians.

Any moral value the war trials might have possessed was seriously undermined by the methods often used to extort confessions. Most notorious and unsavory was the third-degree treatment inflicted upon

15. See pp. 275–77 for the strong circumstantial evidence that the Soviet authorities were responsible for this massacre.

the defendants in the Malmédy trial, a large group of German soldiers accused of killing American prisoners during the Battle of the Bulge.

An Army commission, headed by Justice Gordon Simpson, of the Texas Supreme Court, investigated this matter. Its conclusion was that "highly questionable methods which cannot be condoned" were used in obtaining the "evidence" and "confessions" upon which the many death sentences inflicted in this case were based. Judge Edward L. van Roden, a member of the commission, was more specific in his description. He listed among these "highly questionable methods": beatings and brutal kickings, knocking out teeth and breaking jaws; mock trials with impersonation of priests by investigators; solitary confinement on limited rations. Colonel W. M. Everett, an American officer in two world wars, was appointed counsel for the defendants. He submitted to the Supreme Court of the United States a long affidavit, containing the following statement, among many other allegations of torture and undue pressure:

"The American prosecutors would make many threats of violence and torture, directed toward the mothers, fathers, sisters, wives, and children of various accused unless they signed complete dictated confessions of acts and deeds never committed by them, and acts and deeds of other accused, never witnessed by them."

This suggested the methods of the Gestapo, rather than a "re-education" in the ways of civilized justice. Indeed, it seems doubtful whether the Germans could have been expected to learn any lesson from the war trials except one the Nazis could have taught them: Woe to the vanquished.

In the retrospect of five years it is difficult to recognize even one constructive or hopeful feature of the preliminary peace settlement sketched at Potsdam. The *Economist* uttered an understatement in predicting that the Potsdam settlement would not last ten years. Within two years it had been disregarded by the Soviet Union and modified beyond recognition by America and Great Britain.

Had the Potsdam Declaration, the Level of Industry Agreement of 1946, and Directive No. 1067 been applied in full rigor without compensating outside aid, millions of Germans would have perished of malnutrition and slow starvation. As it was, the first years of the occupation witnessed an abnormally high death rate among the very old and the very young.

Mass starvation was averted only because the more destructive features of these schemes were gradually relaxed or scrapped and because the United States poured a large sum of money into Germany—about three billion dollars by the beginning of 1950. But it would surely have been wiser, more humane, and more economical never to have composed these destructionist plans than to announce them and then go over to slow, painful, piecemeal revision. It is doubtful whether history records any more wasteful process than the American action in assenting to and sometimes initiating destructionist measures in Germany and simultaneously paying out money to avert the consequences of these measures. The cost of satisfying the emotion of blind, undiscriminating vengeance has been absurdly high.

The kind of peace settlement indicated by the Potsdam decisions was brutally unjust and profoundly unwise from the economic standpoint. It also gives the impression of being extremely unstable. Had Europe escaped the politically unsettling effects of the economic crisis of 1929–33, there might have been an adjustment on the basis of existing political frontiers.

It is hard to foresee stability for the grotesque frontiers in eastern Europe that were foreshadowed at Teheran, accepted at Yalta, and given clearer form at Potsdam. The Germans will never be reconciled to the loss of such old authentically German cities as Danzig and Königsberg, Breslau and Stettin. The presence of millions of miserable, unabsorbed refugees will always remind them of what has been lost in the East.

Some of the defects of the German peace settlement were repeated in Austria, although the treatment of that country was less deliberately vindictive. Little Austria was split up into four zones of occupation. Its chances of becoming self-supporting were gravely injured by the Soviet seizure and exploitation of the Zistersdorf oil wells, the Danubian shipping, and many factories, claimed as "German assets."

Not only the Russians, but the western powers kept out of commercial use many hotels which normally housed tourists and added to the Austrian national income. Only the Americans paid the expenses of

their own occupation. In Austria, as in Germany, large American subsidies eased the economic difficulties. But much better economic results could have been achieved at a considerable saving to the American taxpayer if the occupation could have been quickly ended and if
the elastic Soviet claim to confiscate German assets had never been accepted. It had been decided at the Moscow Conference of Foreign Ministers in 1943 that Austria should be regarded as a "liberated" country.
But several years after the end of the war, there was still no formal
peace for Austria. The Soviet Union was still blocking the conclusion of
a peace treaty that would have required a general evacuation of occupation forces.

Peacemaking in the Orient brought its special disappointments.
This was because China, the country on whose behalf the United States
went crusading in that part of the world, turned Communist and proceeded to heap insults upon American diplomatic representatives unprecedented since the days of the Boxer uprising. This was very much
as if Great Britain and France had set up Soviet governments, sent
delegations to pay homage to Stalin, and lost no opportunity to express
their contempt and detestation for the United States. Seldom has retri-
bution for a short-sighted, sentimental, mistaken policy been so swift
and so merciless.

To be sure, the occupation of Japan was smoother and more efficient than the occupation of Germany. General Douglas MacArthur's
authority was, for all practical purposes, unquestioned.

Molotov, following the usual Soviet method of losing nothing for
want of asking for it, had tried to put a Soviet foot inside the door of
the Japanese occupation. On August 11, 1945, when Japan was about
to surrender, Molotov suggested to American Ambassador Harriman
that there should be two supreme commanders in Japan, MacArthur
and the Soviet Marshal Vasilievsky. By this time Harriman had learned
how to say No, and nothing came of this suggestion.[16]

Apart from a small British force which was ultimately withdrawn,
the occupation troops in Japan were exclusively American. The United
States was the source of the funds and supplies which were required

16. Deane, *The Strange Alliance*, 278–79.

to ward off starvation and save the Japanese economy from complete collapse. MacArthur enjoyed a freer hand than General Clay possessed in Germany, for Clay was obliged to reckon not only with the persistent hostility of the Russians, but with frequent divergences of French opinion and occasional disagreements with the British.

Unfortunately American policy in Japan in the first years of the occupation repeated, sometimes in milder form, the blunders which have already been noted in Germany. Economically there was much in common between these two defeated countries. Both were thickly settled lands, incapable of supporting more than a minority of their population by agriculture.

Japan had given food and work to its growing population and balanced its international accounts in the past by processing raw materials—American cotton, for instance, Australian wool, rubber from southeastern Asia—and making a profit on the export of cheap manufactured goods. Japan also benefited from intensive development of its colonial regions, Korea, Formosa, and Manchuria. Japanese passenger ships and freighters plied a lively trade. The Japanese merchant marine was the third largest in the world.

The war shattered these bases of the Japanese economy. Japan lost its overseas possessions and assets. The overcrowded Japanese islands, where over eighty million people live in an area smaller and poorer than California, were forced to receive millions of new inhabitants, Japanese who had formerly lived on the Asiatic mainland and in the adjacent islands. Most of Japan's shipping was at the bottom of the ocean. Its industrial plant was heavily damaged by bombing.

Two salient points about the Japanese situation should have been clear to every competent economist. First, there was no surplus in the Japanese economy that could be devoted to the payment of reparations. Second, if Japan was to get off the American dole and become self-supporting, the Japanese needed for this purpose all the industry, shipping, and foreign trade they could rebuild and regain.

However, the revengeful psychology which found its extreme expression in the Morgenthau Plan prevailed for a time in regard to Japan. Countries which had taken part in the war against Japan were invited to present indemnity bills. Edwin W. Pauley, who as United States Reparations Commissioner had done much to ruin the economy of Central Europe, drew up a plan admirably calculated to wreck the Japanese economy.

This "Little Morgenthau Plan," as it might well have been called, proposed to limit the Japanese merchant marine to 1,500,000 tons, to set a limit of 5,000 tons for Japanese vessels, and to prohibit Japanese ships from calling at any but Oriental ports. The Pauley scheme also called for the reduction of Japanese steelmaking capacity from 8,000,000 to 2,750,000 tons. There were to be drastic cuts in such essential industries as chemicals, railway equipment and rolling-stock, shipbuilding, communications, and electrical power.

Mr. Pauley knew nothing of Japan's economic problems at first hand. There is reason to believe that he was influenced in his decisions by the views of some left-wing "experts" on Japan who saw in an economically ruined Japan the necessary and desirable prelude to a Communist Japan. This same consideration explains the enthusiasm of Communists and fellow travelers for the Morgenthau scheme in Germany.

Fortunately the Pauley blueprint for economic destruction was never realized in practice. The recipients of the prospective loot from Japan squabbled so long and bitterly over their shares that there was time for wiser counsels to get the upper hand in Washington.

The United States Government in May 1949 announced the end of reparations from Japan in a note characterized by economic insight and realism. The communication stressed a point that had apparently escaped the attention of Mr. Pauley: that the Japanese economy could be made to bear additional burdens "only by prolonging or increasing the staggering costs borne by the American taxpayer." American resources "to meet demands from all parts of the world," the note continued, are limited.

Japan, therefore, should be permitted to develop its peaceful industries without limitation. In the words of the note: "The problem facing us is not one of limitation of Japan's peaceful industries, but of reviving those industries to provide for the people's barest wants."

So there was a belated return to sanity on the question of industrial dismantling in Japan. Meanwhile, however, the political picture in the Far East had changed very much for the worse. China passed almost completely under Communist control. This left South Korea, under a precariously weak government, as the only toehold of American influence on the mainland of East Asia. Japan itself threatened to turn into a permanent sub-WPA project.

Nine years after Pearl Harbor, five years after atomic bombs fell on Hiroshima and Nagasaki and introduced the world to a new age of fear, there was no true pacification, no sense of security for American interests in Asia. The aftermath of the crusade was, if possible, even more disillusioning in that continent than it was in Europe.

For the basic assumption on which the crusade had been based, the assumption that the Big Three could and would rule and police the world with unity of purpose, had proved to be one of the most disastrous miscalculations in history. The world organization that was supposed to assure peace and the reign of law and justice had been shown impotent to assure either. By innumerable brawls, on issues large and small, the United Nations had proved themselves the Divided Nations.

# 14

---

## Crusade in Retrospect

America's Second Crusade belongs to history. Was it a success? Over two hundred thousand Americans perished in combat, and almost six hundred thousand were wounded. There was the usual crop of postwar crimes attributable to shock and maladjustment after combat experience. There was an enormous depletion of American natural resources in timber, oil, iron ore, and other metals. The nation emerged from the war with a staggering and probably unredeemable debt in the neighborhood of one quarter of a *trillion* dollars. Nothing comparable to this burden has ever been known in American history.

Were these human and material losses justified or unavoidable? From the military standpoint, of course, the crusade was a victory. The three Axis nations were completely crushed. American power on land and at sea, in the air and in the factory assembly line, was an indispensable contribution to this defeat.

But war is not a sporting competition, in which victory is an end in itself. It can only be justified as a means to achieve desirable positive ends or to ward off an intolerable and unmistakable threat to national security. When one asks for the fruits of victory five years after the end of the war, the answers sound hollow and unconvincing.

Consider first the results of the war in terms of America's professed war aims: the Atlantic Charter and the Four Freedoms. Here surely the failure has been complete and indisputable. Wilson failed to make his Fourteen Points prevail in the peace settlements after World War I. But his failure might be considered a brilliant success when one surveys the abyss that yawns between the principles of the Atlantic Charter and the Four Freedoms and the realities of the postwar world.

After World War I, there were some reasonably honest plebiscites, along with some arbitrary and unjust territorial arrangements. But the customary method of changing frontiers after World War II was to throw the entire population out bag and baggage—and with very little baggage.

No war in history has killed so many people and left such a legacy of miserable, uprooted, destitute, dispossessed human beings. Some fourteen million Germans and people of German stock were driven from the part of Germany east of the Oder-Neisse line, from the Sudeten area of Czechoslovakia, and from smaller German settlements in Hungary, Yugoslavia, and Rumania.

Millions of Poles were expelled from the territory east of the so-called Curzon Line and resettled in other parts of Poland, including the provinces stolen from Germany. Several hundred thousand Finns fled from parts of Finland seized by the Soviet Union in its two wars of aggression. At least a million East Europeans of various nationalities— Poles, Russians, Ukrainians, Yugoslavs, Letts, Lithuanians, Estonians— became refugees from Soviet territorial seizures and Soviet tyranny.

Not one of the drastic surgical operations on Europe's boundaries was carried out in free consultation with the people affected. There can be no reasonable doubt that every one of these changes would have been rejected by an overwhelming majority in an honestly conducted plebiscite.

The majority of the people in eastern Poland and the Baltic states did not wish to become Soviet citizens. Probably not one person in a hundred in East Prussia, Silesia, and other ethnically German territories favored the substitution of Polish or Soviet for German rule. What a mockery, then, has been made of the first three clauses of the Atlantic Charter: "no territorial aggrandizement," "no territorial changes that do not accord with the freely expressed wishes of the peoples concerned," "the right of all peoples to choose the form of government under which they will live."

The other clauses have fared no better. The restrictions imposed on German and Japanese industry, trade, and shipping cannot be reconciled with the promise "to further the enjoyment by all States, great or small, victor or vanquished, of access, on equal terms, to the trade and to the raw materials of the world."

The terrific war destruction and the vindictive peace have certainly not helped to secure "for all, improved labor standards, economic advancement and social security."

In the year 1950, five years after the end of the Second Crusade, "all men in all lands" are not living "out their lives in freedom from fear and want." Nor are "all men traversing the high seas and oceans without hindrance."

The eighth and last clause of the Atlantic Charter holds out the prospect of lightening "for peace-loving peoples the crushing burden of armaments." But this burden has become more crushing than it was before the crusade took place. The "peace-loving peoples" have been devoting ever larger shares of their national incomes to preparations for war.

All in all, the promises of the Charter seem to have evaporated in a wraith of Atlantic mist.

Nor have the Four Freedoms played any appreciable part in shaping the postwar world. These, it may be recalled, were freedom of speech and expression, freedom of religion, and freedom from fear and want. But one of the main consequences of the war was a vast expansion of Communist power in eastern Europe and in East Asia. It can hardly be argued that this has contributed to greater freedom of speech, expression, and religion, or, for that matter, to freedom from want and fear.

The fate of Cardinal Mindzenty, of Archbishop Stepinac, of the Protestant leaders in Hungary, of the many priests who have been arrested and murdered in Soviet satellite states, of independent political leaders and dissident Communists in these states, offers eloquent testimony to the contrary.

In short, there is not the slightest visible relation between the Atlantic Charter and the Four Freedoms and the kind of world that has emerged after the war. Woodrow Wilson put up a struggle for his Fourteen Points. There is no evidence that Franklin D. Roosevelt offered any serious objection to the many violations of his professed war aims.

It may, of course, be argued that the Atlantic Charter and the Four Freedoms were unessential window dressing, that the war was not a crusade at all, but a matter of self-defense and national survival. However, there is no proof that Germany and Japan had worked out, even on paper, any scheme for the invasion of the American continent.

In his alarmist broadcast of May 27, 1941, Roosevelt declared: "Your Government knows what terms Hitler, if victorious, would impose. I am not speculating about all this. . . . They plan to treat the Latin American countries as they are now treating the Balkans. They plan then to strangle the United States of America and the Dominion of Canada."

But this startling accusation was never backed up by concrete proof. No confirmation was found even when the Nazi archives were at the disposal of the victorious powers. There has been gross exaggeration of the supposed close co-operation of the Axis powers. General George C. Marshall points this out in his report, *The Winning of the War in Europe and the Pacific,* published after the end of the war. This report, based on American intelligence reports and on interrogation of captured German commanders, contains the following statements:

No evidence has yet been found that the German High Command had any over-all strategic plan. . . .

When Italy entered the war Mussolini's strategic aims contemplated the expansion of his empire under the cloak of German military success. Field Marshal Keitel reveals that Italy's declaration of war was contrary to her agreement with Germany. Both Keitel and Jodl agree that it was undesired. . . .

Nor is there evidence of close strategic coordination between Germany and Japan. The German General Staff recognized that Japan was bound by the neutrality pact with Russia but hoped that the Japanese would tie down strong British and American land, sea and air forces in the Far East.

In the absence of any evidence so far to the contrary, it is believed that Japan also acted unilaterally and not in accordance with a unified strategic plan. . . .

Not only were the European partners of the Axis unable to coordinate their plans and resources and agree within their own nations how best to proceed, but the eastern partner, Japan, was working in even greater discord. *The Axis as a matter of fact existed on paper only.*[1] [Italics supplied.]

1. Marshall, *Report,* 1–3.

So, in the judgment of General Marshall, the Axis did not represent a close-knit league, with a clear-cut plan for achieving world domination, including the subjugation of the American continent. It was a loose association of powers with expansionist aims in Europe and the Far East.

Of course the United States had no alternative except to fight after Pearl Harbor and the German and Italian declarations of war. But the Pearl Harbor attack, in all probability, would never have occurred if the United States had been less inflexible in upholding the cause of China. Whether this inflexibility was justified, in the light of subsequent developments in China, is highly questionable, to say the least.

The diplomatic prelude to Pearl Harbor also includes such fateful American decisions as the imposition of a virtual commercial blockade on Japan in July 1941, the cold-shouldering of Prince Konoye's overtures, and the failure, at the critical moment, to make any more constructive contribution to avoidance of war than Hull's bleak note of November 26.

The war with Germany was also very largely the result of the initiative of the Roosevelt Administration. The destroyer deal, the lend-lease bill, the freezing of Axis assets, the injection of the American Navy, with much secrecy and doubletalk, into the Battle of the Atlantic: these and many similar actions were obvious departures from neutrality, even though a Neutrality Act, which the President had sworn to uphold, was still on the statute books.

It is sometimes contended that the gradual edging of the United States into undeclared war was justified because German and Japanese victory would have threatened the security and well-being of the United States, even if no invasion of this hemisphere was contemplated. This argument would be easier to sustain if the war had been fought, not as a crusade of "a free world against a slave world," but as a cold-blooded attempt to restore and maintain a reasonable balance of power in Europe and in Asia.

Had America's prewar and war diplomacy kept this objective in mind, some of the graver blunders of the Second Crusade would have been avoided. Had it been observed as a cardinal principle of policy that Soviet totalitarianism was just as objectionable morally and more dangerous politically and psychologically than the German and Japanese brands, the course of American policy would surely have been different. There would have been more favorable consideration for the viewpoint artlessly expressed by Senator Truman when he suggested that we should support Russia when Germany was winning and Germany when Russia was winning.

It was the great dilemma of the war that we could not count on winning the war without Russia and certainly could not hope to win the peace with Russia. But there was at least a partial solution for this dilemma. One of the ablest men associated with the American diplomatic service suggested this to me in a private conversation:

"We should have made peace with Germany and Japan when they were too weak to be a threat to us and still strong enough to be useful partners in a coalition against the Soviet Union."

But such realism was at a hopeless discount in a crusading atmosphere. The effect of America's policy was to create a huge power vacuum in Europe and in Asia, and to leave the Soviet Union the one strong military power in both these continents. Then the United States belatedly began to offer resistance when the Soviet leaders acted precisely as anyone might have expected them to act in view of their political record and philosophy.

An old friend whom I met in Paris in 1946, a shrewd and witty British journalist, offered the following estimate of the situation which followed the Second Crusade:

"You know, Hitler really won this war—in the person of Stalin."

President Roosevelt declared in his speech of May 27, 1941: "We will accept only a world consecrated to freedom from want and freedom from terrorism." The war into which he was steadily and purposefully steering his country was apparently supposed to assure such a world.

The argument that "we cannot live in a totalitarian world" carried weight with many Americans who were not impressed by lurid pictures of the Germans (who were never able to cross the narrow English Channel) suddenly frog-leaping the Atlantic and overrunning the United States. Both in the hectic days of 1940–41 and in the cooler retrospect of 1950 it seems clear that a Nazi Germany, dominant in Europe, and a militarist Japan, extending its hegemony in Asia, would be unpleasant neighbors and would impose disagreeable changes in the American way of life.

It could plausibly be argued that in such a world we should have to assume a heavy permanent burden of armament, that we should have to keep a constant alert for subversive agents, that our trade would be forced into distorted patterns. We would be exposed to moral corruption and to the erosion of our ideals of liberty because the spectacle of armed might trampling on right would be contagious.

These dangers of totalitarianism were real enough. But it was a disastrous fallacy to imagine that these dangers could be exorcised by waging war and making peace in such fashion that the power of another totalitarian state, the Soviet Union, would be greatly enhanced.

Failure to foresee the aggressive and disintegrating role which a victorious Soviet Union might be expected to play in a smashed and ruined Europe and Asia was the principal blunder of America's crusading interventionists. Those who secretly or openly sympathized with communism were at least acting logically. But the majority erred out of sheer ignorance and wishful thinking about Soviet motives and intentions. They were guilty of a colossal error in judgment and perspective, an almost unpardonable error in view of the importance of the issues at stake.

After Pearl Harbor and the German declaration of war, the United States, of course, had a stake in the success of the Red Army. This, however, does not justify the policy of one-sided appeasement which was followed at Teheran and Yalta.

If one looks farther back, before America's hands were tied diplomatically by involvement in the conflict, there was certainly no moral or political obligation for the United States and other western powers to defend the Soviet Union against possible attacks from Germany and Japan. The most hopeful means of dealing with the totalitarian threat would have been for the western powers to have maintained a hands-off policy in eastern Europe.

In this case the two totalitarian regimes might have been expected to shoot it out to their hearts' content. But advocates of such an elementary common-sense policy were vilified as appeasers, fascist sympathizers, and what not. The repeated indications that Hitler's ambitions were Continental, not overseas, that he desired and intended to move toward the east, not toward the west, were overlooked.

Even after what General Deane called "the strange alliance" had been concluded, there was room for maneuvering. We could have been as aloof toward Stalin as Stalin was toward us. There is adequate evidence available that the chance of negotiating a reasonable peace with a non-Nazi German government would have justified an attempt, but the "unconditional surrender" formula made anything of this sort impossible. With a blind optimism that now seems amazing and fantastic, the men responsible for the conduct of American foreign policy staked everything on the improbable assumption that the Soviet Government would be a co-operative do-gooder in an ideal postwar world.

The publicist Randolph Bourne, a caustic and penetrating critic of American participation in its First Crusade, observed that war is like a wild elephant. It carries the rider where it wishes to go, not where he may wish to go.

Now the crusade has ended. We have the perspective of five years of uneasy peace. And the slogan "We are fighting so that we will not have to live in a totalitarian world" stands exposed in all its tragic futility. For what kind of world are we living in today? Is it not very much like the world we would have faced if the crusade had never taken place, if Hitler had been allowed to go eastward, if Germany had dominated eastern Europe and Japan eastern Asia? Is there not a "This is where we came in" atmosphere, very reminiscent of the time when there was constant uneasy speculation as to where the next expansionist move would take place? The difference is that Moscow has replaced Berlin and Tokyo. There is one center of dynamic aggression instead of two, with the concentration of power in that one center surpassing by far that of the German-Japanese combination. And for two reasons this difference is for the worse, not for the better.

First, one could probably have counted on rifts and conflicts of interest between Germany and Japan which are less likely to arise in Stalin's centralized empire. Second, Soviet expansion is aided by propaganda resources which were never matched by the Nazis and the Japanese.

How does it stand with those ideals which were often invoked by advocates of the Second Crusade? What about "orderly processes in international relations," to borrow a phrase from Cordell Hull, or international peace and security in general? Does the present size of our armaments appropriation suggest confidence in an era of peace and good will? Is it not pretty much the kind of appropriation we would have found necessary if there had been no effort to destroy Nazi and Japanese power?

Secret agents of foreign powers? We need not worry about Nazis or Japanese. But the exposure of a dangerously effective Soviet spy ring in Canada, the proof that Soviet agents had the run of confidential State Department papers, the piecemeal revelations of Soviet espionage in this country during the war—all these things show that the same danger exists from another source.

Moral corruption? We have acquiesced in and sometimes promoted some of the most outrageous injustices in history: the mutilation of Poland, the uprooting of millions of human beings from their homes, the use of slave labor after the war. If we would have been tainted by the mere existence of the evil features of the Nazi system, are we not now tainted by the widespread prevalence of a very cruel form of slavery in the Soviet Union?

Regimentation of trade? But how much free trade is there in the postwar world? This conception has been ousted by an orgy of exchange controls, bilateral commercial agreements, and other devices for damming and diverting the free stream of international commerce.

Justice for oppressed peoples? Almost every day there are news dispatches from eastern Europe indicating how conspicuously this ideal was not realized.

The totalitarian regimes against which America fought have indeed been destroyed. But a new and more dangerous threat emerged in the very process of winning the victory. The idea that we would eliminate the totalitarian menace to peace and freedom while extending the dominion of the Hammer and Sickle has been proved a humbug, a hoax, and a pitiful delusion.

Looking back over the diplomatic history of the war, one can identify ten major blunders which contributed very much to the unfavorable position in which the western powers find themselves today. These may be listed as follows:

1. The guarantee of "all support in their power" which the British Government gave to Poland "in the event of any action which clearly threatened Polish independence." This promise, hastily given on March 31, 1939, proved impossible to keep. It was of

no benefit to the Poles in their unequal struggle against the German invasion. It was not regarded as applicable against Russia when the Soviet Union invaded and occupied eastern Poland, with the full understanding and complicity of Hitler.

All this ill-advised guarantee accomplished was to put Great Britain and France into war against Germany, to the great satisfaction of Stalin, for an objective which the western powers could not win. Poland was not freed even after the United States entered the war and Hitler was crushed. It was only subjected to a new tyranny, organized and directed from Moscow.

There is no proof and little probability that Hitler would have attacked the West if he had not been challenged on the Polish issue. The guarantee, more than any other single action, spoiled the best political opportunity the western powers possessed in 1939. This was to canalize German expansion eastward and to keep war out of the West.

2. The failure of the American Government to accept Konoye's overtures for a negotiated settlement of differences in the Far East. The futility of the crusade for China to which the American Government committed itself becomes constantly more clear.

3. The "unconditional surrender" slogan which Roosevelt tossed off at Casablanca in January 1943. This was a godsend to Goebbels and a tremendous blow to the morale and effectiveness of the underground groups which were working against Hitler. It weakened the American and British position in relation to Russia, since Stalin did not associate himself with the demand. It stiffened and prolonged German resistance.

4. The policy of "getting along" with Stalin on a basis of all-out appeasement. The Soviet dictator was given everything he wanted in the way of munitions and supplies and was asked for nothing in return, not even an honest fulfillment of the Atlantic Charter, of which he was a cosignatory. The disastrous bankruptcy of this policy is evident from one look at the geographical, political, and moral map of the world today.

5. Failure to invade the Balkans, as Churchill repeatedly urged. This mistake was the result partly of the policy of appeasing

Stalin and partly of the narrowly military conception of the war which dominated the thinking of the War Department. There was a tendency to regard the war as a kind of bigger football game, in which victory was all that mattered.

6. The public endorsement by Roosevelt and Churchill in September 1944 of the preposterous Morgenthau Plan for the economic destruction of Germany. To be sure, the full extravagance of this scheme was never put into practice, but enough of its vindictive destructionist spirit got into the Potsdam Declaration and the regulations for Military Government to work very great harm to American national interests and European recovery.

7. The bribing of Stalin, at China's expense, to enter the Far Eastern war and the failure to make clear, until the last moment, that unconditional surrender, for Japan, did not mean the elimination of the Emperor. These were grave mistakes, fraught with fateful consequences for American political interests in the Orient. Had the danger from Russia, the undependability of China, and the desirability of enlisting Japan as a satellite ally been intelligently appreciated, a balance of power far more favorable to the United States would now exist in East Asia.

8. The failure, for political reasons, to exploit the military opportunities which opened up in the last weeks of the struggle in Europe, notably the failure to press on and seize Berlin and Prague. Closely linked with this error was the failure to insist on direct land access to Berlin in the negotiations about the postwar occupation of Germany.

9. The persistent tendency to disregard the advice of experts and specialists and base American foreign policy on "hunches" inspired by amateurs and dilletantes. Conspicuous examples of unfitness in high places were Harry Hopkins as adviser on Russia, Edward R. Stettinius as Secretary of State, Henry Morgenthau, Jr., as policy framer on Germany, and Edwin W. Pauley as Reparations Commissioner. A parallel mistake was the laxness which permitted American and foreign Communist sympathizers to infiltrate the OWI, OSS, and other important strategic agencies.

10. The hasty launching, amid much exaggerated ballyhoo, of the United Nations. The new organization was not given either a definite peace settlement to sustain or the power which would have made it an effective mediator and arbiter in disputes between great powers. It was as if an architect should create an elaborate second story of a building, complete with balconies, while neglecting to lay a firm foundation.

These were unmistakable blunders which no future historical revelations can justify or explain away. In these blunders one finds the answer to the question why complete military victory, in the Second Crusade as in the First, was followed by such complete political frustration. Perhaps the supreme irony of the war's aftermath is that the United States becomes increasingly dependent on the good will and co-operation of the peoples against whom it waged a war of political and economic near extermination, the Germans and the Japanese, in order to maintain any semblance of balance of power in Europe and in Asia.

Primary responsibility for the involvement of the United States in World War II and for the policies which characterized our wartime diplomacy rests with Franklin D. Roosevelt. His motives were mixed and were probably not always clear, even to himself. Frances Perkins, Secretary of Labor in his Cabinet and a personal friend, described the President as "the most complicated human being I ever knew."

Certainly Roosevelt was far from being a simple and straightforward character. In an age when Stalin, Hitler, and Mussolini played the role of the popular tyrant, of the dictator whose grip on his people is maintained by a mixture of mass enthusiasm and mass terrorism, Roosevelt showed what could be done in achieving very great personal power within the framework of free institutions. His career after his election to the presidency stamps him as a man of vast ambition, capable, according to Frances Perkins, of "almost childish vanity."

There were probably three principal motives that impelled Roosevelt to set in motion the machinery that led America into its Second Crusade. First was this quality of ambition. What role could be more tempting than that of leader of a wartime global coalition, of ultimate world arbiter? Second was the necessity of finding some means of extricating the American economy from a difficult position. Third was a conviction that action against the Axis was necessary. This conviction was greatly strengthened by the first two motives.

Roosevelt's first Administration, which began at the low point of a very severe depression, was a brilliant political success. He was reelected in 1936 by an enormous majority of popular and electoral votes. But dark clouds hung over the last years of his second term of office. For all the varied and sometimes contradictory devices of the New Deal failed to banish the specter of large-scale unemployment. There were at least ten million people out of work in the United States in 1939.

The coming of the war in Europe accomplished what all the experimentation of the New Deal had failed to achieve. It created the swollen demand for American munitions, equipment, supplies of all kinds, foodstuffs which started the national economy on the road to full production and full employment.

There was the same economic phenomenon at the time of the First World War. The vast needs of the Allies meant high profits, not only for munitions makers (later stigmatized as "merchants of death"), but for all branches of business activity. It brought a high level of farm prices and industrial wages. As the Allies ran out of ready cash, loans were floated on the American market. The United States, or at least some American financial interests, acquired a direct stake in an Allied victory.

Now, the purely economic interpretation of our involvement in World War I can be pressed too far. There is neither evidence nor probability that Wilson was directly influenced by bankers or munitions makers. He had given the German Government a public and grave warning of the consequences of resorting to unlimited submarine warfare. When the German Government announced the resumption of such warfare, Wilson, with the assent of Congress, made good his warning.

Yet the lure of war profits (not restricted, it should be noted, to any single class of people) did exert a subtle but important influence on the evolution of American policy in the years 1914–17. It worked against the success of the mediation efforts launched by House as Wilson's confidential emissary. The British and French governments counted with confidence on the absence of any strong action to back up periodic protests against the unprecedented severity of the blockade enforced against Germany. The American economy had become very dependent on the flow of Allied war orders.

After the end of the war, after depression and repudiation of the greater part of the war debts, the majority of the American people reached the conclusion that a war boom was not worth the ultimate price. This feeling found expression in the Neutrality Act. Roosevelt himself in 1936 described war profits as "fools' gold."

Yet the course of American economic development in World War II followed closely the pattern set in World War I. First the Neutrality Act was amended to permit the sale of munitions. Then, as British assets were exhausted, the lend-lease arrangement was substituted for the war loans of the earlier period. As an economic student of the period says:

> The nation did not emerge from the decade of the depression until pulled out by war orders from abroad and the defense program at home. The rescue was timely and sweet and deserved to be made as sure as possible. Whether the involvement of the United States in the war through progressive departure from neutrality was prompted partly by the reflection that other means of extrication from economic trouble had disappeared, nobody can say. No proponent did say so. Instead, advocates of "all-out aid to Britain," convoying of allied shipping and lend-lease took high ground of patriotism and protection of civilization.[2]

There can be no reasonable doubt that the opposition of business and labor groups to involvement in the war was softened by the tremendous flood of government war orders. It is an American proverb that the customer is always right. Under lend-lease and the immense program of domestic arms expansion the government became the biggest customer.

Ambition certainly encouraged Roosevelt to assume an interventionist attitude. He unmistakably enjoyed his role as one of the "Big Three," as a leading figure at international conferences, as a mediator between Stalin and Churchill. There is a marked contrast between Roosevelt's psychology as a war leader and Lincoln's.

2. Mitchell, *Depression Decade*, 369.

The Civil War President was often bowed down by sorrow over the tragic aspects of the historic drama in which he was called to play a leading part. His grief for the men who were dying on both sides of the fighting lines was deep and hearty and unaffected. One finds little trace of this mood in Roosevelt's war utterances. There is no Gettysburg Address in Roosevelt's state papers. The President's familiar mood is one of jaunty, cocksure, sometimes flippant, self-confidence.

Another trait in Roosevelt's personality which may help to explain the casual, light-hearted scrapping of the Atlantic Charter and the Four Freedoms is a strong histrionic streak. If he originated or borrowed a brilliant phrase, he felt that his work was done. He felt no strong obligation to see that the phrase, once uttered, must be realized in action.

When did Roosevelt decide that America must enter the war? There was a hint of bellicose action in his quarantine speech of October 5, 1937. Harold Ickes claims credit for suggesting the quarantine phrase, which did not appear in earlier drafts of the speech which had been prepared in the State Department. It was like Roosevelt to pick up and insert an image which appealed to him. However, the quarantine speech met such an unfavorable reception that it led to no immediate action.

Various dates are suggested by other observers. Supreme Court Justice Felix Frankfurter, who enjoyed substantial influence and many contacts in Administration circles, asserted in a Roosevelt memorial address at Harvard University in April 1945:

"There came a moment when President Roosevelt was convinced that the utter defeat of Nazism was essential to the survival of our institutions. That time certainly could not have been later than when Mr. Sumner Welles reported on his mission to Europe [March 1940]."[3]

That Roosevelt may have been mentally committed to intervention even before the war broke out is indicated by the following dispatch from Maurice Hindus in the *New York Herald Tribune* of January 4, 1948:

3. Cited in Beard, *President Roosevelt*, 413.

"Prague—President Eduard Beneš of Czechoslovakia told the late President Franklin D. Roosevelt on May 29, 1939, that war would break out any day after July 15 of that year, with Poland as the first victim, and Mr. Roosevelt, in reply to a question as to what the United States would do, said it would have to participate because Europe alone could not defeat Adolf Hitler."

A suggestion by Assistant Secretary of State A. A. Berle that Roosevelt should have become the leader of the free world against Hitler is believed to have influenced the President's psychology.[4]

Admiral James O. Richardson, at that time Commander in Chief of the Pacific fleet, talked at length with Roosevelt in the White House on October 8, 1940. He testified before the Congressional committee investigating Pearl Harbor that he had asked the President whether we would enter the war and received the following answer:

> He [Roosevelt] replied that if the Japanese attacked Thailand, or the Kra peninsula, or the Netherlands East Indies, we would not enter the war, that if they even attacked the Philippines he doubted whether we would enter the war, but that they could not always avoid making mistakes and that as the war continued and the area of operation expanded sooner or later they would make a mistake and we would enter the war.[5]

It is clear from these varied pieces of evidence that the thought of war was never far from Roosevelt's mind, even while he was assuring so many audiences during the election campaign that "your government is not going to war." During the year 1941, as has been shown in an earlier chapter, he put the country into an undeclared naval war in the Atlantic by methods of stealth and secrecy. This point was made very clear by Admiral Stark, then Chief of Naval Operations, in his reply to Representative Gearhart during the Pearl Harbor investigation:

> Technically or from an international standpoint we were not at war, inasmuch as we did not have the right of belligerents, because war had not been declared. But actually, so far as the forces operating under Admiral King in certain areas were concerned, it was against

4. Davis and Lindley, *How War Came*, 65.
5. U.S. Congress, *Report of the Joint Committee*, Part I, p. 266.

any German craft that came inside that area. They were attacking us and we were attacking them.

Stark also testified that, by direction of the President, he ordered American warships in the Atlantic to fire on German submarines and surface ships. This order was issued on October 8, 1941, two months before Hitler's declaration of war.

It is scarcely possible, in the light of this and many other known facts, to avoid the conclusion that the Roosevelt Administration sought the war which began at Pearl Harbor. The steps which made armed conflict inevitable were taken months before the conflict broke out.

Some of Roosevelt's apologists contend that if he deceived the American people it was for their own good. But the argument that the end justified the means rests on the assumption that the end has been achieved. Whether America's end in its Second Crusade was assurance of national security or the establishment of a world of peace and order or the realization of the Four Freedoms "everywhere in the world," this end was most certainly not achieved.

America's Second Crusade was a product of illusions which are already bankrupt. It was an illusion that the United States was at any time in danger of invasion by Nazi Germany. It was an illusion that Hitler was bent on the destruction of the British Empire. It was an illusion that China was capable of becoming a strong, friendly, western-oriented power in the Far East. It was an illusion that a powerful Soviet Union in a weakened and impoverished Eurasia would be a force for peace, conciliation, stability, and international co-operation. It was an illusion that the evils and dangers associated with totalitarianism could be eliminated by giving unconditional support to one form of totalitarianism against another. It was an illusion that a combination of appeasement and personal charm could melt away designs of conquest and domination which were deeply rooted in Russian history and Communist philosophy.

The fruit harvested from seeds of illusion is always bitter.

To recognize the bankruptcy of the illusions for which we fought our Second Crusade is the essential step in curing the consequences of those illusions. American foreign policy, of course, cannot come to a dead stop. Americans cannot wring their hands in hopeless disillusion-ment. To every historical challenge there is an effective response.

The broad goal of American foreign policy is clear. It is to promote world-wide co-operation of anti-Communist nations, to create such a measure of unity, with its consequent power, in the countries that are threatened by Soviet aggression that such aggression will never take place, or will be crushed if it does take place. In the present state of the world this is no sentimental undertaking, no Third Crusade. This is an enterprise vital to American security, and America is the natural leader.

Unfortunately the recognition of America's wartime illusions has been an uneven process. It is even worse that a new and no less perni-cious fallacy besets our peace policies. The State Department, the Quai d'Orsay, and the Foreign Office seem to believe that Germany and Japan can be kept indefinitely in a status of second-class sovereignty; the tremendous significance of the time factor is ignored. There is no indication whatever that Roosevelt, Churchill, or their counselors ever considered whether it is reasonable, whether, in fact, it is possible, to fasten an occupation indefinitely on a large, historically developed, in-telligent, and industrially powerful European people like the Germans without demoralizing them. In the same vein, Allied statesmen have never seen fit to acknowledge the consequences of the peace they gave to Germany after World War I. Under the watchful eyes of the occu-pation authorities the life of Germany may become more and more normal, and her leaders, accepting the inevitable, may show a sincere desire to co-operate. But neither German governments nor occupying powers, however good their intentions, can control the irrational and destructive passions which will develop in the depths of the nation so long as it is not free.

To be sure, the pressure of foreign rule is being alleviated in a halt-ing, piecemeal fashion both in Germany and Japan. In Germany's case, which so far seems more complex and urgent, the London Statute of the summer of 1949 was hailed as proof of great moderation, yet it created endless frictions and squabbles, as will all such half-hearted accommodations. The French proposal of May 1950 for pooling the French and German iron and coal industries certainly contains great constructive possibilities. Yet at the very moment it was made the Germans were forced to watch helplessly while France was expropriating the wealth of the Saar. Nevertheless, the French proposal was warmly welcomed in Bonn. Nothing was said of the fact that, at the conference of foreign ministers in London where Schuman, the French Foreign Minister, made his sensational proposal, Germany was not represented, although matters of vital importance to Germany were on the agenda. Under foreign domination such contingencies will repeat themselves again and again. When a man's head is held under water it makes no difference to him whether it is three inches or twelve feet under.

The memory of the slave acts differently than that of the master. The invisible debt which the victors have been running up ever since the summer of 1945 will be presented to us in full at a fateful hour, when the co-operation of our former enemies may be of crucial importance, unless we have the courage and insight to make the positive step which the challenge of the moment demands. The Germans and the Japanese must be liberated without further delay, in accordance with the principles we have set out to teach them.

The conception of a united western Europe leaving its quarrels to history and capable of resisting Soviet aggression is completely fatuous unless it includes Germany as an active participant in the making of the political, military, and economic decisions on a basis of full equality. Only in this way can the loyalty of the Germans become strong enough to withstand any test contrived by Moscow.

It is time, and high time, for positive, imaginative statesmanship. We can never count on superior strength so long as we support negative policies which fail to utilize the immense potentialities of our former enemies as bastions against Soviet imperialist communism — of a Japan and a Germany, that is, whose powers have not been consumed and exhausted by repression and frustration, if not actively turned against us. The surest way to win the cold war is to end the obsolete shooting war with Germany and Japan with a lasting peace firmly built on mutual respect and interest.

The point of view set forth in this book will challenge powerful American intellectual and emotional interests, but the iron logic of facts will, I believe, confirm these interpretations with the passing of time.

# Bibliography

Agar, Herbert. *A Time for Greatness.* Boston: Little, Brown, 1942.

Alsop, Joseph, and Robert Kintner. *American White Paper.* New York: Simon and Schuster, 1940.

Bailey, Thomas A. *The Man in the Street.* New York: Macmillan, 1948.

———. *Woodrow Wilson and the Great Betrayal.* New York: Macmillan, 1945.

Beard, Charles A. *American Foreign Policy in the Making, 1932–1940.* New Haven: Yale University Press, 1946.

———. *President Roosevelt and the Coming of the War, 1941.* New Haven: Yale University Press, 1948.

Belgion, Montgomery. *Victor's Justice.* Chicago: Regnery, 1949.

Bullitt, William C. *The Great Globe Itself.* New York: Charles Scribner's Sons, 1946.

Butcher, Harry C. *My Three Years with Eisenhower: The Personal Diary of Captain Harry C. Butcher, USNR, Naval Aide to General Eisenhower, 1942 to 1945.* New York: Simon and Schuster, 1946.

Byrnes, James F. *Speaking Frankly.* New York: Harper and Brothers, 1947.

Cardwell, Ann Su (pseudonym of Margaret Low Super). *Poland and Russia: The Last Quarter Century.* New York: Sheed and Ward, 1944.

Carroll, Wallace. *Persuade or Perish.* Boston: Houghton Mifflin, 1948.

Chiang Kai-shek, Mme. *China Shall Rise Again.* New York: Harper and Brothers, 1941.

Churchill, Winston S. *The Aftermath.* New York: Charles Scribner's Sons, 1929.

———. *Blood, Sweat and Tears.* New York: G. P. Putnam's Sons, 1941.

———. *The Dawn of Liberation.* Boston: Little, Brown, 1945.

———. *The End of the Beginning.* Boston: Little, Brown, 1943.

———. *The Gathering Storm.* Boston: Houghton Mifflin, 1948.

———. *The Grand Alliance.* Boston: Houghton Mifflin, 1950.

———. *Their Finest Hour.* Boston: Houghton Mifflin, 1949.

———. *The World Crisis.* New York: Charles Scribner's Sons, 1923–29. 4 vols. in 5.

Ciano, Count Galeazzo. *The Ciano Diaries, 1939–1943.* Edited by Hugh Gibson. Garden City: Doubleday, 1947.

———. *Ciano's Diplomatic Papers.* London: Odhams Press, 1948.

Ciechanowski, Jan. *Defeat in Victory*. Garden City: Doubleday, 1947.

Clay, Lucius D. *Decision in Germany*. Garden City: Doubleday, 1950.

Dallin, David J. *The Rise of Russia in Asia*. New Haven: Yale University Press, 1949.

———. *Soviet Russia and the Far East*. New Haven: Yale University Press, 1948.

———. *Soviet Russia's Foreign Policy, 1939–1942*. New Haven: Yale University Press, 1942.

Dallin, David J., and Boris I. Nicolaevsky. *Forced Labor in Soviet Russia*. New Haven: Yale University Press, 1947.

Dangerfield, Elma. *Behind the Urals*. London: British League for European Freedom, 1946.

*The Dark Side of the Moon*. Written anonymously; preface by T. S. Eliot. New York: Scribner, 1947.

Davis, Forrest, and Ernest K. Lindley. *How War Came*. New York: Simon and Schuster, 1942.

Deane, John R. *The Strange Alliance*. New York: Viking Press, 1947.

*Documents and Materials Relative to the Eve of the Second World War: Dirksen Papers*. Moscow: Foreign Languages Publishing House, 1948.

Dulles, Allen Welsh. *Germany's Underground*. New York: Macmillan, 1947.

Eisenhower, Dwight D. *Crusade in Europe*. Garden City: Doubleday, 1948.

Fay, Sidney Bradshaw. *The Origins of the World War*. 2d ed. New York: Macmillan, 1930.

Finer, Herman. *Mussolini's Italy*. New York: Henry Holt, 1935.

Fotitch, Constantin. *The War We Lost: Yugoslavia's Tragedy and the Failure of the West*. New York: Viking Press, 1948.

Fuller, J. F. C. *The Second World War, 1939–45, a Strategical and Tactical History*. London: Eyre and Spottiswoode, 1948; New York: Duell, Sloan and Pearce, 1949.

Gafencu, Grigore. *Prelude to the Russian Campaign, from the Moscow Pact (August 21st 1939) to the Opening of Hostilities in Russia (June 22nd 1941)*. Translated by Fletcher-Allen. London: Frederick Muller, 1945.

*The German White Paper*. Full text of the Polish documents issued by the Berlin Foreign Office. With a foreword by C. Hartley Grattan. New York: Howell, Soskin, 1940.

Gliksman, Jerzy G. *Tell the West*. New York: Gresham Press, 1948.

Goebbels, Josef. *The Goebbels Diaries, 1942–1943*. Translated and edited by Louis P. Lochner. Garden City: Doubleday, 1948.

Grew, Joseph C. *Ten Years in Japan*. New York: Simon and Schuster, 1944.

Hankey, Maurice Pascal Alers Hankey, Baron. *Politics, Trials and Errors.* Chicago: Regnery, 1950.

Hassell, Ulrich von. *The Von Hassell Diaries, 1938–1944.* Garden City: Doubleday, 1947.

Henderson, Nevile M. *Failure of a Mission, Berlin 1937–1939.* New York: G. P. Putnam's Sons, 1940.

Hitler, Adolf. *Mein Kampf.* Edited by John Chamberlain and others. New York: Reynal and Hitchcock, 1939.

———. *My New Order.* Edited with commentary by Raoul de Roussy de Sales. New York: Reynal and Hitchcock, 1941.

House, Edward Murrell. *The Intimate Papers of Colonel House,* arranged as a narrative by Charles Seymour. 4 vols. Boston: Houghton Mifflin, 1926–28.

Hull, Cordell. *Memoirs of Cordell Hull.* New York: Macmillan, 1948. 2 vols.

Johnson, Walter. *The Battle against Isolation.* Chicago: University of Chicago Press, 1944.

Keynes, John Maynard. *Economic Consequences of the Peace.* London: Macmillan, 1920.

Koestler, Arthur. *The Yogi and the Commissar.* New York: Macmillan, 1945.

Lane, Arthur Bliss. *I Saw Poland Betrayed: An American Ambassador Reports to the American People.* Indianapolis: Bobbs-Merrill, 1948.

Langer, William L. *Our Vichy Gamble.* New York: Alfred A. Knopf, 1947.

Lattimore, Owen. *Solution in Asia.* Boston: Little, Brown, 1945.

Leahy, William D. *I Was There.* New York: Whittlesey House, 1950.

Lehrman, Harold A. *Russia's Europe.* New York: Appleton-Century-Crofts, 1947.

Liddell Hart, Basil Henry. *The German Generals Talk.* New York: William Morrow, 1948.

———. *The Revolution in Warfare.* London: Faber and Faber, 1946.

Lippmann, Walter. *U.S. Foreign Policy: Shield of the Republic.* Boston: Little, Brown, 1943.

———. *U.S. War Aims.* Boston: Little, Brown, 1944.

Lyons, Eugene. *The Red Decade.* Indianapolis: Bobbs-Merrill, 1941.

Macdonald, Dwight. *Henry Wallace: The Man and the Myth.* New York: Vanguard Press, 1948.

Markham, Reuben H. *Rumania under the Soviet Yoke.* Boston: Meador, 1949.

———. *Tito's Imperial Communism.* Chapel Hill: University of North Carolina Press, 1947.

Marshall, George C. *General Marshall's Report—The Winning of the War in Europe and the Pacific.* Published for the War Department in cooperation with the Council on Books in Wartime. New York: Simon and Schuster, 1945.

Mears, Helen. *Mirror for Americans: Japan.* Boston: Houghton Mifflin, 1948.

Mehnert, Klaus, and Heinrich Schulte. *Deutschland-Jahrbuch—1949.* Essen: West-Verlag, 1949.

Mendelssohn, Peter de. *Nuremberg Documents.* London: George Allen and Unwin, 1946.

Mikolajczyk, Stanislaw. *The Rape of Poland.* New York: Whittlesey House, 1948.

Millis, Walter. *Road to War.* Boston: Houghton Mifflin, 1935.

———. *This Is Pearl! The United States and Japan, 1941.* New York: William Morrow, 1947.

Mitchell, Broadus. *Depression Decade: From New Era through New Deal, 1929–1941.* New York: Rinehart, 1947.

Morgenstern, George. *Pearl Harbor.* New York: Devin-Adair, 1947.

Morgenthau, Henry. *Germany Is Our Problem.* New York: Harper and Brothers, 1945.

Namier, L. B. *Diplomatic Prelude, 1938–1939.* London: Macmillan, 1948.

*Nazi-Soviet Relations, 1939–1941.* Documents from the Archives of the German Foreign Office. Edited by Raymond James Sontag and James Stuart Beddie. Publication of the United States Department of State. Washington, D.C.: Government Printing Office, 1948.

Nicolson, Harold. *Peacemaking, 1919.* Boston: Houghton Mifflin, 1933.

Orton, William. *Twenty Years' Armistice, 1918–1938.* New York: Farrar and Rinehart, 1938.

Perkins, Frances. *The Roosevelt I Knew.* New York: Viking Press, 1946.

Petrov, Vladimir. *Soviet Gold: My Life as a Slave Laborer in the Siberian Mines.* Translated from the Russian by Mirra Ginsburg. New York: Farrar, Straus, 1949.

*Polish-Soviet Relations, 1918–1943.* Issued by the Polish Embassy, Washington, D.C.

*The Polish White Book, 1933–1939.* Published by the authority of the Polish Government. London: Hutchinson, 1940.

*Prefaces to Peace, A Symposium consisting of the Following: One World,* by Wendell L. Willkie. *The Problems of Lasting Peace,* by Herbert Hoover and Hugh Gibson. *The Price of Free World Victory,* by Henry A. Wallace. *Blue-print for Peace,* by Sumner Welles. New York. Cooperatively published by Simon and Schuster, Doubleday, Doran and Company, Inc., Reynal and Hitchcock, Inc., Columbia University Press, 1943.

Raczyński, Count Edward. *The British-Polish Alliance, Its Origin and Meaning.* London: Melville Press, 1948.

Reel, A. Frank. *The Case of General Yamashita.* Chicago: University of Chicago Press, 1949.

Roosevelt, Elliott. *As He Saw It.* New York: Duell, Sloan and Pearce, 1946.

Roosevelt, Franklin D. *Public Papers of Franklin D. Roosevelt, Forty-eighth Governor of the State of New York: Second Term, 1932.* Published by the State of New York, 1939.

Rothfels, Hans. *The German Opposition to Hitler, an Appraisal.* Chicago: Regnery, 1948.

Scott, John. *Duel for Europe.* Boston: Houghton Mifflin, 1942.

Sherwood, Robert E. *Roosevelt and Hopkins.* New York: Harper and Brothers, 1948.

Spaight, J. M. *Bombing Vindicated.* London: G. Bles, 1944.

Stettinius, Edward R., Jr. *Roosevelt and the Russians: The Yalta Conference.* Edited by Walter Johnson. Garden City: Doubleday, 1949.

Stimson, Henry L., and McGeorge Bundy. *On Active Service in Peace and War.* New York: Harper and Brothers, 1948.

Stolper, Gustav. *German Realities.* New York: Reynal and Hitchcock, 1948.

Trevor-Roper, H. R. *The Last Days of Hitler.* London: Macmillan, 1947.

U.S. Congress. Joint Committee on the Investigation of the Pearl Harbor Attack. *Hearings before the Joint Committee on the Investigation of the Pearl Harbor Attack.* Congress of the United States, 79th Cong., 1st Sess. Pursuant to S. Con. res. 27. . . . Washington, D.C.: Government Printing Office, 1946. 39 vols.

U.S. Congress. Joint Committee on the Investigation of the Pearl Harbor Attack. *Report of the Joint Committee on the Investigation of the Pearl Harbor Attack.* . . . Congress of the United States, 79th Cong., 1st Sess. Pursuant to S. Con. res. 27. . . . Washington, D.C.: Government Printing Office, 1946.

Utley, Freda. *The High Cost of Vengeance.* Chicago: Regnery, 1949.

Welles, Sumner. *Time for Decision.* New York: Harper and Brothers, 1944.

Wheeler-Bennett, John W. *Munich: Prologue to Tragedy.* London: Macmillan, 1948.

White, William Allen. *The Autobiography of William Allen White.* New York: Macmillan, 1946.

Willkie, Wendell L. *One World.* Reprinted in *Prefaces to Peace.*

Wolfe, Henry. *The Imperial Soviets.* New York: Doubleday, Doran, 1940.

Zacharias, Ellis M. *Secret Missions: The Story of an Intelligence Officer, by Captain Ellis M. Zacharias, U.S.N.* New York: Putnam's, 1946.

# Index

The typeface used for this book is ITC New Baskerville, which was created for the International Typeface Corporation and is based on the types of the English type founder and printer John Baskerville (1706–75). Baskerville is the quintessential transitional face: it retains the bracketed and oblique serifs of old-style faces such as Caslon and Garamond, but in its increased lowercase height, lighter color, and enhanced contrast between thick and thin strokes, it presages modern faces.

The display type is set in Didot.

Book design by Rich Hendel, Chapel Hill, North Carolina
Typography by Tseng Information Systems, Inc., Durham, North Carolina